Dividing the Child

Dividing the Child

Social and Legal Dilemmas of Custody

Eleanor E. Maccoby and Robert H. Mnookin

with Charlene E. Depner and H. Elizabeth Peters

Harvard University Press   Cambridge, Massachusetts   London, England

First Harvard University Press paperback edition, 1994

Library of Congress Cataloging-in-Publication Data

Maccoby, Eleanor E., 1917–
  Dividing the child : social and legal dilemmas of custody /
Eleanor E. Maccoby and Robert H. Mnookin ; with Charlene E. Depner and H. Eliza-
beth Peters.
     p.   cm.
Includes bibliographical references (p.   ) and index.
ISBN 0-674-21294-0 (acid-free paper) (cloth)
ISBN 0-674-21295-9 (pbk.)
1. Divorce—California—Longitudinal studies. 2. Custody of children—California—
Longitudinal studies. 3. Divorce—United States. 4. Custody of children—United
States. 5. Divorced parents—United States—Family relationships.
I. Mnookin, Robert H. II. Title.
HQ835.C2M33 1992
306.89—dc20   92-96
                                               CIP

To the divorced parents who so thoughtfully and patiently participated in our study: from you we have learned about the difficulties but also the great benefits of parental cooperation in the interests of children.

Contents

Preface

This book had its inception in the interdisciplinary setting of the Stanford Center for the Study of Families, Children, and Youth. Both of us, for different reasons, became acutely aware of how little reliable information was available about the social and legal processes of divorce custody decisions. A seminar called "Children and the Law" (for law students, students in the other professional schools, and graduate students in the social sciences) was jointly taught at the Center for several years by Eleanor Maccoby and Michael Wald (Professor of Law). Robert Mnookin, meanwhile, as part of his continuing interest in conflict resolution, had been writing on the relation between the provisions of divorce statutes and the nature of the bargaining that occurred between divorcing couples. It became more and more evident how limited existing social science research was in its ability to furnish reliable information relevant to custody decisions. Merrill Carlsmith, then director of the Family Studies Center, recognized the confluence of our interests and urged us to mount a research program that would fill some of the information gaps we all recognized. Carlsmith provided us with seed money from Center funds, underwriting the initial stages of our work. Subsequent directors of the Center—Michael Wald and Sanford Dornbusch—have continued to support our work, not only financially but by providing an intellectual environment that has been notably stimulating and supportive.

Our major financial support has come from the Institute of Child Health and Human Development (Grant No. R01 HD19386), and we wish to thank our project officer, Jeff Evans, and Wendy Baldwin, Chief of the Demographic and Behavioral Sciences Branch, for their continued interest and support. A grant to Elizabeth Peters (HHS #1530533) also provided an increment of support.

Charlene Depner, trained in survey research at the Institute for Social Research at the University of Michigan, joined the project at its inception. She functioned as a full colleague in the planning phases, and directed the field work throughout the several rounds of interviewing that were conducted during the three years of our longitudinal study. She set up procedures for selecting our sample (from court records of divorce filings) and devised an intensive follow-up system for locating both parents. She hired and trained interviewers, supervised the pretesting of the interview schedule used at each interviewing period, supervised the interviewing and the entry of data, and carried out some of the initial data-reduction steps. She also wrote the appendix on methods for this book, and an early draft of Chapter 4. It is our loss that she was unable to continue with the project through the major phases of the data analysis and write-up of our findings. It is largely as a result of her unstinting efforts that we were able to get high rates of cooperation from potential respondents, many of whom were in highly stressful life situations and were not always initially open to participation in the study. Along with our thanks to Charlene Depner goes our heartfelt gratitude to the mothers and fathers who talked with us so openly, with no recompense other than their hope that by participating, they could help others who might face dilemmas similar to the ones they had encountered.

We cannot sufficiently acknowledge the contributions to the study of our data manager and computer analyst, Sue Dimiceli. The complexities of our large longitudinal data bank have been formidable indeed. For some purposes we have merged data from the two parents; for others we have examined the responses of the two parents separately. We have encountered the usual missing data problems that stem from sample attrition over time in any longitudinal study. More difficult has been the fact that the circumstances of our sample families were extremely varied in terms of where the children lived, how often they saw the nonresidential parent, how parents arrived at a settlement concerning money and child custody; many blocks of questions were applicable only to subsamples of the families, with resulting complexities for constructing composite scores and conducting multivariate analyses. Sue Dimiceli has been the central person in managing these complexities and devising the myriad computer programs that were required. She has been tireless, and her work has been indispensable to the completion of the study.

Professor Elizabeth Peters, in the Economics Department at the University of Colorado, joined the project toward the end of the data-collection phase. She had previously done work on the financial implications of divorce, and agreed to take responsibility for analyzing our study's data on child support and spousal support awards, in the context of the income and assets of the divorcing couples. With her able research assistant, Laura Argys, she provided a detailed analysis of our financial data and wrote an initial chapter draft which subsequently evolved into Chapters 6 and 10 of this book. We have been fortunate indeed to have Liz Peters as a colleague in our work. We also wish to thank Robert Williams, of Policy Studies Incorporated, who provided national CPS data used by Peters for comparison with our own data.

Catherine Albiston was an important contributor to our project over several years' time. She began as an undergraduate assistant, doing a variety of data-processing chores, but after graduation she became a full-time research assistant and assumed major responsibility for searching court records for information on the legal events that led to the divorce decree. She then assisted with data analysis and took the lead in the analysis of the effects of joint legal custody. We are grateful for this help, and especially for her willingness to assist with certain data-analysis problems after she had entered law school. Finally, we wish to thank Julie Cohen, who served as Robert Mnookin's research assistant during the 1990–91 academic year when he was a visiting professor at Harvard Law School, and Tracy George, his 1991–92 Stanford research assistant. Their research, analytical, and editorial talents substantially improved our manuscript.

The manuscript-preparation chores of word processing, preparation of tables, and last-minute incorporation of references were in the able hands of Pat Weaver, who was assisted by Judith Slater. We thank both Pat and Judy for their cheerful competence, initiative in catching errors of all kinds, and sustained interest in all phases of the project.

Several colleagues have read early drafts of chapters. We are grateful to Richard Birke, Christy Buchanan, David Chambers, Andrew Cherlin, Sanford Dornbusch, Elizabeth Kopelman, and Michael Wald for their helpful comments.

We believe this project has been as fully collaborative as interdisciplinary work can be. The order of our names on the cover of this book is alphabetical. We regret that one name has to come before the other. In our own jargon, we refer to this as the "M & M book," and hope others will think of it this way as well.

Eleanor E. Maccoby
Robert H. Mnookin
Stanford University
December 1991

Dividing the Child

1

Introduction

This year, and each year in the foreseeable future, the families of more than one million American children will be disrupted by separation and impending divorce. Divorce forces mothers and fathers to address new questions and requires changes that can affect every aspect of life. Two households must be established where there was only one before. The family economy must typically be radically reorganized: hours of work and jobs may change; income and consumption will not be shared as in the past. Spousal relations are profoundly affected; divorce ordinarily severs the couple's sexual union, and men and women must ask themselves: When will I be ready for a new relationship?

For a childless couple, carrying out the changes involved in divorce can be difficult and agonizing enough. But for a divorcing couple with children, the processes of change are much more complex. A parent must ask: How will I integrate my needs and priorities with those of my children? The responsibility for supporting the children financially must be allocated. In the large majority of divorcing families, both parents have been involved with the children on a daily basis. Simple continuity with the past, in terms of the roles of the two parents in the lives of the children, is hardly possible. The relationship between parents and children must change markedly. Before separation, both parents could be with the child at the same time, and they may have shared responsibilities in ways that no longer will be possible. After separation, arrangements must be made concerning how much time children will spend in each household. Before the divorce can be final, agreements must be reached about custody and visitation. If both parents remain involved, the logistics of sending children back and forth from one household to another must be negotiated and the timing of visits must be arranged, and sometimes modified. To what extent, in spite of the divorce, will the "parental alliance"—the parents' coordination with each other and their mutual support in their executive roles within the family—be maintained? Do the parents agree on rules for the children, and will they back up each other's authority? If parents share responsibility for day-to-day care after the separation, who will take on such everyday tasks as supervising homework, buying clothes, or arranging for medical care? In sum, divorce requires that new arrangements be made for children and that child-rearing responsibilities be allocated.

Parents can experience a rude shock in working out these matters. In many people's minds, the image of divorce is one of a "clean break." The fateful demand "I want a divorce!" implies, to many people, "I want you out of my life." However, parents quickly discover that if both parents want to remain involved in the children's lives, the image of a clean break is an illusion. As Emery has said: "Ironically, having just decided that they can no longer remain married, parents must attempt to cooperate with each other over the children" (1988, p. 109).

Mothers commonly see themselves as having carried most of the responsibility for child-rearing before the separation, and may therefore expect to have sole responsibility afterward. Fathers, however, commonly believe that their contributions to child-rearing (as well as to economic support) have been quite substantial. Although the perceptions of the two parents about their respective roles and family responsibilities may have diverged for some time, parents may not have been aware of the divergence until they decide to separate, at which point they must confront each other's assumptions. It is at this time that one or both parents may begin to search for legal or social standards to support their assumptions about who is entitled to custody of the children.

Until recently, the dominant legal standard created a presumption in favor of maternal custody, particularly for children of "tender years." But an award of sole maternal custody made under this presumption did not, in and of itself, either deprive the father of his legal rights of visitation or eliminate his ongoing obligation to help support the child economically. At the present time, the law in nearly every state insists that in deciding which parent should have sole custody, no custody preference should be given to either simply on the basis of gender: mothers and fathers are said to stand on a level platform before the law.

Some states have gone well beyond simply insisting on formal gender neutrality. Divorcing mothers and fathers are now encouraged to develop cooperative co-parental relations in which both remain substantially involved in the children's lives. For example, the California legislature included in its 1979 revision of the state's divorce statute the following phrase: "It is the public policy of this state to assure minor children of frequent and continuing contact with both parents after the parents have separated or dissolved their marriage."[1] By 1990, nearly every state permitted—and some even encouraged—newer forms of custody in which time with the child and responsibility for the child are more equally divided than in the traditional sole custodian/visitation pattern.

Despite these changes in divorce law, there is no clear consensus concerning the wisdom of dividing children's time between two divorced parents. In *Beyond the Best Interests of the Child* (1973), Goldstein, Freud, and Solnit urge that there should be only one custodial parent. These authors argue that authority over a child's life needs to be clearly allocated to *one* parent, and that children suffer painful loyalty conflicts if they maintain contact with two parents who are not in a harmonious relationship with each other. They recommend that the power to decide whether the child could visit the "outside" parent should be left entirely in the hands of the custodial parent. An implication of their position is that exposure to continuing parental conflict is more endangering to a child than losing touch with a non-residential parent. Some mediators and other mental health professionals, working from the perspective of family systems theory, have also expressed reservations about the wisdom of liberal visitation, recommending that certain constraints be imposed on visitation by the outside parent in the interest of forming firm new boundaries around the family unit made up of the custodial parent and children (Preston and Madison, 1983).

Expressing a different viewpoint about visitation, Strauss and Strauss (1974), in their review of the Goldstein, Freud, and Solnit book, agree that loyalty conflicts might be damaging for children but question whether most divorces were sufficiently acrimonious to create serious risks of this kind. They argue further that allowing the custodial parent full power to block visitation would foster conflict over custody.

Advocates of "frequent and continuing contact" with both parents, while acknowledging the risks of loyalty conflicts, feel that such risks are outweighed by the risks of *not* seeing a divorced parent. They have pointed to the profound grief and sense of abandonment children can experience over the loss of a beloved parent, and the damage such reactions can do to normal development. Early studies of children who were living with their divorced mothers indicated that the children were better adjusted if they were able to visit the father and maintain a close, stable relationship with him.[2]

There has also been little consensus with regard to the wisdom and practicability of the highest level of continued contact with both parents—joint physical custody. Opponents have been concerned about the effects on children of being bounced from one parental household to the other, never having the stability of a coherent life. Proponents, on the other hand, have argued that parents as well as children suffer deeply from the disruption of the parent-child attachment relationships, and have insisted that both parents should have equal rights before the law to maintain their parental relationships with the children. They have also pointed to some early evidence that joint custody is practicable, at least when both parents are highly committed to the children and able to cooperate with each other in matters concerning the children (Steinman, 1981). Under these conditions, most children appeared to adapt well to a divided regime.

More recent studies of the risks and benefits of continued contact with both parents have had mixed results. In his review of research on visitation, Emery (1988) finds no clear evidence linking children's adjustment to a continuing relationship with the outside parent. Emery notes, however, that relationships maintained through visitation may have considerable symbolic value for children whether they affect adjustment or not, and we would add that such relationships may acquire greater meaning at subsequent phases of children's lives—that is, in young adulthood. So far, however, children from divorcing families have seldom been followed long enough to determine long-term effects.

With respect to the feasibility of joint custody, the existing studies once again do not give us a simple picture. Some parents appear to manage this complex arrangement successfully, but others do not (Steinman, Zemmelman, and Knoblauch, 1985). It is becoming increasingly apparent that the impact of either liberal visitation or joint custody depends on the relationship between the two divorced parents. Dividing the child between two parents who are locked in conflict may inflict severe harm and pain on children (Johnston, Campbell, and Mayes, 1985). But at the same time, sustaining a child's relationships with both parents promises important benefits under the right conditions.

Unhappily, crucial information is lacking in much of the debate about these matters. Deciding what arrangements best serve children's needs requires wise and patient judgments from parents, from the professionals involved in the divorcing process in individual cases, and from policymakers responsible for formulating general rules. But exercising wisdom without knowledge is difficult. There are a great number of unanswered questions: To what extent are divorcing parents able to avoid legal disputes? To what extent can divorcing parents develop cooperative co-parenting relationships? What circumstances permit children to maintain membership in two different parental households? It was our hope of shedding light on these and related questions that led us to undertake this study.

This book, based on our empirical study of more than a thousand divorcing families, is about the legal and social realities of how divorcing mothers and fathers make arrangements for their children. Our empirical research does not resolve the most difficult policy questions concerning divorce; value judgments as well as data must always inform sound policy. But such research can inform debate and sharpen the relevant questions.

The Divorce Revolution

Remarkable changes have occurred in the legal and social framework of divorce over the past several decades. Since the 1950s, married women with children have entered the work force in unprecedented numbers. Divorce has become much more common, and social attitudes toward divorce have changed. Between 1969 and 1985, the legal system for divorce throughout the country was transformed by a "no-fault" revolution. In the wake of this revolution, both the standards and the procedures concerning child custody have been transformed. Custody law has been stripped of presumptions based on gender. And the legal system now seems geared to emphasize private dispute resolution, not the regulation of family life of post-divorce families. California, the site of our study, has always been in the vanguard of these changes.

No-fault divorce. Divorce is now commonplace, and in every American state, there are no longer legal impediments for either spouse unilaterally to dissolve the marital bonds. In the past, divorce was both less common and much more difficult to secure. The Anglo-American legal tradition treated marriage as a permanent status that the spouses themselves lacked the legal power to dissolve. Indeed, until 1857 a divorce in England required a separate act of Parliament; civil courts lacked the power to dissolve a marriage. Although in America some states authorized their courts to grant divorce long before England did, a divorce could be granted only after an official inquiry by a judge, who had to determine whether "appropriate grounds," narrowly defined in terms of "marital offenses," existed.

Until 1969, fault—the notion that either the husband or wife had engaged in serious misbehavior—provided the only basis for divorce in every American state. To justify divorce, the innocent spouse was required to demonstrate to the satisfaction of the court that the guilty spouse had committed some marital offense. Under state law, these typically included adultery, desertion, physical or mental abuse, drunkenness, imprisonment, drug addiction, or insanity.

Over a 16-year period, the no-fault revolution essentially dismantled this divorce regime. Between 1969 and 1985, each of the 50 states changed its divorce law to accept "the concept that marriage failure is itself an adequate reason for marital dissolution" (Kay, 1990, p. 6). The no-fault legal reforms both reflected and reinforced changing social realities and social attitudes toward marriage and divorce. Long before the no-fault revolution, family size had been decreasing, and children had become less of an economic asset than they had been in earlier times. Partly in consequence of these changes, there was an increasing belief among American couples that emotional ties between spouses were of fundamental importance[3]—the glue that held successful marriages together. If that glue was missing, why should the state require a demonstration of a marital offense? No-fault divorce simply acknowledged that if either spouse found the marriage emotionally unsatisfying, he or she should be free to exit. Both the increase in the frequency of divorce and the no-fault changes themselves undoubtedly changed attitudes toward divorce. Before the no-fault revolution, divorced persons risked being stigmatized. Someone, after all, had committed a marital offense. But if a marriage breaks down because one spouse no longer finds it emotionally tolerable, and this is no one's fault, stigma is inappropriate. Moreover, as divorce became more common—and rates began to increase substantially in the early 1960s even before the legal revolution—public attitudes softened, which in turn both reduced the stigma and weakened the social constraints holding less successful marriages together.[4]

The removal of gender role stereotypes. In addition to the elimination of fault as the sole ground for securing divorce, a second set of fundamental changes involved the move away from gender stereotypes toward formal gender neutrality.[5] Before 1970, family law reflected and reinforced the ideology of the traditional allocation of responsibilities between husbands and wives: custody standards incorporated presumptions that explicitly favored mothers, while child support and alimony statutes incorporated the notion that fathers would be the primary wage earners. The husband was seen as having the obligation and responsibility of supporting, maintaining, and protecting the family, while child care and day-to-day household management were thought to be the wife's responsibilities.

Legal rules concerning divorce and its aftermath reflected these notions. Although in the nineteenth century the father, as head of the household, was said to have custodial rights, throughout most of the present century the mother was presumed to be the preferred custodian of the children. The mother was particularly favored if the children were young, unless the father somehow showed that the mother was unfit. The father's support obligation toward the children, in theory at least, continued after the divorce, and the law on the books further provided that the wife—particularly if she was the innocent spouse—would receive other economic subsidies through alimony and the distribution of property.

The rebuttable presumption that the custody of a young child should normally go to the mother has now largely disappeared. States now characteristically provide that custody disputes between parents must be resolved by a case-by-case determination of the child's best interest, with no preference given to either parent simply by reason of gender. In the last 10 years, a number of states have taken the additional step of authorizing and even encouraging joint custody—an arrangement under which the parents share responsibility for the children following divorce.[6] This represents a radical departure from the traditional notion that one parent would be the child's custodian and the other parent would simply have visiting rights. There are two types of joint custody: legal and physical. With joint *legal* custody, even though the child may reside with one parent, the mother and father have equal rights to make decisions about the child's medical care, religion, and education. Joint *physical* custody empowers both parents to share day-to-day responsibility for the child's care, and carries with it the idea that after divorce the father and mother should have roughly equivalent roles.

Alimony and marital property rules have also changed in ways thought to reflect greater gender equality. In *Orr v. Orr*, 440 U.S. 268 (1979), the U.S. Supreme Court declared that it was unconstitutional for a state to provide only for the possibility that upon divorce a husband might be required to pay support to his wife, but not vice versa. In some states property distribution rules were also changed. Some laws were changed to reduce judicial discretion, which in the past had sometimes been exercised to protect custodial mothers through disproportionate awards. Instead rules were adopted, often premised upon the notion that marriage is a partnership between equals, that marital property should be divided equally upon divorce.

These legal changes took place in a social context in which gender roles within marriage were changing. In the 1950s, for most married couples with children, the father was the sole wage earner and the mother was a full-time homemaker. Only about one out of four married women with children under 16 worked outside the home in 1950. Today, because married women with children have surged into the workplace, mothers as well as fathers are typically breadwinners.[7] By 1986, more than half (54 percent) of women with children under 6 had a paid job, with the proportion even higher (68 percent) for those with children between 6 and 16. Indeed, Victor Fuchs noted that by the late 1980s, "one out of two new mothers returns to a paid job before her baby's first birthday—four times as many as in 1960" (1988, p. 1). Moreover, about two-thirds of married working mothers are essentially working full time, that is, 35 hours or more per week. And yet, despite these changes, differences in gender roles persist. Married mothers are much more likely to work part time than fathers; mothers earn less per hour; and they typically do much more of the child care and housework within the home.[8]

Private ordering and dispute settlement. Contemporary divorce law has increasingly recognized the legitimacy of "private ordering"—the notion that divorcing parents should have broad latitude to negotiate their own financial and custodial arrangements. This does not mean that law is unimportant; such negotiations, in which one or both parents may be represented by counsel, occur in the shadow of state laws concerning custody, visitation, child support, and marital property. The judiciary functions primarily not to regulate the lives of divorcing families, but instead to resolve those legal disputes that divorcing parents cannot work out. To facilitate this dispute resolution, some states have also adopted new procedures, such as mediation, to help parents resolve divorce disputes without the pain, expense, and delay that were thought to characterize the traditional adversarial approach.

The California Legal Setting

California, the location for our study, has been in the vanguard of the family law revolution. In 1969 California became the first state to adopt a no-fault regime for divorce.[9] The Family Law Act of 1969 provided for the award of child custody "to either parent according to the best interests of the child, *with a preference for maternal custody* if the child is of tender years."[10] This preference for maternal custody, a relic of previous legal tradition, was weakened in 1970[11] and discarded in 1972[12] in favor of a gender-neutral "best interests of the child" standard. By the time the families in our study were divorcing, state law also contained an explicit provision that the gender of a parent not be the basis for preference.[13]

Since 1979, California has gone beyond formal insistence on gender neutrality; it has also enacted legislation designed to encourage arrangements that assure children "frequent and continuing contact with *both* parents."[14] In 1979 California became the first state in the nation to adopt a statute that explicitly authorized joint custody arrangements following divorce. The law not only established a presumption in favor of joint custody when both parents requested it, but also authorized a court to order joint custody in a disputed case.[15] Moreover, the statute suggested that when the parents could not agree on custody, the preferences of the more cooperative parent—that is, the parent more willing to accept a custodial arrangement that provides for continuing participation by both parents—should be favored.

In 1983 California further facilitated private ordering by explicitly differentiating between physical and legal custody.[16] This differentiation between legal and physical custody allows parents more flexibility in negotiating custody arrangements, in that they may adopt joint legal custody while allocating the responsibility for day-to-day physical care (i.e., physical custody) to one parent, not both. Moreover, the statute permits incorporation into the divorce decree of any agreement concerning the allocation of particular responsibilities between parents who have joint legal or joint physical custody.

Finally, California law emphasizes the resolution of custody disputes without the need for judicial intervention. Since 1981, California has mandated mediation for parents engaged in any sort of custody dispute.[17] This mediation is usually court-annexed, but a private mediator chosen by the parents may also be used. If mediation fails to resolve the conflict over custody, the family proceeds to a custody evaluation. As with mediation, custody evaluation is usually performed by a court-appointed evaluator, but occasionally it is done by an evaluator of the parents' choice.[18] If disagreement over custody continues after the evaluation, each parent may respond to part or all of the report before there is a contested hearing. At any point before or even during the hearing, the parents may elect to settle the custody dispute before the judge decides.[19]

The Focus of Our Study

The various reforms in California family law appear to reflect three intertwined purposes: *first*, a desire to encourage greater equity between mothers and fathers, both with respect to child-rearing and in the workplace; *second*, a desire to deregulate divorce and promote private ordering by changing the substance and process of divorce law to diminish the fault-based, adversarial nature of the legal process, and instead to encourage parental cooperation; and *third*, a desire to foster and protect the welfare of the children in divorcing families by ensuring their continued access to both parents to the maximum practicable degree. The reforms—and their relationships to legal conflict, to co-parenting, and to stability and change in the post-separation roles of mothers as compared with fathers—provide the focus for our study of how divorcing parents make arrangements for their children. Four clusters of questions are central to our inquiry.

1. *Gender role differentiation.* How are parental responsibilities in fact divided after divorce? By what processes are arrangements arrived at, and how similar are mothers and fathers in their post-separation parental roles?

2. *Legal conflict.* How much legal conflict is involved in the resolution of issues about custody, visitation, and financial support? When there is conflict, how is it resolved?

3. *Contact: maintenance and change.* As time passes, how viable do the different arrangements for custody and visitation prove to be? Do arrangements that seemed to fit the family circumstances at the time of parental separation become obsolete as family circumstances change? How flexibly can families adapt their arrangements to such changes?

4. *Co-parenting relationships.* How commonly are divorced parents able to cooperate in regard to the daily lives of the chil-

dren? When both parents remain involved with the children, how frequently are the co-parental relationships instead characterized by conflict, in which the parents fight, or by disengagement, in which they avoid conflict by not communicating?

As we have seen, many of the legal changes adopted in the last twenty years were enacted in order to create greater gender equity. Much of the recent debate over custody standards and procedures has concerned whether the new regime (or certain of its elements) systematically and unfairly favors fathers or mothers. Many advocates for mothers have claimed that the gender-neutral best interests standard disfavors mothers and operates to deprive women of a critically important bargaining chip with which to counter attempts to reduce spousal and child support (Polikoff, 1982; Neely, 1984; Weitzman, 1985).[20] For example, Singer and Reynolds (1988) boldly claim that "Proponents [of joint custody] ignore what studies increasingly confirm: divorcing husbands routinely and successfully use the threat of a custody fight to reduce or eliminate alimony and child support obligations. The success of such 'custody blackmail' has been identified as a major cause of the impoverishment of divorced women and their children." But in fact, no *empirical* studies exist supporting such a contention; instead, several good *theoretical* analyses have been offered.[21] Advocates for fathers counter that the best interests standard is gender-neutral only in theory, and that in reality judicial biases favoring mothers perpetuate a maternal presumption (Roman and Haddad, 1978).[22] Good empirical data are needed to inform this debate. What proportion of divorcing mothers prefer sole custody at the time of divorce? Do the preferences of fathers frequently differ? When parental requests for custody conflict, in what proportion of cases are the outcomes favorable to fathers?

Although most custody conflicts are resolved through negotiation rather than adjudication, little reliable information exists about the proportion of divorcing parents who disagree over custody or the number of cases that require mediation, custody evaluation, or adjudication.[23] When parental preferences are in conflict, how is that conflict resolved? How many cases are actually subjected to judicial determination? How does conflict affect the terms of the divorce decree? Today advocates for divorced mothers and divorced fathers each claim that the present system is biased,[24] and commentators have argued that the discretionary best interests standard creates uncertainty about judicial outcomes, and thus increases the likelihood of legal conflict.[25]

In our study we will examine the changing realities that underlie the legal labels found in the divorce decree. The terms of the divorce decree do not always determine where the children actually live or how much they visit their non-custodial parents, even at the time the divorce becomes final. And as time passes, changes in family circumstances may call for changes in the way children's time is divided between the two parents. For example, one or both parents may remarry; one or both may move to a new residence; a child may change schools. It has been widely reported that non-residential fathers tend to drop out of the children's lives as the time since parental separation lengthens and circumstances change. But some non-residential parents do remain involved, and indeed, one of the objectives of the revision of the California custody statutes was to keep them involved. We know very little about the stability of different arrangements for custody and visitation. We suspect that there is a good deal of "hidden" modification (that is, modification not reflected in legal modification actions), but the extent of such change needs to be documented.

In addition, our research provides an opportunity to discover whether the involvement of both parents is more likely to be sustained over time if they have initially adopted one of the newer custodial arrangements (joint physical or legal custody).

We are very interested in the issue of co-parenting after divorce, and the extent to which parents are able to cooperate in raising their children. Camera and Resnick (1988) traced the impact of parental conflict on children's adjustment in mother-custody, father-custody, and intact (two-parent) households, and found that interspousal conflict is more strongly related to children's adjustment difficulties in single-parent situations than it is when the children's parents are not divorced. However, they were able to recruit only ten father-custody families, and no joint-custody families were included. We wished to examine a wider variety of residential arrangements for children, and in addition to the more commonly studied mother-custody families, we include substantial groups of families in which the children either live with their fathers or spend nearly equal amounts of time in both parental households. We also consider how parental conflict and cooperation affect children's ongoing contact with their non-custodial parents. In these ways, we hope to generate information that will help to explain some of the connections between family structures and outcomes for the child that others have reported.

Researchers have expressed particular interest and concern about joint custody and the requirements for parental cooperation that it presumably imposes. We wished to look beneath this new legal label, to learn how in fact parents share responsibilities. Proponents claim that joint custody, because it emphasizes shared parental rights and responsibilities, fosters parental cooperation (Bartlett and Stack, 1986); critics have feared that joint custody might be used to resolve custody conflicts between parents who are fundamentally at odds with each other and who will be unable to cooperate in parenting following divorce.[26] Once again, information about the actual operation of the legal system is needed. How common is joint custody? How frequently is it imposed by courts or used by mediators or warring lawyers to resolve highly conflicted divorce custody battles? When it has been awarded as a conflict-resolution strategy, can parents sustain it, and can they even become cooperative?

Research Design and Methods

To explore these questions, we studied approximately 1,100 California families as they made post-separation arrangements for their children. All of these parents filed for divorce in either San Mateo County or Santa Clara County between September 1984 and April 1985, and all had at least one child under age 16 at the outset of the study. Because we wanted to trace a process, we conducted three separate telephone interviews with these parents over a three-year time span. In addition, we examined court records to determine the sequence of legal events and its relationship to the day-to-day lives of families. The result, we hope, is an improved understanding of the realities of the divorce process and the actual custodial arrangements made for children—not as suggested by the law on the books or from formal court documents, but as reported by parents engaged in the process.

Our research design emphasizes four features, which we outline here (a detailed discussion of our methodology and data-set conventions is given in Appendix B). First, because divorce is not a single event but a dynamic process of family breakup and reorganization, we wanted a longitudinal approach that would capture critical events as they occurred. Accordingly, we conducted a series of three interviews with divorcing parents. The first (Time 1, or T-1) occurred shortly after the petition for divorce was filed. In the most common case, the first interview occurred about three months after the divorce filing, which

in turn usually occurred about three months following parental separation. Thus, the first interview took place about six months after separation. The second interview (Time 2, or T-2) took place one year after
the first (one and a half years after separation), when many of the
divorces had been completed. The third (Time 3, or T-3) occurred after
two more years had passed, three and a half years after separation. At
this time, protracted divorces were ending and families had had time
to establish new routines and relationships.

Second, we followed a cohort of families who were all initiating the
divorce process at roughly the same time. The use of a cohort design
ensures that differences between groups are not simply attributable to
variation in the time since divorce (Kessler, 1983). However, because
a cohort is created by the onset of the divorce process, the design
does not permit contemporaneous collection of information prior to its
onset. To obtain a sufficiently large cohort of divorcing families, we
used the filing of the divorce petition to form our cohort. Thus, although we could examine post-filing parental interactions as they un-
folded, we could not assess directly the relationships that existed when
the family was intact. Like other researchers, we resorted to retrospective measures to fill in the picture to some degree.

Third, we made every effort to locate and recruit both parents for
our study. Family researchers have severely criticized the traditional
practice of relying exclusively on mothers' reports of family events,
and have argued that a balanced perspective on family interactions
during and after divorce is impossible without sampling the opinions of
both mothers and fathers (Safilios-Rothchild, 1969). In divorce-related
research, however, it is particularly difficult to induce participation by
both parents (Hetherington, Cox, and Cox, 1982). Locating both parents is difficult for this highly mobile population, and then there is
the issue of whether, once located, both agree to participate. Other
researchers have reported that limiting a sample to only those families
in which both parents agree to participate produces a sample that is
severely biased in comparison with the universe of all divorcing families (Hiller and Philliber, 1985; Scanzoni, 1965). Accordingly, we
sought but did not require participation by both parents. Of the 1,124
families in the T-1 data collection, 44 percent had both parents participating, 39 percent had only the mothers participating, and 17 percent
had only the fathers involved. In the final year of the study, we made
a concerted effort to locate non-resident parents not previously interviewed, and added 43 mothers and 110 fathers to the final round of
interviews.

Finally, we attempted to develop a sample broad enough and diverse enough to permit comparison of subgroups of families. Although the relative merits of alternative forms of custody have been fiercely debated, few empirical investigations actually provide comparative data about two or more custody arrangements. Similarly, many studies of divorce have focused on children within one specific age range. Most research evidence in this area is also limited to the white middle-class population. For our study, we restricted our work to two counties in northern California, Santa Clara and San Mateo counties. Examination of the demographic characteristics of these two counties revealed a broad range of age, education, income, and ethnicity. Using the methods described in Appendix B, we obtained a sample with great diversity in family characteristics, including the age, number, and sex of children and the socioeconomic status of parents.

Early studies of divorce looked for direct connections between family structure and child adjustment. More recent work has been concerned with process, and has included observations of parent-child interaction in single-parent and two-parent families. Using this information, researchers have sought to illuminate the way in which family structure translates into family process and how this process then affects outcomes for the children.[27] In our study of the divorce process, we start even earlier in the causal chain. Rather than take post-divorce family structures as givens, we ask which families select which post-divorce arrangements and why, how different arrangements function for families in different initial circumstances, and how stable these arrangements are.

Previous research has established that post-divorce events have important effects on the adjustment of individual parents and children.[28] For the purposes of this study, we did not attempt to determine the adjustment of individual children (or parents). We focused instead on how custodial arrangements are set in place and how they work out over time. A follow-up study has been done, consisting of interviews with the children in our sample families who were between the ages of 10 and 18 at that time (Buchanan, Maccoby, and Dornbusch, 1991). These interviews, which took place four and a half years after the parental separation (one year after the conclusion of the present study), assess the children's adjustment to the post-divorce arrangement and their relationships within each of the parental households.

We should point out that readers will encounter considerable variation in the number of cases available for the different analyses we present. We lost a small proportion of our initial sample at each subsequent interview (primarily as a result of parents' having moved and left no forwarding information). Therefore, the number of cases is smaller for later interviews than at Time 1, and when we want to chart changes over time, we have usually confined the analysis to those families for whom we had data at all three interviewing periods—880 families. For a number of our research questions, we use family-level information which either parent is able to report—for example, information about where the children are living, the number of children, who filed for divorce, and so forth. For such information, it does not matter whether we interviewed the mother, the father, or both parents, and our number of cases is equal to the number of families in which we interviewed at least one parent. However, for some purposes we wish to present data separately for mothers and fathers; for such comparisons there are more mothers than fathers available, and the total number of parents is greater than the total number of families. When we wish to compare the experiences of mothers and fathers in the same families, we must confine the analysis to only those families in which both parents were interviewed—a much smaller number than the family total.

In chapters that deal with legal outcomes of divorce negotiations, we have based our analyses on the subsample of families with final divorce decrees by the fall of 1989. In chapters that deal with co-parenting, the analysis is based on those families in which the children were spending time in both parental households. There were additional instances in which certain questions were asked only of the subgroup of parents for whom they were relevant (for example, questions about supervising homework were asked only when parents had children old enough to be in school). Readers should be prepared, then, for the fact that different research questions call for the analysis of different subgroups in our sample, and that the number of cases in different tables will vary considerably.

Overview of the Book

The book is divided into four main parts. This chapter and the next two provide the necessary introduction for our study. Chapter 2 analyzes the tasks facing divorcing parents with respect to family functioning, and provides an analytical framework for understanding the process of decision-making and divorce bargaining between spouses. Chapter 3 introduces the families in our study by describing their social and economic characteristics before they filed for divorce, and shows how our sample families from San Mateo and Santa Clara counties compare with families from the rest of the nation. We also show what proportion of our sample families had a traditional division of parental responsibilities (where before divorce the mother was primarily responsible for child-rearing and did not work outside the home) as compared to less traditional roles.

The second part of the book examines the initial arrangements that parents establish for children at the time of divorce. In Chapter 4 we examine where the children actually resided and how frequently they visited non-residential parents at Time 1 of our study—typically about three months after the couple filed for divorce but before the conclusion of the formal divorce proceedings. Chapters 5, 6, and 7 concern the legal process of divorce. In Chapter 5 we examine the custodial provisions of the divorce decree. Chapter 6 describes the economic provisions of the divorce decrees for our sample families. We analyze the factors that determine the probability and size of child support awards and spousal support awards, as well as the factors that determine the disposition of the family home. Building on the two preceding chapters, Chapter 7 concerns the extent to which parental conflict characerizes the legal process of divorce.

In the third part of the book we investigate the changes that occur with time in the de facto arrangements for children's residence and visitation, as well as the nature of the parenting and co-parenting patterns developed by divorced parents. Chapter 8 explores changes in the initial residential and visitation arrangements, and analyzes the factors that relate to change. In particular, we focus on the extent to which non-custodial fathers maintain contact with their children in the years immediately following the divorce.

From our interviews, we learned that in a substantial majority of our families, both the father and the mother had some continuing contact with the children following parental separation. Chapter 9 explores how these couples manage co-parenting relationships when the children are spending time in both households.

Chapter 10 deals with changes in economic status over time, and compares the economic well-being of the custodial parent's household with that of the non-custodial parent's household in the years following the divorce. We also investigate the level of compliance with support obligations by non-custodial parents (typically fathers), and examine the effect of compliance on economic well-being relative to pre-divorce levels.

The final section of the book, consisting of the concluding chapter, draws together the important themes of our work and explores the implications of our findings for all those concerned with making arrangements for the children of divorce: parents, lawyers, mediators, judges, and policymakers. We also explore the implications of our study for understanding the limits of the law—the extent to which it is realistic to think that family law can substantially change the roles of mothers and fathers after divorce, or encourage greater parental cooperation.

2

Understanding the Processes
of Divorce

Because the status of being married officially comes to an end on the day when a divorce decree is issued, divorce might be thought of as a single event. But of course divorce is in fact a continuing process—one that begins long before and may continue long after the date of legal dissolution. The goal of this chapter is to provide a framework for understanding the various ways in which the relationship between divorcing spouses must be transformed, and the profound challenges posed by the process.

It is helpful to consider four distinct relationships between a married man and woman that must be transformed.[1] In the *spousal divorce* the intimacy—sexual, psychological, and social—beween husband and wife must be brought to an end. The *economic divorce* requires that the previous economic relationship based on a single household be transformed. The *parental divorce* requires the spouses to redefine their respective parental roles because of the new arrangements required for the children. And the *legal divorce* requires a process aimed at producing a written document specifying the custodial and financial arrangements that will govern after the dissolution. Though interconnected, these four aspects of divorce involve different processes, and they may differ greatly in how difficult they are for a couple to manage.

The primary focus of our book is the parental divorce and its legal context. Nevertheless, the spousal and economic divorces may each create difficulties that affect how parents make arrangements for their children. In this chapter we sketch briefly some of the implications of the spousal and economic divorces and then focus on the parental divorce itself, and how the parental roles of mothers and fathers may be changed. We conclude with an analysis of the legal divorce, exploring the extent to which there are opportunities for divorcing parents to escape from the "zero-sum game," and, through cooperation, to make both better off.

The Spousal Divorce

The spousal divorce is concerned with ending the intimate relationship between a husband and wife, apart from money issues and the relationship with the children. It involves a process of disengagement which typically begins long before the divorce petition is ever filed and may not end until long after the final decree. Because it involves the failure of a marriage, the spousal divorce almost always involves great emotional distress. It leaves wounds which take time to heal. Many writers have described the process of adjustment as an emotionally difficult journey, with predictable stages. In the eyes of one or both spouses, the marriage may have been troubled for months or even years before a separation occurs. The decision to separate is often an anguishing one, about which one or both may feel deep ambivalence. The period surrounding separation often marks a crisis in which very strong emotions erupt. Some may act in exaggerated and very uncharacteristic ways.

For many, the process of disengagement creates an enormous sense of loss and failure. Although the legal system may now characterize divorce as "no fault," spouses often feel a need to apportion blame, to oneself and to the other, for the failure of the marriage. Grief and longing are often felt as the relationship is relinquished. Even after separation, the attachment between spouses typically persists and is responsible for the lingering feelings of loneliness and depression that characterize the separation process for most people. The fact that one may choose to leave one's mate does not negate the longing for the comfort of the other's presence or their daily interactions (Weiss, 1975).

The two spouses do not necessarily go through the process of disengagement and psychological recovery at the same rate. Commentators have suggested that in adjusting to divorce, spouses often go through stages, and that the "psychic wounds" characteristically heal at different rates. Often one spouse may have begun planning for the end of the marriage months or even years before the other spouse becomes aware that there is a serious problem in the marriage. For one spouse, the act of physical separation may be preceded by a gradual emotional separation, but "this movement towards separation is rarely a mutual effort. More likely it begins when one of the spouses decides that the marital distress or dissatisfaction is not likely to disappear or change" (Ahrons and Rodgers, 1987, p. 56). Many researchers have shown that the decision to end the marriage is rarely a collaborative one, in which both spouses share equally. More characteristically one spouse has a greater desire for the marriage to end, and often the decision is very much a one-sided one. In a psychological sense, one spouse is leaving and the other spouse is left. And they often experience different emotions: "Initiators, or leavers, identify their predominant emotion as guilt. They feel responsible for the breakup and for inflicting pain on the other. The assenters, or left, most usually feel anger and want to punish the spouse" (Ahrons and Rodgers, 1987, p. 62).

For some the emotional healing process may be fast, while for others the wounds may never heal. More commonly, there will be residual scars, but, over time, most divorcing spouses do heal themselves and establish new relationships, and to varying degrees a new life. There is no guarantee, however, that the pace of psychological adjustment or the end result will be the same for the two spouses.

Because of these differing rates of adjustment and the emotional nature of the spousal divorce process, it can pose serious difficulties for the way parents make arrangements for their children. If one parent still does not want to disengage, he or she can use the children as a lure to keep the other parent engaged; or one parent may try to punish the other by blocking access to the children. Such maneuvers can complicate enormously the possibilities of establishing cooperative co-parenting relationships. Moreover, the psychological turmoil and substantial emotional distress can jeopardize deliberate and well-informed decision-making, as well as creating or exacerbating the risk of legal conflict.

The Economic Divorce

A divorce means that two households must be created where there was only one before, and this fact typically requires a difficult reorganization of the family economy. For divorcing couples, the formation of two households poses an economic challenge for three reasons: the loss of economies of scale; the gender-based division of labor that characterizes many households; and the existence of joint consumption.

One reason for the difficulty of the economic divorce is the extra costs imposed by the formation of a second household. One household is typically more efficient in economic terms than two (that is, because

of economies of scale). The establishment of a second household necessarily imposes additional costs—for housing, for furniture, and for
housewares in the short run. Over time, adjustments can be made in
either or both households by spending more on housing and less on
other items, or by a combination of strategies. Whatever the adjustments, the loss of the economies of scale means that there is an economic loss that must be borne by someone. Although housing represents the most conspicuous example, economies of scale may also
arise with respect to medical and automobile insurance, and the use
of various durable goods such as washing machines or freezers that
come in sizes larger than a single user needs.

A second reason for the economic strains imposed by divorce relates
to the gender-based division of labor which, as we will show in Chapter
3, characterizes many households. Husbands and wives in many
households have traditionally exchanged specialized services, with
men contributing their higher income to the household while women
to a greater degree specialized in providing child care, nurturing, cooking, and housekeeping services. As is well known, to some degree the
traditional marriage—with a strict division of labor and completely
distinct roles—is breaking down. Married mothers and fathers often
are both in the labor market today, and some parents do share domestic responsibilities. But our findings in Chapter 3 are consistent with
the substantial body of research that shows that a significant amount
of division of labor within the family still exists (Hochschild, 1989;
Thompson and Walker, 1989). Fathers work longer hours outside the
home, earn more, and do substantially less housework and child care.[2]

When couples stop living together, the terms of the ongoing exchange that prevailed during marriage necessarily must be redrawn.
"So long as they remain married, men are content to trade their higher
income for the nurturing, child-care services, cooking, and house-
cleaning they receive from their wives" (Furstenberg and Cherlin,
1991, p. 29). When the relationship dissolves, however, the old exchange can no longer continue. As part of the process of divorce, the
exchange of many services simply comes to an end. After the divorce
a woman does not characteristically prepare meals or clean house for
her ex-husband on a regular basis. A man will not typically mow the
lawn or fix the car for his ex-wife. In the couple's role as parents, a
division of labor may or may not be maintained after divorce. If the
mother provides the bulk of the child-care services after separation, it
is possible for the father to compensate her for these services through
providing support. But from the father's perspective, he no longer

receives the same bundle of services, and indeed no longer has the same access to the child. Before, he could see the child every day, and on an ongoing basis enjoy the child's company and experience the rewards of parenthood. If by reason of separation he only sees the child during visitation, this is hardly the same. In any event, the creation of two separate households means that the terms of the previous informal exchanges of money and services are substantially modified.[3]

A third reason for the difficulty of the economic divorce concerns joint consumption: the custodial spouse and the children must essentially share the same standard of living, because they consume together. It is not practical to provide high-quality housing for a child without also providing it for the custodial spouse. Similarly, it would be difficult and expensive to provide the custodian and child with different diets or different social milieus. Joint consumption creates a dilemma concerning how the financial burdens imposed by divorce should be shared. Our legal and cultural norms reflect the notion that children should not bear the economic costs of divorce, and that, other things being equal, the two spouses should bear the loss equally. Joint consumption makes this impossible for all but the most prosperous families: either the children must bear some part of the economic loss, or the non-custodial parent must bear much more of the extra financial burden imposed by divorce than the custodial spouse.

The economic impact of divorce varies greatly from one family to another, depending on each parent's earnings, on whether the parents own a house, on how many children they have, and so forth. Consider, for example, the case of a traditional family with one young child in which the mother was a homemaker not employed outside the home and in which the father was earning a mid-level income that did not allow for many luxuries but supported a reasonably comfortable standard of living before the divorce. After the separation, the father moves out and rents a small apartment, where the child comes for overnight visits. He now keeps up his apartment on his own, prepares his meals, and does his own laundry—all household tasks formerly done by his wife. The mother wants to stay in the family home with the child, but the father finds it financially impossible to keep up the mortgage payments on the house in addition to paying his own rent. The mortgage payments can only be managed if the mother goes to work, but her entry-level earnings will be low, and she may have to move to cheaper quarters. Whether she moves or not, some portion of the father's paycheck will be needed to support her household.

We can contrast this case with one in which both parents have been working at mid-level jobs, earning similar amounts, and sharing household chores and the care of their two school-age children as evenly as possible. This couple might decide to continue sharing child-care responsibilities after their separation. They agree to a joint-custody plan in which the children spend every other week with each parent, and since they have comparable jobs, they further agree that there should be no support paid by either parent. Even with this egalitarian history and agreements, divorce brings severe economic pressures in its wake. The parents now need two homes, each large enough to accommodate two children. If the father moves out and agrees to find housing within the same school district so that the children can conveniently go back and forth, it would double their previous housing costs if he were to get housing of comparable quality to the family home. The alternative is for the parents to sell their present home and for each spouse to move into considerably smaller quarters—perhaps in a less desirable school district. Note, too, that each parent will now be spending less total time with the children. Moreover, the parents will no longer be able to exchange household services in ways that made a single household more efficient: when the husband cooked before, he prepared a meal not only for the children but for his wife as well. Now each must spend time on meal preparation, and on various other household tasks that before were shared.

Many couples will fall somewhere between the fully traditional and the fully egalitarian pre-separation patterns described above, but whatever the balance has been, there will be no escaping the greatly increased costs of two households compared to one. The parents' joint incomes can hardly sustain a standard of living in the two new households that will be comparable to the one they previously enjoyed.

The Parental Divorce: Co-parenting before and after Separation

While parents are dealing with the distress of the spousal divorce and the relentless pressures of the economic divorce, they must also redefine their parental roles and responsibilities. We now turn to the parental divorce, and examine in some detail the ways in which divorcing parents characteristically must modify their old patterns. Before doing so, it is worth emphasizing that this task is enormously complicated by the spousal and economic divorces. Separating spousal roles from parental roles is not an easy matter. In families in which both parents wish to remain involved in the children's lives, and in which the children will be spending some time in both households, the parents will need to deal with each other as co-parents, even though they are no longer spouses. The two aspects of their relationship—the spousal and the co-parental—had previously been interwoven, and to terminate one while maintaining the other is an entirely unfamiliar issue which many parents are unprepared to handle. And these spousal and parental transitions occur at the same time when the old family economy, in which all family members engaged in formal exchanges within a single household, must come to an end.

In focusing on this central concern of our study, how divorce changes parental roles and responsibilities, we begin by considering in some detail what co-parenting involves in pre-divorce families. Then we examine the changes in the co-parental relationship that occur when parents move into separate households while each continues to see the children. From the perspective of family systems theory, we consider the implications of these changes for post-separation family organization and therapeutic approaches.

Co-parenting in Pre-divorce Families: The Parental Alliance

In the past, most research on how parents socialize a child focused on the mother-child pair. More recently, the role of fathers in child-rearing has been given more attention, and two aspects of the paternal role in the family have been emphasized: the father's role in giving support (both emotional and material) to the mother as major child-rearer, and his direct interactions with the children. The interest in fathers' role in child-rearing emerged partly in response to pressure for gender equality. Feminists asked why women should be the ones primarily responsible for child-care duties. Because women have traditionally occupied the primary child-rearing role in all human societies— particularly for young children—one question posed for child development researchers was whether this had to be so. In a sense, the question many studies addressed was: can men "mother" as well as women? Work by Parke and O'Leary (1976) illustrates this approach.[4] They observed fathers and mothers interacting one-on-one with infants, and found fathers to be as skillful in bottle-feeding, and as gentle and responsive, as were mothers.

Although it appears that fathers, like mothers, can successfully nurture even very young children, in most American families the two parents do not have the same functions in child-rearing. When fathers are asked what it means to be a father, they are likely to mention first their role as breadwinner. Studies show that most two-parent families with young children—even those where both parents are working—adopt a division of labor such that the mother assumes more responsibility for child care and household management while the father brings in a higher portion of the family income. If either parent is to reduce the time spent in outside employment in order to care for children, many families find that it makes more economic sense for the family as a whole for the mother to be the one who does so.

Lamb and colleagues (1987), summarizing a considerable body of research, report that although there is great variation among families in the extent of the father's involvement in child-rearing, fathers on the average are considerably less involved even when mothers are working. On average, fathers are "available" (that is, present and accessible) to their children for about half as much time as are mothers; mothers spend about three times as much time in face-to-face interaction with children as do fathers. And mothers are overwhelmingly more likely to be the person *responsible* for the children—the only person at home with them, the one who stays home from work with them if they are ill, the person who arranges the child care, makes medical appointments, takes the children to lessons and doctor's appointments, decides about their clothing, and so forth. It terms of the time spent as the responsible parent, mothers outweigh fathers nine to one.

When one considers the "role overload" that many women experience when they are both working outside the home and carrying the major responsibility for child care, it may come as a surprise to learn that many are not enthusiastic about their husbands' taking on a larger role with the children. Yet this is the case (Pleck, 1983), and there is evidence that when economic circumstances force a reversal of roles—with the mother as the major wage earner and the father staying home with the children—mothers express considerable dissatisfaction with the way their husbands are managing the household. It would seem that many if not most women wish to retain their dominant role in the management of household and children.

While the division of child-care labor has been extensively studied, the nature of parental cooperation in dealing with children has not been examined in as much detail. However, family systems theorists have contributed to our understanding of some of the elements of co-parenting relations. They tell us, first of all, that families are indeed systems, having their own dynamic properties, boundaries, and subsystems. In well-functioning two-parent families, the strongest and most cohesive dyad is the one between the mother (wife) and father (husband) (Feldman and Gehring, 1988). Children perceive the parental pair as jointly exercising authority, and as being affectively close.

Patricia Minuchin (1985), in discussing the family, points out that much interaction between parents and children goes on when both parents are present, and the mother-father-child triad has its own dynamics in the socialization of the child. Minuchin gives an example of an interaction that was observed while the parents of a young child were being interviewed:

> The two-year-old knocks over a box of chalks and they spill out onto the carpet.
>
> Mother (soft voice): "Brian, pick them up, please." (She turns back to adult conversation.)
>
> Father (voice raised slightly): "Brian, put the chalks in the box." (Pause; voice stronger): "Brian, put the chalks in the box!"
>
> Mother: "Yeah, come on. Don't muck up the carpet." (Adult conversation resumes. Child is examining the chalk.)
>
> Father: "Brian, listen! You're not supposed to have the chalk on the carpet. Now pick them up. Come on."
>
> Child: "I'm doing it."
>
> Father: "You're not. You're playing. Come, pick them up first. Quickly. If I get up, you know you will. Now come on!"
>
> Adult discussion resumes. Mother glances at child, stands up and goes to him, kneeling and talking softly. As he dallies over the chalk, she says, "Don't throw them. Put away all of them." Father, seated, says "Come on," and watches as the mother tells the child he will have to sit on her lap and not play if he doesn't pick them all up. The child says, "I want to play," and gathers the chalk up more quickly. Father relaxes and mother returns to the adults. (Minuchin, 1985, p. 296)

The dynamics of this interaction are complex. Possibly, the mother sees a confrontation brewing between the father and child, and moves to forestall it. But the major feature of the interaction is that the two parents are working together in the exercise of joint authority.

A similar dynamic may be seen in the following incident, recently observed by Maccoby:

> Six-year-old girl exuberantly runs out the back door of her home, bumping into the sliding screen door and knocking it off its track. Father gets up to reset the screen, saying irritably:

"Janie, that's the *third* time you've knocked that door off."
Janie: "I didn't do it."
Father: "Yes you did!"
Janie: "No I didn't!"
Father leaves door, goes to girl, holds her shoulders firmly, looks directly into her face, and says loudly: "Don't tell me you didn't do it. I *saw* you. You didn't mean to, but you *did* do it."
Child wails and goes to mother. Father returns to door. Mother puts arm around daughter, rubs her back, says: "It's all right, honey. You didn't mean to. But you have to be more careful. So daddy won't always have to be fixing the screen door."

Here the roles of the two parents were different—mother as comfort-giver, father as disciplinarian. Also, their momentary socialization goals were somewhat different: the father was focusing on truth-telling, the mother on being considerate of another family member. Yet they were mutually supportive. In many families, instances of joint parenting such as these may be fairly rare—most of the time, only one parent at a time directly interacts with a child, although in family dinner-table conversations, three-way exchanges do occur. The point is, however, that it may not take many instances of jointly-exercised parental authority for the children to form a picture of their parents as a mutually reinforcing team.

Most parental couples not only adopt a division of labor in terms of child-rearing roles and responsibilities; the father and mother may also have different characteristic styles of interaction with children. In both the vignettes, the mothers were to some extent mediating between the father and the child. That is, they softened the impact of the fathers' power-assertive style, while supporting him in his attempts to teach relevant lessons to the child. There is evidence that in most families mothers do more of the work of sustaining positive moods among family members than fathers do; fathers are observed generally to be more power-assertive in the way they speak to children (Gleason, 1987).

But fathers do much more than merely play the "heavy" role of authority figure. From the earliest period of the child's life, fathers typically spend a higher proportion of their interactive time in play than mothers do (Parke and Tinsley, 1981; Russell and Russell, 1987), and they do more joking. While father-child play involves more roughhousing, mother-child play involves more reciprocal role-taking in fantasy scripts (Maccoby and Jacklin, 1983). In addition, mothers are the primary comfort-givers for children at times of distress. Moreover, they chat more with them, and spend more time listening to what they have to say. Indeed, mothers appear to be better able to understand what a very young child is saying at a time when the child's speech can be quite unclear (Gleason, 1987). Russell and Russell (1987) report that although mothers issue more directions than fathers to school-age children (second-graders)—for example, telling the child to take a bath, come to the table, put away toys—mothers also consult the child's viewpoint more, and respond more positively than fathers do when the child makes an independent decision. Perhaps as a consequence, the children in their study expressed their feelings more freely to their mothers.

Our interpretation of the existing research is that while the affectional bonds are normally very strong between the children and each of the parents, typically there is more reciprocal give-and-take between mothers and children in the course of daily life, even though fathers may be the favorite playmates. One corollary of the maternal style is that mothers usually know more about the child's interests, friends, preferences, and goals. Adolescents report that their mothers know them better than their fathers do, even though they regard their two parents as equally important as standard-setters (Youniss and Smollar, 1985). In many households, then, the two parents play complementary roles in the lives of their children.

How a parent interacts with a child may depend, according to some research, on whether the parent is alone with the child. Per Gjerde (1986) has observed mothers and fathers interacting with their teenage children, either one-on-one or in the mother-father-child trio. He found that a parent's mode of interaction with the children does change somewhat, depending on whether the other parent is present. Fathers appeared to be somewhat inhibited in the presence of the child's mother, and when alone with the child, interacted more freely and became more relaxed and humorous. When both parents are present many fathers regard the management of the children as more in their wives' domain than their own, and they are careful about invading her territory. Mothers, on the other hand, interacted with teenage sons more comfortably and more assertively when their husbands were present. Thus, fathers may serve as "backup" authority, helping to keep children—especially sons—in line. Many a boy has heard his father say: "Young man, I don't want to hear you talking to your mother like that." Lytton (1979), in observing parents with much younger children, found that mothers were more effective in controlling their 2-year-old sons when the father was present than when he was not.

We do not have comparable information on the effect of a mother's presence on children's compliance to their fathers' demands, but suspect that her presence would not make as much difference, considering that there is evidence that fathers are usually more successful in exacting compliance even when the mother is not there. For example, in observations of mothers and fathers interacting separately with a preschool child, Hetherington and colleagues (1982) found that children complied more readily to a father's than a mother's demands, in both intact and divorced families. Furthermore, it has been reported that school-age children treat fathers as though they were more powerful than their mothers (Cowan, Drinkard, and MacGavin, 1984). Thus, mothers on the average may derive more benefit from their spouse's authority backup than do fathers.

During marriage, successful parents forge a parental alliance. When parents are closely allied, they make most decisions concerning the children jointly; or at least, they have an understanding concerning which decisions need to be discussed and which can be left to either parent acting singly. Allied parents also relieve each other of child-care duties when one parent is ill, overstressed, or subject to special demands outside the home. At such times, the other parent will step in to manage or entertain the children. When the children simply need someone to stay with them at times when no formal child care has been arranged, one parent will usually "sit" with the children so that the other can do necessary errands, or participate in out-of-home functions or recreational activities to which the children cannot be taken.

The parental alliance also involves agreeing on rules for the children, backing up the other parent's authority, and conveying an atmosphere of mutual respect and affection. Even in well-functioning families, of course, parents do not always manage to present a united front, and children become expert at finding weaknesses in the parental alliance. As they grow older, children learn which parent is more likely to soften a particular rule under particular circumstances. They try out "divide and conquer" tactics: for example, saying, "But Mom, Daddy said I could." They quickly learn whether their parents are communicating well enough so that each knows what the other has demanded or decided. Parents with a strong alliance learn, for their part, to respond to a child's demands with "We'll see" or "I'll talk to your mother (father)," so as to allow themselves time for working out a joint strategy.

In two-parent households, each parent may at times protect children from potentially damaging behavior by the other parent. Hetherington and colleagues (1982) have called this parental "buffering." Their research suggests that in intact families, one well-functioning parent can shield children from the risks entailed in exposure to a depressed, abusive, or neglectful parent. Parents know each other's behavior patterns well enough so that one parent can often anticipate a blowup on the part of the other parent, and may be able to forestall it. If one parent does become enraged or drunk or potentially abusive, the more stable parent may be able to get the children out of reach of the endangering one. In less extreme situations, if a parent has misgivings about something the other parent is doing vis-à-vis the children—for example, doing things that frighten them, or allowing too much or too little autonomy—there are opportunities for the parents to discuss the issue and perhaps influence each other's parental style.

Co-parenting as the Parental Alliance Breaks Up

New family structures. In some divorcing families, the parental alliance has already begun to crumble before the couple actually separates. One parent may form an alliance with the child to exclude the other parent, thus forming what family therapists consider an unhealthy subsystem (Minuchin, 1985). Parents may also compete for the children's loyalty, and differences in their values and standards may have become evident to all family members. Recent evidence indicates that parents in conflict do not hold their children to as high standards as do parents who have a harmonious relationship (Goldberg, 1990). This research suggests that as the parental alliance weakens, the behavior standards for the children decline. If parents quarrel openly in front of the children, and show contempt for each other, the atmosphere of mutual respect that underlies their joint authority and effective co-parenting is seriously weakened. In some families, however, the decision to separate is rather sudden (perhaps triggered by one parent's discovery of the other's extramarital affair), and the parental alliance may have been well maintained up to the point of separation.

When the parents do actually separate, the parental alliance must obviously be profoundly affected. For children and adults alike, the separation of spousal roles from parental roles is difficult. The mere fact of spousal divorce means that one parent (or both) no longer considers the other lovable as a spouse. Even when a mother says to a child: "I don't love your father any more, but *you* should (may) love him," the message is a mixed one. The kind of teamwork that was illustrated in the vignettes presented earlier can hardly occur when each parent is operating from a different household.

Divorce requires that the division of child-rearing responsibilities must be renegotiated. In order to understand the degree and kind of co-parenting that can occur following divorce, we now consider the nature of the post-divorce family structure or structures that take the place of the pre-divorce structure. When therapists or mediators deal with couples who have passed the point of attempting reconciliation, a major goal is to help the couple dampen or at least manage their interpersonal conflict so that they can complete their spousal detachment from each other while still being able to do necessary business together concerning the children. Still, there are some differences among therapists concerning the kind of family structure that should be the outcome. One set of theorists suggests that so long as a child is continuing to spend time with both parents, the child is a member of a single family structure that includes both parents. The pre-divorce family structure continues (or can, or should continue) as a structural entity, and is merely reorganized so that the non-resident parent becomes an extended family member in the same sense that grandparents are: living in a different household, but nevertheless linked to the resident family by family ties and obligations. A contrasting viewpoint suggests that the prior nuclear family structure no longer exists, and is replaced by *two* new structures, organized within each of the two parental households. In the case of a child who spends time in both households, the child is a member of two families.

These differences in viewpoint are more than merely semantic. They affect the way mediators and family therapists define the goals of intervention. Working from the first point of view, for example, Isaacs and colleagues (1986) say:

> We place special emphasis on problem solving—parent with parent, and parent with child—that allows family members to struggle face to face with each other during the process of reorganizing the unit. We view the immediate family (mother, father and their children) as the unit of direct intervention. (Isaacs, Montalvo, and Abelsohn, 1986, p. 5)

> The unit has to maintain some subsystems, shed others, and develop new ones. In working with subsystems, we follow two elementary principles: we support those that will help the family fulfill its functions, and we attempt to limit the influence of antagonistic groupings. (p. 6)

> Separation and divorce need not herald the death of the family. For some, separation can be a transition and not an end. The well-being of parents and children can be enhanced as the family—albeit considerably changed—attempts to remain a viable, self-propelled and interprotective unit. (p. 219)

These therapists make it clear that a guiding principle of their therapeutic efforts is to prevent either parent from "abdicating"—to keep both parents involved and functioning together as co-parents.

In contrast, Preston and Madison (1984), two therapists working in the Family Court of Australia, see the post-divorce family as made up of the custodial parent and children. For a child living with the mother, the mother's household is "home" for the child, even if the child visits the father. The boundary around the old system is gone, and a new boundary is formed around the mother and children. The father does not have a place within this new boundary. His visits may be experienced as intrusions, particularly if visitation is imposed against the wishes of the primary parent. Preston and Madison argue that visitation arrangements should have rules that give the new family (that is, the mother-child dyad) control over the conditions of the father's presence in their household. They say:

> Following separation, the family boundary becomes disturbed. The departure of one spouse from the family makes this boundary diffuse; it becomes more permeable and less able to provide a sense of security and containment for the members of the family. This is because of disturbance in the spousal sub-system which is responsible for maintaining the family boundary. The important task in the initial period after separation is to re-establish the boundary around the family. Disputes over access (visitation) can serve to prevent the formation of a clear family boundary. (Preston and Madison, 1984, p. 39)

In short, Preston and Madison believe that access by the father should be limited and/or clearly regulated in the interest of strengthening the boundary around a new family structure that does not include him.[5]

We are not completely satisfied with either view about the changes in family structure. Let us consider first the most common residential situation, that in which the children are living with the mother and maintaining some degree of contact with a non-residential father. Certainly if the father is continuing to pay child support, he is joining with the mother in the enormously important function of providing food and shelter for the family. In this sense, he continues as part of the original nuclear family. Yet in other equally important respects, he is not part of this family because of the spousal divorce. He no longer has a key to the house; he cannot arrive at the house and expect to join the family for dinner; he does not share in the plans the mother and children have for their joint activities, nor in their confidences with one another. The child's family household is not the father's "home," and normally he no longer shares in the household upkeep and chores. It has been said that home is the place where "they always have to take you in." A divorced non-resident father does not have the right to be "taken in," nor to have his needs considered by other family members, and he no longer functions as a co-parent in the day-to-day rearing of the children. Indeed, it may be said that a couple's decision to divorce is in effect a decision no longer to be members of the same family.

A non-resident father is not a member of an extended family, in the same sense that grandparents are. In sociological writings, the term "extended family" usually refers to a network of kin (people related by blood, marriage, or adoption) who exchange goods and services. Thus members of the extended family might baby-sit for the nuclear family, help in finding jobs for the parents or the young people as they grow into adulthood, help to provide the down payment for a house, and so on. In addition, members of an extended family usually share important symbolic occasions: birthdays, holidays, weddings, funerals. Usually, loyalty, a common identity, and pride mark an extended family. Clearly the children's father and his parents are not part of the mother's extended family as so defined. They are kin to the *child* (related by blood ties), but not kin to the extended *family* of which the child and mother are the central system.

As we see it, divorce necessarily involves the formation of at least one new family structure, having its own boundaries. When one parent simply disappears from the children's lives at the time of divorce, the family is "reconstituted" as a single-parent family. It may later be transformed in structure once more with the addition of a stepparent. When the children continue to spend time with both parents, this need not imply that mother, father, and children are now a "reconstituted" version of the original family. True, from the *child's* standpoint, both parents (and both sets of grandparents) may still be seen as members of the child's family (Funder, 1991). But when both parents remain involved in the children's lives following divorce, we believe that from a structural standpoint it is more accurate to say that a single family (both nuclear and extended) has been replaced by two family structures, and that the child may be a member of both.

Do any vestiges of the old boundary around the original family as a unit remain? This, we think, is a matter of degree, and varies from family to family. Clearly, it depends on whether, and in what way, the parental alliance is maintained. There may be no residual vestiges in circumstances where the divorced parents no longer communicate with one another concerning the children. On the other hand, there are situations in which divorced parents cooperate actively, attempting to coordinate rules for the children in the two households and jointly making decisions about the children's lives. Here, one aspect of the old family unit continues to exist, but the structure is qualitatively very different from its predecessor. The old family unit was one whose members lived together, shared many plans and activities with one another, and had unlimited access to one another. The new version of the original mother-father-child "unit" involves only a limited sharing of information and plans about the child (which can be seen as a limited overlap between the two family structures). Other aspects of the family life are separate, even in this "ideal" case of high parental cooperation. Even for those parents who succeed in the important task of developing a cooperative co-parenting relationship, we see their parental unit not as a simple continuation of their old co-parenting processes but as something that must be constructed anew to fit their greatly changed circumstances.

Single parenting in separate households. We have seen that in intact families, mothers and fathers frequently have somewhat different roles and interactive styles where parenting is concerned. These differences, we believe, have implications for the way the two parents will function as single parents. In view of the division of labor that typically prevails in pre-separation households, with mothers having the predominant role in child-rearing, we may expect that there would be considerable continuity in the way mothers carry out parenting functions during the times when the children are with them following the separation. And indeed, Hetherington and colleagues (1982) have reported that the quality of a mother's parenting after divorce can be fairly well predicted from her pre-separation parenting activities. The way divorced fathers interacted with their children when the children were with them was not so predictable, however. Fathers, as single parents, or even as visiting parents, typically have more to learn than single mothers do.

Nevertheless, for mothers there are important changes. Although the mother has the advantage of greater experience in household management and day-to-day child care, she must continue to do these things when there are increasing demands on her time for other activities (for example, increased working hours outside the home). The spousal backup for her authority is largely absent. Furthermore, children tend to believe that parenting is primarily the responsibility of mothers rather than fathers. Consequently, they do not experience (or at least, do not express) any particular indebtedness to custodial mothers for their caretaking, whereas they do express such appreciation to custodial fathers, who are seen by the children as doing something beyond what might be expected (Ambert, 1982). In short, in the eyes of children, being cared for by one's mother is a right; being cared for by one's father is more a privilege. Hence, children may feel they "owe" more respect and obedience to a custodial father, and may be less responsive to a custodial mother's attempts at control. There is reason to expect, then, that custodial mothers may encounter more difficulty in maintaining discipline. Furthermore, the additional financial pressures and the lack of a partner to share household chores and child-care duties can produce sufficient stress to make the mother more irritable toward the children, less responsive, and less patient.[6] For some mothers, on the other hand, the father's departure from the household may relieve stress and simplify parenting.

Single fathers, we predict, will have a different set of problems during the times when they have responsibility for the children. Discipline should not pose any special difficulties for them. For non-residential fathers who see the child only on brief weekend visits—particularly if the children do not stay overnight—the father may become mainly a "pal," playmate, or friend and not so much an important authority figure. But for fathers who have their children with them for any substantial portion of residential time, the "playmate" relationship must be transformed into a managerial one. As noted above, fathers may have an advantage in terms of the children's readiness to comply to parental directives. Hetherington and colleagues (Hetherington, Cox, and Cox, 1982) report that the young children in their study obeyed their divorced fathers more readily than their divorced mothers. However, all these fathers were non-custodial, and we have no information concerning how these influence patterns would work out with custodial fathers.

There is probably great variability among custodial fathers in what and how much they have to learn. A small group of fathers may have assumed primary parental management duties before the divorce, sometimes because their wives were unwilling or unable to assume them. For many fathers, however, assuming the primary parental role will be new. When the children are young, fathers who have not been especially vigilant before must learn to pay attention to small noises (or silences) that signal impending dangers or otherwise call for parental action. They must plan agendas for the children, and modify their own schedules to fit in with the children's schedules. They must monitor the whereabouts, friendships, activities, and moods of the children if they are to provide effective guidance, control, and support.

Fathers, like mothers, may experience some parental gains as well. Now they can interact directly with their children without the mother's mediation. Fathers who have taken on a major role in child-rearing report that they get to know their children much better than they did in a traditional father's role, and feel closer to them (Russell, 1982). But, at least initially, their lack of familiarity with the details of the children's lives may make it more difficult to monitor the children's whereabouts and supervise their activities. In Chapter 9 we explore the differences and similarities between residential mothers and residential fathers in the nature of the difficulties they encounter in child-rearing during the post-separation period.

Co-parenting after separation. In some families, divorce means that one parent essentially drops out of the parental role—that is, he or she seldom sees the children, and does not participate in child care or child-rearing. For such families, the question of parental cooperation hardly arises. In other families, both parents continue to be involved, and for these families important new issues emerge: What kind of agreement can the parents come to concerning the amount of time the children will spend with each parent? How will they divide responsibilities for getting the children back and forth? Should they operate independently, or should they try to achieve some form of coordination between the two households with respect to standards of behavior set for the children, discipline, chores, allowances, privileges, and so forth? When important decisions need to be made concerning the child's life (for example, what school the child should attend, medical care, religious training), should the parents plan to discuss each issue and decide jointly? What decisions should be left to the independent decision-making of whichever parent has the child with him/her at the time?

It is possible for parents who are both seeing the children to carry out their parental functions almost entirely separately from each other—that is, to practice "parallel" parenting. Alternatively, parents can maintain contact with each other in connection with their joint responsibilities for the children—and this contact can be either cooperative or conflicted. Although we have argued that the parental alliance can no longer function as before, it is certainly possible for divorced parents to create a new co-parental relationship that permits them to do business together concerning the children in a cooperative and mutually supportive way. Indeed, this is the goal of many mediators and family therapists who work with divorced parents. Yet clearly, many parents are so caught up in the emotional turmoil of their spousal divorce that they cannot construct a co-parental relationship.

The parental divorce is especially complex in cases of joint custody. A joint custody decree implies that parents will share responsibility for the children after divorce. Joint legal custody gives both parents the right and responsibility to be involved in decisions about the children's education, medical care, and religious training. When the decree is for joint physical custody, this suggests that the two will share in day-to-day responsibility for the upbringing of the children. Such arrangements presumably call for a considerable degree of cooperative co-parenting. However, little is known about how joint-custodial parents manage their co-parental functions: the extent to which they are able to cooperate, the degree of conflict, the amount of joint decision-making, and the way they carry on their parental business together. In fact, we do not know how co-parental functions are managed between divorced parents in *any* of the three custodial arrangements. In Chapter 9 we will examine these processes. Clearly, joint decision-making and other forms of cooperation should be possible when both parents are eager to sustain each other's involvement with the children. But what about cases in which joint custody is ordered over the objections of one of the parents? Or cases where the parents agree to it because they can find no other solution to a serious conflict over custody? The nature of co-parenting under conditions in which parents have initially been in conflict about custody has seldom been examined, and we will consider this matter in some detail in the chapters that follow.

A final word should be said about "buffering." Hetherington and colleagues (1982) have noted that as time goes on following parental separation, the quality of children's functioning becomes more and more dependent on the quality of the residential parent's functioning, and less and less related to characteristics of the non-residential parent. This can have either positive or negative implications—sometimes both—as far as the children are concerned. A competent residential parent can raise the children without having to worry about interference from a spouse or—in more extreme cases—about protecting the children from the other parent's endangering behavior. On the other hand, the children are left more vulnerable to the residential parent in terms of that parent's mood states, lack of parenting skills, or life style.

Parents functioning in two different households can hardly serve as effective buffers or mediators between the children and the other parent when the children are at the other parent's house. For a parent who is deeply committed to the children's welfare, this can be one of the most frustrating situations a divorced parent faces. Some parents are in the fortunate position of feeling that the former spouse is entirely reliable as a parent. But others are not; they remember all too well the former spouse's flash points and weaknesses. Indeed, they are probably more aware of these weaknesses than of the other parent's strengths. Some of their concerns will surely be unrealistic, but others will be accurate appraisals of kinds of situations that can arise between a given parent and child in the course of ordinary life situations. In the chapters that follow, we will explore the frequency and nature of such parental concerns.

The Legal Divorce

To divorcing spouses and their children, family law is inescapable. The legal system affects when a divorce may occur, and how it must be procured. It may influence the consequences of divorce as well. Nevertheless, the influence of the legal system on the way particular parents divide child-rearing responsibilities is likely to be highly variable: it may influence some families a great deal, and others much less so. Our goal is to provide a framework for understanding the complex role of law at the time of divorce.[7]

As we see it, divorce law primarily provides a framework for private ordering and a procedure for the resolution of legal disputes between divorcing spouses. For some families, the legal system will exert a powerful influence on the allocation of parental responsibilities, and on the terms of the economic and parental divorce. Consider a divorcing couple so locked in conflict that a judge must decide the custodial and support provisions of the divorce decree. In such a case, the judge is essentially determining the arrangements for the children by applying relevant legal doctrine. For other families, however, divorce law may have little effect. Consider divorcing parents who establish their post-divorce arrangements without any legal conflict and without considering the formal legal standards that a judge might apply in court. For a couple like this, the legal proceeeding is nothing more than a required formality, in which the petition is uncontested and a judge simply rubber-stamps a decree. Some families will obviously fall between these two extremes. These couples may resolve the custodial and financial issues posed by divorce through negotiations, where each parent is represented by counsel. Although a judge may never need to decide any issue, the bargaining may take place in the shadow of the law, and thus is influenced if not determined by the legal system. One purpose of this chapter is to consider how the rules and procedures used in court for adjudicating disputes may affect decision-making, not just in those cases decided by a judge but for those divorces where the legal issues are resolved outside of court.[8]

Private Ordering

Legal doctrine separates the potential consequences of divorce into four distributional questions, which relate closely to the economic and parental divorce. The questions posed by the legal divorce are the following: (1) how should the couple's property—the stock of existing wealth owned separately or together—be divided? (marital property law); (2) what ongoing claims should each spouse have on the future earnings of the other? (alimony law); (3) what ongoing claims should a child have for a share of the earnings or wealth of each of his parents? (child-support law); and (4) how should the responsibilities and opportunities of child-rearing be divided in the future? (child-custody and visitation law).

These four strands of law, and the procedural mechanisms for their implementation, have conventionally been seen by legal commentators from a highly regulatory perspective. Analysis seems premised on the notion that the distributional consequences of divorce are to be determined through judicial or administrative proceedings in which legal standards are imposed from above on the divorcing spouses. As we suggested in Chapter 1, we see the primary function of contemporary divorce law not as imposing order from above, but rather as providing a framework within which divorcing couples can themselves determine their post-dissolution rights and responsibilities. This process by which parties to a marriage are empowered to create their own enforceable legal commitments is a form of private ordering. To what extent does state law permit parties to make their own law by private agreement?

The parties' legal power to determine the consequences of divorce depends on the presence of children.[9] When the divorcing couple has no children, the law generally recognizes the power of the parties upon separation or divorce to make their own arrangements concerning marital property and alimony. In California, for example, the couple's agreement allocating their property and establishing the amount and duration of spousal support can, if the parties wish, be made binding and final—that is, not subject to later modification by a court.

In families with minor children, existing law imposes some formal doctrinal constraints on private ordering. For those allocational decisions that directly affect children—that is, child support, custody, and visitation—parents lack complete power to make their own law. Judges, exercising the state *parens patriae* power, are said to have responsibility to assess whether the custodial and support arrangements for the children are appropriate.[10] Private agreements concerning these matters are possible and common, but parental agreements cannot entirely bind the court, which, as a matter of official dogma, is said to have an independent responsibility to ensure that the arrangements serve the child's welfare. Thus, the court has the power to reject a parental agreement and order some other level of child support or some other custodial arrangement it believes to be more desirable. Moreover, even if the parties' initial agreement is accepted by the court, it lacks finality. A court may, at any time during the child's minority, reopen and modify the initial decree in light of any subsequent change in circumstances. Parents lack the legal power to deprive the court of this jurisdiction.

Available evidence on how the legal system processes undisputed divorce cases involving minor children suggests that parents actually have broad powers to make their own deals. Typically, separation agreements and uncontested decrees are rubber-stamped in cases involving children. The parents' broad discretion is not surprising for several reasons. First, getting information is difficult when there is no dispute. The state usually has very little resources for a thorough and independent investigation of the family's circumstances. Furthermore, parents may be unwilling to provide damaging information that may upset their agreed arrangements. Second, the applicable legal standards are extremely vague and give judges very little guidance as to what circumstances justify overriding a parental decision. Finally, there are obvious limitations on a court's practical power to control the parents once they leave the courtroom. For all these reasons, it is not surprising that most courts behave as if their function in the divorce process is *dispute settlement*, not child protection. When there is no dispute, busy judges or registrars are typically quite willing to rubber-stamp a private agreement in order to conserve resources for disputed cases.

Reexamination of the four doctrinal strands from the perspective of spouses who are negotiating their own settlements suggests several important conclusions. First, the legal rules for property, support, and custody may influence, but they certainly need not control, how parents make arrangements for children. Instead, in ways we shall describe, we see the relevant legal doctrine as creating bargaining endowments that *may* affect the economic divorce and the parental divorce.

Second, from the perspective of spouses negotiating outside of court in a regime that permits private ordering, the boundaries between these various doctrinal strands are not so clear. Marital property, alimony, and child-support issues are all basically problems of money, and the distinctions among them may become very blurred. Third, custody standards permit parents potentially to divide parental responsibilities and the time the child spends with each in a wide variety of ways—many different sorts of custody arrangements are possible. Finally, the money and custody issues are likely to be linked together.

The Money Element of the Bargain

Alimony and child support. California child support rules involve guidelines in which tables are provided that suggest the minimum child support that should be paid in light of the relative earnings of the two parents, the number of children, and the amount of time the children spend in each household. The spousal standards are much less clear-cut: alimony is said to depend on the length of the marriage, the relative earning capacity of the two spouses, and their other assets. Not only are the considerations used in establishing child support and spousal support somewhat different, but legal doctrine also provides different rules for the duration. Spousal support terminates automatically on remarriage or death, and it may terminate earlier if the parties agree or a court so decides. Child support, on the other hand, normally ends only when a child reaches maturity or is emancipated.

Notwithstanding these differences, from the economic perspective of bargaining spouses, alimony and child support may seem interchangeable: both involve periodic money payments and, indeed, will often be paid by a single check from the non-custodial parent. A father may find it psychologically easier to pay child support, which will presumably help only his children, than alimony, which explicitly helps his former spouse. But this characterization hardly imposes much of a practical constraint. A custodial spouse is not required to keep track of how child support money is spent, and the courts do not supervise child support expenditures once a payment has been made. Even if a court were concerned with how transfer payments are spent, accounting would be extremely difficult because of joint consumption.

Lump-sum payments versus payments over time. California is a community property state. Upon divorce, the legal rule is that all property accumulated during a marriage from the earnings of either spouse is treated as community property and is divided equally between the spouses.

From a bargaining perspective, an important distinction is between a lump-sum transfer of money or property, typical of a community property division, and payments over time, whether alimony, child support, or a combination of the two. When a recipient is receiving money over time, he or she faces the risk that the promise may be broken, or may be enforceable only at considerable expense. Periodic alimony or child support payments thus pose risks of noncollection that are avoided by a lump-sum settlement. Lump-sum and periodic transfers are also taxed differently under the Internal Revenue Code.

Despite these important differences, during bargaining it is theoretically possible to convert lump-sum offers into offers involving flows over time. For any set of time preferences, one spouse can in principle convert a money flow over time into a present-value equivalent. Moreover, a recipient can always discount the value of a promise to reflect the perceived risks that the full amount may never be received. Finally, the tax consequences of alternatives can be evaluated and compared.

For those fortunate families with significant assets, this ability to compare different packages may have important implications for private bargaining. When a sophisticated couple has sufficient economic resources, the two spouses and their lawyers may attempt to seek out circumstances in which a different characterization, because of tax effects or differences in risk or time preferences of the parties, can make both spouses better off.

On the other hand, for most families this may be no more than a theoretical possibility because of the limited amount and special nature of the property to be divided. Few divorcing couples have savings that are substantially greater than their debts, or own much in the way of stocks, bonds, or other investment assets. Even for solidly middle-class divorcing couples, the only major assets are typically the equity in a family home, and perhaps certain vested pension rights. For many, their property consists entirely of clothing, household effects, and one or perhaps two automobiles.

Custody

The remaining element of the bargain concerns the custodial duties and rights of the parents. Custody is said to be governed by the best interest of the child test, with no preference based on gender. This standard obviously provides broad discretion. By varying the time the child spends with each parent, and by assigning particular child-rearing tasks to one parent or the other, a divorce settlement may divide prerogatives and obligations in many different ways. At the extreme, one parent may be entirely responsible for the child all the time, with the other spouse having no contact with the child. Or divorcing parents may agree to share child-rearing responsibilities equally after divorce through joint physical custody; for example, the child may live with each parent one-half of the time, with the parents together deciding where and how the child should be educated, who the pediatrician should be, and so forth. Between these extremes, many other alternatives are often possible.

The Relationship of Custody and Money

The preceding analysis suggests that in most cases divorce bargaining has two elements: money and custody. From a bargaining perspective, even these two elements may be linked for any of several reasons.

First, under California law at the time of our study, the amount of child support to which a parent is entitled is a function of the percentage of time the child is to spend with each parent. A parent without custody is obviously not entitled to receive child support. In cases where parents are sharing day-to-day responsibilities for child-rearing, the amount of the child support transfer may depend upon the relative time the child spends with each parent, as well as upon the parents' comparative incomes.[11]

A second reason the two are linked is that the negotiating process itself provides opportunities for the parties to link money and custody issues. One troubling possibility relates to strategic bargaining. Some commentators suggest that many fathers use custody as a bargaining chip: they may threaten to contest custody when the real goal is to coerce the mother into accepting less support.

A third reason why money and custody issues may be linked is that, over some range of alternatives, each parent may be willing to exchange custodial rights and obligations for income or wealth. Economic analysis suggests as much. Although this notion may offend some, a contrary assertion would mean that a parent with full custody would accept no sum of money in exchange for slightly less custody, even if the parent were extremely poor. Faced with such alternatives, many parents might prefer to see the child a bit less often and be able to give the child better housing, more food, more education, better health care, and some luxuries. Suppose, for example, that a mother was reluctant to let the children go on regular visits to their father, but believed that she could only receive child support from her ex-husband if she agreed to visitation. She might well agree; and her ex-husband might be more willing to pay support if he could be assured of seeing the children.

In most states, formal legal doctrine seeks to prohibit these connections between custody and money: in a suit brought to collect overdue support payments, a father cannot defend on the ground that his ex-wife did not permit visitation. Nor have courts permitted a custodial parent to cut off visitation because of a failure to pay support. Nevertheless, it is often time-consuming and expensive to enforce promises in court. There can be substantial advantages, therefore, from the perspective of one or both bargainers, in having piecemeal bargains that spread support payments over time and, as a practical matter, link the custody issues (especially visitation) with the financial issues. If a father who values visitation fails to make support payments, then, quite apart from the mother's ability to enforce his promise in court (which may often be too slow and expensive to be effective), the mother may believe that she can retaliate by informally cutting off the father's visitation or making it more difficult. Even though this tactic has no legal validity, it is nevertheless likely to be faster, cheaper, and more effective than court enforcement. Similarly, a father may believe that his ability to cut off support will ensure that the mother will keep her word concerning visitation. The links between support and visitation are reinforced not only by the parties' power to take self-help measures, but also by important cultural values. Many believe that support obligations and visitation rights are inextricably tied together in terms of what it means to be a parent. A father who fails to support his children, at least when he has the financial capacity to do so, may in popular perception no longer be entitled to maintain a relationship with his minor children if the custodial mother objects. Similarly, a mother who purposely prevents a father from maintaining his relationship with his children after a divorce may be viewed as no longer entitled to his support.

Toward a Theory of Divorce Bargaining

Ideally, a bargaining theory would allow us to predict how alternative legal rules would affect negotiations between particular spouses and what kind of deal, if any, they would strike. Such a theory might be combined with knowledge of how the characteristics that determine bargaining behavior are distributed among divorcing couples. Alternative rules and procedures could then be compared by evaluating the patterns of outcomes that would result under each. Unfortunately, no existing theory of bargaining allows confident prediction of how different legal rules and procedures would influence outcomes.

What follows is not a complete theory. Instead, we identify several factors that seem to be important influences on or determinants of the outcomes of bargaining, and then offer some observations on the bargaining process. The factors are (1) the preferences and commitments of the divorcing parents; (2) the bargaining endowments created by legal rules that indicate the particular allocation a court will impose if the parties fail to reach agreement; (3) the degree of uncertainty concerning the legal outcome if the parties go to court, which is linked to the parties' attitudes toward risk; and (4) transaction costs and the parties' respective abilities to bear them.

Parental preferences. Money is important to both parents. Each would like to emerge from the divorce negotiations as economically well off as possible, and there is no reason to believe that either values financial security more than the other. Preferences with regard to custody, however, can differ considerably between parents.[12] Some parents are more willing than others to expend the time and energy—and make the necessary sacrifices—involved in rearing children. High willingness stems partly from taking pleasure in spending time with the children and seeing their development, partly from a strong commitment to the children's welfare, and partly from a sense of confidence in being able to handle child-rearing tasks competently. Some parents, who lack either the interest, the commitment, or the confidence, may prefer to have a relatively small share of child-rearing responsibilities, or even none at all. Many, both fathers and mothers, like to find a balance between their outside interests, including commitment to careers, and their child-rearing commitments, and such parents may be more willing to share child-rearing responsibilities with their former spouse than parents whose primary and most satisfying role is caring for children.

A wide variety of prerogatives and duties are associated with child-rearing, and parental preferences may vary among them. A parent may value very highly some tasks, such as reading the child a bedtime story, and place negative value on others, such as shopping for school clothes. Preferences may vary depending on how involved a parent has been in day-to-day child-rearing activities: some may want to become more involved, some less, and some may simply seek to sustain the same level of involvement they had before the separation. How well can a divorcing parent assess accurately his or her own preferences concerning custodial alternatives? Making such assessments is difficult and complicated. The information each parent has relates to the actual division of child-rearing tasks in an ongoing family. As we have seen, dissolution or divorce inevitably alters this division, and the parent may discover new advantages or disadvantages to child-rearing responsibilities. Moreover, the parents' own needs may alter drastically after divorce. A parent interested in dating may find the child an intrusion in a way that the child never was during marriage.

In addition, a parent's interest in children (and confidence in being able to manage their care) may vary according to the children's age. Because children and parents both change, and changes may be unpredictable, projecting parental preferences for custody ten years into the future is a formidable task. Nevertheless, most parents have some self-awareness, however imperfect, and no third party (such as a judge) is likely to have better information about a parent's tastes, present or future.

Parental preferences, of course, will not generally be determined solely by self-interested judgments; a theory must take note of possible altruism or spite. One hopes that parental preferences reflect a desire for their children's happiness and well-being, quite apart from any parental needs. For example, a father may commit himself to child support payments beyond what he predicts a court would require, simply because he does not want his children to suffer economic detriment from a divorce. A mother may agree to substantial visitation for the father because she thinks this is good for the children, even though she personally despises the father and wants nothing more to do with him. Similarly, either or both spouses may feel compassion toward a former spouse, and attach weight to his or her happiness and desires.

At the other extreme, one can easily imagine preferences that reflect spite and envy. A spouse may simply have a strong wish to punish the other spouse, regardless of the detriment to himself/herself or to the children. An angry parent, enmeshed in the spousal divorce, may engage in a protracted and largely hopeless custody fight, exhausting his or her financial reserves and bringing emotional torment to the children, simply to punish the former spouse.

How legal rules create bargaining endowments. Divorcing parents do not divide family wealth and custodial prerogatives in a legal vacuum; they bargain in the shadow of the law. The legal rules governing alimony, child support, marital property, and custody give each parent certain claims based on what each would get if the case went to trial. In other words, the outcome that the law will impose if no agreement is reached gives each parent certain bargaining chips—an endowment of sorts.

Two primary endowments are conveyed by the existing divorce laws in all states: (1) non-custodial parents have a right to visitation, unless they are shown to be unfit; (2) non-custodial parents have an obligation to pay child support to custodial parents, within limits based upon need and ability to pay. Parents bargain in the knowledge of these two constraints; both know that if either tries to abrogate the rights of the other in either of these respects, the aggrieved party can go to court with reasonable expectations that his or her rights will be protected. The legal rules and case law relating to marital property and alimony may also entitle a mother to a determinate share of the husband's assets. In negotiations under these conditions, a rational spouse would never consent to a division that left him or her worse off than if he or she insisted on going to court. The range of negotiated outcomes would be limited to those that leave both parents as well off as they would be in the absence of a bargain.

Nevertheless, we would not necessarily expect parents to split custody and money the way a judge would if they failed to agree. In a state where the courts usually award physical custody to the mother—along with some child support—with "reasonable" visitation to the father, the father might well negotiate for more child time and the mother for less. Suppose, for example, that a mother needs to get further education in order to become self-supporting. Even though she wants full custody and a court would probably award it to her, she knows she would have difficulty managing full-time single parenting, at least for the first few years following the separation. Suppose that the father has taken a job with less out-of-town travel, so that he would be in a better position to expand his share of child time, and proposes that they try joint physical custody. The mother realizes that, under the court's child support guidelines, she would get less child support with joint than with sole custody. But the father offers to pay her tuition for further training. She might consider this the best bargain under the circumstances. In any event, because the parents' situations differ with regard to their readiness and ability to manage child-care responsibilities, it will often be possible for the parties to negotiate some outcome that makes both better off than they would be if they simply accepted the result a court would impose.

The Question of Risk

Legal rules are generally not as simple or straightforward as is suggested by the last example. Often the outcome in court is far from certain, with any number of outcomes possible. Indeed, existing legal standards governing custody are striking for their lack of precision and thus provide a bargaining backdrop clouded by uncertainty. The California standard for resolving custody disputes is the "best interests of the child." Except in situations when one parent poses a substantial threat to the child's well-being, predicting who will get custody under this standard may be difficult indeed, especially given the rejection of any presumption in favor of maternal custody. Similarly, the legal standards governing alimony are also vague and allow courts broad discretion in disputed cases.

Analyzing the effects of uncertainty on bargaining is an extremely complicated task. It is apparent, however, that the effects in any particular case will depend in part on the attitudes of the two spouses toward risk—what has been called "risk aversion." This can be illustrated by considering a mechanism suggested in *Beyond the Best Interests of the Child* for resolving custody disputes between equally acceptable spouses: they would draw straws, with the winner getting full custodial rights and the loser none.

Drawing straws, like flipping a coin, gives each parent a 50 percent chance of receiving full custody, but also a 50 percent chance of receiving none. Some parents would be willing to take the risk of getting none of the child's time in order to have a good chance at full custody. Others would be entirely unwilling to take the risk of losing contact with the child, and rather than toss a coin, would give up the chance for full custody in return for an assured fraction of the child's time. A parent who would accept a certain outcome of partial custody in order to avoid the gamble—the chance of losing the coin flip and receiving no custody—is risk-averse. Other parents may be risk preferrers: they would rather take the gamble and have a 50 percent chance of winning full custody than accept the certain outcome of splitting the child's time.

We do not know the likely consequences of one parent being more risk-averse than the other; probably the more risk-averse of the two parents is at something of a bargaining disadvantage. However, the reality of custody litigation is more complicated, and the knowledge of the parties much less complete, than in our hypothetical case. The parties in the example know the standard for decision and the odds of winning custody in court. But in real situations, the exact odds of various possible outcomes are not known by the parties; often they do not even know what information or criteria the judge will use in deciding.

Transaction Costs

Costs are involved in resolving the distributional consequences of separation or divorce, and in securing the divorce itself. The transaction costs that the parties must bear may take many forms, some financial and some emotional. The most obvious and tangible involve the expenditure of money. Professional fees—particularly for lawyers—must be paid by one or both parties. In addition, there are filing fees and court costs. More difficult to measure, but also important, are the emotional and psychological costs involved in the dispute-settlement process. Lawsuits generally are emotionally burdensome; the psychological costs imposed by bargaining (and still more by litigation) are particularly acute in divorce.

The magnitude of these transaction costs, both actual and expected, can influence negotiations and the outcome of bargaining. In the dissolution process, one spouse, and that spouse's attorney, can substantially affect the magnitude of the transaction costs that must be borne by the other spouse. It is generally the case that the party better able to bear the transaction costs, whether financial or emotional, will have an advantage in divorce bargaining.

In divorce, transaction costs will generally tend to be (1) higher if there are minor children involved, because of the additional and intensely emotional allocational issues to be determined; (2) an increasing function of the amount of property and income the spouses have, since it is rational to spend more on negotiation when the possible rewards are higher; and (3) higher when there is a broad range of possible outcomes in court. Our analysis of transaction costs certainly suggests that most divorcing spouses would seek to avoid adjudication and instead resolve their disputes by less expensive means. Divorcing spouses usually have no incentive to take cases to court for their precedential value. Unlike insurance companies, public-interest organizations, and other "repeat players," a divorcing spouse will generally have no expectation that an adjudicated case will create precedent, or that precedent created will be of personal benefit in future litigation.

Given the advantages of negotiated settlements, why would divorcing spouses ever require courtroom adjudication of their disputes? There are a variety of reasons why some divorce cases will be litigated.

Spite. One or both parties may be motivated in substantial measure by a desire to punish the other spouse, rather than simply to increase their own net worth.

Distaste for negotiation. Even though it costs more, one or both parties may prefer the adjudicative process (with third-party decision) to any process that requires a voluntary agreement with the other spouse. Face-to-face contact may be extremely distasteful, and the parties may not be able to negotiate—even with lawyers acting as intermediaries—because of distrust or distaste.

Calling the bluff: The breakdown of negotiations. If the parties are heavily engaged in strategic behavior and get carried away with making threats, a courtroom battle may result, despite both parties' preference for a settlement. The negotiations may resemble a game of "chicken," in which two teenagers set their cars on a collision course to see who turns first. Some crack-ups may result.

Uncertainty and risk preferences. The exact odds for any given outcome in court are unknown, and it has been suggested that litigants typically overestimate their chances of winning. To the extent that one or both of the parties overestimate their chances of winning, more cases will be litigated than in a world in which the outcome is uncertain but the odds are known. In any event, when the outcome is uncertain, settlement prospects depend on the risk preferences of the two spouses.

No middle ground. If the object of dispute cannot be divided into small enough increments—whether because of the law, the practical circumstances, or the nature of the subject at issue—there may be no middle ground in which to strike a feasible compromise. Optimal bargaining occurs when, in economic terminology, nothing is indivisible.

In sum, there are reasons why some cases might be litigated. But our theory would certainly suggest why the overwhelming majority of divorces would be resolved through negotiation—not adjudication.

The Task Facing the Spouses: Is Divorce a Zero-Sum Game?

One view of divorce bargaining sees it as a process in which any benefit to the wife must necessarily come at the husband's expense, and vice versa. Both the money issues and the custody issues do have distributive elements, with a zero-sum characteristic. When a divorcing couple must divide $1,000 in a checking account, a division that gives a $100-larger share to the mother must necessarily give the father a $100-smaller share. Similarly, if a father must transfer more of his paycheck to the mother's household by way of support, there is less available for him to spend on himself. Dividing the child's time can also be seen to have this distributive feature. While the child is spending time in one household, this necessarily means that the child cannot be simultaneously with the other parent.

For those who see the money and custody issues in these purely distributive terms, there is a tendency to see the process necessarily as a competitive one. Thus, divorce negotiations can be seen as adversarial, with a winner or a loser. For a person who conceptualizes divorce as dividing a pie of fixed size, "every slice I give to you is a slice I do not get; thus I need to claim as much of the value as possible by giving you as little as possible" (Lax and Sebenius, 1986, p. 33). The mind-set of competitive negotiators has been described as follows:

> To win at negotiating—and thus make the other fellow lose—one must start high, concede slowly, exaggerate the value of concessions, minimize the benefit of the other's concessions, conceal information, argue forcefully on behalf of principles that imply favorable settlements, make commitments to accept only highly favorable agreements, and be willing to outwait the other [negotiator]. The hardest of bargainers threaten to walk away or retaliate harshly if their one-sided demands are not met; they may ridicule, attack, and intimidate their adversaries. (Lax and Sebenius, 1986, p. 33)

From this vantage point, the actual bargain that is struck through negotiations—indeed, whether a bargain is struck at all—will depend on the negotiation process. During this process, each party transmits information about his or her own preferences to the other. This information may be accurate or intentionally inaccurate; each party may promise, threaten, or bluff. Parties may intentionally exaggerate their chances of winning in court in the hope of persuading the other side to accept less. Or they may threaten to impose substantial transaction costs—economic or psychological—on the other side. In short, there are a variety of ways in which the parties may engage in strategic behavior during the bargaining process.

Opportunities for strategic behavior exist because the parties often will not know with certainty (1) the other side's true preferences with regard to the allocational outcomes; (2) the other spouse's preferences or attitudes toward risk; and (3) what the outcome in court will be, or even what the actual odds in court are. Although parents may know a great deal about each other's preferences for money and children, complete knowledge of the other spouse's attitudes is unlikely.

The polar opposite view of divorce, often emphasized by those in favor of divorce mediation, rejects the image of "win-lose" but instead suggests "win-win" outcomes, in which both parents can presumably derive great value through cooperation. Negotiation theory does in fact suggest that there may be a variety of circumstances in which one party's gain need not be another's loss. If the pie can be made larger, both parents can share in the gains and receive larger slices. By cooperating in negotiations, parties can "create value" and improve the outcome from each party's point of view.

First, and most fundamentally, the father and mother may share certain interests that are not competitive. One fundamentally important interest that ideally the parents share is the well-being of their children. If a child does well, it is possible for both parents to derive benefits. Therefore, arrangements that benefit a child, whatever they may be, potentially create joint gains for both parents. To the extent that parents can cooperate in co-parenting, opportunities for the children may well be improved, and thus both parents may benefit.

Divorcing parents may have other shared interests as well. Reducing the costs of divorce—financial and emotional—once again may benefit both parents. To the extent that parents can cooperate in the process of divorce, and thus reduce transaction costs, the money saved is available for division between the two households. Large expenditures on lawyers, or on the process of divorce, on the other hand, shrink the size of the pie available for distribution. Similarly, both parents may share a long-run interest in the financial independence of the wife. By subsidizing additional education for the mother, thus increasing her independent earning potential, a father may benefit not only his wife but himself as well because of her decreased dependence.

Another important potential source of joint gains relates to the parties' preferences, and flows from differences, not similarities. The zero-sum characterization no longer holds once one acknowledges the possibility that the parents, because of their preferences, may attach different relative values to the custody and money elements. This means that there can be gains—and value created—through trades. The basic principle is simple: through negotiation one aims to discover and match what one side finds to be relatively cheap with what the other finds or expects to be more valuable. A vegetarian will trade his chicken for a carnivore's cabbage, and both will be better off. Similarly, if a mother places a higher value on her commitment to child-rearing (in comparison to earning more at a job), and a father does not, they can both be made better off if the children live with the mother.

Divorcing couples, through constructive negotiations, may continue to have opportunities to create joint gains. There may be opportunities to take advantage of economics of scale by sharing baby-sitters, health insurance, or play equipment. Parents may have different capabilities that complement each other. For instance, a father who is an engineer may be able to help the children with math homework over the phone much more efficiently than the mother who is an English teacher.

How can parents best achieve outcomes that create joint gains? There is a great deal of writing about this issue, both concerning negotiations in general and divorce in particular. The essential recommendations are similar: parents should avoid locking themselves into fixed positions, or making threats; they should fully and honestly disclose their own interests; they should communicate clearly and in an empathetic way, and try to understand the interests of the other party; and they should rationally and creatively search for alternatives that are mutually beneficial. Divorce is seen as a joint problem, in which the husband and wife cooperatively search for solutions. If parents are able to develop a cooperative relationship, they can often both derive benefits, during the course of the legal divorce and also with respect to co-parenting thereafter.

Why Cooperation May Be Difficult

As we have suggested, opportunities may exist for divorcing parents to make arrangements in ways that may make both themselves and their children better off than some alternatives. On the other hand, our discussion of the spousal, economic, and parental divorces suggests a number of potential barriers to cooperation.

The strong emotions attending the spousal divorce may pose a formidible barrier to collaborative, cool, and rational problem-solving. Joint problem-solving and negotiation work best with clear communication and good listening skills. Many couples lacked these skills during the marriage itself, and divorce is obviously an extremely difficult time to develop them. Indeed, many couples may replay in the divorce process old and dysfunctional patterns of dealing with each other during the marriage, and these patterns may make cooperation difficult or impossible

Basic features of the economic divorce also make cooperation more difficult. As noted, the size of the economic pie shrinks because of divorce and the extra expenses of sustaining two households. Social psychologists have pointed out that negotiators find it much more difficult to allocate losses than to divide potential gains. In this sense, the economic reality of shrinking resources undoubtedly inhibits cooperation and augments conflict.

Parents are usually inexperienced negotiators. But even if they were more skilled, they would face an inescapable tension between cooperative moves to create value and competitive moves to claim value. This feature of negotiations, called the "negotiator's dilemma" by Lax and Sebenius, suggests that cooperative moves—if they are not reciprocated by the other side—can indeed lead to exploitation. One spouse, after all, can cooperate in making the pie much bigger, but nevertheless be left with a very small slice. Where there is a lack of trust, each side may be fearful that if he or she makes a cooperative move that is not reciprocated, he or she will end up being exploited. On the other hand, the inability to create value through cooperation may mean that opportunities are missed to create joint gains that can be distributed fairly.

In sum, this analysis suggests why divorcing couples may gain substantial advantages when they can reach an agreement concerning the distributional consequences of divorce. They can minimize the transaction costs involved in adjudication; they can also avoid its risks and uncertainties, and negotiate an agreement that may better reflect their individual preferences. But there are certainly barriers that may make unlikely the sort of collaborative problem-solving approach that might contribute to the best sorts of outcomes.

The Range and Limits of the Law's Effects

Because of the changes brought about in the wake of the no-fault revolution, in one sense the law is now less ambitious: less is attempted by way of explicit regulation. Instead, the contemporary legal regime focuses primarily on dispute resolution, and provides a framework for private ordering. Because the parties must go through a legal proceeding in order to get a divorce, divorcing parents cannot escape the legal system entirely. Moreover, when there are minor children, the legal process requires review of the arrangements for the children, and the process itself may introduce professionals—attorneys representing individual parents; mediators; and judges—any of whom may have influence in particular cases. Finally, we have suggested that the rules that are applied in the cases that do require adjudication create bargaining endowments that may well affect outcomes.

There are also a number of reasons to believe that much divorce decision-making takes place outside the law's shadow, however. In an area so intimately touching family life, legal norms and institutions may be less important than in other areas of conflict. For example, with respect to custody, many divorcing couples may have quite traditional values—both parents may simply assume that it is right and proper for the mother to have custody of the children. There may be no discussion of alternatives. Moreover, although contemporary legal doctrine may indicate that issues concerning custody, child support, and marital property are not to be influenced by an assessment of which parent is more at fault in terms of the breakdown of the marriage, notions of fault very much influence the behavior of divorcing parents.

In legal doctrine, custody is not supposed to depend on which parent has more financial resources. Although it might be thought that custody ought to go to whichever parent can afford to provide a better house in a better school district, along with other advantages of affluence, legal doctrine says that no parent should be disadvantaged in a contest for custody because of poverty. Instead, the standard is that the custody decision should be independent of the relative financial status of the two parents, and after the custody decision is made, a wealthier parent should pay child support to a less well off custodial parent to ensure the adequacy of the child's standard of living. In practice, however, we suspect that parents sometimes do take into account the relative ability of the two parents to support the child, and in our study we will look for evidence as to whether this is the case.

The influence of legal norms may also be dampened because of costs. It is expensive to find out what legal endowments one has: indeed, the transaction costs of invoking and enforcing the formal legal norms may be so great, in relationship to the stakes, that the threat to insist on what one is entitled to may in some circumstances not be very credible.

One of the goals of this book is to explore how the law and the social realities of family life intersect, and this will lead us into a study of several related issues. We will be interested not only in the extent to which some of the newer arrangements—joint physical custody and joint legal custody—are being adopted, but also in how these families (apart from legal labels) actually share responsibilities. Our theory has also suggested the importance of parental preferences, particularly with respect to custody. In Chapter 5 we show the extent to which the custodial preferences of mothers and fathers differ, and the frequencies with which their preferences conflict. Our analysis above has pointed to several possible linkages between the transfers of money between the two parents and the relative share of the children's time that each parent receives. We will explore the extent to which the amount of child support awarded to a parent appears to be a function of the amount of time a child is spending with each parent, and the extent to which continued visitation and compliance with support obligations appear to be related.

The theory of divorce bargaining does not necessarily lead to predictions about whether there will be much or little legal conflict, but it does have clear implications concerning the procedures by which conflict is likely to be resolved. A central claim of the theory is that because parents would prefer to minimize the transaction costs of the divorce, there will be a strong tendency to avoid adjudication and instead to resolve disputes through less expensive means. Chapter 7 explores in some detail the extent to which legal conflict characterizes divorce, and shows the relative frequency with which different means of dispute resolution are employed.

We are also interested in exploring the extent to which strategic, hard-nosed bargaining characterizes the process of legal divorce. By comparing what parents said they really wanted in terms of custody with what they asked for in their legal papers, we have developed a rough, although hardly perfect, measure of the extent to which parents may be exaggerating their custodial preferences in order to gain some bargaining advantage. We are also able to suggest the extent to which parents, perhaps to avoid conflict, may actually request less custody than they might prefer. In Chapter 7 we assess the claim that mothers who secure their preferred custodial arrangements in high-conflict custody cases do so only by paying a price in terms of less financial support. In Chapter 9 we consider to what degree the hostility generated by legal conflict in the spousal divorce subsequently invades co-parental relations.

3

Characteristics of the Families Studied

To set the stage for our study of the post-separation experiences of the families in our sample, we begin by describing a few aspects of their situations at the time the separation occurred. We told the parents at the time of our first contact with them that we would not be delving into the "story" of their divorce—the history of the interpersonal conflicts they had undergone, nor the precipitating incidents that had crystallized their decision to separate. The only question relevant to this large array of issues was: "Which one of you was the first to want to end the marriage?" (The majority—nearly two-thirds—of both mothers and fathers told us that it had been the mother; most of the remaining third said that the father had been the instigator, though a small group said it had been mutual.) Overwhelmingly, though, our focus was on the children, on what would be happening in their lives as a result of the parental separation. Consequently, we have only a small amount of information about the pre-separation family situation, although certain characteristics of these families at the time of the breakup can be described.

Family Resources

At the time of their divorce, most of the families in our sample (72.4 percent) lived in Santa Clara County, California, with a smaller number living in San Mateo County. These counties lie to the south and west of San Francisco Bay. The area includes what is known as Silicon Valley, and to many this connotes a well-educated, high-income population working in high-tech jobs. In fact, many of the jobs in the Silicon Valley high-tech industries are semi-skilled.[1] The largest area of population concentration in this region is the sprawling city of San Jose, which has some affluent suburbs but is largely made up of working-class neighborhoods, including pockets of first- and second-generation immigrants. It is not surprising, then, that a sample drawn from the court records of divorce filings in these two counties should be diverse indeed.

As Table 3.1 shows, about a third of the parents in our sample had only a high school education or less. A fifth of the mothers and nearly a third of the fathers were college graduates. The largest number were in between these upper and lower education levels; that is, they had gone to a local two-year community college or had taken some kind of occupational training following their graduation from high school. Pre-separation earnings also covered a wide range, from a group of families in which the fathers had had no regular earnings during the immediate pre-separation period to a few families in which the fathers had been earning more than $100,000 a year; the most common level of earnings for the fathers was close to $35,000. A larger proportion of the women than the men were either not working outside the home or working part time (53 percent) before the separation, and those who were working were earning only about half as much, on the average, as the employed men. The most common level of earnings for the employed women was $15,000 or $16,000 a year, but there were substantial numbers earning under $10,000, as well as a few who earned more than $40,000. In relation to the cost of living in this area—in particular, the high cost of housing—it may be seen that the majority of the sample did not approach the level of affluence commonly associated with Silicon Valley professionals. The more important point to be kept in mind, however, is the great diversity of the economic circumstances faced by these families at the time of the parental separation.

In the most common case, couples were separating after four to eight years of marriage (the median was seven years), although a substantial minority had been married more than ten years. Nearly half of the separating couples had only one child, and most of the rest had only two.

Comparison with a National Sample

We were interested in investigating how the families in our sample compare with divorcing families elsewhere in the country, and whether divorcing families who live in this narrow geographic region are demographically distinct. There was no national information that was exactly comparable, but we did find some data from a national survey

Table 3.1 Characteristics of the parents in our sample

	Percentage of mothers	Percentage of fathers
Years of schooling completed		
Less than high school	9.3%	11.2%
Finished high school	29.6	22.4
Trade school, some college	40.1	35.3
Finished college	10.9	14.1
Some or finished graduate or professional training	10.1	17.0
	100.0%	100.0%
	(N = 1,108)	(N = 1,107)
Preseparation annual earnings[a]		
None (not working)	30.8	6.9
Under $10,000	16.7	3.3
$10,000–$19,999	27.9	17.9
$20,000–$29,999	17.6	21.9
$30,000–$39,999	4.8	22.5
$40,000–$49,999	0.6	12.1
$50,000 or more	1.6	15.3
	100.0%	100.0%
	(N = 838)	(N = 809)
Ethnicity		
Anglo	79.4	77.9
Hispanic	11.2	12.0
Black	2.4	3.1
Asian or Filipino	5.9	4.9
Native American (Indian)	0.7	0.8
Other	0.4	1.3
	100.0%	100.0%
	(N = 1,014)	(N = 959)
Employment: hours per week		
Not employed	31.0	6.8
Less than 15 hours	2.2	0.4
15–29 hours	9.9	2.1
Part time, hours not reported	11.2	4.2
30–39	8.5	6.1
40 or more	30.0	43.5
Full time, hours not reported	7.2	37.0
	100.0%	100.0%
	(N = 832)	(N = 817)

Table 3.1 (cont.)

	Percentage of families
Number of children from this marriage	
One	47.2
Two	40.9
Three	10.0
Four	1.6
Five or more	0.4
	100.0%
	(N = 1,124)
Age of youngest child (at time of first interview)	
Under 3	31.9
3–5	31.2
6–8	14.5
9–11	10.1
12–14	9.5
15 or more	2.8
	100.0%
	(N = 1,124)
Length of marriage (until separation)	
Less than 3 years	14.5
3–5 years	24.2
6–8 years	15.2
9–11 years	12.9
12–14 years	13.6
15 or more years	19.7
	100.0%
	(N = 1,089)

Note: The numbers of cases vary for the different items of information in this table. Information concerning ethnicity, income, and working hours was not obtained in the mail questionnaire that was the source of data for a subgroup of the families at Time 1. We were able to fill in ethnicity information from subsequent interviews for some of the T-1 mail-survey families.

a. Preseparation earnings are in 1984 dollars.

Table 3.2 Comparison of means of national sample and our sample*

	U.S. mothers divorced during 1984	Mothers in our sample (divorce finalized 1984–1988)
Mother's age	34.9	32.8
Percentage white[a]	86.6	88.4
Education (years)	12.3	13.7[b]
Labor force participation (%)	84.2	83.9[c]
Annual earnings[d]	$10,504	$18,607[c]
Number of children	1.8	1.7
Duration of marriage (years)	12.3	10.7

 * For this comparison, we have omitted the families in our sample in which the children were living with fathers, or in split or "other" arrangements. The national sample includes only those divorced mothers whose children were living with them.
 a. Eleven percent of our mothers were Hispanic, a group which includes people of more than one race. For this table, we have counted Hispanics and Anglos as "whites."
 b. The California education data were reported in categories which were made comparable to the national data by using means within each educational category for the CPS sample.
 c. At Time 3.
 d. Earnings are converted to constant 1985 dollars. Means based on employed women only.

taken in 1986 in which information was given for a group of 209 mothers who had finalized their divorces in 1984 and who had their children living with them.[2] We have compared these mothers with the mothers in our sample who also had their children living with them (excluding father, split, and "other" custody). Since most of our families had not finalized their divorces until 1986 or later, we took Time 3 data for comparison of those items that changed with time since separation.

Table 3.2 shows that our sample is quite similar to the national sample with respect to the age of the mothers, their race, their rate of employment, and the number of children. The average duration of marriage in our sample is a little lower. The more striking differences have to do with education and income: our mothers' earnings by Time 3 were substantially higher than those in the national sample of women whose divorces became final in 1984. In part, this no doubt reflects the fact that the mothers in our sample had, on the average, one year more of education than the mothers in the national sample, and this may have qualified them for somewhat better jobs. However, the cost of living is substantially higher in this area of California than in the nation as a whole. It is therefore very difficult to determine whether our mothers' earnings would enable them to achieve a substantially higher standard of living.

To what extent will we be able to generalize our findings to other regions? Two counties in California certainly cannot be regarded as representative of the United States, to say nothing of other places in the industrialized world. Other Western nations have a stronger "safety net" for the support of families and children than does the United States, a fact which may mitigate the post-separation stresses for single parents in those societies. Other parts of the United States have a different ethnic mix from that in our sample. However, our modest comparative information indicates that Californians are not a breed apart. They are demographically similar to people elsewhere who are undergoing divorce and must face the difficult issues of allocating financial resources and arranging for the care of children. They also have in common with other divorcing families a state of emotional distress which greatly affects the quality of their decision processes. Perhaps the most important point to make about our sample, however, is that like divorcing families elsewhere, they run the gamut of socio-economic levels and family circumstances. One of the questions we will be asking is whether and how these kinds of variations affect the process of divorce and its outcomes.

Division of Family Responsibilities

Most of the children in the sample families were quite young—in nearly two-thirds of the families, the youngest child was under 6 years old (see Table 3.1). In only 12 percent of the cases were all the children older than age 11. Most of these couples, then, were at a point in their family lives where child-care requirements were substantial because the children were young enough to require intensive investment of parental time for child-rearing.

When a parental pair are raising children together, there are two major functions that must be performed: providing for the economic support of the family, and providing day-to-day care for the children. Of course, some families hire child-care help and others rely upon unpaid help from relatives, but for the present, we will be concerned with the involvement of the two parents themselves in the two major family roles.

Families vary greatly in the way the economic support and child-care responsibilities are divided between the two parents. The traditional arrangement has been for the father to work full time and provide all or most of the economic support, while the mother does all or most of the child care and little or no paid work outside the home. Many modern couples strive for an egalitarian ideal in which both parents work full time outside the home (relying upon paid help for child care during their working hours), and in which the two parents share child-care duties equally during non-working hours. In practice, there is a continuum between fully traditional and fully egalitarian arrangements, a common one being for the mother to work less than the father and do more of the child care, while she nevertheless has some outside earnings and the father participates substantially but not equally in child care. Wherever along this continuum a couple falls, the "deal" can be perceived by both as fair so long as the trade-off of outside work versus child care is regarded as commensurate and agreeable to both.

It is difficult, however, to assess in objective terms how equitable a couple's division of responsibilities actually is. The realities of the labor force are such that the father frequently has a higher-paying job. Sometimes this simply reflects the fact that he is older than his wife and has had more time to move up in his career; or the father may have more education, and thus may be qualified for a higher pay level over and above the value of his years of work experience; or he may have the kind of job where hourly pay is relatively good, but which is essentially closed to women (for example, in the building trades), while his wife works in a poorly paid "women's job" (such as beautician or caregiver in a day-care center); or the mother may have taken time out (or dropped to part time) for childbearing, resulting in a loss of earning power. Whatever the reason, there will be many families in which, even though both parents are working full time outside the home, the father is earning considerably more. Should we regard it as equitable for the wife to be doing more of the child care (and house-work) because she is bringing in less money for the support of the household? Clearly, men and women might have quite different perspectives in answering this question.

When it comes to the parents' perceptions of their relative roles in child-rearing, we may also expect some discrepancies. Sociologists Furstenberg and Cherlin (1991) have noted that husbands and wives commonly have different stakes in marriage, and therefore different perceptions of the costs and benefits of a marital relationship.[3] Psy-

chologists Ross and Sicoly (1979) have identified a common phenomenon which they call "egocentric bias"; they have shown that when
people are engaged in joint enterprises, individual participants usually
exaggerate their own contribution to the joint outcome and underestimate the contribution of their partners. In one of their studies, they
questioned husbands and wives concerning how much each contributed to various joint tasks (including housework and child care), and
found that each spouse claimed to be doing more than his or her partner acknowledged. A similar situation is reported by Hetherington and
Clingempeel (in press), who found that husbands claimed to be doing
more of both housework and child care than they said their wives were
doing, while the wives were claiming exactly the reverse. A variety of
reasons may be given for such discrepancies in perception: for example, people always know what they themselves have done in a collaborative activity, but they may not be aware of (because they were
not present, or because they did not notice) what a partner did; or it
may be that their own activities are more available for recall. And,
of course, people's perceptions are selective in self-serving, ego-
enhancing ways. Whatever the reason, egocentric bias is endemic, and
we may expect it to affect what each parent truly believes about how
much he or she was contributing to pre-separation family functioning.

It seems reasonable to expect that the perceptions of the two parents
concerning their respective contributions to the family before the divorce might have some bearing on how they would negotiate the terms
of their divorce. We have therefore attempted to describe the way in
which the families in our sample had worked out their pre-separation
division of labor with respect to child care and economic support,
taking into account any differences in the perspectives of the two parents as they recalled their earlier situation. Our assessment can only
be approximate, considering that we have limited information concerning the pre-separation situation.

Contributions to Economic Support before Separation

At Time 1, we asked parents to report their own and their former
spouse's pre-separation earnings. We were also able to estimate the
level of paid work each had been doing, distinguishing roughly between
those not employed, those employed part time, and those working full
time.[4] From this information we were able to estimate the balance of
responsibilities for economic support. Husbands and wives usually did

Table 3.3 Division of economic responsibilities before the separation

Work roles	Percentage
Father employed, mother not working or working less, earning less	49%
Employed equally, father earning more than 60 percent of joint earnings	18
Employed equally, earnings roughly equal (each between 40 and 60 percent of joint earnings)	22
Mother employed, father not working or working less, earning less	11
	100%
	(*N* = 797)

Note: Families are omitted if both parents were unemployed. "Employed equally" usually means that both parents were working full time, but there are a few families in which both were working part time.

not differ in what they reported about their respective earnings or working hours, and therefore we have combined their two reports into a single estimate of their respective roles, shown in Table 3.3.

The table shows that the bulk of our families were fairly traditional in their division of economic responsibilities before the separation. In two-thirds of the cases the fathers were the major wage earners. In only about a fourth of the cases were the two parents' economic roles equivalent, and in only 11 percent were the mothers the major breadwinners.

Involvement in Child-Rearing before Separation

At Time 1, we asked about each parent's pre-separation involvement with the children. We wanted to establish a frame of reference for the parents to use in giving us their answers, and so used a rather long preamble for our question, as follows:

> We are interested in the ways that parents were involved in their children's day-to-day care and activities before the separation. Of course there are many different possibilities, depending on the age of the child and the circumstances of your life. Some examples are things like taking the child to the doctor, shopping for clothes, the basics of feeding, dressing, and putting to bed. In addition, you could think of things like playing with the child, giving advice, or making decisions, or talking with the child about something important in his or her life. Thinking of what's

Table 3.4   Responsibilities for child-rearing before the separation

	Mother's report (N = 926)	Father's report (N = 672)
Mother was more involved	84%	42%
Two parents were equally involved	13	30
Father was more involved	3	28
	100%	100%
Mean involvement of mothers	8.92	7.69
Mean involvement of fathers	4.72	7.52

relevant to you, how involved were you in your children's lives before the separation? Use a scale from 1 to 10, where 1 is someone with low involvement, and 10 is someone with high involvement.

After the parents had rated their own pre-separation involvement, they were asked to rate that of the former spouse on the same 10-point scale. Thus, for each parent it was possible to compare the two ratings, and determine whether the parent reported having been more, less, or equally involved in child-rearing, relative to the former spouse. Here the perceptions of the two parents did commonly differ, in some cases quite strongly. In Table 3.4 we show how the two parents evaluated their relative involvement, including the reports of all the parents we interviewed at Time 1, regardless of whether their spouses were also included in the sample. The fathers said they had been much more involved than mothers as a group gave them credit for. Some of the differences might be due to the fact that the fathers we interviewed were a somewhat selected sample, in that they were undoubtedly more involved with their children than the fathers we were not able to locate for the study. However, when we examined only those families in which both parents were interviewed, differences were still strongly evident between mothers and fathers in their estimates of their respective child-rearing roles before the separation (see Table 3.5). It remains true, then, that the large majority of mothers saw the pre-separation child-rearing roles as having been traditional, and almost none of them believed that the father had been more involved than they themselves were. By contrast, although a plurality of fathers agreed that the division of responsibility was traditional, over half claimed equal or more involvement.

Why did the two parents differ so greatly in their judgments about which of them had been more involved in child-rearing? Perhaps they were using different frames of reference—the fathers might have been rating themselves relative to other fathers based on an implicit assumption about a father's role; mothers may have, more commonly, directly compared their own involvement with that of the fathers. Or the two might have been giving different weight to different aspects of child-rearing: fathers to joint activities with the children, mothers to caretaking. Whatever the reason, we believe the differences in perception are real and may be important in the way couples negotiate their divorce once they have decided to separate.

The Intersection of Work and Child-rearing Roles

The discrepancies between fathers' and mothers' perceptions of their respective pre-separation contributions to child-rearing might have different implications, depending on how economic responsibilities had been divided. For example, a father who believed that he had been sharing child-rearing equally but doing more of the breadwinning might have a different view of his "rights" (to either money or custody) after separation than a father who thought that both the child-rearing and economic responsibilities had been shared equally.

In Table 3.5, we have included only those families in which both parents were interviewed, and have cross-classified the division of economic responsibility by mothers' and fathers' perceptions of their respective child-rearing roles. We can see that despite the large differences in perceptions about child-rearing, both mothers and fathers were describing a division of labor that was traditional in certain respects. In more than two-thirds of the families, the fathers were the major providers of economic support; in half the cases (according to the fathers) or 85 percent of the cases (according to the mothers), the mothers carried the major responsibility for child care. Especially striking is how rare the fully egalitarian or androgynous families were: only 2 percent of the mothers and 9 percent of the fathers claimed that the two parents were participating equally in both child-rearing and breadwinning functions. Perhaps even more striking is the absence of families in which the traditional roles were reversed, with the father doing more of the child care while the mother was the major earner (2 percent of fathers and no mothers reported this kind of "househusband" situation).

We did not ask the parents how equitable they thought their pre-separation division of family responsibilities had been, but we can see

Table 3.5 Intersection of work and child-rearing roles

	Mother's report	Father's report
Mother more involved with children		
Father employed, mother not working or working less, earning less	41%	26%
Employed equally, mother earning less	19	9
Employed equally, earning equally[a]	21	9
Mother employed, father not working or employed earning less	4	3
Both equally involved with children		
Father employed, mother not working or working less, earning less	7	13
Employed equally, mother earning less	2	6
Employed equally, earning equally[a]	2	9
Mother employed, father not working or employed earning less	2	3
Father more involved with children		
Father employed, mother not working or working less, earning less	0	9
Employed equally, mother earning less	1	6
Employed equally, earning equally[a]	1	5
Mother employed, father not working or employed earning less	0	2
N = 450 (where both parents interviewed)	100%	100%

a. "Earning equally" means that each spouse earned between 40% and 60% of their combined income.

that their differences in perceptions about child-rearing roles might imply some differences in their feelings about how fair the arrangement had been. From the maternal perspective, a large group of women (44 percent) could be said to have been carrying more than their share of family responsibilities, in that they were working at least as many hours outside the home as their husbands but also doing more of the child-rearing (we could call this group "second shift" mothers). Only half as many fathers agreed that their wives were carrying a double burden. By contrast, 34 percent of the fathers said that they were doing as much or more of the child-rearing while also doing more of the breadwinning—an arrangement which they could regard as inequitable. Only 10 percent of mothers were willing to concede that their ex-husbands had been carrying a greater share of the joint economic and child-care responsibilities.

If parents expect to be able to continue, after separation, with levels of child-rearing involvement that are similar to those that prevailed before the separation, we may predict that most mothers will feel that they have a right to custody of the children. Many fathers, on the other hand, will feel that they have a right to a larger share of the children's time than their wives will see as reasonable. Thus, the differential perceptions that we have charted above might well lead to fairly substantial amounts of conflict over custody. In Chapters 5 and 7 we will examine what the two parents say they want in terms of custody, and whether the amount of legal conflict is related to the differences in perceptions described here. We will be interested, too, in whether these discrepant perceptions have anything to do with the kind of co-parenting relationship that divorced couples are able to set up in the cases in which the children spend time in both parental households after the separation.

We have been describing what we know about the situation of our sample families as they entered the divorce process. We now turn to our central enterprise: the analysis of the divorce process itself, as it unfolds over a three-year period of time.

4

Initial Residence and Visitation

When couples with children separate, they face a period of months or even years during which the terms of their legal divorce will be worked out and a custody decree issued. Meanwhile, practical decisions must be made about where the children will live and how frequently the children will see their non-residential parents. In some families, the parents seem not to have made explicit decisions nor arrived at a considered agreement concerning these matters—the children's residence is something simply taken for granted by both parents, and a visitation pattern is drifted into as convenience dictates. In other families, initial residence and visitation are matters for active discussion and decision-making, and sometimes for dispute.

In the present chapter, we will be concerned with the initial division of the child's time between the two parents: where the children in our sample actually lived in the period immediately following separation, and how much visitation with non-residential parents occurred. It is to be expected that these initial arrangements may not remain in place as family circumstances change and negotiations between the parents (and their attorneys) proceed. In Chapters 5, 6, and 7 we will examine in detail the processes whereby legal agreements are reached and disputes resolved. In Chapter 8 we will consider the changes that occur over time in the amount of time children spend with each of the two parents.

A child's contact with two divorced parents can take many forms. Of major interest is the pattern of time spent in the two residences in "normal" portions of the school year. Thus, in considering the child's contact with the two parents, our attention is focused on the division of children's residential time apart from holidays and summer vacations. As noted in Chapter 1, all parents were interviewed during the school year, and we asked parents in detail about the time each child spent with each parent during typical two-week periods of the school year. If residential parents said that there was no regular or typical visitation pattern—for example, that the non-resident parent could pick up the children for visitation whenever it was possible and convenient—then the visitation for the previous two weeks was entered as the best estimate of the situation prevailing for that family. A two-week period was chosen as the best time unit for analysis because an arrangement for children to visit their non-custodial parent every other weekend has been traditional, and we presumed it would still be common.

A word about terminology is needed here. We will use the terms "legal custody" and "physical custody" in later chapters to refer to the two aspects of custody specified in the divorce decree. In other words, "custody" is a legal label. Thus "joint physical custody" is one type of physical custody that can emerge in the legal settlement. We use the term "residence," or sometimes "de facto residence," to refer to the place where the children actually live at a given time. We use the term "dual residence" to designate a residential arrangement in which the children are spending at least four overnights with each parent in a typical two-week period.[1] When discussing families in which the children reside mainly with one parent (rather than being in dual residence), we will sometimes refer to the residential parent as the "primary" parent, and the non-residential parent as the "outside" parent. The distinction between custody and residence is important because, as we will demonstrate in later chapters, a child's actual residential living arrangements do not always correspond to what the legal label suggests.

A number of analysts of divorce have asked how much difference it makes, in terms of the well-being of children in divorcing families, whether they live with the mother, with the father, or in some form of dual-residence arrangement. In all such studies, however, the thorny issue arises as to whether any differences among children living in these different residential arrangements can be attributed to the residential arrangement itself, or whether they reflect "self-selection" factors. By self-selection factors we mean factors that led families to adopt a given residential arrangement in the first place. For example, children might live with their father because the mother was ill, or because she was unable to care for the children for some other reason. Or dual residence might be chosen more often by couples in which both parents had relatively high incomes, so that they could both maintain residences large enough for regular occupancy by the children. Little information is available on what such self-selection factors might be, and one of our objectives is to provide such information as a guide to what factors need to be controlled when residential effects are studied.

In this chapter, we first show the proportion of our sample families who had adopted each of the various residential and visitation arrangements at the time of our first interview—usually about six months after the parents separated and three months after they filed for divorce. Next we examine the background factors associated with families' adopting each of the three major residential arrangements. Finally, we consider the reasons parents gave for adopting the residence arrangement that was in place at Time 1.

Where Were the Children Living Initially?

The families in our sample were initiating their divorces during a time when the ethos favored joint custody when it was practicable. Assumptions about the value of such an arrangement were built into the revised California divorce statute, and presumably these legal changes had come about because the climate of opinion favored them. If our families were affected by this social climate, we might expect that a substantial number would already be dividing their children's residential time between the two parents, even in the period before formal legal issues were settled and divorces became final.

As Table 4.1 shows, however, in the large majority (two-thirds) of the families in our sample, the children were living with their mothers—the traditional residential pattern. Fifteen percent of the families had set up a dual-residence arrangement in which the children were spending a third or more of their time with each parent in a typical two-week period. It is difficult to say whether this frequency of dual residence should be regarded as high or low. We suspect this represents an increase from earlier times, and that California's rate may be higher than other regions. However, we do not have comparable information from national samples, nor from California at earlier periods, to tell us whether a 15 percent rate of dual residence represents an important change.

In view of the increasing pressure upon fathers to take a more active part in child-rearing, and the larger number of fathers interested in doing so, we may ask whether an increasing number of fathers are assuming the major role in child-rearing following divorce. Here we

Table 4.1   De facto residence of children and visitation patterns at Time 1[a]

Live with mother		67.6%
No regular visitation with father[b]	18.3%	
Only daytime visits with father	19.6	
Overnight visits with father	29.7	
Dual residence		15.0
4–6 overnights with father[c]	10.1%	
7–10 overnights with father[c]	4.9	
Live with father		9.5
No regular visitation with mother[b]	2.8%	
Only daytime visits with mother	2.6	
Overnight visits with mother	4.1	
Split residence[d]		2.2
Parents still living together		5.0
Live with neither parent		0.7
		100.0%

a. This table is based on the 1,124 families in the study at Time 1.
b. No visitation during regular portions of the school year.
c. Per 2-week period during the school year.
d. Split residence means that one or more children live with one parent while one or more live with the other.

do have some comparable data, and our rate of 9.5 percent of families with father residence does *not* appear to reflect an increase. Figures from the 1980 census indicate that, in the nation as a whole, 13.4 percent of single-parent families were headed by a man (reported in Laosa, 1988). In a national-sample study of families of 11- to 16-year-old children conducted in 1981, Furstenberg and colleagues reported that approximately 10 percent of children in single-parent households were living with their fathers. Our finding of 9.5 percent of families with father residence, then, does not indicate that this arrangement was becoming a more popular choice for California families divorcing in the mid-1980s than it was at earlier times or other places in the United States.

There were small groups of families who did not initially fit into the usual categories of mother, father, or dual residence. In 5 percent of the families the separating couple were still living together. This pattern sometimes reflected the high cost of housing, in that the parent who was leaving had not yet been able to find an affordable place to live. In other cases, however, both parents believed (sometimes on the advice of attorneys) that a parent who had maintained continuous residence with the children would have a better chance of getting physical custody, and neither parent wanted to jeopardize his or her chance of custody by moving out.

How Much Initial Visitation Occurred?

In about three-quarters of the mother-residence families at Time 1 of our study, the children either had daytime or overnight visits to their fathers during typical two-week periods in the school year. As Table 4.1 shows, overnight visitation was the most common practice, followed by daytime visits, with the "no contact" group being the smallest. Among the smaller group of children living with their fathers, over 40 percent had overnight visits with their mothers, while in about a third of the father-residence families the children did not see their mothers during typical portions of the school year. Some of the "no contact" children did, however, see their non-residential parents on holidays, birthdays, or during summer vacations.

Other researchers have reported that a high proportion of divorced fathers drop out of their children's lives and have no contact (Furstenberg et al., 1983). For the families in our study, Table 4.1 shows this certainly was not true six months after the parents separated. Children were no longer seeing their fathers in only 18 percent of the families. In all the others, children were either visiting their fathers during typical portions of the school year, living with them part of the time, or having their major residence with their fathers. And even some of the 18 percent who lived with their mothers and did not have a visitation arrangement for seeing the fathers nevertheless saw him during vacations or on special occasions. For children to lose contact with their mothers so soon after the separation was even more rare—in only about 3 percent of our families were the children not seeing their mothers during typical two-week periods, and as we have seen, in most cases the children lived with their mothers all or part of the time.

Background Factors Associated with Initial Residence

Parental education and income. It is widely believed that dual residential arrangements appeal especially to the affluent and highly educated. For example, Rothberg (1983), who studied 30 joint custody parents in New York, concluded: "The figures clearly indicate the population moving toward joint custody is upper-middle class and highly educated, with greater access to job flexibility and financial security" (p. 46). Another study, however (Lowery, 1986), with a very small number of joint custody families, did not find them to be different in these background characteristics from sole-custody families. In our own study, we first omitted those families in which the children were not living in one of the three major residential arrangements at T-1, and for the remaining sample, compared the three residential groups on a variety of background characteristics. We found that dual residential arrangements were adopted by a wide range of families from varied backgrounds, so that dual residence for children was not by any means exclusively chosen by the well-educated and affluent. Nevertheless, our dual-residence families included a somewhat higher proportion of parents with college degrees (27 percent of dual-residence mothers, and 37 percent of dual-residence fathers) than did the sole residence group. Dual-residence families were also somewhat more likely to have high incomes, though the majority of families in all three groups had incomes in the middle or lower range (see Table 4.2).

Employment status. The relationship between the employment status of the two parents and their children's residence is interesting. About 10 percent of the fathers in our study were not working for pay at Time 1. Such fathers were significantly less likely to have the children living with them, or to share in a dual-residence arrangement, than were employed fathers. Indeed, only 3 of our 79 unemployed fathers were primary custodians, and none of these had been "house husbands" before the separation. It would appear that the inability of unemployed fathers to provide economic support was of overriding importance in the decision about where the children would live—more important than the fact that, being unemployed, they might have had more time to care for children. Mothers who were not working for pay, by contrast, were slightly *more* likely to have the children living with them. Among the 20 percent of mothers who were not working for pay, 76 percent were the primary residential parent, as compared with 71 percent for employed mothers. We see a reflection of traditional sex roles here: although most of the mothers in our sample were working for pay, those who were not included some traditional homemakers who had been devoting themselves to the care of their families before the divorce; for them, a non-working caretaker role represented continuity. Their economic support came mainly from

Table 4.2   Relation of children's residence to socioeconomic factors

	Children's residence at T-1			
	With mother	Dual	With father	Chi^2
Mother is a college graduate (%)	20	27	12	8.69*
Father is a college graduate (%)	28	37	22	5.33†
Mother has a professional job (%)	26	32	26	2.14
Father has a professional job (%)	33	42	42	6.24*
Mother's annual earnings greater than $25,000 (%)	16	28	16	13.21**
Father's annual earnings greater than $50,000 (%)	18	25	21	5.15†
Mother is not working for pay (%)	21	13	25	5.56†
Father is not working for pay (%)	13	2	5	16.10***

†$p \leq .10.$
*$p \leq .05.$
**$p \leq .01.$
***$p \leq .001.$

child-support and alimony payments from their former husbands, or from welfare. The placement of children with these mothers appears to have been based on their experience as caretakers, rather than on their ability to support the children.

Age and sex of children. When families had more than one child, the children almost always lived in the same household. The effort to "keep the children together" overrode any considerations of the individual characteristics of the children, such as their age or sex. However, the children's age and sex could and did affect the residential decision in families with only one child, or where the children were similar in age and/or sex. To show the relation of children's age and sex to their residence, we have taken each child (rather than each family) as our unit of analysis. We have excluded the children whose parents were still living together at Time 1. Figures 4.1 and 4.2 show that while the large majority of both boys and girls lived with their mothers, a somewhat higher proportion of boys than girls lived in dual residence or with their fathers. Infants and toddlers almost always lived with their mothers. From age 3 through age 8 we see the highest rates of dual residence. In the preteen and teenage years, dual resi-

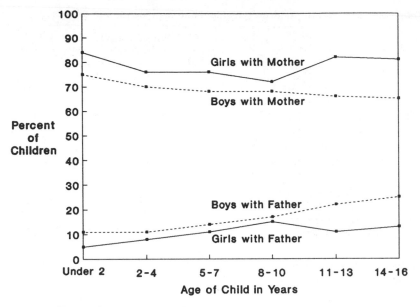

Figure 4.1   Mother or father residence by age and sex of child, T-1.

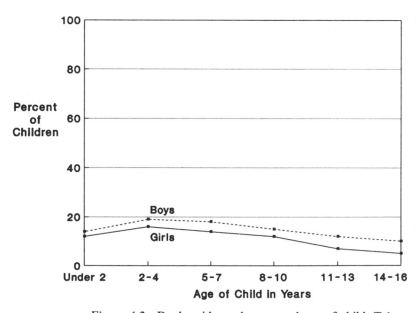

Figure 4.2   Dual residence by age and sex of child, T-1.

dence became much less common, and the proportion of children living with their fathers increased. The majority of the children in our sample families were quite young at the time of our first interview—half the children were under age 6. It will be interesting to see whether there is a shift to higher frequencies of dual and father residence as the children grow older (see Chapter 8).

Two other aspects of family composition were associated with residence. One-child families were somewhat more likely to elect dual residence at Time 1 (19 percent of such families, compared to 13 percent of families with more than one child). And if either of the parents had other children from a prior marriage, they were unlikely to adopt dual residence. Indeed, among the relatively small group of families in which the mothers had other children, fathers had the children of the present marriage living with them in 18 percent of the cases, as compared with only 9 percent when the mother had no other children.

Housing circumstances. The majority of the families in our study were renters, but for those who did own a home, we found that home ownership was associated with the children's residence. When a mother lived in a home that she owned, the children were very unlikely to live with the father (only 1 percent of this group did so). We have information about father's home ownership for only a minority of our sample families, but for the 378 families providing this information, the results are striking: in families in which the father owned the house he was living in ($N = 128$), only 39 percent had children living with the mother—the rest had adopted either dual (30 percent) or father (31 percent) residence.

If the father was living in a temporary residence at Time 1, he was slightly less likely to have the children living with him. If the mother's residence was temporary, however, this did not affect the likelihood of the children living with her.

Reasons for Adopting the Initial Residential Arrangement

So far we have few clues as to the reason why so many families adopted maternal residence when the parents separated. Certainly, it did not happen because mothers were better able to support the children—the mothers' earnings were much lower than those of the fathers, and the child-support payments provided by fathers did not make up the difference (see Chapter 10). When we asked parents at Time 1 why they had adopted their present residence arrangement for the children, their most common answers had to do with logistics. In particular, the parents' work schedules, the children's school hours, and the distance between households were frequently cited. As an example, one primary-resident mother said: "I think this 50-50 stuff is crazy. It's not practical. My two oldest are in school. They [would] have to leave their father's house an hour earlier to get to school. That's no way to live."

When such reasons were cited, the probabilities were higher that the children would be living with their mother. In some cases the choice rested on the fact that the mother had remained in the family residence, and the children's schools, out-of-home activities, or care arrangements were located nearby. But in other cases it was not obvious why the logistical problems described (such as the parents' work schedules) should be easier for the mother than for the father to solve. The preference for mother residence does not seem to rest on the fact of the mother having more time available to take care of the children. Four-fifths of the mothers with primary residence worked outside the home, most full time. Indeed, mothers who were working over 40 hours a week were no less likely to have the children living with them than were mothers who had a lighter work schedule.

We noted in Chapter 3 that whether mothers work for pay or not, they usually have management responsibility for child-rearing, and we now ask: to what extent do the residential arrangements reflect simple continuity in the division of responsibility for child-rearing that prevailed between the father and mother before they separated?

Continuity in division of parental responsibilities. Some researchers studying family structure have characterized the post-divorce residential arrangement as an outgrowth of parenting commitments and behaviors established during the marriage. Steinman (1981), drawing on a study of a small group of families that elected dual residential arrangements, observed that they were characterized by (1) a history of shared parenting during the marriage, and (2) a strong ideological commitment to the continued involvement of both mother and father in the life of the child. Watson's (1981) comparison of joint and father custody revealed that fathers in both arrangements had a strong commitment to parenting that was based on extensive involvement in child-rearing. Lowery (1986) reported that families adopting mother residence were less likely to have a strong ideological commitment to the father's participation in child-rearing.

By contrast, both Hetherington and colleagues (Hetherington, Cox, and Cox, 1982) and Wallerstein and Kelly (1980) have reported that the father's post-divorce participation with children, and his behavior toward them, has little to do with their pre-separation role in child-rearing. We need to know more, then, concerning how much continuity there is in paternal involvement. The issue is an important one, in that advocates of certain modifications in divorce statutes have recommended that custody decisions should be made in part on the basis of such involvement. For example, Judge Neely of West Virginia (1984) advocated the awarding of custody to the parent who has been the primary caretaker. He recognized that this would be synonymous with maternal custody in the majority of cases, but he wanted to make the language of the law more gender-neutral, and also to allow for exceptions, giving fathers a larger post-divorce role in families where they had in fact played a major role in child-rearing prior to parental separation.

California divorce law does not embody any presumption in favor of primary caretakers, though in practice in disputed cases, some weight is undoubtedly given to maintaining continuity in the caretaker role. The information given to us by parents about their pre-separation involvement with the children (Table 4.3) indicates that they seldom took this factor into account in initially choosing dual or father residence, instead of mother residence, for the children.

Fathers who shared their children's residential time in a dual residence arrangement at Time 1 had been very slightly more involved with the children prior to the separation—according to their own reports, not the mothers'. More important is the fact that when children were living with their fathers, this did *not* reflect continuity from the pre-divorce situation. That is, those fathers who were assuming primary responsibility for the children had not been exceptionally involved when the family was intact. The salient factor seems to be that in the father-residence families, the *mothers,* on the average, had had a somewhat lower level of involvement than was true for the other custodial arrangements. Among the 71 fathers with primary residential responsibility whom we interviewed with the long standard interview, 19 (27 percent) rated their former wives at 5 or lower on the 10-point scale in terms of prior involvement with the children. We see, then, that there is a subgroup of father-residence families in which the mother had been a relatively uninvolved parent—a factor that evidently weakened the mother's claim to become the single primary caretaker. In this sense, we have continuity—continuity of low maternal involvement in a small group of families. For these families, the options that many parents have in arriving at a decision about residence were considerably constrained.

Table 4.3 Pre-divorce involvement of each parent with the children, as rated by fathers and mothers

| | Children's residence | | | |
	With mother	Dual	With father	*F* values
How involved was mother?				
As rated by mother ($N = 652$)	8.9	9.0	8.9	n.s.
As rated by father ($N = 470$)	8.1	7.9	6.9	8.59***
How involved was father?				
As rated by mother ($N = 652$)	4.5	4.8	4.9	n.s.
As rated by father ($N = 470$)	7.2	7.7	7.1	2.75†
% mother rates self as having been:				
Less involved than father	2%	3%	0%	
Equally involved	13	11	22	
More involved	85	86	78	
	100%	100%	100%	
	($N = 401$)	($N = 130$)	($N = 91$)	
% father rates self as having been:				
Less involved than mother	52%	38%	37%	
Equally involved	28	34	29	
More involved	20	28	34	
	100%	100%	100%	
	($N = 298$)	($N = 102$)	($N = 71$)	

Note: Means are on a 10-point scale, by children's T-1 residence.
† $p \leq .10$; *** $p \leq .001$.

There were constraints, too, for a much larger subgroup among the families adopting mother residence. More than two-thirds of the mothers in this group rated their former husbands at a 5 or lower on the pre-divorce involvement scale, and 42 percent rated them at 3 or below. Among the non-residential fathers whom we interviewed (probably a more involved group than the fathers we could not locate), 71 out of 298 rated themselves at 5 or less on their pre-divorce involvement with the children. Depending on which parent's report is given more weight, we see that there is a group of fathers ranging from one-fourth to perhaps half of the fathers of mother-residence children whose pre-divorce involvement with the children had been low enough to make them unlikely prospects for taking on major child-rearing responsibility, in the absence of extraordinary circumstances.

The important point, however, is that in many families, both fathers and mothers agreed that the mother had been the primary parent before the separation, and in these families, the mothers were especially likely to have the children living with them. Comments volunteered by some parents underscored the importance of continuity. Some comments by fathers are illustrative:

(Father of two children aged 5 and 3): "[Ex-wife] is more suited to bring up the kids than myself under the circumstances. It's the woman's role to bring up the kids. She is the guiding force behind the children. She has more desire to be a mother—more prepared to take on the kids than me; I couldn't give the kids the time they need to bring them up."

(Father of two sons aged 10 and 2): "It's crucial to me to have time with the boys. [But] I don't have the kind of place where they can be with me and feel at home. And they are much more attached to their mother than to me. The younger one needs a mother."

(Father of a 1-year-old daughter): "I don't know how to be with a baby very well. She's very attached to her mother. I don't really like to be with her. She screams a lot and I'm not used to that. She doesn't like being away from her mother—doesn't like being here. It's most sensible [for her to be with mother]."

We suspect that the fact that mothers have been the primary caretakers in most of our families also creates an assumption that living with her is the default option. That is, if fathers want to share custody and have the necessary resources (including time and adequate living quarters), other options aside from mother residence are considered. But if the fathers are not in this position, then in many cases the assumption of both parties is that the mothers will take the children, usually regardless of *her* resources and time schedule:

(In a family with a girl aged 6, a boy aged 3, Mother says): "I'd like to have them see him more. It's his schedule. I can't force him to take the children." (Father says): "The hours I work leave only weekends. I want a weekend to myself and one for the kids. I can't afford baby-sitters, so I didn't take them [more]."

A number of fathers seemed to assume that the choice about the division of children's time was theirs to make, and that the mother would pick up whatever responsibilities the fathers did not choose to take on:

(Father of three children, aged 15, 13, and 10): "I'm not a very good parent. Parenting is a difficult thing that I am not willing to handle at this time."

"I have three children, and do not have sufficient space at this time. My job requires frequent out-of-state travel, and child care would be difficult."

Some of these examples reflect relatively low commitment to the children on the part of the father. In many of the families who initially adopted mother residence, however, the fathers expressed strong continuing commitment, and readiness to provide backup support for the children if and when it should be needed.

Trust in the quality of the ex-spouse's parenting. No doubt, one reason many parents have the children live with the parent who has been doing most of the child-rearing all along is that they believe experience implies competence. However, the connection is by no means invariable. Some mothers trust a father who has been relatively uninvolved to be a competent parent when he is on his own with the children. Other mothers are considerably worried. And some fathers fear that their former wives cannot cope adequately with child-rearing when the father is no longer there to help and mediate, even though the mother was the primary caretaker during the marriage.

There were a number of points in our interviews when some parents made free comments (not in response to a specific question) about the situation for the children in each other's households. There were also specific questions about any misgivings the parents might have about the adequacy of the care their children would receive in the other household. (See Chapter 8 for details of the answers to these questions.) The interviewers compiled from these free comments and specific questions any mention by one parent of concerns about the children's well-being in the other household. In some cases the misgivings were strong, based on concerns about the other parent's drinking, drug-taking, or abusive behavior. Some parents felt that the former spouse was not sufficiently attentive to cleanliness, diet, or safety, or that he or she left the child alone too much. Others were concerned about life-style issues: allegedly unsound or weak values, the presence of untrustworthy people at the other household (including the other parent's new boyfriend or girlfriend), too much television, lack of homework supervision, and so forth. Nearly two out of three mothers mentioned some inadequacy in the father as a caretaker for the children. Some excerpts from the interviews with mothers help to convey the range of their concerns:

(Mother of two boys, one aged 18 months, the other 5 years): "It isn't just for a day at a time—we're talking about three days in a row. And he [dad] just wasn't changing him enough and cleaning him up right. He has a sensitive skin and every time he came home he had a horrible rash. His skin was either bleeding or ready to bleed. It was so bad, and the little guy was in such pain that I wanted to cry. I couldn't take care of him without hurting him. I would be buying medicine and taking him to the doctor and would just get him OK when it was time for him to go back to his dad again . . . He [dad] doesn't have the patience . . . It is irritating to him to have to stop what he is doing to change the baby."

(Mother of 5-year-old daughter): "He can't take care of her very well. He lives with two single men, and they keep guns around because they are police officers. He says he can't tell them [housemates] what to do."

(Mother of 4-year-old daughter): "I sometimes doubt that he can take care of her. One night at 11:00 she called and said she was just eating dinner. And if anything serious happens, he calls for me to take care of it."

(Mother of 2-year-old daughter): "Her dad has a history of both alcohol and drug problems. I don't like him driving with her in the car. He wants overnight visitations, and I say 'not at her age.' I know eventually . . . but at 2½, if he gets soused, she can't take care of herself."

(Mother of 5-year-old boy): "He's irresponsible and leaves our son alone. He left Jimmy with a baby-sitter, and Jimmy called in the middle of the night hysterical because the baby-sitter had left and he was alone. Recently, his dad took Jimmy skiing and told him his lift ticket said he could go by himself; Jimmy was hit by an out-of-control skier."

About 40 percent of fathers mentioned doubts about the mother's child-rearing competence. Examples of such cases are given in the following section.

As Figure 4.3 shows, when the children were living with their mothers, mothers were twice as likely to express concern about the father's parenting as he was to do so about hers. In father-residence families the situation was the reverse: here two-thirds of the fathers, and only one-third of the mothers, mentioned deficiencies in the other's parenting. These figures suggest that when parents are making their initial decision about which parent will have major day-to-day responsibility for the children, they take into account which parent will probably be more competent in the parental role. Of course the two parents do not always agree about this, and their disagreements about which one is the better parent can spark custody disputes. It is worth noting, too, that in more than half of the cases (56 percent) in which the father

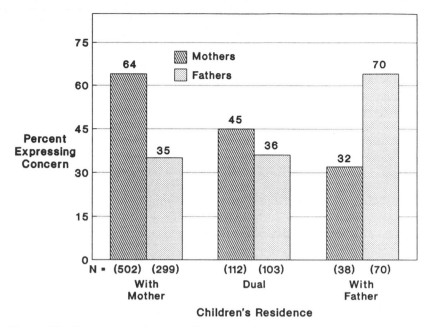

Figure 4.3 Percentage of parents in each residential group who express concerns about other parent's child-rearing.

expressed misgivings about the children's welfare in the mother's household, the children were nevertheless living with the mother. By contrast, in only 3 percent of the cases in which the mothers were concerned about the father's child-rearing competence were the children living with him.

Hostility between the two parents. How might hostility between the parents influence the residential arrangement for children that a family adopts? We might expect that couples electing to share the child's residential time between them would understand that to do so, they would have to continue dealing with each other, at least minimally. If so, it might be that dual-residence families are drawn mainly from relatively "friendly" divorces—couples whose hostility to each other could be kept within bounds. On the other hand, when both parents are intensely hostile, it may be that they use a dispute over who will have the children as one manifestation of their anger, and divide the children's residence initially because they are too hostile to resolve their dispute in any other way.

As Figure 4.4 shows, the ratings of parental hostility at T-1 are only

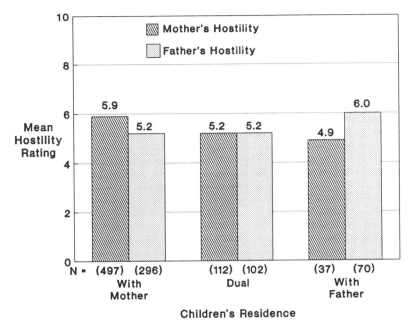

Figure 4.4 Mothers' and fathers' (interviewer-rated) hostility toward former spouse by children's residence.

slightly (though significantly) related to where the children were living at that time. Residential parents were rated as somewhat more hostile than non-residential ones, and parents who were sharing the children's residential time fairly evenly between the two households were comparable to non-residential parents in terms of their hostility. But within each residential group the variation in levels of hostility was great, with the average levels of rated hostility being near the midpoint of the scale for the parents in each residential group. The groups did differ, however, with respect to the weighting of parental hostility, compared to other factors, in the residential decision. We will now consider the constellation of factors in each of the residential arrangements individually.

Reasons for Residence with the Father

We have seen that both low levels of maternal pre-divorce involvement in child-rearing (according to the father's report) and fathers' concerns about the children's well-being in the mother's care were factors increasing the probability that children would live with the father. By contrast, the father's prior involvement did not appear to affect the residential decision. We also noted that when mothers were concerned about the quality of the father's child-rearing skills, the children were very unlikely to be living with him. How do these various factors combine? When we consider them jointly (in multiple regressions), we find that the father's level of pre-separation involvement with the children continues to be unimportant in predicting the children's residence, and this is true regardless of whether one relies upon the mother's or the father's rating of his involvement. But the other three factors each make independent and significant contributions to the prediction: children were more likely to live with their fathers initially if (1) the mother was relatively uninvolved with the children before the separation (according to the father's report), (2) the father lacked trust in the child-rearing environment the mother could provide, and (3) the mother did *not* express lack of trust in the father's child-rearing environment. Of course these factors could add together, and the combination of low prior mother involvement and father mistrust was particularly strong in increasing the probability of father residence. Nevertheless, no combination of the factors increased the probability above 40 percent, and the pull toward mother residence that we have discussed earlier was still strong.

Some excerpts from interviews will illustrate the kinds of situations that underlie these results:

(Father of two sons, aged 8 and 11): "I wanted custody of the kids. It was mutually agreed upon. She has no place to stay. For the last six months she has been camping out, staying with friends, couldn't provide care. I'm more emotionally stable . . . The boys have both male and female aspects. I provide the father image, my mom and sister the mother image."

(Father of two boys, aged 6 and 3): "She is trying to relive her childhood, partying and so on, so I took the children into my home which is a better environment for them. She sees them when she wants to. Their mother spoils them, lets them do what they want, doesn't teach them. It's a circus where she lives, people in and out all day and all night telling my children what they can and cannot do in their own home."

(Father of two children, aged 8 and 9): "It's unstable where she is. She doesn't stay in one place. It's not a suitable environment. When she gets her act together, she can see them. She has no money to take care of them. And I can give them more personal time. There's a lot of love in this house, between the kids, my fiancée, and I. I don't feel their mom is there for them. I feel I'm the sole custodian. She doesn't want the responsibility. This may change when they get older.''

(Father of son, aged 3): ''I'm a better parent. My wife left to 'expand her life style.' She's had several live-in boyfriends, which is the reason I don't allow any overnight visits.'' (Mother says): ''Basically, I wasn't ready to have a kid. I don't have any money, or a car. Having him with his dad is the right thing to do until I get myself together.''

(Mother of a 3-year-old daughter): ''I was too young to handle her by myself. Her father offered a stable place for her, and I knew he was a real good father.''

In the first three cases, we did not have interviews with the mothers, so we do not know what their perspective would have been. But as the last two excerpts show, we do have some interviews with the mother in which she concurred that the father would provide a better environment for the children, at least until the mother could reorganize her life.

We wish to stress, however, that the cases of diminished maternal functioning described above are by no means the only kinds of families adopting father custody. We cannot say exactly what proportion of father-custody cases could legitimately be classified as cases of maternal deficit; it depends on how much weight we want to give to mothers' versus fathers' reports about the mother's prior involvement, and how seriously we want to take the fathers' allegations of an unsuitable environment in the mother's household. We estimate that there may be somewhere between one-quarter and one-half of the father-residence cases in which the maternal-deficit factor is involved. Since only 10 percent of our sample adopted father custody at Time 1, this means that approximately 3 to 5 percent of the mothers in our sample families were not functioning competently enough in the maternal role to warrant maternal or dual residence—a very small percentage.

What about the families who adopted father residence for other reasons? A wide range of additional reasons are given, and it is difficult to group them into major categories. But several reasons appeared often enough to be worth mentioning:

· In families with older children, the choice was sometimes left to the children. When they chose to live with their fathers, the choice might reflect conflict with the mother, or the child's perception that fewer demands would be made (and more ''freedom'' allowed) in the father's household. In other cases, the father was the parent who remained in the family home, and the children wanted to stay in the same school and be near their friends. In one or two cases the child's choice reflected a fairly crass evaluation that the father had more money and could provide a more affluent life.

· In several cases, the mother needed to continue education, or was trying to get job training in order to establish herself financially, after which she hoped to have the children with her.

· The mother worked very long hours, or nights and weekends, or had more than one job, and couldn't afford baby-sitters to cover such times.

· The mother was the one to leave the marriage, and the father was extremely angry and/or hurt. In such cases she might relinquish the child to him, feeling that it would be too unfair to take away both his marriage and his children. (Such relinquishment was more likely if she had children from a previous marriage.) Or the father might claim that the mother had forfeited her right to the children when she walked out, and refuse to let her take them.

Two themes ran through a number of the father-residence cases. The first is the father's use of such phrases as "I won't allow" or "I wouldn't let her" or "she can't have" or "so I decided"—phrases which reflect power assertion by the fathers. In a few cases, the fathers even said: ". . . and so I went over and took the children." Mothers sometimes said that they did not feel able to resist when the fathers asserted their right to be the one who would make the decisions.

A second theme running through the father-residence cases was the mothers' economic insufficiency. In a number of families, either the father or the mother would say that she could not afford to have the children with her. This no doubt reflects the generally lower level of education, and the poor job skills, of many of the non-resident mothers in our sample. Our father-residence families were the group with the greatest discrepancy in education between the mothers and the fathers, meaning that the group included a number of families in which the father had a much better educational foundation for adequately paid work than did the mothers. In one such family the father said:

(Father of 1-year-old son): "We felt that it would be better for me to have custody, because she didn't have time to be with him or money to support him. She's working two jobs, and rides buses."

Our first interviews occurred before divorce negotiations had been completed, and some of these mothers might later obtain awards of enough child support from their former spouses to enable them to sustain a household. What we see at Time 1, however, is that whatever temporary financial arrangements were made left some mothers too impoverished to maintain a household for the children.

A subgroup of father-residence cases was marked by the father's intense hostility toward his former wife. By and large, these were different cases from those of maternal deficit described earlier (the two measures were uncorrelated in the father-residence group). When we consider the father's hostility and his concerns about the mother's child-care competence jointly, we find that the two factors make independent and significant contributions to the probability that the children will live with their fathers. This analysis appears to indicate that some fathers have taken the children in a spirit of angry retaliation against wives who, the fathers believe, have wronged them. As one such father put it:

(Father of son, aged 3): "She walked out on me. She walked out on our son. There is no reason she should end up getting him. To our son's eyes it would look like I left him. She left, it was her choice."

A mother who had left an angry husband paints a very dark picture:

"He threatened to kill me if I took Kevin. You know what? He would have. He's beaten me up twice before. I see Kevin every other weekend now. The only thing I could do to make this divorce easy on Kevin was to give Kevin to his father. It's not worth losing my life over. The next time he would kill me. That's how angry he is at me for leaving."

In other cases in which children were living with highly angry or hurt fathers, however, the mother was not merely yielding to his anger, but complied with his demand for custody out of her own feeling of guilt over disrupting his life and that of the children.

It is important to note that in the mirror-image case—when the *father* had been the one more eager to leave the marriage—he was less likely to have the children living with him than was otherwise the case. We suppose that he was responding to the *mother's* anger and hurt by being more yielding about custody than he might otherwise have been.

Visitation with Fathers

As we have seen, in most of the mother-residence families the children were seeing their fathers during regular portions of the school year. We may ask whether the kinds of factors that affect father residence also affect whether children who live with their mothers are allowed overnight visits with the father. To a moderate extent, the answer is yes. In the mother-residence families in which mothers expressed misgivings about the environment in the father's household, 36 percent were sending their children for overnight visits at Time 1, as compared to 53 percent of the families in which the mother expressed no such concerns (Chi square = 13.09, $p < .001$). Although *residence* with fathers did not reflect high levels of a father's pre-separation involvement with the children, visitation with him did: when the mother had rated the father at less than 5 on the 10-point involvement scale, the children had overnight visits in only 37 percent of the cases, as compared with 49 percent when the mother reported the father to have been more involved.

Reasons for Adopting Dual Residence

We have seen that dual-residence families had more resources, on the average, than either mother-residence or father-residence ones, in the sense that dual-residence families included more well-educated and high-income fathers and mothers. Nevertheless, the families with dual residence covered a wide socioeconomic range, and there were clearly factors other than resources which determined their choice of this initial arrangement.

Earlier, we asked whether parents were more likely to elect dual residence if they had sufficiently low levels of hostility toward each other so that they felt confident of being able to cooperate in child-rearing. We saw that although dual-residence parents had somewhat lower hostility ratings, on the average, than primary-custody parents, the differences were not great—less than 1 step on the 10-point scale. The average for the dual-residence parents fell at the midpoint of the scale—5.2—and their ratings covered the range from very low to very high. Thus we can say that although there may be somewhat fewer highly hostile parents among the dual-residence families, there are nevertheless many with high levels of hostility toward the former spouse, and we must search further for the factors that led couples to opt for dual residence.

Perhaps the most outstanding characteristic of dual-residence families is that *both* parents were strongly committed to maintaining strong parental relationships with their children. The fathers did not want to be mere "weekend dads." In a relatively small number of cases, in answering our question about their reasons for choosing dual residence, both parents expressed an ideological commitment to the principle that the two parents should always be equally responsible for the rearing of children, whether divorced or not. More commonly, the fathers had insisted on sharing the child's time more equally than the mother would have wished. Some excerpts from interviews will illustrate their respective points of view:

> (Father of 2-year-old son): "I want to be a father. I won't let a divorce stand in my way. I'm coming from the point of view that I feel it's important for the child to have the benefit of both parents. That a father has just as much equal stake in raising the child and influencing the child's growth. I also feel that it's important for both parents to have time for themselves, to do whatever they have to do. It's not good for a child to be with one parent continuously where that parent feels tied down . . . So, I'm trying to strike a balance where our son gets the benefit of both of us and at the same time we're able to pursue our own interests."
> (Mother in this family says): "I have been a consistent parent. I have a better understanding of my son's needs. I find joint physical custody totally unfair to the child. A child needs certain grounding, stability and roots. Bouncing from one home to the other does not allow that stability."

> (Father of girl aged 13 and boy aged 11): "We fought about it. She's very busy. I am too. We both wanted the kids. The kids wanted to be with each of us. [Ex-wife] is increasingly wrapped up in her career."

> (Mother of 2-year-old son): "He [ex-husband] wants as much time as I have. I miss my son. I'm so used to having him here. The actual leaving, seeing him go . . . it wasn't my idea to dissolve . . . I try to think what's best for [son]. I've always been around. If being with his father would be proven to be better, I'd do it, but it would be hard. His room is here, this is his house."

Summary Comment

At the time of our first interview, typically about six months after separation, maternal residence was the overwhelming norm. Dual-residence and father-residence families are distinct groups, each relatively small, which must be viewed against the backdrop of this "norm." In attempting to understand why children were living with their fathers or in dual residence, we had to consider why children were *not* living with their mothers, since maternal residence continues to be the preference of the large majority. As we summarize our findings on initial residence, it is useful to turn the question around and ask: why do so many families begin post-separation life with the children living with their mothers?

It appears that the initial decision concerning whether the children would live with the mother, with the father, or with both parents did reflect to some extent the resources of the family. In our sample, the families with dual residence included a somewhat higher proportion of high-income and better-educated parents. However, there was a wide range of both income and education in each of the three residential groups. Fathers who were unemployed at the time of our T-1 interview were particularly unlikely to have residential responsibility for children at that time. If either parent lived in a house that he or she owned, the probability that the children would live with that parent was increased. We interpret this to mean that there was a tendency for children to remain in the family residence, with whichever parent was the one who assumed possession of the house. In general, however, the relative economic resources of the two parents were clearly not the determining factor in deciding where the children would live. We did see some cases in which the parents indicated that the children were living with the father because he could support them and the mother could not, but the majority of children were living with their mothers despite the fact that the fathers had substantially higher incomes.

Family composition had some effect on the residence decision. Dual residence was more likely to be adopted by one-child families than by larger families. Boys of all ages were more likely than girls to live with fathers or in dual arrangement, while girls more often lived with mothers. Very young children were almost always in their mothers' residential care, while children between ages 2 and 9 were somewhat more likely to be in dual residence and adolescents to be living with their fathers. However, the large majority of children of all ages and both sexes lived with their mothers. When the mother had children from a prior marriage, a somewhat higher proportion of the children from the current marriage lived with their fathers. Taken together, the composition of the family and the economic resources of the two parents make some difference in the residential decision, but these factors do not begin to explain the great preponderance of maternal residence that we—and others who have chronicled post-divorce family structure—have found.

Does marital fault explain the predominance of mother residence after divorce? We saw that when fathers were the first to want to end the marriage, they were less likely to have the children living with them. And conversely, when the mother was the one most eager to leave the marriage, children were somewhat more likely to be living in dual or father residence. Today no-fault divorce laws are nearly universal in modern societies, and in deciding about the custody of the children, the question of who is the more aggrieved partner is not supposed to be taken into account. But there is evidence that in the private negotiation that occurs at the time of separation, "fault" is indeed considered, at least with respect to the transfer of money and property (see McDonald, 1986, chap. 9); and in reaching an initial agreement concerning the children's residence, it appears that some parents in our sample did consider who was the more aggrieved party. We do not know whether these trends reflect feelings of guilt such that the leaving parent allowed the spouse to have more say over custody, whether the "wronged" parent became a tougher bargainer, or both. In any case, we must now ask: did the mothers more often have the children living with them because fathers were more often the ones who wanted to leave the marriage? The answer is unequivocally no. Both parents reported that the number of mothers who were the first to want to break off the marriage greatly outnumbered fathers who were the first to want to leave—the ratio of mother to father "leavers" was more than two to one. Of course, women might want to leave because of wrongs they believed their husbands had done them, so their leaving might not entail much guilt. In any case, guilt over leaving the marriage could clearly not be the reason why so many fathers were ceding residential responsibility for the children to their former wives.

Does the balance of power during the marriage explain why most children live with their mothers? We noted a theme in a number of the interviews with residential fathers reflecting power assertion on their part. Conversely, there were a number of non-residential fathers who said they would have liked to have more of the children's residential time, but that their wives would not "let" them have anything more than visitation. Does the preponderance of maternal residence imply that mothers, by and large, have more decision-making power in matters affecting the family? We saw in Chapter 3 that mothers usually have more management responsibility within families, but this does not imply greater power vis-à-vis their husbands. Researchers studying power relationships within intact families have concluded that it is almost impossible to determine whether it is a husband or a wife who wields more power (Broderick, 1975). Usually, a married pair pursue many joint goals where their interests converge, so that a conflict of wills is not involved. With respect to issues over which they differ, each is usually able to influence the other, although with somewhat different techniques of persuasion. There is no reason to believe that mothers gain residential responsibility for children following the parental separation because they have wielded more power throughout the history of the marriage. (Perhaps it is the law that empowers them; this is something we will consider in Chapters 5 and 6.)

We believe the strong "tilt" toward mother residence flows from a cluster of factors. First, as we have seen, more mothers than fathers have been primary caretakers of the children before the separation. According to the perceptions of many parents, experience and competence in managing parental functions go hand in hand. Most fathers appear to feel confident that their former wives are good mothers, and can continue to be so after the breakup. The majority of mothers, on the other hand, have misgivings about the adequacy of the care provided for the children in the husband's post-separation household. We have seen that parental trust or mistrust in the ex-spouse's parenting skills has an important bearing on where the children will live.

When we asked parents for the reasons why they had adopted their initial residence pattern, we have noted that the most common replies had to do with logistics—where the residence was located in relation to the parents' jobs and the children's schools; how much driving would be necessary between households; who would have the time (and an available car) to take the children back and forth on various days of the week. When such issues were mentioned by either the mother or the father, the children were highly likely to be living with the mother. A number of researchers studying family organization and economics (Joshi, 1984; Funder, 1986) have noted that married women with children, when they work, are much more likely than their husbands to have chosen jobs in which the work demands are compatible with child-rearing. This need not mean that they work part time—it can mean that they work closer to home or school, or that they take jobs in which they do not need to travel or work overtime on short notice. In so doing, they have accepted jobs which, on average, are at a lower level than the jobs they would be qualified for and could get if they did not have children. Thus most mothers, before the separation, have already made the adjustments in their work schedules that enable them to work while carrying the major responsibility for child-rearing. Fathers, by and large, have not done so. To take on additional child-care responsibilities would require many fathers to make new work-schedule adjustments (see Lamb et al., 1985, on the diminished earnings and career prospects of fathers who are highly involved in child-rearing). When faced with this reality, most fathers appear reconciled to ceding the children to the mother's day-to-day care.

We have been examining the conditions that led to families' adopting the form of residential custody for their children that was in place at the time of our first interview, usually about three months after the couple had filed for divorce. At the time of this interview, then, the couples had not completed the legal formalities that would eventuate in their final divorce. We have seen that the parents in our sample differed widely in the level of hostility they expressed toward each other, and it is to be expected that some of them would manage the processes of negotiation and bargaining with relatively little conflict while others would become embroiled in intense legal battling. We will want to explore to what extent the legal negotiations affect the subsequent de facto residences of children. In the next two chapters we will turn to an analysis of the bargaining and conflict-resolution processes, and will try to identify some of the conditions that determine the extent and nature of legal conflict.

5

Child Custody: What Parents Want and Get

The California legislature substantially modified custody law not only to remove the presumption that mothers would ordinarily be the custodians of young children following divorce, but also to allow and even encourage more androgynous arrangements in which both parents would share responsibilities through joint physical custody or joint legal custody. Is this what divorcing parents want, or do most still express a preference for a traditional arrangement in which the children live with the mother and the father visits? To what extent do divorcing mothers and fathers now differ in their preferences for custody and in their behavior in the legal system?

In this chapter we begin our examination of the way parents resolve the legal issues concerning divorce. In order to be able to compare parents' custody requests with the outcomes of their negotiation process, we have based the analyses in this chapter on the 933 families in our sample whose divorces were final by the fall of 1989. For these families, we were able to go to the court records to determine the provisions of the final decrees. The focus here will be on custody, and it will be recalled that California law now differentiates between physical custody, which concerns where the child resides and the allocation of everyday child-rearing responsibilities, and legal custody, which involves the allocation of authority for major decisions relating to the child's education, religion, and health care. We begin with physical custody, focusing on the relationship between parental desires and parental requests, and between parental requests and custodial outcomes. We then examine a similar set of questions with respect to legal custody.

Physical Custody

Parental desires. In our first interview, we asked each parent what he or she would personally like in terms of residential custody, regardless of what in fact had been or would be requested in the legal proceeding. As shown in Table 5.1, the difference between the desires of mothers and those of fathers is striking. The overwhelming majority (82 percent) of mothers indicated that they wanted sole physical custody of their children. Only 15 percent of the mothers indicated a desire for joint physical custody, and fewer than 2 percent said they wanted the father to have physical custody. By contrast, roughly equal proportions of the fathers desired joint custody, father custody, and mother custody. Nearly 70 percent of the responding fathers expressed a desire for a form of residential custody other than mother custody.

It is likely that our results for fathers reflect some degree of selection bias. We suspect that the 548 fathers who did agree to participate in our study might on average have been somewhat more involved with their children than the fathers whom we could not locate or who refused to participate. Had we been able to interview every father in our 933 familes with completed divorces, a somewhat higher percentage of fathers—perhaps one-half—might have expressed a desire for maternal custody.[1] Nevertheless, our results indicate that there are large numbers of fathers who say they would prefer joint physical custody or father physical custody to the more traditional mother physical custody arrangement.

Table 5.1 Distribution of physical custody wanted

	Percentage of mothers (N = 752)	Percentage of fathers (N = 548)
Custody wanted		
Mother	82.2%	29.4%
Father	1.7	32.5
Joint	14.8	35.4
Split[a]	0.7	1.8
Other	0.7	0.9
	100.0%	100.0%

a. Split residence means that one or more children live with one parent while one or more live with the other.

The relationship of custody desires to custody requests. The contrast between the stated preferences of mothers and fathers surely suggests the possibility of conflict in a high proportion of cases. But the court records reveal that in fewer than one-quarter of the cases was there actually a conflict between parental requests for custody.[2] In more than three-quarters of the cases, either the petition and response asked for the same custodial arrangement or no response was filed. Given the stated preferences of fathers and mothers, why were there so few conflicting petitions and responses?

The primary explanation turns out to be that many fathers do not act on their stated desires. When we compared parental desires with what parents actually requested on the divorce petition or response filed with the court, the gender differences are striking: mothers are more likely to act on their stated desires than are fathers. For example, Table 5.2 reveals that nearly 80 percent of those mothers who said they wanted sole physical custody requested this arrangement, whereas fewer than 40 percent of the fathers who said they wanted sole physical custody filed such a request. For those fathers who wanted joint custody, more than half either made no request or requested sole physical custody by the mother. Many fathers did not bother to file a physical custody request. Nearly 40 percent of the fathers who told us what they would really like in terms of custody failed to make *any* request, whereas only 17 percent of the mothers

Table 5.2 Distribution of physical custody requested by type wanted

| | Type of custody wanted | | | | | |
| | Percentage of mothers[a] | | | Percentage of fathers[a] | | |
	Mother (N = 618)	Joint (N = 111)	Father (N = 13)[b]	Mother (N = 161)	Joint (N = 194)	Father (N = 178)
Requested on petition						
Mother	78.6%	33.3%	—	36.0%	10.8%	12.4%
Joint	6.8	30.6	—	18.0	40.2	19.7
Father	0.5	3.7	—	1.9	6.2	37.6
No request	14.1	32.4	—	44.1	42.8	30.3
	100.0%	100.0%	—	100.0%	100.0%	100.0%

a. Excludes 10 mothers and 15 fathers who wanted/requested split or non-parental custody.

b. Percentages omitted because of very small sample size.

Table 5.3   Congruence between custody wanted and custody requested

	Physical custody	
	Percentage of mothers (*N* = 728)	Percentage of fathers (*N* = 519)
Requested what they wanted	81.7%	56.1%
Requested more than they wanted	6.7	9.8
Did not request as much as wanted	11.5	34.1
	100.0%	100.0%

Note: Excludes parents who wanted split or non-parental custody. If a parent made no request, it is presumed that the request of the other parent was acceptable to him/her and was that parent's request by default.

failed to make a request. We considered the possibility that a parent might not have made a request for physical custody in the legal papers because the other parent, as petitioner, had already requested what he or she wanted. We discovered that in a majority (56 percent) of the 128 cases where the mother made no request, the father in fact had petitioned for the mother's stated preference. For the 210 fathers who made no request, on the other hand, the mother made a consistent request in only 42 percent of the cases. Indeed, as Table 5.3 reveals, when we took into account those cases in which the father simply did not file a petition or response and instead treated the mother's request as his own, it turned out that more than a third of the fathers in our sample did not ask for as much physical custody as they had told us they wanted.

Why did so many fathers who said they wanted joint physical custody or sole father custody fail to act on their stated preference? A number of explanations are possible. On average, fathers may well hold their custodial preferences with less intensity than mothers. In our Time 1 interview, we asked parents to rate themselves and their spouses on a 10-point scale on their "feelings about custody, where 1 is someone who doesn't really care much about which kind of custodial arrangement is made and 10 is someone who is extremely determined to get the exact custody he or she wants." When we compared self-reports of mothers who wanted sole custody with self-reports of fathers who wanted joint or sole custody, we found a statistically significant difference: mothers rated their feelings about custody somewhat higher than did fathers (mean for mothers = 8.8; for fathers = 8.4). These means, however, are both very high, and the difference between them, while statistically significant, is small. We also compared self-reports for fathers who wanted joint or sole custody and filed requests with those of fathers who wanted the same forms of custody but did not file requests. Not surprisingly, fathers who filed requests rated their feelings about custody significantly higher (8.6) than fathers who did not file a request (8.1).

For some fathers, their stated preference may have reflected more what they thought they should want in terms of physical custody rather than the arrangement that they ended up concluding would be realistic or practical for them. Some fathers may have declined to act on their preferences either because they were less experienced in the day-to-day management of the children's lives or because they came to recognize that they would find it too difficult to coordinate the demands of their jobs with the demands of child-rearing. Actually taking on primary child-rearing responsibilities would represent a substantial change for most fathers, and many might wish they could do so (and express that preference in the interview) but hesitate to make the commitment even though they genuinely wanted to live with their children. Some may have unselfishly concluded that despite their own preferences, maternal custody would better serve the needs of their children. Others may simply have decided that, given the mothers' determination to have sole physical custody, the chances of securing some other result were too remote to justify the necessary effort and family stress. Whatever the reasons, many fathers who said they wanted a nontraditional form of physical custody never made a corresponding request in the formal legal proceedings.

The comparison of desires and requests in Table 5.3 also suggests the possibility of strategic behavior in which a parent exaggerates his or her custodial request, perhaps in the attempt to create a bargaining chip. We found that 10 percent of the fathers and 7 percent of the mothers requested more physical custody in their petition or response than they told us they wanted. Indeed, approximately 20 percent of the fathers who said they wanted maternal custody in fact requested joint physical custody or father physical custody. The data indicate that some mothers might be playing this game as well; 33 percent of the small group of mothers who expressed a desire for joint physical custody requested sole maternal custody in their papers.

On the other hand, such requests may not reflect strategic behavior at all if at the time of the petition or response a parent's preference in fact had changed from that reported to us at the time of our initial interview. A request for more custody may indicate a true change, although for most fathers only a month or two separated the interview and the time when the petition or response was filed. In Chapter 7 we examine closely the troubling claim frequently voiced by experts and practitioners that fathers who in fact prefer for the mother to have sole custody are successfully pressuring mothers to accept less support by creating custody conflict.

Outcomes in cases without conflicting requests. For nearly 80 percent of our cases, the parents did not make conflicting requests,[3] and in most of these 705 cases the divorce decree eventually provided for the outcome that was requested in the petition. (Table 5A.1 in Appendix A shows the distribution.) In 134 of these cases, however, the decree provided for some other custodial arrangement, even though the legal papers indicated no evidence of parental conflict. Typically, the final decree was not issued until a year or more after the petition was filed, and in the interim family circumstances and parental preferences could of course change. An analysis of those cases in which the outcome differed from the uncontested request shows a pull toward mother custody.

For more than 500 of these 705 cases, the uncontested request was for mother physical custody. In nearly 90 percent of these cases, sole physical custody was in fact awarded to the mother. By contrast, for the 47 cases in which the uncontested request was for father custody, only about 75 percent resulted in sole physical custody for the father; 12 percent resulted in mother physical custody and 12 percent in some other form of judgment. It is worth noting, however, that there were more than ten times as many cases where the uncontradicted request was for mother physical custody rather than for father physical custody.

Only slightly more than half of the cases in which the uncontested request was for joint physical custody resulted in a joint physical custody decree. The proportion resulting in mother custody (31 percent) was nearly four times higher than that resulting in father custody (about 8 percent).

Outcomes in cases with conflicting requests. Our analysis of the cases in which the parents made conflicting physical custody requests shows that the mothers' requests were granted about twice as often as the fathers' requests (see Table 5.4). Of these 198 cases in which there was a conflict, the mother was granted the custody she requested in 117 cases, the father was granted the custody he requested (or more)

Table 5.4   Outcome for physical custody when parents' requests conflict

	Custody requested		
Mother's request: Father's request:	Mother Joint ($N = 131$)	Mother Father ($N = 53$)	Joint Father ($N = 14$)
Outcome:			
Mother	66.4%	45.3%	0.0%
Joint	28.2	35.9	42.9
Father	2.3	11.3	42.9
Split	3.1	7.5	14.2
	100.0%	100.0%	100.0%

Note: Excludes four families with petitions requesting split or non-parental custody.

in 52 cases, and the remaining 29 cases resulted in a compromise between the two requests in the custody allocated.

The most common form of conflict arose when the mother requested sole physical custody and the father requested joint physical custody. In about 67 percent of these 131 cases the divorce judgment provided for sole physical custody for the mother, while in about 30 percent of the cases the result was joint physical custody. In the few remaining cases, either the father got sole custody or there was split custody, with each parent taking one or more children. In other words, the mother was denied sole physical custody in only about a third of these cases.

The second most common form of conflict involved each parent requesting sole physical custody. This was true for about 6 percent of our sample, some 53 cases. Two important observations can be made about these cases. First, the outcome in these cases was sole mother custody (45 percent) four times as often as sole father custody (11 percent). Second, in more than a third of the cases in which the mother and father each requested sole custody, the outcome was joint physical custody. This suggests that joint physical custody sometimes may be used, whether through negotiation or adjudication, as a way of "splitting the difference" to resolve this extreme form of conflict. We investigate this hypothesis in Chapter 7.

In only 14 cases was there conflict because the mother requested joint physical custody and the father requested sole custody. Only in this category of cases does it appear that mothers and fathers were equally successful (43 percent) in securing their desired outcome.

Table 5.5   Residence at separation by outcomes of cases with conflicting requests

| | Residence at separation | | | | | |
| | With mother | | Dual residence | | With father | |
	N	%	N	%	N	%
Outcome:						
Mother/joint conflicts:						
Mother	74	70	11	65	2	40
Joint or father	31	30	6	35	3	60
Mother/father conflicts:						
Mother	18	67	5	42	1	12
Joint	8	30	5	42	5	63
Father	1	3	2	16	2	25

Is it possible to predict the outcome in cases in which the requests of the parents conflict from information known at the time the petition is filed? As indicated earlier, in our Time 1 interviews we determined whether the children were initially residing with the mother, with the father, or with both parents at the time of separation. Our analysis revealed that the children's place of residence at the time of the initial separation appears to have a very powerful influence on the outcome when parents have conflicting custody requests.

Once again, however, our data reflect a gender difference. Table 5.5 shows that when children are residing with the mother at the time of separation, the father rarely succeeds in defeating her request for sole mother custody. When the children are living with the father, on the other hand, although the father's chances improve significantly, they are not as high. In those cases where there is dual residence at the time of separation, the father's chances of securing his requested custodial arrangement are not as high as the mother's, but are better than when there is mother residence. There were 23 cases in our sample in which the children either had dual residence or resided with the father, where the mother requested sole custody and the father requested joint physical custody. Mothers won in 13 of these cases and fathers won in 10—not quite 50-50 odds, but still a high percentage of wins by fathers by comparison with the sample as a whole.

That residence should influence the custody outcome is hardly surprising. When children are residing with one parent, as long as they are doing well, it is unlikely that an evaluator will recommend a change or a judge will disturb the status quo. This appears to be particularly true when the children are living with the mother. Therefore, in cases where the father is requesting joint physical custody but the children are living with the mother, fathers are probably advised by their lawyers that it is unlikely that they could prevail in a trial or secure an evaluation that would recommend against mother custody.

Lawyers are, of course, aware that where the children are residing may strongly influence the eventual outcome. Regrettably, this may in some cases lead them to advise parents to play "chicken" and refuse to move out of the house for fear of harming their future custody claims. As mentioned earlier, in about 10 percent of our cases both parents remained in the family home at the time the petition was filed. For most of these families, we suspect that the parents were attempting to save money rather than to gain an advantage with respect to custody claims.

Legal Custody

In our interviews with parents, we also asked about their desires concerning legal custody—that is, the allocation of decision-making about such matters as the child's education, religion, and health care. From the court records, we determined what each parent requested, the extent to which the initial requests conflicted, and the outcomes found in the divorce decrees. We discovered that joint legal custody has now become the norm in California.

Parental desires. There was much greater similarity between the desires of mothers and fathers regarding legal custody than regarding physical custody. A majority of both mothers and fathers wanted joint legal custody, and most of the remainder indicated a desire that they (not their spouse) should have sole legal custody. For mothers, about 60 percent indicated a desire for joint legal custody, with the remainder indicating a desire for mother legal custody. For fathers, the percentage preferring joint legal custody was even higher: 75 percent of the fathers wanted joint legal custody, about 17 percent wanted father legal custody, and 6 percent desired mother legal custody.

The relationship of custody desires to custody requests. Comparison of parental requests and desires regarding legal custody reveals a strong pull toward joint legal custody. In about two-thirds of the cases, only one parent made a request, and that request was usually for joint legal custody. When both parents made the same request, that request was almost always for joint legal custody. For those mothers who said they preferred joint legal custody, there was very little slippage in terms of requests. The overwhelming majority either requested joint legal custody, or made no request in circumstances where the father had requested joint legal custody. Only 10 percent of such mothers asked for sole legal custody. For fathers, the pattern is even more striking: all but 2 percent of the fathers who wanted joint legal custody either made that request on a petition or a response or made no request in circumstances where the spouse had requested joint legal custody. Moreover, many parents who initially expressed a desire for sole legal custody ended up requesting joint legal custody or filing no request when their spouse petitioned for joint custody. This was true for more than 62 percent of the mothers, and nearly 83 percent of the fathers.

Conflicting requests were rare with respect to legal custody. In only 100 cases, or about 11 percent of our sample, did mothers and fathers petition for different forms of legal custody. Almost all of these were cases in which the mother asked for mother legal custody and the father asked for joint legal custody. In cases where the parents did not disagree on legal custody, the most common outcome was joint legal custody.

The relationship of legal custody outcomes to parental requests. Whether the requests conflicted or not, the outcome was usually joint legal custody. In two-thirds of our sample, one parent requested joint custody and the other either agreed or filed no request. Nearly all of these cases resulted in joint legal custody. Moreover, when there were conflicting requests, if either parent asked for joint legal custody, that was usually the outcome. For example, in 72 cases the mother asked for mother legal custody and the father requested joint legal custody. In 86 percent of these cases, the result was joint legal custody. The only important exception was in circumstances where the father made no request and the mother requested mother legal custody; the outcome was joint legal custody in only 32 percent of these cases. In sum, for 79 percent of our entire sample, the divorce decree provided for joint legal custody; mother legal custody was the outcome for nearly all the remaining cases.

This overwhelming tendency for California divorce decrees to provide for joint legal custody is of recent origin. Before 1979, there was no statutory reference to any form of joint custody. Pilot studies that sampled Santa Clara County divorce decrees granted in October of 1979 (before any joint custody legislation went into effect) and in October 1981 (shortly after the first provisions were enacted) suggest the explosive growth of the use of joint legal custody. In the 1979 decrees, only 25 percent of the judgments provided for any form of joint custody.[4] In 1981, 37 percent of the final decrees provided for some form of joint custody.[5] By way of contrast, in our sample, where the divorces became final between 1985 and 1989, 79 percent of the decrees provided for some form of joint legal custody.

The Role of Lawyers

Does the presence of lawyers influence custody requests or outcomes? We determined from the court records which parents had legal representation during the divorce proceedings and divided our sample families into four groups: (1) neither parent had a lawyer; (2) only the mother had a lawyer; (3) only the father had a lawyer; (4) both parents had lawyers. We then examined the pattern of custody requests and outcomes for each group.

One or both parents were represented by legal counsel in the divorce proceedings in 80 percent of our sample families. Both parents were represented in nearly half (47 percent) of the cases. When only one parent consulted a lawyer, that parent was much more likely to be the mother (24 percent) than the father (9 percent). In part, this disparity results from the fact that petitioners are usually much more likely to be represented by counsel than respondents. Our sample followed this pattern; mothers were the petitioners in about two-thirds of the cases. The percentage of father petitioners represented by counsel (76 percent) was not statistically significantly different from the percentage of mothers who were petitioners and were represented by counsel (79 percent). However, when mothers were respondents, they were more likely to be represented by counsel than fathers who were respondents: 55 percent of mother respondents but only 46 percent of father respondents were represented by counsel. This difference is statistically significant.

Effects on legal custody requests and outcomes. Given the prevalence of joint legal custody, we were particularly interested in learning whether the presence of lawyers may have affected the diffusion of this form. It appears that the involvement of lawyers did have an impact on both requests and outcomes. In cases in which both parents were legally represented, the outcome involved joint legal custody 92 percent of the time. At the other extreme, joint legal custody was awarded to only half the families in which neither parent had a lawyer.

When only one parent was represented, the frequency (77 percent) fell between the two extremes. (Table 5A.2 in Appendix A shows the distribution.)

The presence of lawyers seems to have influenced legal custody requests as well. First, we found that parents with lawyers were more likely to request joint legal custody than those without lawyers. Second, we examined desire/request discrepancies and looked at the cases in which a parent said that he or she desired sole custody but nonetheless requested joint legal custody. Those with attorneys were more likely to request joint legal custody, with 50 percent of the mothers and 51 percent of the fathers doing so, even though they said in the interviews that they desired sole legal custody.[6] In short, lawyers appear to have encouraged their clients to ask for joint legal custody. This is consistent with the fact that more joint legal custody was awarded when at least one party had an attorney.

Perhaps the most striking evidence that lawyers are key in bringing about a high proportion of joint legal custody outcomes stems from our analysis of one particular subgroup in which the numbers were large enough to make some interesting comparisons. There were 153 cases in which the mother requested mother legal custody and the father made no request. Despite the mother's initial request, and the absence of any conflicting request, one-third of these cases resulted in joint legal custody. As Figure 5.1 shows, the presence or absence of lawyers appears to have had a profound impact even in these 153 cases. Joint legal custody was awarded in 82 percent of the cases in which both parents had an attorney but in only 11 percent of the cases where no attorneys were involved. When only the mother had an attorney, joint legal custody was the outcome 39 percent of the time. In none of these cases did only the father have an attorney. This would suggest that lawyers appear to encourage their clients not only to request joint legal custody but also to push for joint legal custody even when this has not been initially requested in the petition. We suspect that mothers are told by their lawyers that (1) everyone is doing it, and (2) as a practical matter, they are not giving up any real authority and that it may improve the father's satisfaction with the overall agreement.

Effects on physical custody requests and outcomes. The relationships between legal representation and physical custody requests and outcomes were more complex than for legal custody, as Figure 5.2 illustrates. Regardless of group, mother physical custody was the most common outcome, ranging from a low of 49 percent of the cases when

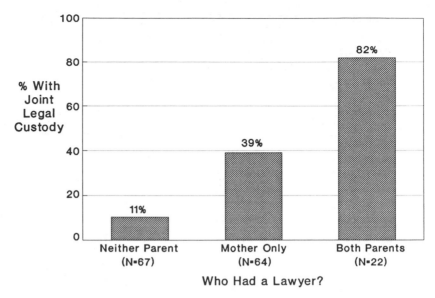

Figure 5.1 Relationship of the percentage of joint legal decrees to having a lawyer, in cases where the mother requested mother legal custody and the father made no request.

only the father had a lawyer, to a high of 86 percent when only the mother did. Father physical custody was quite rare, with one exception: when only the father had a lawyer, he gained physical custody about a third of the time. Similarly, joint physical custody was only slightly more frequent than father physical custody, but it was the result in 29 percent of the cases when both parents had legal counsel.

In short, for physical custody, a parent with an attorney was more likely to gain custody than a parent of the same gender without a lawyer. But this hardly demonstrates a causal relationship between outcomes and the presence or absence of a lawyer. When parents have conflicting custodial preferences, it would seem obvious that those parents who are willing to fight for custody will typically seek legal counsel. On the other hand, it is possible that lawyers may sometimes persuade a parent to ask for custody when without such legal advice the parent would not have pursued the matter.

We also explored the extent to which having a lawyer may influence the discrepancy between what parents say they desire and what they request in their legal papers. In some cases, lawyers may encourage their clients to make custody requests they might not otherwise make.

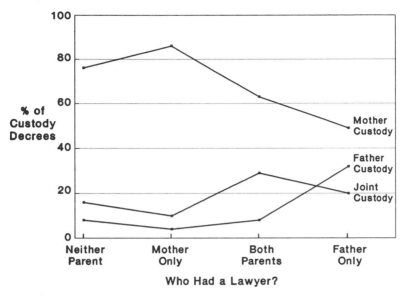

Figure 5.2 Percentage receiving mother, father, or joint physical custody as a function of who has a lawyer. (This subgroup excludes 36 families with split or non-parental custody and 10 with missing information regarding employment of lawyers.)

For mothers, we found no relationship between legal representation and a desire/request discrepancy. Mothers nearly always requested what they wanted—86 percent of mothers who made a request in a petition or response in fact requested the form of custody they said they preferred, which was almost always mother custody. This was not true for fathers, however. Fathers with an attorney were *more* likely to request what they wanted than fathers without a lawyer. Indeed, only 21 percent of fathers without counsel even made a request, whereas 80 percent of fathers who were represented by counsel did so. These differences are statistically significant.

As noted earlier, only a small number of fathers and mothers (44 and 35, respectively) requested more physical custody in the petition than they indicated they desired in their interview. Our analysis suggests that the probability of either parent's requesting more physical custody than he or she desired was higher among those parents who had lawyers than among those who did not. Of the 35 women who said they desired joint physical custody but in fact requested sole physical custody, 30 (or 86 percent) were represented by counsel. In our sample as a whole, only 70 percent of mothers were represented by counsel. For fathers, 41 of the 44 men who asked for more custody than they said they desired were represented by counsel, and only 55 percent of all fathers in our sample were represented by counsel. There is, of course, no way to know for certain whether these requests represented strategic behavior and, if so, whether the lawyer encouraged the request. Nonetheless, the results suggest that a parent represented by a lawyer is more likely to ask for more custody than he or she says she wants, although it should be emphasized that the total number of parents who did this was a small proportion of our entire sample.

Summary Comment

The distribution of custodial outcomes (see Figure 5.3), as well as our findings with respect to parental desires and requests, demonstrates both continuity and change in terms of the actual operation of the legal system in California. Mothers plainly remain the primary custodians of children following divorce: they receive sole physical custody of the children in two out of three cases, while fathers have sole physical custody less than 10 percent of the time.

The evidence concerning joint custody, however, suggests substantial change as well. Joint physical custody was the outcome in nearly a fifth of these California divorces. These families, while a minority, now represent a substantial minority. Although no historical data exist to provide a baseline, the fraction of northern California families with joint physical custody has no doubt increased, and it would appear to be much higher than the fraction reported in other regions of the country at the same time. How do these families fare? A decree providing for joint physical custody is meant to suggest that the parents substantially share day-to-day child-rearing responsibilities, and it is assumed that these parents generally establish cooperative co-parenting relationships. In Chapters 8 and 9 we will return to these issues.

The fact that about 80 percent of our sample families now have joint legal custody suggests dramatic change, but the fundamental question is what this change means. It appears that lawyers were important agents of change in this regard and often may have suggested joint legal custody in situations where one or both parents had not otherwise considered it. For about half of our families (48.7 percent), the decree provided for mother physical custody and joint legal custody. Is there any evidence to suggest that this legal label has some effect on the post-divorce behavior of parents? Joint legal custody is presumed to

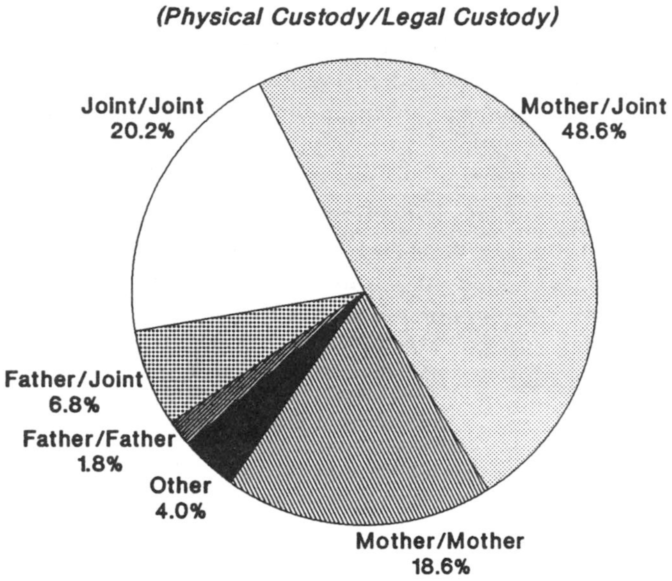

(Physical Custody/Legal Custody)

Figure 5.3   Distribution of custodial decrees (*N* = 933).

encourage shared decision-making between parents and "frequent and continuing contact" between non-residential parents and their children. Are parents in families with joint legal custody in fact more likely than parents in families with mother legal custody to consult with each other concerning education, religion, or medical care for their children? When the children in fact reside with the mother, are fathers with joint legal custody more likely to visit their children regularly? Are they likely to comply better with their support orders? Later chapters will explore these questions.

Despite the evidence of change, our examination of custodial outcomes suggests very substantial gender differentiation. The overwhelming majority of mothers still want sole physical custody of their children, and this is usually the outcome. While many fathers expressed a preference for a less traditional arrangement, mothers were much more likely than fathers to act on their desires by filing a specific custodial request. Many fathers do not file a conflicting request in their legal papers, in spite of their expressed preference. And in cases where they do, and the requests conflict, mothers succeed twice as often as fathers in securing their preferred outcome. In short, although gender stereotypes are no longer embedded in the statute books themselves, and California law is certainly viewed as sympathetic to more androgynous forms of physical custody, the actual custodial outcomes still reflect profound gender differentiation between parents: the decree typically provides that the children will live with the mother.

What about the father? In addition to custody issues, divorcing spouses also must reach agreement on issues relating to child support, spousal support, and the division of marital property. In the traditional allocation, fathers are expected to provide the primary support for their children. Is the pattern of outcomes for money issues also heavily gendered? Are child support, spousal support, or marital property outcomes related to custody outcomes in any consistent, predictable way? In the next chapter we turn to the economic arrangements for the children.

6

The Economic Provisions of the Divorce Decree

In this chapter we examine the economic outcomes of the divorce process. From the vantage point of divorce law, the economic provisions of the divorce decree have three separate elements: child support, spousal support, and division of marital property. We are primarily concerned with the child-support and spousal-support provisions that are incorporated into the divorce decree. What are the principal determinants of whether child support or spousal support is ordered, and what determines the amounts of those awards if they are ordered? To what extent are the custody provisions related to the economic terms of the decree, including the disposition of the house? In a later chapter we consider the implications of the financial provisions of the divorce decree for the standard of living that the two parents can maintain after the separation, and also examine how the impact of the economic divorce decisions changes with time.

We had good measures of child support and spousal support in our study, but only limited data on the division of marital property, except for the family home. In our view, the fact that we had no accurate measure of other marital property at the time of the divorce does not constitute a serious limitation, for two reasons. First, few divorcing couples with children have substantial net worth—most are young, and their stock of property typically consists of clothes, furniture, and an automobile. Outstanding debts often offset a large part of this value. For those with valuable property, the only substantial assets are typically the equity in the family home and perhaps some retirement benefits. Second, California is a community property state, and its law provides for equal division (in value if not in kind) of community property on divorce. Although nothing in the law prohibits unequal divisions, anecdotal evidence suggests that nearly all divorcing couples in California follow the equal division rule.

Child Support

Child support awards are more strictly regulated than other types of wealth transfers between divorcing spouses. California has had advisory child support guidelines since the early 1980s, and the use of such guidelines is increasing across the country. In the 1988 Family Support Act, Congress mandated guidelines for all states. Under the guideline in effect at the time of our study, the amount of the child support award depends on the number of children, the income earned by each parent, and the amount of time that the children will spend with each parent. Although during our study California required only that these guidelines be used to determine support during the pendency of the divorce,[1] in practice the schedules undoubtedly had a significant effect on the final award as well. However, as we shall see, the schedules did not entirely determine how much child support would be awarded.

Probability of Award

We found that in 83 percent of our sample families, the decree provided for child support. The likelihood of a child support award, however, varied with which parent was awarded physical custody (or whether the couple were awarded joint custody). Figure 6.1 shows that fathers were ordered to pay child support in 89 percent of mother-physical/mother-legal custody cases and in 96 percent of mother-physical/joint-legal custody cases. By contrast, only 36 percent of non-custodial mothers were ordered to pay child support to custodial fathers. In joint physical custody cases, the gender effect is even more striking. Nearly 70 percent of fathers but only 2 out of 176 mothers in joint physical custody families were ordered to pay child support.[2]

Since the fathers in our sample were earning more than twice as much as the mothers, on the average, it is easy to understand why more non-custodial fathers than mothers should be ordered to pay child support. In Figure 6.2 we compare the incomes of fathers and mothers in each of the custodial groups. We see that in cases in which the mother had physical custody but legal custody was joint, the fathers earned more than twice as much as the mothers. In families in which the mothers had both physical and legal custody, however, the income differential between the two parents was not nearly as great—

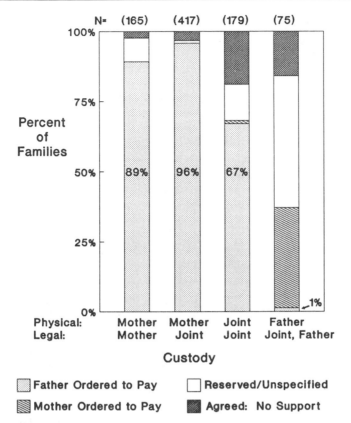

Figure 6.1 Child-support orders by custody arrangement. (The sample used in this figure excludes 54 cases with split custody or other custodial arrangements.)

which no doubt accounts for the fact that somewhat fewer fathers in the latter group were ordered to pay support.

Especially interesting is the case of families who had joint custody—both physical and legal. Although fathers in this group earned even more than fathers in the mother-physical/joint-legal group, only 67 percent were ordered to pay child support. This is a substantial number, but nonetheless is much smaller than the 96 percent found when the mother had physical custody. Thus in about a third of the families in which the children were spending substantial amounts of time in each parental household, neither parent was ordered to pay support to the other. In two-thirds of the cases the father (not the

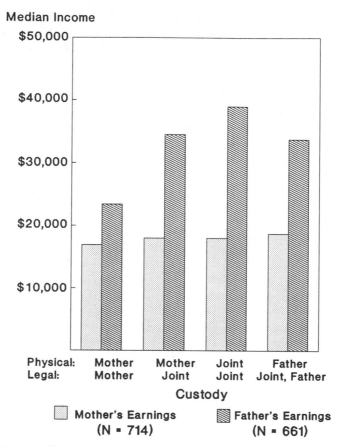

Figure 6.2 Median annual earnings by custody arrangement. (The sample used in this figure excludes 54 cases with split custody or other custodial arrangements.)

mother) was ordered to pay—a finding consistent with the fact that in the joint custody cases, although both parents had to maintain households large enough to accommodate the children, the mothers had much lower incomes with which to do so.

Does the fact that fathers are more often ordered to pay stem in any degree from traditional gender stereotypes concerning fathers' greater obligations to provide economic support? Perhaps, but we cannot be sure. In the small group of father-custody families in which the mother earned at least as much as the father ($N = 13$), the mother was almost always ordered to pay child support to the father—suggesting that mothers and fathers were receiving equal treatment. However, when the mother's income was less than the custodial father's, she was ordered to pay only 28 percent of the time, while in the 86 families in which custodial mothers earned more than the fathers, 76 percent of the fathers were ordered to pay. In these latter cases, the mothers, though earning more than the fathers, were still not high earners, and the father's contributions may have been thought to be needed despite his low earnings. By contrast, in the small group of father-custody cases with relatively high mother earnings, the father was usually also a high earner (mean earnings, $40,000 per year), so he may not have appeared to be in need of contributions from the mother. In other words, it was not only the earnings of the two spouses relative to each other, but the absolute level of the custodial parent's earnings, that appears to have influenced the probability of a child support award.

What other factors influence whether a child support award is ordered? As we saw earlier, there are four factors which the law specifies as relevant: the income of the father, the income of the mother, the number of children, and the division of the children's residential time between the two households. Since these factors are related (for example, higher-income fathers get a higher share of child time, on the average), we used regression analysis to explore the relative weights of the different factors in predicting the probability of an award. We added to the regression several other factors, beyond the statutory ones, that we thought might affect the probability of an award. Because mothers rather than fathers were the recipients of child support in the overwhelming majority of families, we rephrased our question to read: what are the factors that determine whether a father will be ordered to pay child support to a mother? We excluded father-custody cases from the analysis.

Of the four statutory factors, we found that the father's income and the number of overnights spent with the father are both significant determinants of a grant of child support. The probability of an award increased by 0.5 percentage points for each additional $100 per month earned by the father, and decreased by 0.5 percentage points for every $100 decrease in the father's monthly earnings. The probability of an award dropped by 4.4 percentage points for each additional overnight spent with the father. Mainly, what we are seeing here is the "joint physical custody effect" noted earlier. In addition, the probability that the father would be ordered to pay child support was higher by 12 percentage points for families in which the mother was not employed outside the home prior to the initial separation. If the father was the one who wanted to end the marriage, the probability of an award increased by 12 percentage points.

Theoretically, the custodial arrangement can have two potentially offsetting effects on the probability that a father will agree or be ordered to pay child support: a "cost" effect and a "caring" effect. When children spend more overnights with their father, he must incur the costs of providing additional housing and food, as well as other child-care expenses. To the extent that he incurs costs related to visitation and child care, he is less likely to want to provide for child-rearing expenses incurred by the mother as well. On the other hand, fathers who spend more time with their children may care more about the children and may be more willing to pay support. Our regression analysis confirmed both the "cost" and the "caring" effects. Although additional overnights spent with the father decreased the probability of a child support award, the probability of an award was 17 percent lower when the father had no regular contact with his children.

Amount of Award

In cases in which fathers were ordered to pay child support, we computed the amount of the award as a percentage of his gross earnings. Figure 6.3 shows how these percentages varied as a function of custodial arrangement and number of children. When mothers had physical custody, the percentage of the father's gross earnings awarded as child support did not depend on whether the couple had joint *legal* custody: if they had only one child, the portion of his income the father was ordered to pay was 10 percent for both joint legal and mother legal custody cases, and the figures for two-child families similarly show that joint legal custody made little difference in the amount of the award.

Regardless of the legal custody arrangement, the award for two-child families in cases where the mother had sole physical custody was more than two-thirds higher than that for one-child families. For joint physical custody families, however, the child support award for two-child families was on average only slightly higher than that for one-child families, and the average award for two-child families was a substantially lower percentage (8 percent) of the father's gross income. Once again, then, we see a "joint custody effect," with the amount of child support paid to mothers being smaller in joint-custodial families, particularly if they have more than one child.

We conducted a more detailed analysis of award levels (to be paid

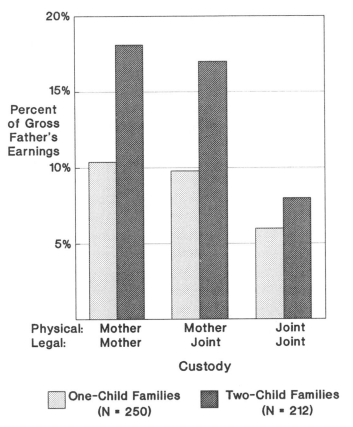

Figure 6.3 Awards as a percentage of the father's gross earnings. (This group excludes zero awards, cases where the mother was ordered to pay, and family support. Forty-four cases with split custody or other custodial arrangements and 76 cases with father sole custody arrangements were eliminated from the sample used. Child-support awards were taken from the court record, and father's earnings were measured in the first survey after the divorce was final.)

by fathers to mothers), first using regression to predict award levels from the four variables included in the child support guidelines. Each of the four statutory factors was independently and significantly related to the amount of awards, but together they only predicted 36 percent of the variation in award levels. If all court awards were based exclusively on the formula given by the regression, the four variables together should have been much more powerful. Several factors could contribute to the unexplained variation. First, our measurements of

Table 6.1   Factors predicting the amount of child-support awards fathers were ordered to pay

	Effect on award amount (in dollars per month)
Father's monthly earnings (for each $100)	4.97*
Mother's monthly earnings (for each $100)	−2.99*
Number of children (for each additional child)	130.22*
Nights with father (each night in 2-week period)	−13.38*
Father's earnings squared	−.01*
Father was first to want out of the marriage	29.19
Couple owned a home	33.24
Father a college graduate	84.04*
Mother not employed prior to separation	44.27*
Father has no contact with children (during school year)	−7.22
R^2	.54
Number of cases	367[a]

a. This table is based on cases with mother custody or joint physical custody, where the divorce was final by the end of the study, where all the above items of information were available, and where the father was ordered to pay child support.

* $p \le .05$.

the variables may be inaccurate. For example, the guidelines refer to adjusted after-tax income, but in our survey respondents reported pre-tax earnings and did not give us information about unearned income. Second, because the guidelines are only advisory, child support awards may reflect some individual and judicial discretion. Finally, the award may reflect additional factors not stated in the child support guidelines.

To test this last possibility, we added several more potential explanatory variables to the regression model. The four statutory factors used in the initial regression analysis continued to have significant effects, but the power of the model as a whole was increased, and it now explains approximately half the variance in the amount of child support awarded. Table 6.1 indicates the relative weights of the various factors, in terms of the dollar amounts added to the award for each increment in the predictor variable. Thus, the table shows that a father who earned $4,000 per month would have to pay about $50 more per month in child support than one who earned $3,000, other things (such as number of children) being equal. We included a squared term for the father's income to capture any nonlinear effects of earnings. The results for this term show that child support awards increase with the father's earnings, but at a decreasing rate. Lower child support awards were given when the children spent more overnights with their fathers (that is, when the children were in joint custody). In addition, awards were larger when there were more children, going up by $130 per month for each additional child.

We found that additional variables that may reflect the father's ability and willingness to pay have a positive effect on awards even after controlling for income. Better-educated fathers (who may have greater long-term earning potential) were ordered to pay more; so were fathers in families in which the couple owned a home, probably reflecting greater wealth. Mothers who were not employed prior to the initial separation received somewhat higher monthly child support awards—$44 more per month—than employed mothers. We also see a modest effect of "guilt feelings," or at least feelings of responsibility for the divorce: when fathers were the first to want to end the marriage, child support awards were somewhat higher.

Although the "cost" effect described above influences the amount as well as the probability of child support awards, we found no significant offsetting "caring" effect. Whether or not the father had any contact with his children during regular portions of the school year (not including vacations) had no statistically significant effect on the size of the award.

The fact that nearly half of the variation in award size remains unexplained suggests that discretion may play a substantial role in child support determination. It is possible that ignorance of the county guideline schedule may also affect the amount of child support awarded. We asked respondents if they had used the child support guidelines to help determine the child support award, and found that the awards were on average $58 higher per month for families that said they used the guidelines than for families that did not, after controlling for the number of children, the parents' incomes, and the number of overnights. Chapter 7 addresses the question of whether the extent of legal conflict appears to affect the economic terms of the divorce decree.

Spousal Support

Unlike child support, which nearly all of the decrees provided for, spousal support provisions were found in only 30 percent of the decrees.[3] We once again conducted regression analysis, first to determine what factors seemed to influence whether there would be any spousal support at all, and then, for those families with spousal support provisions, to predict the amount of the award.

The California statute governing spousal support provides that the decision whether to award such support should be based on the incomes of the two spouses. Not surprisingly, regression analysis revealed these two variables to be significant predictors of the probability and size of awards. The incomes of the two spouses explain more than 30 percent of the variation in the level of the award. The award increased by $15.43 per month for each additional $100 per month earned by the father and decreased by $15.09 for each $100 per month earned by the mother.

Another statutory factor to be considered in awarding spousal support is the duration of the marriage. We found that in cases where spousal support was awarded, the couple had been married more than 12 years on the average—two years longer than the average for the rest of the sample. Once income and the other factors in the regression were controlled, duration of marriage no longer significantly predicted whether there would be an award of spousal support. However, given that there was an award, its *amount* was affected by the length of the marriage: the award increased slightly for each additional year of marriage.[4]

A number of other variables affected the probability that an award for spousal support would be granted. Home ownership increased the probability of an award by 16 percentage points, and if the husband was college-educated the probability increased by 15 percentage points. If the husband was the one who wanted to end the marriage, the probability of an award increased by 12 percentage points. If the mother was not employed prior to the initial separation, the probability of an award increased by 18 percentage points. The mother's age at the time of marriage and the age of the youngest child at the time of divorce did not affect either the probability or the amount of an award. These additional variables, together with duration of the marriage, brought the explained variation in the amount of the award to 50 percent.

Disposition of the Family Home

In our sample, there were 411 families who owned a home and provided information about its disposition. We found that the mother kept the home in 37 percent of these cases, the father kept the home in 26 percent, and in the remaining 37 percent the home was sold and the proceeds divided between the spouses. The disposition of the home was unrelated to the father's income, but mothers who either kept the family home or were in families where the home was sold had significantly higher incomes than mothers in families where the father kept the home. The duration of the marriage was also significant. Families in which the father kept the home had shorter marriages on average than families in the other two groups.

When one parent kept the house, the amount of the transfer made to the other parent was almost identical regardless of whether it was the mother or the father who kept the house. The form of the transfer was different, however. When the father kept the house, the mother received a cash transfer payment in about two-thirds of the cases. When the mother kept the house, she generally relinquished other assets and paid cash in only about 30 percent of the cases.

We found a strong relationship between the disposition of the home and the physical custody decree. Figure 6.4 illustrates that the odds that a parent will keep the house increase with the amount of physical custody granted to that parent. Even after adjusting for the physical custody decree, however, our data reveal a slight pull toward the father in the disposition of the home. Among homeowning families, 45 percent of mothers with sole physical custody and 76 percent of fathers with sole physical custody kept the house. Nineteen percent of fathers in mother physical custody families but only 4 percent of mothers in father physical custody families kept the family home after divorce. When there was joint physical custody, fathers and mothers were equally likely to keep the home, but the home was more often sold than awarded to either parent. The home was also sold in 36 percent of mother physical custody cases. Given their lower incomes relative to fathers, it is likely that many custodial mothers would face difficulty maintaining mortgage payments.

Children's de facto residence is not always the same as the physical custody arrangement specified in the decree. When we examine the relation of actual residence to the disposition of the family home, the results are much the same as those shown in Figure 6.4, with one exception: when children actually *reside* in both households, the parents are less likely to sell the home than if they merely have a joint physical custody decree. When the parents have joint physical custody but the children live with the mother, there is greater likelihood that

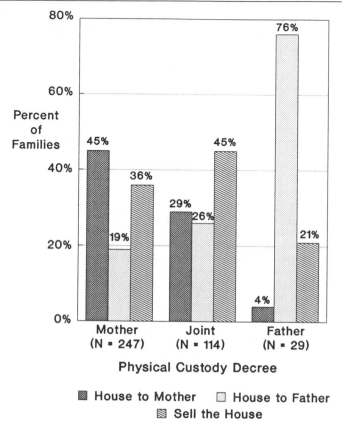

Figure 6.4   Physical custody decree and disposition of the house.

the home will be sold. Among families with joint physical custody decrees, 71 percent of mother-residence families but only 30 percent of dual-residence families sold the family home.

Standards of Living after Divorce

In Chapter 10 we will examine in detail how the standards of living of mothers and fathers (and their respective households) changed over the three and a half year period following their separation. For the present, we will sketch in only roughly the situation that prevailed at Time 1, and the impact that the child support awards and spousal support awards we have been discussing had on the economic level of the two households.

We saw earlier that most of the women in our study had been work-

Table 6.2   Employment and earnings of mothers and fathers compared, before and after separation

	Mothers	Fathers
Before separation		
Percentage employed	72.9	94.3
Median hours, if employed	41.0	45.0
Median annual earnings		
for those employed	$15,079	$31,070
for all cases	$10,357	$30,097
Joint earnings	$40,454	
Time 1		
Percentage employed	79.5	90.0
Median hours, if employed	42.5	45.0
Median annual earnings[a]		
for those employed	$18,000	$34,000
for all cases	$15,288	$31,000
Median child support award	+ $3,348 per year	− $3,348

Note: This table is based on 856 families in which either the father or the mother was interviewed at Time 1.

a. Earnings are expressed in 1985 dollars.

ing for pay outside the home before the separation, and that they usually worked full time. Nevertheless, there were more mothers than fathers who did not work for pay, and those who did work had somewhat shorter working hours. Their earnings, however, were substantially lower than those of their husbands, and the differential was too great to be accounted for by their lower hours. In short, when the mothers were working, they had lower-paying jobs. As shown in Table 6.2, the women in the sample (including both those who were employed and those who were not) were earning in the usual case about $10,400 before the separation, compared to the $30,100 being earned by the men. The median joint earnings before the separation, then, were a little over $40,500, of which the women were earning only about a fourth.

By Time 1, a few more women had gone to work, and those who were employed were working about one more hour per week. Partly for these reasons and partly because of increases in pay levels, the median earnings of employed women were now $18,000, but their husbands were still earning almost twice as much ($34,000). If we think in terms of earnings alone, the standard of living that could be maintained was obviously much lower in the mothers' households. But of course, the payments fathers were ordered to make in the form of child and spousal support were intended to redress this differential to some extent. How far did they go toward doing so? Almost all the mothers who had physical custody were to receive child support, and the most common amount awarded was $300 per month, or $3,600 per year. If we add this amount to the mothers' Time 1 earnings, and subtract it from the fathers', we find that the mothers' income at Time 1 was now nearly two-thirds of the fathers', but the differential was still great. Fewer than a third of the mothers were receiving spousal support in addition, and although the average amount of such support ($500 per month) was enough to redress the income imbalance considerably in some cases, it was usually awarded in the cases of the greatest husband/wife income discrepancy and was not available to most mothers, and so the income discrepancy remains great even when spousal support is taken into account.

Because the mother usually retains primary custody of the children, straightforward comparisons of mothers' and fathers' incomes after divorce will generally overstate the economic well-being of mothers, since they must support a larger household. Most of our families had either one or two children, so the mothers were supporting a two- or three-person household, in contrast to the father's one-person household, during the immediate post-separation period (before either parent remarried). In Chapter 10 we adjust our calculations to reflect the size of each parent's household. For the present, we simply point out the following fairly obvious facts: each parental household has a lower level of income resources after the divorce than their joint household formerly had. But the drop in resources is much greater for the mothers than for the fathers, and the amount fathers pay to mothers in the form of child support and spousal support does not make the two households even approximately equivalent.

How similar are the awards in our sample to those awarded in other parts of the United States? To answer this question, we compiled some descriptive numbers from a national survey of alimony and child support that was conducted in 1986.[5] Table 6.3 compares this nationally representative sample of women who were divorced during 1984 and who had custody of their children at the time of the survey with similar women from our study. To make the two samples as comparable as possible, in this table we restrict our sample to those mothers with sole or joint physical custody. As the table shows, child support

Table 6.3 Comparison of financial awards with national sample

	U.S. mothers divorced during 1984[a]	Our sample[b]
Any child support award[c]	84.7%	89.6%[d]
Child support award positive/per month[c]	$300	$387[d]
Child support received for those with positive awards	$214	$300
Any spousal support award[c]	8.1%	30.5%[d,e]
Spousal support award positive/ month[c]	$540	$561[d,e]
Spousal support received if due	$444	$371
Child support compliance[f]	63.1%	70.8%
Received full child support	52.4%	52.1%
Received zero child support	22.9%	17.7%
Spousal support compliance	70.1%	61.9%
Received full spousal support	66.7%	41.7%
Received zero spousal support	16.7%	28.0%

a. The sample is taken from the 1986 March/April *Current Population Survey* (CPS) of Alimony and Child Support. Spousal support and child support receipt refers to the year 1985.
b. The sample consists of families with mother sole or joint physical custody who had completed their divorce by the third interview. Spousal support and child support receipt are reported for the third interview.
c. Some divorce settlements specify a token award of one dollar in order to retain jurisdiction over the settlement. We convert all one-dollar awards to zero.
d. Some decrees indicate that there is not yet an agreement about child support or spousal support. We treat these cases as having no award at final judgment. There are two joint custody cases where the decree specifies that the mother pays child support to the father. We treat these cases as having no award made to the mother.
e. Any spousal award includes all mothers who were ever awarded support. Some of the women who were originally awarded spousal support are not still eligible to receive support by the Time 3 interview. Sixty-two percent of the divorce decrees granting spousal support limit the time during which this support is owed. The median duration of awards with limits is three years. By the third survey, 34 percent of these limits have expired. In addition, no spousal support is owed to women who have remarried. Thus, only 19 percent of the sample are due spousal support by the third interview. Spousal award positive/month includes only those still due spousal support at the third interview.
f. Child support and spousal support compliance are defined as the amount received as a percentage of the amount that is due.

award rates are slightly higher for our sample: almost 90 percent of mothers with sole or joint custody were awarded child support compared to 85 percent in the United States as a whole. Both the award level and the child support receipt for those with positive awards are also higher in our sample. These differences may be due, in part, to the higher levels of earnings in our sample. Indeed, the percentage difference in earnings is somewhat greater than the percentage difference in the level of awards. Compliance with child support awards is fairly similar across the two samples. About two-thirds of what is owed is actually paid; half of the fathers pay in full, but about 20 percent pay nothing at all.[6]

One notable difference between the two samples relates to spousal support. The award rate for spousal support in our sample—30 percent—is much higher than the award rate for the United States as a whole—8 percent. The level of the award, however, is slightly lower than the U.S. average, and the extent of compliance with the award is also lower. It may be that in other states only fathers with relatively higher income are required to pay spousal support, and that these men have greater ability and propensity to pay.

Summary Comment

Like custody awards, the pattern of child support awards is heavily gendered. This result is not particularly surprising. Because fathers on average earn much more than mothers (see Table 6.2), they are more likely than mothers to be ordered to pay child support. Similarly, the fact that custodial fathers are more likely than custodial mothers to keep the family home is not surprising given the need to maintain mortgage payments.

Despite the income differential between fathers and mothers, however, it appears that custodial mothers assume primary responsibility for supporting their children after divorce. Even assuming full compliance, support payments constitute only a fraction of post-divorce family income for these mothers. As a result, the standard of living for fathers and that of custodial mothers and their children diverge sharply after divorce.

Joint physical custody further reduces the probability that a mother will be awarded child support. For those joint physical custody mothers who do receive child support, moreover, the amount of support awarded is slightly lower than that awarded to their mother physical custody counterparts. The "joint decree effect" on child support is probably due in part to the cost effect of increased visitation. This effect is particularly striking given that fathers in joint physical custody families earned more on average than fathers in families with mother physical custody (see Figure 6.2).

Do fathers comply with support orders, or do support payments drop off over time? If compliance patterns do change over time, do these changes bear any relationship to changes in the children's residence and visitation patterns? Does the nature of the ongoing interaction between divorced spouses affect compliance with child support? Given the amount that fathers pay, how much recovery do we see in the standard of living of maternal households as time passes? How much difference does remarriage make? We will address these questions in Chapter 10.

The significant amount of unexplained variation in the probability and amount of child support awards raises the question of whether conflict between the parents may affect negotiation over child support—or negotiation over other provisions of the divorce decree. As discussed earlier, there is a strong theoretical argument that conflict between divorcing spouses may have significant effects on the outcome of divorce bargaining. The next chapter asks: do the gendered patterns of custody and economic outcomes that we observed vary with the degree of legal conflict? How does conflict affect the use of joint custody arrangements?

7

Conflict over the Terms
of the Divorce Decree

How much legal conflict do divorcing parents have in establishing the financial and custody terms of the decree? The general perception is that legal disputes are very common. Newspapers describe the bitter and protracted divorces of the rich and famous, and television and movies dramatize courtroom battling. The accounts of judges, court personnel, and lawyers tend to reinforce the perception that legal conflict is frequent, for these professionals focus on the problems of resolving highly conflicted divorces. In this chapter we examine (1) the extent to which legal disputes characterize divorce, (2) the processes used to resolve such disputes, and (3) whether the pattern of outcomes varies according to the degree of conflict. We are particularly interested in assessing the extent to which joint physical custody is being used to resolve conflicted cases.

Chapter 5 showed that the expressed preferences of the parents often conflict: 80 percent of all mothers say they would prefer sole maternal physical custody, while more than half of the fathers say they would prefer some nontraditional custodial arrangement. This finding suggests the possibility that legal conflict between divorcing parents might be very common. On the other hand, the fact that only 22 percent of the divorcing couples in our sample filed conflicting physical custody requests suggests that for most families the legal conflict, if any, must have involved divorce bargaining that occurred *before* the formal legal papers were filed.

We also saw in Chapters 5 and 6 that custody outcomes and support awards are highly gendered. Mothers much more often receive custody, and non-custodial fathers are much more often ordered to pay child support than are non-custodial mothers. In examining legal conflict, then, we must be alert to gender-related factors.

For those couples who do have legal disputes, by what process is the dispute resolved? California has constructed an elaborate divorce process that includes mandatory mediation and then custody evaluation as prerequisites to trial. Some critics of mandatory mediation have charged that mediation is inadequate to resolve most custody and visitation disputes, and that a mandatory system simply renders the divorce process even more costly and cumbersome. Do most families who experience conflict require judges to resolve their disputes, or are the intermediate procedural stages effective? How frequently must a judge adjudicate the terms of the custody or visitation provisions of the final decree? To what extent does court-annexed mediation or court-ordered evaluation lead to negotiated resolutions before disputes reach the judge? What proportion of cases is resolved through negotiation without resort to a neutral third party?

We also investigate whether the pattern of custody outcomes varies with the degree of legal conflict. We are primarily concerned with two questions. The first concerns gender. As shown earlier, mothers receive sole physical custody in the overwhelming majority of cases. Does the proportion of custody outcomes favorable to fathers as opposed to mothers change as the conflict becomes more intense? Some critics have argued that mandatory mediation coercively and systematically forces mothers as a class to accept unfavorable outcomes (Grillo, 1991). Others argue that judges, who are typically white males, rule against women more often than men (see Polikoff, 1982). Does the pull toward mother physical custody revealed in Chapters 4 and 5 dissipate or intensify as the divorce progresses through increasingly formal stages of dispute resolution?

The second question about the pattern of outcomes concerns the extent to which joint physical custody is being used to resolve highly conflicted cases. We know from Chapter 5 that joint physical custody was the outcome for about 20 percent of families in the sample. Does the proportion of joint physical custody outcomes remain the same at different levels of conflict? California law authorizes courts to order joint physical custody even in contested cases, and some policy analysts have expressed the fear that mediators often urge parents to adopt joint physical custody decrees as a way of resolving conflict. Critics of joint custody arrangements have charged that such arrangements will operate to the detriment of the children by prolonging parental and family strife. How often is joint physical custody being used to resolve the more conflicted cases?

Finally, we explore the claim that mothers who "win" custody in

disputed cases must often secure their preferred custodial arrangements by accepting less economic support. As explained earlier, when
parents negotiate the terms of the decree, custody and money issues
may be linked. Economic theory suggests that disputes may be resolved through trade-offs, in which one parent may give up some
financial support to avoid the risks of a custody fight. Commentators
have argued that in practice many fathers threaten a custody fight to
bring about a settlement requiring a lower level of support. Is there
systematic empirical evidence to suggest that where there is conflict
over custody, mothers, in fact, receive less support?

Patterns of Legal Conflict

Few studies have attempted to determine in a systematic way the
extent to which legal conflict characterizes the divorce process. The
conventional wisdom among scholars is that comparatively few custody cases require adjudication: estimates commonly range between
10 and 20 percent (Mnookin and Kornhauser, 1979). Empirical studies
that do exist rely exclusively on information from court records, and
therefore have no measure of the degree of legal conflict resulting from
bargaining that left no traces in the formal legal record.[1]

To determine the extent of conflict over custody and visitation issues, we used two sources of information—parental interviews and
court records—to construct three measures of conflict. From the interviews with parents, we ascertained their subjective perceptions of the
degree of legal conflict concerning the custody and money issues for
those families who participated in our Time 3 interview. From the
court records for each family, we determined the stage in the legal
process at which custody issues were resolved for the 933 families
whose divorce was final by the fall of 1989. Finally, we constructed a
measure that combined both sources of information.

All three measures—the parent's assessments, the court record information, and our conflict scale—indicate that most divorcing families
have little legal conflict over custody. The common perception of widespread conflict is a myth: most parents resolve the custody and money
issues without substantial conflict, and it is extremely uncommon for
disputes to require resolution by a judge.

Parental Reports

For one measure of legal conflict, we asked each parent at Time 3 to
rate on a 10-point scale the degree of conflict over custody and visita-

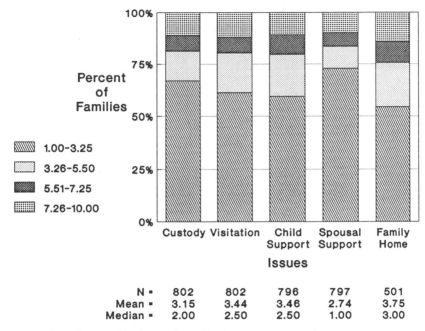

N =	802	802	796	797	501
Mean =	3.15	3.44	3.46	2.74	3.75
Median =	2.00	2.50	2.50	1.00	3.00

Figure 7.1 Parental ratings of conflict for each issue in divorce settlement. (Scales are available only for those families who were interviewed at T-3.)

tion issues before finalization of the divorce, as well as the degree of conflict over money issues—child support, spousal support, and the disposition of the family home. We developed a score for each family in the sample by averaging the responses of the two parents.[2] For each of the issues relating to custody or money, a substantial majority of the families indicated that they experienced little conflict.[3]

The first two columns in Figure 7.1 show that most parents report little legal conflict over custody or visitation issues. More than 40 percent of our families reported custody conflict levels of 1.0, and 75 percent were below 5.0. For visitation, about one-third of all families gave a score of 1.0, and two-thirds reported 3.5 or lower. For both custody and visitation issues, fewer than 10 percent of families rated their levels of conflict at 8.0 or higher.

Similarly, most parents reported very little conflict concerning financial issues. Moreover, regression analysis suggests that for each money issue, with the exception of alimony, the level of reported legal conflict bore no relationship to the amount of the award. When asked to rate the extent of conflict over child support, most parents reported low levels of conflict (mean = 3.46; SD = 2.72). A third of our families had a conflict score of 1.0, and the median for the 796 families who responded to this question was 2.5. Only a quarter of the families had scores above 5.0, and only about 5 percent reported scores of 10.0.

Low conflict ratings for child support issues are no doubt due in part to the influence of California's child support schedules, which indicate the expected amount of child support for parents with different levels of income and different numbers of children. Although at the time of our study the law required only that these schedules be used to determine temporary support—that is, support during the pendency of the divorce—in practice the schedules have substantial influence on permanent orders as well. Again, regression analysis, using the basic formula described in Chapter 6, Table 6.1, suggests that parental conflict over child support has no effect on the level of awards.

Our sample families reported even less conflict over spousal support than over child support (mean = 2.8). This result is not particularly surprising; for many families, the duration of the marriage was not long enough and the father's income not high enough to qualify the mother for spousal support under California law. Parents from 60 percent of our families rated conflict over spousal support at 1.0 on a 10-point scale. In most of these cases, the mother apparently made no serious attempt to secure spousal support.

About 10 percent of the families did rate spousal support conflict at 7.5 or higher, and 5 percent of the families gave a rating of 10.0. As discussed in the previous chapter, the most important determinants of spousal support are the husband's earnings and the length of the marriage. When these variables are held constant, however, the higher the family conflict rating for spousal support, the higher was the award. It may be that women who fight for spousal support are able to secure more spousal support, but these women may simply have better claims because of other characteristics we are unable to measure.

Among the sample families who owned homes, conflict over disposition of the family home was somewhat more common than conflict over child support or spousal support. Although about a third (34 percent) of the families who responded to this question gave a conflict rating of 1.0 and half the families gave ratings of 3.0 or lower, 25 percent rated their conflict level at 5.5 or higher, and 6 percent had ratings of 10.0.

As discussed in the previous chapter, the disposition of the family home appears to be strongly related to both the physical custody decree and the children's residence during the initial separation.[4] We determined that there was no relationship between the degree of conflict over the family home and its disposition. The mean level of conflict for families whose home was sold was somewhat higher than for families in which one parent retained the home, but the difference was not statistically significant.

Court Records

The parental interviews provide a subjective measure of the degree to which parents experienced legal conflict, but the 10-point scale does not suggest at what stage in the legal process decisions about the legal arrangements were made. Rather than relying on the recollection of the parents for this information, we examined the court records to determine for the custodial issues when the decision was made. For this purpose we used six categories, as shown in Figure 7.2. The court record information discloses a conflict pyramid, with a smaller and smaller percentage of cases resolved at each successive stage.[5] The vast majority of cases reached successful resolution of custody issues with no direct judicial involvement. The thick base of the pyramid, which contains half the families in our sample, consists of families with uncontested divorces, in which there was no conflict between the petition and the response concerning custodial arrangements. Often

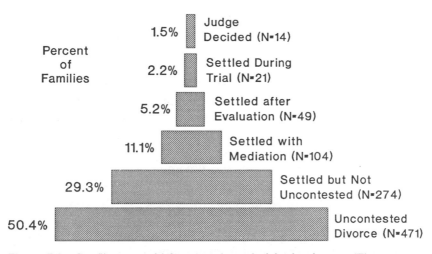

Figure 7.2 Conflict pyramid for custody and visitation issues. (There were 933 cases in which the parents had divorced by September 1989, and where there was also information concerning physical custody outcomes in the court record.)

the parties attached a separation agreement to the petition that spelled out their agreement concerning custody and visitation. In many instances, however, the petitioner secured a default judgment incorporating the provisions requested in the petition because the other parent had not even bothered to file a response.

Cases in the second tier of the pyramid, about 30 percent of our sample, were also resolved without the need for mediation, evaluation, or trial. This was a diverse group of cases. Although most of these court records showed little evidence of legal conflict, many indicated that one parent or the other requested some court action in addition to filing a petition or a response. Some cases involved requests to establish interim support during the pendency of the divorce; others involved orders to show cause or restraining orders. In all of these cases, however, the custody and visitation terms of the divorce decree were settled through negotiations.

The remaining 20 percent of the cases required involvement by a neutral third party associated with the court system to resolve a custody or visitation dispute. About 11 percent of our sample cases were resolved after custody mediation, and another 5 percent required the further step of a custody evaluation. At the top of the pyramid are the 4 percent of cases that actually required a custody trial. In half of these cases the custody issue was resolved without a final judicial ruling—the parents finally settled, either on the courthouse steps or during the trial itself. For only 1.5 percent of the cases—only 14 families—did the judge actually have to decide the custody or visitation issue.

A Combined Measure of Conflict

Alone, neither the court records nor the interview data tell the whole story about legal conflict. Although the court record reveals the stage at which the dispute was resolved, the location of a particular case on the conflict pyramid does not necessarily correspond to the intensity of the conflict experienced by the divorcing parents. For example, bitter negotiations extending over many months may result in settlement before any petition is filed; in such a case the court record would indicate an uncontested divorce. In other cases, a thick court record may reflect the lawyer's personal style rather than the degree of conflict between the parents. Rather than simply calling the opposing attorney to arrange for interim child support, some lawyers as a matter of course file an order to show cause and demand a hearing, and only then negotiate.

Yet we were equally reluctant to rely solely on parental reports to capture the extent of conflict over custody and visitation issues. Parents from different families could rate similar legal conflict very differently for personal reasons. For example, to avoid any implication that the children were upset by parental conflict over custody, some parents might give a very low conflict rating even though the court record clearly indicates intense battling that required third-party intervention. Conversely, even if the divorce is uncontested and there is no evidence that the other parent ever disagreed with the petitioner's custody request, a sensitive father might nevertheless rate custody conflict as 7 on the 10-point scale because he remembers a single intense argument with the mother over the custodial arrangement at the time of separation.

Examination of the court records and the interview information together revealed that in most cases the two measures of conflict concerning custody and visitation are consistent and reinforcing.[6] As one progresses up the conflict pyramid, the median parental conflict reports steadily climb. Cases that fall within the lower two tiers of the conflict pyramid tend to have low parental conflict ratings (with medians of 2 and 3 respectively), while cases in the top three tiers of the pyramid (involving custody evaluation or trial) have median scores of 10.0 (see Table 7.1).

For some cases, however, the two measures yield strikingly different results. Although parents whose divorce was uncontested nearly always reported little legal conflict, some 16 families (4 percent of this group) rated the conflict as high—8.0 or more. This certainly suggests that some families have bitter disputes concerning the custodial terms

Table 7.1   Parents' subjective ratings of conflict by mode of resolution

Subjective rating	Uncontested divorce ($N = 402$)	Settled but not uncontested ($N = 237$)	Settled with mediation ($N = 80$)	Settled after evaluation ($N = 45$)	Settled during trial ($N = 20$)	Decided by judge ($N = 14$)
1.00–3.25	68%	56%	27%	9%	—	7%
3.26–5.50	20	24	23	15	5	7
5.51–7.75	8	7	21	9	20	14
7.76–10.00	4	13	29	67	75	72
Total	100%	100%	100%	100%	100%	100%

Note: 135 cases did not have interview data to provide subjective conflict ratings.

that are resolved through intense negotiations that occur *before* the legal papers are filed. In addition, there is considerable variation in parental ratings for cases that were settled but not uncontested. Thirty of these families (13 percent of this group) reported very high conflict in the interviews. The most variation in parental ratings was seen in cases resolved through mediation. More than half of these families gave conflict ratings of 5.5 or greater, but nearly as many gave lower ratings. Indeed, the parents in about 30 percent of the mediated cases reported that they experienced little or no conflict. These data suggest that some couples used court-annexed mediation to get information or advice rather than to resolve a dispute.

We decided that it would be useful to construct a single measure of legal conflict that combined information from both sources. For each family, we started with the family-level parental conflict rating for custody and visitation, measured as described in note 2. Because the conceptual distinction between conflict over custody and conflict over visitation is unclear, especially in cases involving joint physical custody requests, we chose whichever of the two ratings was higher. We partitioned the 10-point interview scale into four equal segments (the rows in Table 7.1) and used the court record information to assign each case to one of four tiers of the conflict pyramid. The matrix in Table 7.A1 (in Appendix A) shows the conflict rating we assigned to each combination.[7]

Figure 7.3 shows the proportion of our sample falling into each of the four custody conflict ratings. About 75 percent of the families that had completed the divorce by September of 1989 had either negligible (51 percent) or mild (24 percent) conflict. For the 51 percent of families that experienced negligible conflict, the divorce was uncontested and the parental interview information suggested that there was no basic disagreement concerning custodial arrangements. The evidence suggests, however, that for approximately 25 percent of the families in our sample, resolution of the legal issues concerning custody and visitation was not so easy. We determined from the court records and the interviews that these families experienced substantial (10 percent) or intense (15 percent) conflict. We should acknowledge that this combined measure may somewhat underestimate the overall level of legal conflict, since we could construct the measure only for those families which had completed the divorce by September 1989 *and* in which at least one parent participated in the Time 3 interview. We had Time 3 interviews for 118 families who had not yet completed the divorce by September of 1989—more than four years after the petition had been

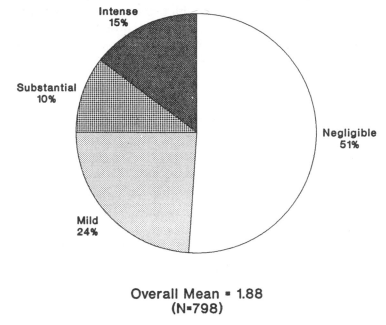

Overall Mean • 1.88
(N•798)

Figure 7.3   Proportion of sample in each of four custody conflict levels.

filed—and there is evidence that on average these families may have experienced somewhat more legal conflict.[8]

Statistical Profile of Intense-Conflict Families

Why do some families have intense conflict over custodial issues while most do not? What makes these families different? Are there demographic factors associated with high-conflict divorces, and is there a way to identify these families when they first enter the legal system? It may be that the actual process of divorce is somehow different for these families, and that this difference affects their ability to compromise and end their dispute. Understanding the preferences and behavior of parents in high-conflict families may provide insight into how to manage their legal conflict. To explore these issues, we compared the characteristics of intense-conflict families (Level IV on our conflict scale) with those of families in Levels I–III. This comparison revealed no significant demographic predictors of intense conflict, with the exception of the employment status of the parents.[9]

We thought it likely that parents with higher earnings would be more likely to be involved in intense legal conflict, if only because they can better afford the legal fees, than their poorer peers. Doing legal battle, after all, is expensive. The data suggest, however, that conflict in intense-conflict families was not generated by the parents' access to financial resources to support a battle for custody. The earnings of fathers and mothers in intense-conflict families were not significantly different from those of their counterparts in lower-conflict families.

The employment status of the parents, however, did prove to be statistically significant in a gendered way. The percentage of mothers not employed outside the home in the intense-conflict group (24 percent) was significantly higher than for lower-conflict families (18 percent). On the other hand, there were significantly *fewer* unemployed fathers in the intense-conflict group (4 percent) than in lower-conflict families (11 percent). In other words, an unemployed father is less likely to be involved in a custody fight, while a mother not working for pay is more likely to be.

This difference between fathers and mothers most likely reflects a traditional allocation of gender roles. Although an unemployed father might be thought to have more time available for child care, his inability to fulfill the traditional father's obligation to support his children makes him less likely to be involved in custody conflict. For a mother, the lack of paid employment suggests a traditional homemaker's role prior to separation, which may make it more likely that she will fight for sole maternal custody in the divorce process. These data also suggest that the custody dispute in intense-conflict families did not stem from fathers' increased involvement with the children as a result of mothers' employment. Comparison of intense-conflict families with lower-conflict families on a number of other demographic variables, such as the parents' age, race, and education, yielded no significant differences. (See Appendix Table 7.A2.)

Not surprisingly, parents who experienced intense conflict over custody took significantly longer (14.5 months) than parents in the lower conflict levels (11.8 months) to complete their divorces. Intense-conflict parents spent an average of 13.4 percent of their combined incomes on legal fees, whereas parents in lower-conflict families spent only about 5 percent. In fact, one intense-conflict family spent a total of $81,000 in legal fees. While the demographic data indicate that intense-conflict families do not have legal battles simply because they can afford to do so, these families do pay a price for their conflict in both time and money.[10]

The relation between legal conflict and the preferences and actions of parents also was not surprising. Recall from Chapter 5 that almost all mothers (82 percent) reported that they wanted sole physical custody. This percentage remained essentially consistent regardless of the level of conflict—80 percent and 84 percent for low- and high-conflict mothers respectively. Significantly more intense-conflict mothers (77 percent) than lower-conflict mothers (68 percent), however, asked for what they wanted on their petitions or responses.

Also recall that fathers overall had a much more even distribution of custody desires than mothers; roughly one-third desired mother custody, one-third father custody, and one-third joint custody. Intense-conflict fathers, however, were more likely than lower-conflict fathers to want joint or father custody. While 33 percent of lower-conflict fathers wanted mother custody, only 10 percent of intense-conflict fathers wanted the same. Although a greater proportion (90 percent) of intense-conflict fathers wanted joint or father custody, two-thirds of lower-conflict fathers wanted these forms as well. Significantly more intense-conflict fathers (52 percent) than lower-conflict fathers (35 percent), however, requested what they wanted. Furthermore, 66 percent of lower-conflict fathers who did not request what they wanted made no request at all. Thus, legal conflict could not simply be predicted on the basis of the custody preferences stated by the father, because many fathers expressed nontraditional preferences while few acted on them.

What Underlies Conflict?

We have seen that legal conflict occurred with about equal frequency in families of different socioeconomic levels; parental age and race were also not related to the incidence of legal conflict. Thus we were not successful in trying to identify a demographic profile of high-conflict families that differentiated them from the larger number of low-conflict families. What factors, then, do seem to lead families into legal conflict?

Parental hostility. A first and most obvious factor, we might think, would be the intensity of anger, jealousy, and feelings of betrayal that the two parents harbor toward each other. Surely we might expect that an intensely angry parent would seek revenge through trying to wrest custody of the children from a spouse to whom custody was supremely important. The threat to ''take the children away'' is a potent one in the interpersonal battle between divorcing parents, and many divorce mediators report that custody battles may merely be the arena in which parents are attempting to hurt each other and get revenge for their perceived injuries at the hands of the former spouse. In view of such reports, we are surprised that parental hostility does not play a stronger role than it does in generating legal conflict.

At the end of each T-1, T-2, and T-3 interview, the interviewers made an overall rating (on a 10-point scale) of the parent's hostility toward the former spouse. Interviewers were trained to focus on the *affect* being expressed—the tones of voice that conveyed anger or contempt, as distinguished from liking, empathy, or compassion—as well as on the content of what was being said. For each couple, a score called "maximum hostility" was derived, reflecting the highest hostility rating given to either spouse in a given interview round. The correlations of these maximum hostility ratings with the amount of legal conflict were as follows: T-1, .16; T-2, .28; T-3, .22. Each of these correlations is significantly above zero, but they are nevertheless small. The low level of these correlations is particularly surprising considering that the two measures are to some degree confounded. That is, when interviewers rated hostility, they were not blind to the amount of legal conflict the couple had engaged in, and their ratings were undoubtedly influenced by whether the couple had been involved in an intense legal struggle. The low level of correlations means that the interviewers were able to rate hostile affect to some degree independently of what they knew about the legal process that had occurred. More important, the low correlations mean that there were many intensely hostile parents who did not express their anger through legal conflict—and conversely, that some of the parents who did engage in legal conflict were *not* intensely angry, but were struggling over custody or visitation for reasons other than (or in addition to) their anger toward each other. Inter-spousal hostility, then, is one factor associated with high legal conflict, but it only contributes to a modest degree.

Age of the children. Parents were somewhat more likely to engage in legal conflict when their children were young: 30 percent of the families whose youngest child was under age 3 engaged in legal conflict that was either substantial or intense, as compared with only 19 percent of the families whose youngest child was age 11 or older. Of course, parents with older children have been married for a longer period of time, on the average, than parents of younger children. We thought it possible that short marriages were more likely to be marked by legal conflict, and if so, that our finding on the age of the children would be merely an artifact of length of marriage. This did not turn out to be the explanation, however.[11] We do not know why legal conflict should be more common for families with young children. Possibly, fathers fear that young children will forget them if they do not find a way to guarantee continued contact, whereas they have confidence that with older children, with whom a close relationship has already been established, the relationships can be sustained without legal guarantees. It could also be the case that the older children expressed custodial preference to which both parents tended to defer.

Pre-separation involvement in child-rearing. We saw in Chapter 2 that the two parents often did not agree on how much each had been involved in the day-to-day rearing of the children prior to the separation. Fathers frequently claimed that they had been equally or even more involved than their wives, while the mothers almost universally claimed that they had done more of the child-rearing than their husbands. If parents expect that the post-divorce division of the child's time between the two parental households should reflect the history of their respective roles in child-rearing, then it is a reasonable hypothesis that there will be more legal conflict over visitation and custody when the parental perceptions diverge substantially than when they do not. In families in which both parents participated in a standard interview at Time 1, we compared the perceptions of the two parents with respect to how each evaluated their respective pre-separation roles in child-rearing. A couple in which both parents said that the mother had done most of the child-rearing would be rated as having no discrepancy in perception; a couple in which the father claimed that he had been equally involved, while the mother rated herself as a "10" on involvement and her ex-spouse as a "3," would have a large discrepancy in perceptions. Table 7.2 shows that high legal conflict (substantial or intense) was quite rare (only 12 percent) among couples who agreed on what their pre-separation roles had been. By contrast, 44 percent of the couples with a large discrepancy in perceptions engaged in substantial or intense legal conflict.

Concerns about the child's well-being in the other parent's household. In Chapter 4 we showed that parents' concerns about the quality of the environment that would be provided by the other parent were related to the decisions about where the children were living at the outset of our study. At Time 1, we asked each parent: "Do you personally find anything upsetting about your children going to spend time with (your ex-spouse)?" As we noted earlier, many parents expressed confidence that the children would be well cared for in the other household. However, 30 percent of mothers and 23 percent of fathers did express concerns in response to this question, and an additional group

Table 7.2   Relation of legal conflict to discrepancies in parental perceptions of their pre-separation involvement in child-rearing

Amount of legal conflict	Difference in perception of pre-separation child-rearing involvement (T–1)			
	None (N = 66)	Slight (N = 129)	Considerable (N = 128)	Large (N = 66)
Low	62%	53%	50%	29%
Moderate	26	26	29	27
Substantial or intense	12	21	21	44
	100%	100%	100%	100%

Chi^2 24.48; df 6/382; $p \leq .0001$.

Note: This table is based on families in which both parents had standard interviews at Time 1. Each parent rated self and former spouse on pre-separation child-rearing involvement. The column "None" means that the two agreed on how involved each had been (or in a few cases, that they attributed greater involvement to the other than the other claimed).

mentioned such concerns at other points in the interview. In Chapter 9 we consider in detail the nature of these concerns; here it is sufficient to say that parental concerns covered a considerable range with respect to how serious the problems appeared to be. Some concerns had little to do with the quality of care the child would receive in the other household (for example, some parents resented the influence of the other parent's new partner). But some parents were worried about whether the child would be adequately supervised and protected from hazards in the other household. In particular, 8 percent of the mothers in our sample, and 4 percent of the fathers, expressed concerns over the other parent's abuse of drugs or alcohol, and the effect such problems might have on the ability of a former spouse to handle child-care responsibilities when the children were visiting. Table 7.3 shows how each parent's concerns (as expressed in their answers to a specific question about "finding it upsetting" for the child to spend time in the other household) were related to legal conflict. We see that if either parent answered "yes" to the question about being upset over the child's well-being in the other household, the likelihood of legal conflict was elevated. A father who won physical custody of a 10-year-old boy through an intense legal battle provides an example. He reports: "She's a Disneyland mom. I couldn't get my son to bed. I had to deal with settling him down after the visits with his mom. My custody was

Table 7.3 Relation of legal conflict to parents' concerns about children's well-being in other household

| | Are you concerned about child's welfare in other household (T–1)? | | | |
| | Mothers | | Fathers | |
Amount of legal conflict	Yes ($N = 206$)	No ($N = 477$)	Yes ($N = 122$)	No ($N = 407$)
Low	42%	56%	32%	55%
Moderate	24	24	29	25
Substantial or intense	34	20	39	20
	100%	100%	100%	100%

Note: Chi^2 16.6, $p \leqslant .0001$ (mothers); Chi^2 23.2, $p \leqslant .0001$ (fathers).

mandated by the courts. There was one major consideration and that was his mom's manifest inability to get him to school on time. He was late or absent 75 percent of the time [when he was with her]."

It is important to note, however, that there were a number of parents having concerns that could be regarded as serious who did not resort to legal conflict. For example, in the case mentioned in Chapter 4 in which the mother was worried about her 3-year-old visiting a father's household in which loaded guns were left unsecured, the mother did not bring an action to stop visitation but attempted to solve the problem (so far unsuccessfully) by negotiating with the father.

How much credence can be given to parents' allegations about the competence of the other parent to care for the children? Certainly we should expect that if parents cannot agree on custody or visitation and are entering into a legal conflict, each should be involved in "case-building" against the other, with each attempting to show that his or her own household is the better environment for the child.[12] Thus it may be that the relationship between parental concerns and legal conflict merely reflects reporting bias or rationalization on the part of parents who are looking for support of their own case. On the other hand, it may be that parents are more likely to carry their dispute over visitation and custody to higher levels of legal conflict if they have valid reasons to believe that the other parent's household is in fact not beneficial (or is endangering) for the child. We believe that both explanations are probably true to some degree, but our data do not permit distinguishing between them.

The Relative Importance of Factors

Which of the various predictors of legal conflict discussed above carries the most weight? When we put them all into a joint prediction equation, the order of importance of those that remained significant is as follows:[13]

1. Father's concern over child's well-being in mother's household.

2. Father's hostility toward mother.

3. Mother's concern over child's well-being in father's household.

4. Discrepant perceptions of pre-separation child-rearing roles.

It is interesting that the father's hostility toward the mother at Time 1 should be significantly more related to legal conflict than the mother's hostility toward the father. We interpret this as reflecting the fact that mothers are likely to get the custody they want unless the father puts up firm opposition; the strength of the father's motivation to fight for custody, then, is more important in determining whether there will be a legal dispute.

In sum, our examination of possible factors related to legal conflict reveals that there is no demographic "type" of family that is more likely than other families to experience legal conflict, although the proportion of mothers not working for pay and employed fathers is higher in intense-conflict families. Wealthy and poor, old and young, all kinds of divorcing parents are represented among the minority who experience substantial or intense conflict. For many of these families, legal conflict over custody may reflect relationship issues between the spouses that existed long before the divorce process began—issues which we did not examine in our study, except to assess the level of hostility each parent harbored toward the other when the study began. As mentioned earlier, intense hostility was somewhat related to the occurrence of high levels of legal conflict, although the relationship was not a close one. What does seem clear is that parents involved in high levels of legal conflict often had very different perceptions of how much each had been involved in the children's lives before the separation. When fathers believed they had been closely involved, they were more likely to press for their rights to time with the child, while mothers who thought the father had *not* been substantially involved were more likely to resist such demands—perhaps because they did not fully trust the father's competence to provide adequate care and supervision. Parents involved in high legal conflict often expressed serious concerns about the adequacy of the other spouse's parenting capacity and the quality of the child-rearing environment that would be provided in the other household. We do not know how justified these accusations were; we can only report that they are part of the psychological profile of high-conflict families.

Outcomes and Conflict

We saw in Chapter 5 that in cases where the parents made conflicting custody requests, the mother secured her requested choice about twice as often as the father. Now we explore whether the pattern of outcomes varies with the intensity of conflict. We discovered that as one moves up the conflict pyramid, the proportion of joint custody decrees and father custody decrees increases.

We first looked at the outcomes for cases involving conflicting requests in which each parent asked to have sole physical custody. Such cases represented only 5 percent of our sample (some 53 families), and the variations in outcome patterns should therefore be interpreted with caution since there are only a few cases within the various tiers of the pyramid. Table 7.4 shows that on average, these cases resulted in mother physical custody four times as often as father physical custody. For cases within the top three tiers of the pyramid (settled after evaluation, settled during trial, or decided by a judge), the ratio of mother custody to father custody is no different from that in cases settled at earlier stages in the divorce process. However, for more than a third of the cases in which the mother and father each requested sole physical custody, the outcome was joint physical custody. There is a striking

Table 7.4 Conflict pyramid and outcomes of mother/father request conflicts

Mode of resolution	Physical custody outcome			
	Mother	Joint	Father	Split
Judge decided	3	1	1	—
Settled during trial	2	3	1	1
Settled after evaluation	5	5	—	1
Settled with mediation	8	8	2	1
Settled but not uncontested	6	2	2	1
Total	24	19	6	4

Table 7.5 Conflict pyramid and outcomes for mother/joint request conflicts

	Physical custody outcome	
Mode of resolution	Mother	Joint or father
Judge decided	2	3
Settled during trial	3	3
Settled after evaluation	8	8
Settled with mediation	20	6
Settled but not uncontested	54	20
Total	87	40

Note: Four cases which resulted in split custody were excluded.

increase in the proportion of compromise outcomes at successively higher levels of the conflict pyramid.

The more common conflict (127 cases, or 10 percent of our sample) occurred when the mother requested sole physical custody and the father requested joint physical custody. Nearly 80 percent of these cases did not require evaluation or trial. The overall ratio of mother custody to joint custody outcomes is about 2 to 1, as described in Chapter 5. However, for these cases the proportion of joint or father custody decrees also increases dramatically as one moves up the conflict pyramid. As shown in Table 7.5, cases that were settled without the need for custody evaluation or trial resulted in mother custody 74 percent of the time and joint custody or father custody only 26 percent of the time. By contrast, for those cases requiring evaluation or trial, sole mother custody was the outcome only about half the time. Because evaluations are sealed after resolution of a case, we could not examine the evaluators' recommendations, but it is likely that the ultimate resolution followed the recommendation for most cases.

Many critics of joint physical custody have expressed concerns that it is too often being used to resolve custody conflicts (see, for example, Singer and Reynolds, 1988). They fear that such use will divide the child between two parents, who will continue to fight long after the decree has been issued. Table 7.6 demonstrates that joint physical custody is in fact being used to resolve highly conflicted cases. The table shows the percentage distribution of custody outcomes for each tier of the conflict pyramid. Because the number of cases settled after evaluation, during trial, or by a judge is small, we combined the data for the top three tiers to compute the percentages. The combined data

Table 7.6   Physical custody outcomes by mode of resolution

	Physical custody outcome				
Mode of resolution	Mother	Joint	Father	Split	Total
Resolved after evaluation or trial (*N* = 84)	44%	40%	11%	5%	100%
Settled after mediation (*N* = 104)	63%	25%	6%	6%	100%
Settled but not uncon-tested (*N* = 274)	70%	19%	7%	4%	100%
Uncontested divorce (*N* = 471)	70%	17%	10%	3%	100%

show that use of joint physical custody becomes more frequent toward the top of the pyramid.

In the bottom two tiers of the pyramid (uncontested divorces and settled but not uncontested cases), 70 percent of cases result in mother physical custody and fewer than 20 percent in joint physical custody. For cases that are settled with mediation, there is a slight increase in the rate of joint physical custody awards and a small drop in awards to mothers. At the top of the pyramid, 40 percent of cases result in joint physical custody—nearly as many as result in sole mother custody (44 percent). Recall that only a small number of the cases at the top of the pyramid were actually decided by a judge; most cases reached negotiated resolutions. However, each of these cases required a custody evaluation prior to resolution, and it is likely that such evaluation would have a profound and coercive effect on subsequent negotiations. There is also some evidence that court-annexed mediation may encourage joint physical custody, although the proportion of mother physical custody outcomes (63 percent) is only slightly lower than for the two lower tiers (70 percent).

Examination of the distribution of custody outcomes using our four-point conflict scale also suggests the use of joint physical custody to resolve more highly conflicted cases: 23 percent of the joint physical custody cases but only 11 percent of mother physical custody cases involved intense conflict (Level IV). When we included families with substantial conflict (Level III) in the analysis, this disparity remained: 35 percent of the joint physical custody families but only 20 percent of the mother physical custody families experienced high levels of

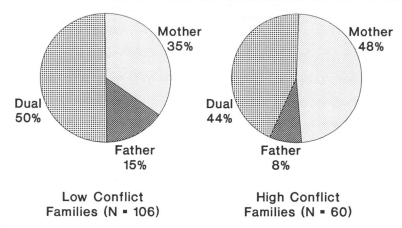

Figure 7.4 De facto residence for high and low conflict, joint custody families.

conflict. Again, nearly all of these cases reached negotiated settlements and did not require resolution by a judge.

We defer until Chapter 9 our analysis of how parents with joint physical custody decrees manage their co-parenting relationship. For now, one further aspect of the relationship between legal conflict and custody outcome is worth emphasizing. For those families with joint custody decrees, we compared the de facto residence—that is, where the children were actually living at Time 3—for the 60 high-conflict families (Levels III and IV) and the 106 low-conflict families (Levels I and II). As Figure 7.4 shows, the differences (though not statistically significant) are suggestive. In half (48 percent) of the high-conflict joint physical custody families, the children were in fact residing with the mother at Time 3; this was true of only 35 percent of the low-conflict families. To put it another way, in two-thirds of the low-conflict joint physical custody families, children in fact spent four or more overnights with the father in a typical two-week period, but this was true of only slightly more than half of the high-conflict families (52 percent).

Did these 29 high-conflict families that combined joint physical custody decrees with mother residence shift from dual residence to mother residence after the decree was issued? Or was the custody conflict simply resolved by putting a joint physical custody label on a preexisting relationship? We looked at residential stability between Time 2 and Time 3 for those families that had completed their divorce by Time 3, and found that high-conflict families were no more likely than low-conflict families to change residential patterns during this period.

This result suggests that some highly conflicted cases are being resolved by adopting the joint physical custody label although in fact the children reside with the mother.

The Gender Issue Revisited

We have found that although mothers receive sole physical custody in the vast majority of cases, the proportion of joint or father custody outcomes approaches 50 percent for high-conflict families. At first blush, this finding would appear to disprove allegations that the California divorce process reflects and perpetuates gender bias. Why, after all, shouldn't a 50-50 distribution of outcomes suggest gender neutrality?

Both advocates for women's rights and advocates for fathers' rights would probably reject this reading of our findings, and in fact the presence or absence of gender bias in the legal process is not so simple to establish. A fathers' rights group might well argue that since the overall gender ratio in cases where there are conflicting requests is 2 to 1, the law in action still reflects a maternal presumption. Why, after all, would fathers who conceded custody at lower levels of the conflict pyramid have settled for less than they wanted if they believed they had a 50 percent chance? Advocates for women, on the other hand, would counter that our findings demonstrate that escalation of legal conflict over custody clearly operates to the benefit of fathers. As we demonstrated in Chapter 3, before divorce mothers are the primary caretakers of children far more often than men. Thus, a 50-50 distribution of outcomes should be considered neither fair nor neutral. Rather, a "fair" distribution of outcomes should reflect differences in the caretaking base rate for mothers and fathers.

In different ways, both sorts of critics object to the fact that the gender ratio changes as one moves up the pyramid. This change in itself, however, is no proof of gender bias at all: it might simply reflect a selection bias built into the divorce process. Even if one assumes that on average mothers in fact have stronger custody claims than fathers, it is certainly plausible to assume that fathers with relatively stronger claims to custody might well constitute a higher proportion of those who continue to fight and reach the top of the conflict pyramid. If fathers without strong claims are more likely to settle earlier in the process, then one would expect a higher proportion of fathers at the top of the conflict pyramid to "win."

Alternatively, suppose that, on the merits, custody claims of mothers were, on the average, no stronger than the claims of fathers. (Imagine a judge going into her chambers and flipping a coin in all contested cases.) The outcome ratios might still vary by conflict level if most mothers simply cared more about the custodial outcomes than most fathers, and were therefore more prepared to escalate the conflict to a higher level rather than settle for less than their preferred custodial alternative. Because it takes time and energy to work one's way up the conflict pyramid, this would imply that only in a small minority of families would the father be prepared to pay the price, even though those who did so might have a 50 percent chance of prevailing.

Finally, there is a good theoretical argument that in a world of rational actors the distribution of outcomes at the top of the conflict pyramid should approach 50/50,[14] especially in divorce cases.[15] Otherwise, either fathers as a class or mothers as a class would be systematically overestimating their odds of success.

Without some objective measure to indicate how cases would be resolved in a gender-neutral world, it is impossible to determine whether the existing pattern of outcomes reflects gender bias. There is no independent measure of each child's best interests against which to measure the actual outcomes in disputed cases. But one thing does seem reasonably clear: our finding that the gender ratio of custody decrees at the top approaches 50-50 even though the overall ratio among conflicted cases is closer to 2 to 1 in favor of mothers demonstrates neither the presence nor the absence of gender bias.

Trade-offs between Money and Custody in Divorce Bargaining

Because mothers receive the custodial arrangements they prefer about twice as often as fathers, a critical question for cases involving custody conflict is whether mothers who "win" custody after a struggle pay for this victory by accepting less financial support. In divorce bargaining, it is possible that fathers who request custody may be using mothers' overwhelming preference for sole physical custody strategically to lower their support obligations or to garner a larger share of the marital property.

As suggested in Chapter 2, there is certainly a plausible theoretical argument that by threatening to fight over custody, some fathers could persuade some mothers to accept less support. Moreover, in Chapter 5 we presented evidence that suggests that a small number of fathers requested joint custody in their petition or response even though they told our interviewers they preferred sole mother custody as an outcome. This finding at least suggests the possibility of strategic behavior in which a custody claim is being used by a father to gain economic leverage. Finally, parental reports of custody conflict and child support conflict are correlated,[16] and this certainly reinforces the commonsense notion that there must be some linkage between custody and money issues. We therefore examined the relationship between conflict over custody and conflict over money.

The task of evaluating bargaining behavior through statistical analysis is a complicated one. Our approach was to use regression analysis to determine whether, after holding other relevant variables constant, the amount of support awarded to a mother who secures sole physical custody is affected by the degree of legal conflict. In other words, did mothers who experienced higher conflict secure their preferred custodial arrrangement only by accepting less money?[17]

We began by determining what other factors might affect the size of support awards. As noted earlier, child support awards in San Mateo and Santa Clara Counties are heavily influenced by child support schedules. These schedules take into account the income of both parents, the number of children, and the amount of residential time each parent spends with the children.[18] In addition to these factors, we hypothesized that the child support award might be lower in families with joint custody decrees even after controlling for time spent with the children. Regression analysis of child support awards for families with mother custody or joint physical custody suggested that joint physical custody decrees tended to have a significant negative effect on support awards (see Table 7.7).

We further hypothesized that those parents who experienced high levels of conflict over custody might be those most prone to strategic behavior. Because intense negotiation through lawyers may occasion a high degree of conflict that would not be reflected in court record information, we used parents' ratings of conflict over custody (a 10-point scale) rather than our combined conflict measure for this analysis. We predicted that higher levels of conflict would be related to lower child support awards, after holding constant other factors that affect the size of the support award. Because joint custody decrees tended to affect the level of the child support award, we looked at families with mother custody and joint custody decrees separately.

For families with mother physical custody, regression analysis incorporating the statutory factors described above and parental ratings of conflict over custody yielded no statistically significant relation between conflict over custody and the level of support. (See Table 7.8

for the regression results.)[19] We repeated the analysis for total support (that is, the sum of child support and spousal support) and reached the same conclusion. In other words, when we analyzed the support awards for those several hundred mothers who clearly achieved the custodial outcome they preferred (sole mother physical custody where the children in fact resided with the mother), we found no statistically persuasive evidence that those mothers who experienced more legal conflict had to give up support to win the custody they wanted.

We were frankly surprised by these results, given the theoretical argument mentioned earlier, the anecdotal evidence that some fathers do use custody claims as a strategic lever, and the frequently heard claims by feminists that the many women who must negotiate for child custody pay a "price" in terms of support. One theoretical challenge to our finding should be acknowledged at the outset. If an implicit and credible threat to contest custody existed across all cases, and this implicit threat could secure the same economic concessions as an explicit threat, even where there was no measurable conflict, then the regression variable for conflict would not capture the "price" being extracted. In other words, low-conflict mothers may be paying the same price for custody because of this implicit threat. Between businesses, for example, a friendly letter that made no explicit threats might nonetheless extract a concession. In the context of divorce negotiations, given the economic needs of custodial mothers and an explicit support schedule, we find it implausible that mothers who report no conflict would nevertheless make economic concessions because of an

Table 7.7 Regression predicting child-support awards

	Parameter estimate	*t*-statistic	Standardized beta
Intercept	296.45		
Father's earnings[a]	0.03	11.06****	0.42
Mother's earnings	−0.02	−2.39*	−0.09
Number of children[b]	160.97	10.35****	0.40
Overnights with father[c]	−12.51	−3.05**	−0.14
Joint decree	−51.03	−1.85†	−0.08

†$p \leq .10$; *$p \leq .05$; **$p \leq .01$; ****$p \leq .0001$.
a. Father's earnings minus $2,000.
b. Number of additional children past the first.
c. Overnights in a two-week period.

Table 7.8   Regression predicting child-support awards: mother decree families

	Parameter estimate	*t*-statistic	Standardized beta
Intercept	303.00		
Father's earnings[a]	0.03	10.10****	0.44
Mother's earnings	−0.02	−2.01*	−0.09
Number of children[b]	163.05	9.46****	0.42
Overnights with father[c]	−3.86	−0.69	−0.03
Conflict over custody	−6.45	−1.42	−0.06

*p ≤ .05; ****p ≤ .0001.

a. Father's earnings minus $2,000.

b. Number of additional children past the first.

c. Overnights in a two-week period.

implicit threat. Moreover, if fathers are making implicit threats, it is plausible that mothers would provide a higher conflict rating.

We think there are a number of more likely explanations. For one thing, California child support schedules and community property rules—both of which introduce more certainty into the outcome if a case is contested—may make it easier for mothers to resist strategic claims by fathers. A second possible explanation is that the strategic use of custody claims may actually be quite infrequent. Most fathers may well consider such a tactic unfair and reprehensible, which in our view it plainly is. Moreover, a threat must be credible to get results. It may be very difficult for a father who does not really want custody to threaten effectively. Because each parent typically knows how involved the other was in child-rearing before the divorce, it may be very difficult for a father to exaggerate his experience, competence, or willingness to carry substantial custodial burdens.

Some fathers who might be tempted to bluff about wanting custody may not do so because they believe that the mother will in fact resist and that mothers almost always win contested cases unless they are shown to be incompetent or unfit, despite the surface gender neutrality of the law on the books. It may well be the common perception of both fathers and mothers that when push comes to shove, mothers nearly always win custody—that a strong maternal preference still operates. And indeed it may. Although our own evidence suggests the ratio is 50-50 for the most highly conflicted cases, the overall ratio for cases with conflicting requests is 2 to 1. In any event, it is the perception of the odds, not the reality, that should influence behavior.

There is another group of mothers, smaller in number, who were not unequivocal "winners" of custody. These are mothers whose children reside with them for ten or more overnights in a typical two-week period, but whose divorce decrees provide for joint physical custody. For these mothers, a higher degree of legal conflict does appear to be associated with *lower* child support awards. Our regression model indicates that within the group of mothers with joint physical custody decrees, conflict over custody was a significant negative predictor of child support levels (see Table 7.9). The regression equation suggests that for every 1-point increase on our 10-point custody conflict measure, these joint physical custody mothers lost on average $16 per month in child support.[20]

In interpreting these results, it should be emphasized that out of some 900 families in our sample, there were only 29 high-conflict mothers who ended up with joint physical custody decrees and mother residence. Although nearly half of the high-conflict joint physical custody families ended up with such a result, such cases (high-conflict/joint-custody/mother-residence cases) represent less than 3 percent of our total sample. It is by no means clear how one should interpret this finding. We cannot know whether the fathers in these families were behaving strategically or not. On the one hand, if these fathers genuinely wanted a residential arrangement in which the children in fact lived with them a substantial part of the time, they too lost. It may be

Table 7.9 Regression predicting child-support awards: joint decree families

	Parameter estimate	*t*-statistic	Standardized beta
Intercept	366.47		
Father's earnings[a]	0.05	4.40****	0.37
Mother's earnings	−0.03	−1.76†	−0.14
Number of children[b]	138.64	3.86***	0.32
Overnights with father[c]	−22.50	−3.57***	−0.29
Conflict over custody	−16.49	−2.02*	−0.16

†$p \leq .10$; *$p \leq .05$; ***$p \leq .001$; ****$p \leq .0001$.
a. Father's earnings minus $2,000.
b. Number of additional children past the first.
c. Overnights in a two-week period.

that both parents preferred this compromise to further litigation. On the other hand, some of these fathers may have preferred all along that the children reside with the mother.

Summary Comment

Our data suggest that the common perception that conflict is the norm for divorcing parents is largely unfounded. Three-quarters of the families we studied experienced little if any conflict over the terms of the divorce decree. Moreover, almost all of the high-conflict cases were settled through negotiation, some of which included court-annexed mediation or a court-ordered evaluation. Only a trivial number of cases (about 1.5 percent of our sample) required a formal adjudication. Although no comparative data exist from an earlier period, our findings certainly suggest that the procedural innovations adopted in California to reduce reliance on adversary proceedings and promote resolution through negotiation have proved successful in reducing the number of adjudicated custody cases. Moreover, this study confirms the important role that mandatory court-annexed mediation now plays in the custody dispute settlement process in California.

For the minority of families, about 25 percent, that do experience substantial legal conflict, we were unable to isolate any demographic variables that differentiate them from lower-conflict families. Their psychological profile indicates that in these families, the parents—the fathers in particular—harbor especially high levels of hostility toward the former spouse. Moreover, fathers in these families believe they were more involved in the lives of the children before the separation than the mothers do. A further manifestation of parental discord is that in high-conflict families, each parent is more likely to express misgivings about the quality of care the child receives in the other household. In many cases, trained mediators or attorneys could probably identify families with these characteristics at the start of the divorce process.

Our most disturbing finding is the frequency with which joint physical custody decrees are being used by high-conflict families to resolve disputes. Of the 166 cases in which the decree provides for joint custody, 36 percent involved substantial or intense legal conflict. For about half of the high-conflict joint physical custody cases (29 cases), the children in fact resided with the mother, and these cases certainly demonstrate that the label of joint physical custody often does not reflect the social reality. They also may suggest the difficulty of sustaining dual residence unless both parties want to make the arrangement work.

We found that, contrary to popular perception, most divorce decrees do not reflect a trade-off between custody and money issues. We believe that child support schedules and community property rules substantially constrain such trade-offs. Moreover, for the reasons discussed above, it may be very difficult for fathers to engage in strategic behavior that appears credible to their spouses. Things are much more complicated, however, for those high-conflict families who end up compromising with a joint physical custody decree while maintaining de facto mother residence. For these families, the father is paying support as if he had substantial day-to-day responsibility for the care and upkeep of the children, yet acquiescing in an arrangement that allows him little actual contact with the children. The mother, on the other hand, takes on a degree of responsibility for the children commonly associated with sole physical custody, yet accepts a slightly smaller level of support—one more appropriate for shared parental responsibility under a dual residence arrangement. In short, for these families, the outcome may well be a compromise in which neither parent got what he or she wanted. On the other hand, for fathers who never really wanted to have the children reside with them a substantial portion of the time, this outcome may represent the success of hard-nosed, strategic bargaining.

Our analysis of families with joint physical custody decrees thus adds an additional wrinkle to the gender issue. Although the proportion of cases that result in mother physical custody decreases as the level of custody conflict increases, almost half of the high-conflict cases that result in joint physical custody end up with the children residing with the mother. Consequently, fathers'-rights advocates might allege that these mothers have "won." On the other hand, advocates for women's rights would suggest that since these women receive less support than they would have received had the decree reflected the reality of the residential arrangement, both they and the children "lose."

In considering the effect of legal conflict on custody outcomes, it is important to remember that framing the issue in terms of "winning" and "losing" fails to capture the complex nature of the negotiations surrounding resolution of the custody dispute. Parents who "win" custody also "win" the responsibilities and difficulties that attend raising the child, and a parent who has sole custody may face these responsibilities largely unaided. In addition, the financial burden of child-rearing is considerable, particularly for women who have never been employed outside the home. Moreover, even if one parent gets the custody arrangement that he or she initially requested, the other parent may not necessarily have "lost." It is possible that parents who initially disagreed over custody have come to believe that the custodial arrangement requested by one parent was best for the child. If they are correct, the resolution of their conflict has produced a "win/win" situation.

Nevertheless, our results clearly demonstrate that the process by which the legal conflict is resolved may have a significant effect on the pattern of outcomes. Moreover, substantial conflict may translate into a "loss" either for the parents or, more important, for the children involved. Accordingly, it is important to determine whether the effects of legal conflict on custodial arrangements persist or change over time.

From a policy perspective, we are particularly concerned about joint custody children who do reside in both households and are therefore shuttled back and forth between parents who have had high legal conflict. We found some 25 joint physical custody cases in which the children were, in fact, spending at least a third of their school-year residential time with each of two parents who had had substantial legal conflict. What becomes of these children? Is the arrangement stable? Does the fighting stop, or do the children feel caught in the middle of a continuing parental warfare? And for families in which the children live primarily with one parent and visit the other, does legal conflict lead to change in the residence and visitation patterns in the years following the divorce? In particular, for high-conflict families where the children reside with the mother, does the amount of contact between the children and their father decrease over time? What effect do custody outcomes and initial conflict levels have on parental cooperation in post-divorce child-rearing? Can those joint physical custody families who experienced high conflict nevertheless create and sustain cooperative co-parenting relationships? Do custody outcomes and initial conflict levels affect the parenting skills of divorced spouses, and do mothers and fathers experience the same difficulties? The remaining chapters explore these and related issues.

8

Continuity and Change in Children's Residence and Visitation

Existing studies of divorce have usually not considered the distinction between the physical custody arrangement specified in the divorce decree and the children's actual residence. The large-scale studies of compliance with child support awards (for example, Chambers, 1979) have seldom asked whether the children's actual residence corresponded with the custody decree on which the support award had been based (Peters, Argys, Maccoby, and Mnookin, 1992). Studies concerned with family process or children's adjustment have usually classified families according to the children's current residence, without regard to how long the children had been living in this arrangement or how it compared to the divorce decree (for example, Camera and Resnick, 1988). Indeed, little is known concerning how commonly children move from one parental household to the other after the parents have separated. As far as visitation is concerned, there has been considerable interest in the "dropout" of non-residential parents, but the frequency with which visitation *increases* has seldom been documented, and we know little concerning the circumstances that affect whether visitation increases, decreases, or remains the same.

Our study fills some of these information gaps. In Chapters 5 and 7 we noted that the realities of where the children lived and how much they visited with the non-custodial parent did not always correspond with the provisions of the formal divorce agreement. Our first objective in this chapter is to see how well the provisions of divorce decrees match the realities of family life as time passes and families adapt to changed circumstances.

After examining the relation between the legally decreed physical custody and the children's actual residence, we turn to our study of stability and change. For this purpose, we use a subsample of our cases: those families for whom we have data at all three interviewing times ($N = 880$, henceforth called "panel" families). We first chart the frequency of change in the children's residence. Then, for the children living primarily with one parent (excluding the dual-residence cases), we describe the patterns of visitation and how they changed, asking in particular whether or not visitation with outside fathers was affected by an award of joint legal custody. We then examine the reasons why change did or did not occur in the amount of contact children had with each of the parents, considering residence and visitation jointly. We examine stability and change in relation to (1) children's sex and age; (2) residential moves; (3) parental remarriage or repartnering; (4) economic resources of both parents; and (5) the relationship between the parents.

In assessing how the child's time is divided between the parents, we recognize that a good deal of children's time may be spent in settings where neither parent is present (such as day care or school). Even in these situations however, one parent usually has primary responsibility for the child's whereabouts and welfare. Except for children who live with someone other than a parent, we assume that a child's de facto physical custody is divided between the parents in such a way that if time with one parent increases, time with the other decreases. Although we measure a child's time with each parent mainly in terms of where the child sleeps, the underlying concept we mean to deal with is the proportion of time during which each parent is *responsible* for the child.

We have seen that mothers usually have the predominant role in the care of children at the time of the initial separation. As the date of the separation recedes into the past, many questions surface: what happens to the roles of the two parents as time goes on? Is there a trend toward fathers taking on more, or less, responsibility as the two separate households become more fully established? We have already seen that at Time 1, a substantial majority of the children in our families were maintaining contact with both parents. To what extent is this high level of contact with both parents sustained? What circumstances enable parents to maintain contact, and what circumstances break it off? Does a decree that provides for joint legal custody make any difference in whether the non-residential parent maintains contact with the children?

During the three and a half post-separation years covered by our study, many types of changes occurred in the situation of the two parents that had the potential to affect the children's residence and visitation. Some parents remarried, or were joined by a new live-in partner to whom they were not (yet) married. Some of the parents changed jobs and/or moved (sometimes quite far away from the original locale). The relationship between the two parents sometimes changed, as the passage of time allowed angry passions to cool and lives to become stably reorganized. In addition, the children grew older. We saw in Chapter 4 that initial residence was related to the children's age: children in middle childhood were more likely to have dual residence than children in other age groups; and children of ages 11 and older were less likely to have dual residence and somewhat more likely to live with their fathers. In this chapter we will investigate whether the developmental changes occurring over a three-year period triggered changes in the residence and visitation arrangements that our sample families adopted.

In Chapter 1 we noted that the evidence supporting beneficial effects of contact with non-resident fathers was thin and inconsistent. The effects appeared to depend, at least in part, on how well the two parents were able to cooperate. It is possible that the changes parents made in the arrangements for the children were determined partly by the parents' ability to cooperate. If a child's contact with the non-residential parent falls primarily among those families in which parents cannot cooperate, and is maintained primarily in those families where they can, then we will have identified a self-corrective process operating for the benefit of children. On the other hand, it is possible that a substantial number of families maintained the children's contact with both parents despite continuing high levels of conflict between them. We therefore examine how the changes in children's residence and visitation relate to the parents' ability to cooperate.

Relationship of the Physical Custody Decree to Actual Residence

We saw earlier that in cases where parents had conflicting requests, physical custody was more likely to be awarded to the parent with whom the children were living at the time of the initial separation—in other words, "possession" was "nine tenths of the law." However, there were some cases where the legal agreement concerning physical custody differed from the initial residential arrangements. It is reasonable to expect that the negotiations couples go through in the process of reaching their legal agreement would make some difference in where the children live and how much visitation occurs. We therefore first

examine the correspondence between children's actual residence before and after the divorce, and the terms of the physical custody decree. We then ask: when the legal decree did not correspond with the
initial residence, did the children's actual residence shift to the residence called for in the legal agreement?

In exploring these questions, we focused on 783 families who had a
legal divorce decree by Time 3, and for whom we had residence data
at both Times 1 and 3. Some families had reached a firm agreement
concerning physical custody at Time 1, before the divorce became
final. The majority finalized the divorce during the following year (before the Time 2 interview), but some were still in the process of settlement until shortly before the Time 3 interview. Table 8.1 shows how
the children's de facto residence at Times 1 and 3 compared to the
physical custody agreement embodied in the divorce decree. There
was no greater correspondence after the divorce was finalized than
there was before. In fact, the proportion of families with joint physical
custody awards that actually had what we have defined as dual residence dropped, from 52 percent to 45 percent. The correspondence
was greatest for the families in which physical custody had been
awarded to the mothers; in a large majority of such families, the children were living with their mothers at both Times 1 and 3. For the
much smaller group awarded father physical custody, correspondence
was high at Time 1 (82 percent) and somewhat lower at Time 3 (71
percent).

The relatively low level of correspondence for families awarded joint
physical custody reflects, at least in part, some informal agreements
between parents that they would specify joint physical custody in their
legal settlement, but that the children would actually live with the
mother, at least for the first few years. Such informal agreements were
usually meant to keep residential options open for the future while
maintaining mother residence as the preferred short-term arrangement.
In some cases, however, as we saw in Chapter 7, a joint physical
custody decree emerged from extended conflict over custody, in which
fathers secured a joint decree but did not assume the level of de facto
contact required for our dual-residence classification.

It is tempting to conclude from Table 8.1 that the legal decree made
no difference in the children's de facto residence, and that changes
in residence were based on other aspects of the families' changing
circumstances. We will demonstrate that other circumstances did indeed play the major role. There is reason to believe, however, that the
negotiations over the legal decree did affect the children's residence

Table 8.1   Correspondence of actual residence at Time 1 and Time 3 with physical custody decrees

	Legal settlement: physical custody			
	Mother ($N = 519$)	Father ($N = 68$)	Joint ($N = 167$)	Split ($N = 29$)
Children's de facto residence, Time 1				
With Mother	87%	6%	33%	31%
With Father	1	82	7	17
Dual	7	7	52	3
Split	1	1	2	35
Parents living together	4	2	5	14
Other	—	2	1	—
	100%	100%	100%	100%
Children's de facto residence, Time 3				
With Mother	85%	9%	38%	34%
With Father	4	71	12	14
Dual	8	15	45	14
Split	2	1	3	34
Parents living ɔgether	—	1	1	4
Other	1	3	1	—
	100%	100%	100%	100%

Note: Based on all cases with a final judgment and residence data at both T-1 and T-3 ($N = 783$). Numbers are percentage of families in each custodial group having each de facto residence.

for some families. Consider the following facts that emerged from our data:

· When the legal decree confirmed the residential arrangement already in place at Time 1 ($N = 579$ families), that arrangement was much more stable (that is, 84 percent were still in place at Time 3) than when the decree and Time 1 residence did not match (only 45 percent still in place).

· When the initial residence and the physical custody decree did not match ($N = 111$ families), some (35 percent) made a residential shift that brought them into conformity with the decree. A much smaller proportion (16 percent) moved out of an initial arrangement even though the divorce decree had validated it.

· In one group of families ($N = 41$), physical custody was awarded to the mother although the children were not initially living with her. Two-thirds of these families had moved into conformity with the decree by Time 3—that is, the children were then living with their mothers. By contrast, among the 70 families awarded joint or father physical custody when the children were initially not living in these arrangements (most were living with mothers initially), only 15 percent moved into conformity.

It would appear that the legal decree can function to confirm residence with the mother if it exists initially, and to bring it about if it does not exist initially. The decree is much less powerful in moving children out of maternal residence once such an arrangement is established.

Stability and Change in Children's Residence

When we simply tabulate the proportion of families having each kind of residential arrangement at each of the three time periods, we see astonishingly little change (see Figure 8.1). At each time, two-thirds of the children were living with their mothers, and about one-sixth were in dual residence. Over time, we charted a slight increase in the proportion living with fathers,[1] and also a slight increase in the number of split-residence families, with 3.4 percent having one or more children living with one parent while one or more children lived with the other at Time 3.

Do the stable proportions shown in Figure 8.1 mean that few if any individual families changed residential arrangements between Time 1 and Time 3? By no means. Instead, there were many compensating shifts, with some families moving into a residential arrangement while an equivalent number of other families moved out. As shown in Figure 8.2, mother residence was the most stable arrangement. However, since the *number* of families with mother residence at Time 1 was so much greater than that for the other arrangements, the absolute number moving in and out of maternal residence was approximately equivalent to the number moving in and out of other, less stable, arrangements. Father residence was fairly stable (with 70 percent of the families who initially adopted this pattern remaining there at Time 3), and dual residence less so (54 percent the same at Time 3 as at Time 1). Less than a third of the very small group of families who initially had a split-residence arrangement for their children continued in this pattern. The proportion of families with dual residence did not decline

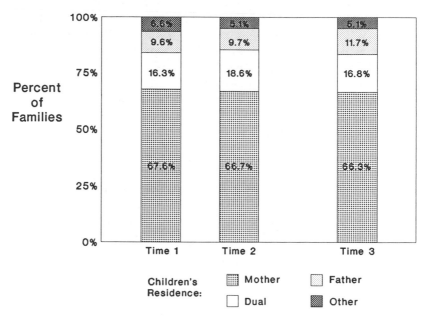

Figure 8.1 Children's residence at T-1, T-2, and T-3 (based on the 880 families providing data at all three time periods; families in a given residential arrangement at T-1 were not always the same families as those in this arrangement at later times).

over time—indeed, it increased slightly—so that the families who abandoned this pattern during the three-year period of the study were replaced by a slightly greater number who adopted it after beginning in either a mother-residence or a father-residence arrangement.

When families that initially adopted mother residence at Time 1 did not maintain this arrangement, the majority of these changers shifted to dual residence by Time 3, with smaller subgroups going to father or split residence. For families starting out with dual residence who did not maintain this arrangement, most shifted to mother residence—it was more than twice as likely that children shifting out of dual residence would go to mothers as opposed to fathers. Among the smaller group of families initially adopting father residence, those who shifted were almost equally likely to shift to dual as to maternal residence.

We analyzed stability in another way, taking children rather than families as the unit of analysis: we asked how many children in each residential arrangement at Time 3 had been in that arrangement *throughout* the three-year period between Time 1 and Time 3. Some children who started in one residence, switched to another, and then returned to their initial residence at Time 3; we have included them in the "residence unstable" group in Figure 8.3. We found that only 19 percent of the children living with their mothers at Time 3 changed residence at any time since Time 1. For the children in either dual or father residence at Time 3, however, the situation was quite different: in both these groups *half* (51 percent) made at least one change.

In sum, the apparent stability in residential arrangements over the three-year period masked a good deal of internal shifting by families that moved from one kind of arrangement to another in compensating numbers. This further supports our view that parental gender matters.

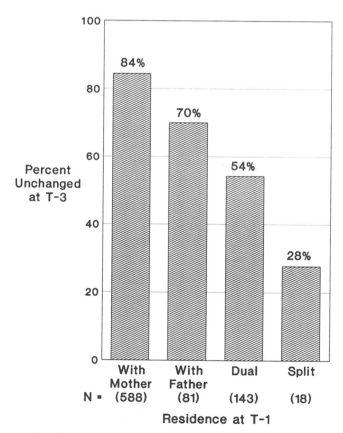

Figure 8.2 Stability of residence (percentage of families where the children retained the same residence at T-3 as T-1; based on 880 families providing data at all three time periods).

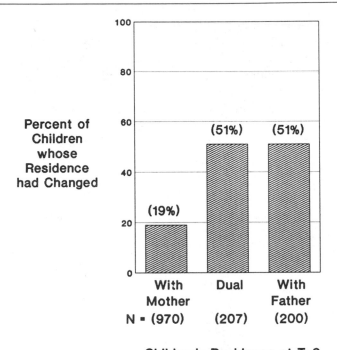

Percent of Children whose Residence had Changed

Children's Residence at T-3

Figure 8.3   Percentage of children in each T-3 residential group whose residence had changed at least once between T-1 and T-3.

The most stable arrangement was mother residence, and more than 80 percent of the children living with their mothers at Time 3 had lived there since Time 1. In contrast, among children living with their fathers or in dual residence at Time 3, only half had lived there all along. This last fact has some important implications: in any efforts to understand the impact of different residential arrangements on children's adjustment, it is imperative to determine how long children have been living in their current residence, and to distinguish the effects of residential instability from the question of whether it makes a difference which parent children live with.

Visitation with Non-residential Parents

We saw in Chapter 4 that at Time 1, most of the children who were living primarily with one parent visited the non-residential parent, although there was great variation in the kind and amount of visitation.

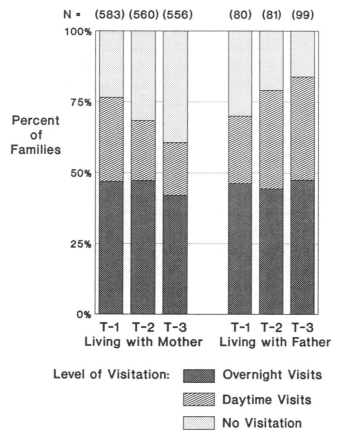

Figure 8.4 Visitation with "outside" parent for families in which children lived with one parent (based on families providing data at all three time periods).

We focus here on visitation during typical two-week periods of the school year, not including visits during Christmas, spring, or summer vacations. How did the frequency of such visitation during typical two-week periods change with time?

Figure 8.4 shows the level of visitation in families in which the children were living primarily with either the mother or the father, at each of the three time periods of the study. Families with dual, split, or "other" residence are excluded, and families are classified according to the children's residence at the time the visitation pattern was being reported.[2] In the majority of families where the children lived primarily with one parent at T-2 and T-3, visitation with the non-residential parent was maintained, and the visits most commonly involved overnight stays. The most common pattern was for these visits to occur on alternate weekends. Sometimes the children spent Friday and Saturday nights and were returned on Sunday; sometimes they spent three weekend nights, or Saturday and Sunday nights, in which case the non-residential parent usually took them to preschool or school on Monday morning. The majority of families had set up a regular pattern for visitation, but a substantial group (about 20 percent of those having some visitation) said that they did not have a definite schedule. Some of these parents said explicitly that they had an agreement permitting the non-residential parent to see the children whenever he or she wanted to or found it possible within the demands of a variable work schedule. For example, one non-residential father was an airline pilot whose work schedule took him out of town on different days from week to week, and visitation was adjusted accordingly.

In families with a primary and an "outside" parent, actual visitation varied considerably. Some children never saw the "outside" parent, or only on rare occasions when that parent happened to be in town and got in touch. Other children saw their non-residential parent only during vacations. Still others saw their outside parent fairly often, but only for daytime visits. For example, when the child lived with the mother, the father might drive by and take the child to school every morning, or pick the child up from school or day care. Some non-residential parents took their children out to dinner once or twice a week, and perhaps spent a few hours helping with homework, but brought the child home by bedtime. Some spent a half-day or a whole day with their children during the weekend.

The proportion of mother-residence families in which the children had overnight visits with their fathers remained quite constant over time. However, there was a drop in daytime visitation and an increase in the proportion of families in which the children had no visits. By the end of our study, the proportion of mother-residence children who were no longer visiting their fathers during regular portions of the school year reached 39 percent. For the father-residence families, the time changes in visitation with the mother were quite different; there was a shift from no visits to daytime visits. Between Time 1 and Time 3, the proportion having daytime visits to the mother rose from 16 percent to 36 percent, while the proportion having no visits dropped from 39 percent to 18 percent.[3] We saw earlier that among father-residence families at Time 3, a much higher proportion (compared to mother-residence families) had not been in this arrangement over the three-year span since Time 1. Was the difference in visitation between mother-residence and father-residence families due to this difference in residential stability? That is, did some children maintain high levels of visitation with the mother because they had recently been living with her? We do not find this to be the significant factor: when we looked only at those families in which the children had been in the same T-3 residence over the three years, the same picture emerged as that shown in Figure 8.4.[4]

Stability of visitation arrangements. Among both mother-residence and father-residence families, the proportion of families in which the children had overnight visits with the non-resident parent remained fairly constant over the three years of the study. However, this does not imply that once individual families adopted overnight visitation, all continued to have them. As in the case of residence, compensating changes occurred. Figure 8.5 shows the stability of each visitation pattern. Although the proportion of mother-residence families in which the children had no usual school-year visitation with their fathers increased from Time 1 to Time 3, almost a quarter of the families that initially had no visitation established some by Time 3. Thus, within the overall picture of declining visitation with fathers, there were countervailing subgroups, and for a substantial minority of mother-residence families, visitation with fathers *increased* over time. Daytime visitation was by far the least stable arrangement, giving way over time to either no visitation (most commonly) or to overnight visitation.

We have not charted stability for the small group of families who retained father residence over the three years ($N = 52$ families), since the subgroups for different visitation arrangements were very small. However, the relevant figures are as follows: for the 22 families in which the children initially had overnight visits with their mothers, 13 continued to have them at Time 3; for the 13 families initially having only daytime visits, 6 were still in this category at Time 3; for the 17 families initially having no mother visitation, only 5 still had none, while in 12 of these families the children were visiting their mothers, most often for daytime visits.

Figure 8.5 shows that daytime visitation is notably unstable in mother-residence families. Among families initially adopting this arrangement, 40 percent no longer had school-year visitation arrangements of any kind at Time 3, and only 5 percent shifted into dual or father residence. This contrasts with the group of mother-residence families who were maintaining overnight visitation with fathers at Time

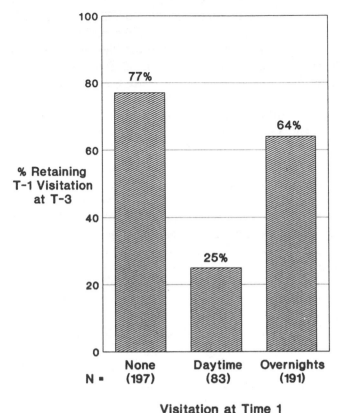

Figure 8.5 Stability of visitation with father for mother-resident families (based on 471 families in which the children resided with their mothers at all three time periods).

1: in only 16 percent of these families were the children no longer visiting their fathers at Time 3; about two-thirds were still making overnight visits; and 19 percent had shifted to dual or father residence.

An interesting sidelight on visitation concerns the number of trips that children made back and forth between households. For children who spent overnights with their non-residential parent at all three time periods, the *number* of overnights in a typical two-week period did not drop over the three years of our study. However, the number of trips between households dropped significantly, from a mean of 2.2 round trips in two weeks at Time 1 to a mean of 1.5 at Time 3. Even among the children in dual residence, the number of round trips made between households declined. Families appeared to find ways, as time passed, to cut down on the amount of driving between households without sacrificing visitation time.

Daytime visitation was much more likely to be irregular than overnight visits, which were almost always prearranged according to a regular schedule agreed upon by the two parents. Irregular visitation was strongly associated with instability in visitation arrangements. It appears that daytime visitation is a fragile arrangement. For many families, it signals the early stage of loss of contact with outside fathers, although there are some families who began with irregular daytime visitation and shifted to more stable overnight arrangements as the two parents established stable residences.

When did the children last see their non-resident parent? At Time 3, parents were asked when each child had last seen the outside parent. Among the children we have put in the "no visitation" category, there were quite a few who saw the outside parent during vacations and holidays. Parents reported at Time 3 that nearly two-thirds of the children had seen the outside parent within the previous month (see Table 8.2). Only 13 percent of the children living with their mothers had not seen their fathers within the past year, and among children living with their fathers, only 7 percent had not seen their mothers during that time. Thus we can see that the likelihood of a child maintaining some contact with the non-resident parent at Time 3 was very high.

The impact of joint legal custody. We saw in Chapter 5 that joint legal custody (as distinct from joint *physical* custody) has become enormously popular in California. It was embodied in the decrees of a substantial majority of the families in our study. By explicitly allowing for joint physical custody even when physical custody was not joint, the framers of the California statute no doubt hoped to encourage non-resident parents to stay involved in the lives of their children. Specifically, the hope was that awards of joint legal custody would enhance the amount of contact children had with their outside parents, allow such parents to be involved in major decisions concerning the children, and increase the willingness of such parents to continue contributing financial support to the children. When children are living with the mother, is a father more likely to visit if he has joint legal custody?[5]

This question is not an easy one to answer. We cannot simply select the mother-residence families and compare those having joint legal custody with those having mother legal custody, because the two groups differ so greatly on other dimensions (see Albiston, Maccoby, and Mnookin, 1990, for details). Mother-residence families with joint legal

Table 8.2 When children last saw outside parent (T-3; percentage of children)

	Live with mother, last saw father: ($N = 1,016$)	Live with father, last saw mother: ($N = 214$)
Within the last month	63.9%	66.8%
1–2.9 months ago	10.4	12.2
3–5.9 months ago	6.9	7.4
6–11.9 months ago	6.0	7.0
12–23.9 months ago	6.5	3.3
Two years or more	6.3	3.3
	100.0%	100.0%

custody decrees, by comparison with mother-residence families who had mother legal custody, were characterized by the following:

· Fathers with higher incomes and better education.

· A higher proportion of employed fathers.

· Fathers who were more hostile toward the mothers at Time 1.

· Mothers who were *less* hostile toward the fathers at Time 1.

· Fathers who were having more overnight visitation at Time 1.

As we saw in Chapter 4, several of these factors were associated with high rates of visitation at Time 1, before the legal custody decree had been issued, and might be more than sufficient to produce a higher rate of visitation at Time 3 among the joint legal custody fathers, regardless of the effect of the award itself. Table 8.3 shows how one factor, father's income, is implicated in the amount of T-3 visitation: higher-income fathers were much more likely than other fathers to have visits with their children at Time 3. The table suggests a tendency for fathers at each income level to visit more if they have joint legal custody. However, this effect is not statistically significant[6] and, in fact, disappears if all the other factors listed above are controlled. (See Albiston, Maccoby, and Mnookin, 1990, for a fuller report.) Our conclusion is that when fathers of mother-residence children are awarded joint legal custody, this has no effect on sustaining their contact with the children, once the factors associated with being awarded joint legal custody in the first place are taken into account.

Table 8.3 Relation of joint legal custody to children's contact with non-resident fathers at T-3, by father's T-3 income (mother-resident families only)

Father's income at Time 3	Percentage of families in which children have visitation with fathers	
	Mother physical custody, mother legal custody (*N* = 121)	Mother physical custody, joint legal custody (*N* = 328)
Under $15,000	17%	30%
$15,000 to $30,000	48%	54%
$30,000 to $70,000	54%	59%

Note: This table is based on 449 families who had completed their legal divorces by the end of our study, and in which the children were living with their mothers at Time 3. Included as having visitation are those families in which children either have overnights with the father, or at least 8 hours of daytime visitation during usual two-week periods of the school year.

Conditions Affecting Change in Residence and Visitation
Gender of the Child

In Chapter 4 we reported that although a large majority of boys and girls lived with their mothers initially, boys were somewhat more likely to live with their fathers or in dual residence than were girls, who more often lived with their mothers. This situation did not change with time. The proportion of the two sexes in the various residential arrangements remained constant (see Table 8.A1 in Appendix A). Although there continued to be some bias toward children living with the same-sex parent, the amount of this bias did not change over the three years of our study. While we had expected that more boys than girls might shift into father residence, particularly among preteens growing into adolescence, this did not prove to be to the case. Although a child's entry into puberty may sometimes be a trigger for a residential move, the move is not more likely to be to the same-sex parent's household. There were some instances in our sample in which a girl of 12 or 13 would move to the father's household when a mother's new partner moved in with the mother, presumably because the presence of the new partner represented an unknown and possibly threatening factor for the daughter. Cases of this kind balanced the small group of boys who moved from mother to father residence for other reasons. Also, teenagers of either sex sometimes moved away from a residential parent's household when parent-child conflict was high, regardless of whether they were living with a same-sex or opposite-sex parent.

The likelihood of visitation with the outside parent did not depend on the child's sex. For children living with their mothers, boys and girls did not differ in their pattern of visitation with the father at Times 1 and 2 (see Table 8.A2 in Appendix A). At Time 3, boys were slightly more likely to be spending overnights with their fathers, but the basic picture is one of gender neutrality. Among children living with their fathers, boys and girls had almost identical patterns of visitation at Time 1, but at Times 2 and 3, girls were somewhat more likely to be spending overnights with their mothers, boys to have only daytime visits or none at all.[7]

Effect of Children's Developmental Changes

We saw in Chapter 4 that children's age had some bearing on where they would live. The probability was high, and equally high in all age groups, that children would live with their mothers. However, the probabilities of father residence were higher for older children, and the probabilities of dual residence were higher for children between the ages of 3 and 8 than they were for the preteen and teenage children. Thus, in deciding on the initial residential arrangements, parents evidently took the developmental level of the children into account when other circumstances permitted. Some parents told us they did not find dual-residence arrangements workable for infants and toddlers, for whom they felt a single familiar place to sleep was especially important. Others said that teenagers had a greater voice than younger children in decisions about where they were to live and how much they would visit, and that children of this age tended to avoid arrangements in which they would have to sleep in two different houses. This preference is further reflected in the fact that older children who visited their fathers were more likely than younger ones to make daytime visits only, rather than overnights.

At Time 3, the children in our sample families were three years older than they had been at Time 1. Children who had been infants or toddlers were now preschoolers or kindergartners; children who had been in the early grade-school years were now preteens. Our question was: did the residence and visitation arrangements initially adopted carry over despite the developmental changes implied in three years of growth, or did families adapt their arrangements to make them more appropriate for their children's changed developmental level?

To answer this question, we studied the 1,386 children for whom we had residential data at all three time periods, and who were under 15 years of age at Time 1 (see Table 8.A4 in Appendix A). We found that by and large, children did *not* move out of dual residence as they reached the age when at least some might have been expected to do so. Thus at Time 1, 16 percent of children aged 6–8 were in dual residence, as compared with only 11 percent of children aged 9–11 and 9 percent of those aged 12–14. Three years later, when the children who had been aged 6–8 at Time 1 were now aged 9–11, 17 percent of them were in dual residence—a higher proportion than might have been predicted by the Time 1 age curve.

A similar situation prevailed with respect to visitation. We studied the 772 children who were living with their mothers at all three time periods (and who were under age 15 at Time 1) to see whether the frequency of overnight visitation with fathers changed as the children grew older (see Table 8.A5 in Appendix A). On the basis of the situation at Time 1, we expected overnight visitation to increase for children who were under age 3 at Time 1—that is, at Time 3 they might be considered old enough for overnights. At the other end of the age curve, we expected that children who had moved from the preteen years to the teen years would be less likely to have overnights as they grew old enough to prefer a single sleeping place. However, our expectations were not borne out. As Figure 8.6 shows, the youngest children did *not* increase their overnights as they grew into the pre-school years; the children who had been 9 to 11 years old at Time 1 did *not* show a declining rate of overnight visits as they moved into the 12–14 age bracket; and the children aged 6–8 at Time 1 continued throughout the study to be the group least likely to lose contact with their fathers and most likely to maintain overnights.

These findings do not mean that patterns of residence and visitation, once established, become fixed. Many families change their arrangements as time goes on. However, our findings on age trends do indicate the following: parents appear to establish their initial arrangements for residence and visitation with certain assumptions about what will be workable for children of different ages. However, as children grow older, families do not systematically adopt the residence and visitation pattern found to be characteristic (at Time 1) of the next-older age cohort. Thus, the developmental changes that are taking place in the children do not appear to trigger reassessment of the arrangements that were initially established. Other factors bring about changes, but the parental assessments of whether their arrangements need to be changed seem not to depend on such age-related factors as whether children are entering preschool or grade school, entering puberty, or becoming cognitively more mature.

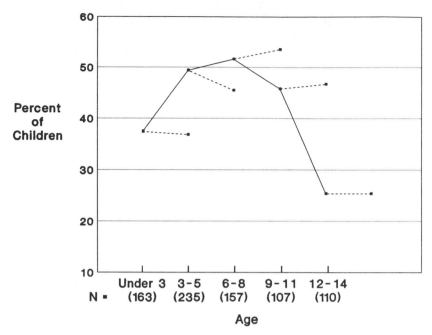

Figure 8.6 Proportion of children in mother residence at all three time periods who spent overnights with father, by age (*N* = 772). Solid line shows T-1 incidence of overnights by age group; dotted lines show each group three years later (T-3).

There is one exception to this generalization. The likelihood that children would live with their fathers did increase with age, and as each age group became three years older, the rate of father residence moved up to a level appropriate for the new age cohort a child had entered (see Figure 8.7). We suspect these changes reflect the fact that children require less child-care time and involvement as they grow older, and that fathers feel more comfortable about caring for them (or that mothers grow more comfortable about allowing them to be in the father's care) as they grow old enough that they no longer require moment-to-moment supervision, and are either in school or able to be left on their own for longer spans of time.

An Index of Change

So far, we have found that a child's sex had very little to do with changes over time in the amount of time a child would spend with each parent. Moreover, a three-year increase in the children's ages did not appear to trigger changes in visitation patterns, nor did it affect

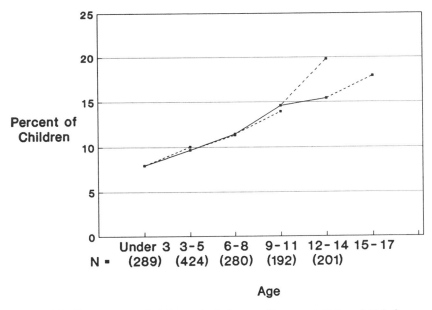

Figure 8.7   Percentage of children in father residence, at T-1 and T-3, by age (children with data at all three time periods). Solid line shows T-1 incidence of father residence by age group; dotted lines show each group three years later (T-3).

whether the child would be in dual residence, although the chances that children would be living with their fathers did increase slightly. Surprisingly, the negotiations over the legal and physical custody to be specified in the divorce decree did not seem to bring about significant changes in where the children would live or how much they would visit the non-residential parent. Yet we saw at the beginning of this chapter that there were indeed changes, over the three years of our study, in the amount of contact children had with their parents.

We turn now to a set of factors which might be important in bringing about these changes. In attempting to identify and describe these factors, we have considered changes in residence and visitation simultaneously, enabling us to plot the amount of contact the child has with the two parents on a continuum. Living with one parent is seen as a greater degree of contact with that parent than merely visiting him or her. Steps on a father-contact scale are as follows:

1. Live with mother, no visitation with father.
2. Live with mother, daytime visits with father.

3. Live with mother, overnight visits with father.

4. Dual residence.

5. Live with father, overnight visits with mother.

6. Live with father, daytime visits with mother.

7. Live with father, no visitation with mother.

The amount of contact that children have with their mothers would be the reverse of this scale, so that a 7 on a father-contact scale would become a 1 on a mother-contact scale. In forming the father-contact scale, we have considered daytime visits to be a lesser form of visitation than overnight visits. This reflects our earlier findings that daytime visitation was less regular, less stable, and more likely to drift into non-visitation than was overnight visitation. In assessing change in contact, we subtracted each family's T-1 score on the above contact scale from its T-3 score. Families which experienced an increase in father contact received positive scores, and those with a decrease received negative scores. Of course, the change score that a family could receive was constrained by its initial position—families receiving a 1 at Time 1 could only increase, if they changed at all, while families in the middle of the scale could change in either direction. For this reason, we have examined changes separately for families who initially adopted mother, dual, or father residence. Examination of the scores reveals that most changes in the distribution of children's time between the two parents were only one-step changes. This means that for mother-residence families, increases in father contact usually took the form of a shift from no visitation to daytime visits, from daytime visits to overnights, or from overnights to dual residence, while decreases usually took the form of a shift from overnights to daytime visits or daytime visits to no visitation. There were only 18 families who increased by three or more steps, signaling a change from no visitation to dual or father residence.

In a similar vein, we see that for families starting out with dual residence, those who shifted usually did so by only one step. In *all* cases in which the children moved from dual into father residence, increases were only one step, indicating that the children continued to have overnights with their mothers. Those who moved from dual into mother residence were more equally divided between those having overnights with father and those having lesser degrees of contact. An exception to the one-step pattern occurs among the relatively small group initially having father residence: in this group, there were approximately as many families in which the children had two or more steps of increase in contact with their mothers as there were families having one-step increases.

Using our index of change, we may now examine a list of factors that might affect changes occurring as time goes on in the division of children's time between the two parents.

Residential Moves

Often there is considerable time, effort, and expense involved in transporting children back and forth between parental households. These costs undoubtedly increase when parents move farther apart. What effect do such moves have on visitation?

At Time 3, when parents reported that there had been changes in the amount of time the children were spending with each of the two parents, we asked why these changes occurred. Residential moving was the most common response. In the large majority of cases, moving meant an increase in the distance between the parental households. While fathers were somewhat more likely than mothers to move, they were generally equivalent to mothers in their rate of making moves that had an impact on the children's residence or visitation.

The major means of transportation for our families was the automobile (only a few parents lived so far apart that air travel was called for, or so close that the children could walk or bike), and it was the non-residential parents who did most of the driving. At each interview, we asked how far apart the two parental residences were in terms of driving time. The average distance between households was initially less for couples with dual residence, and this distance changed very little over the three years of the study. Average distance increased moderately for mother-residence families, and somewhat more for the father-residence ones. However, averaging conceals a good deal of residential moving. In about a third of the families for whom we have driving-distance information at both Times 1 and 3, one or both parents had made residential moves that increased driving time by at least 20 minutes. A smaller number (nearly a fifth), however, had moved at least a few minutes *closer*. Figure 8.8 shows the changes in father contact that occurred between Times 1 and 3 in families with initial mother or dual residence, and how these were related to changes in the distance between parental residences occurring in the same time period. It is clear that when the parents moved farther apart, the children saw their fathers less. For mother-residence families, father contact dropped off only when driving distance increased by over an hour. Dual-residence arrangements were more vulnerable to shorter-distance moves. The father-residence families (not shown in Figure 8.8) were the exception: although there was a trend for decreasing mother contact with increasing distance, it was neither significant nor linear. For this group, it seems that changes in residence and visitation—which were frequent—were usually triggered by factors other than residential moves, whereas such moves were powerful triggers for mother-residence or dual-residence families.

Remarriage and "Repartnering"

Remarriage of one or both of the parents can trigger a reevaluation of the arrangements for residence and custody of the children of the for-

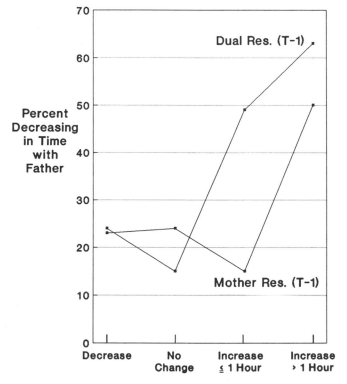

Change in Distance between Households,
T-1 to T-3 (in Driving Time)

Figure 8.8 Residential moves and changes in contact with fathers from T-1 to T-3. (The numbers of cases for the four distance groups are as follows: mother residence: 65, 159, 92, 88; dual residence: 29, 54, 33, 19.)

mer marriage. Remarriage often entails a residential move, and as we have seen, such moves often affect the time-sharing arrangements for children. Equally or perhaps even more important are the facts that some new spouses are ready and willing to take on the stepparent role while others are not, and that some children are ready and willing to accept a parent's new partner while others are not. It is not surprising that dual-residence arrangements are especially likely to break down when one of the parents remarries as this arrangement presumably entails frequent contact with former spouses—something new spouses could hardly be expected to applaud.

We have information for 794 mothers and 769 fathers concerning whether they had remarried by Time 3.[8] Twenty-eight percent of the mothers and 29 percent of the fathers had done so. Figure 8.9 shows how a mother's remarriage is related to change in children's time with her. When mothers remarried, the children spent somewhat more time with them, on the average, and somewhat less time with their fathers, than was the case for mothers who were still unmarried by Time 3. This was true regardless of where the children had been living at Time 1. When fathers remarried (data not shown), the effect appeared to depend somewhat more on where the children had been living, although the numbers of cases were too small to confirm the trend. For children initially living either with their mothers or in dual residence, a father's remarriage had little effect either on the children's residence or on the likelihood that they would visit their fathers. For children initially living with their fathers (many of whom increased their contact with their mothers over the three years of the study, as we have seen), the increase in mother contact tended to be less pronounced if the father had remarried. However, this tendency does not approach statistical significance. Our overall conclusion is that when a mother remarries, the children are drawn toward her household and away from the father's, while a father's remarriage has little impact on his contact with his children. We can only speculate about the reasons for these differential effects: possibly the fact that mothers enjoy a much greater improvement in their economic situation through remarriage than fathers do enables these mothers to expand their child-care responsibilities (by allowing them either to reduce working hours or hire more child-care help); or it may mean that stepfathers may be more willing to accept children from a previous marriage than stepmothers are.

Remarriage often entails a residential move, which frequently triggers changes in the amount of contact children have with each of

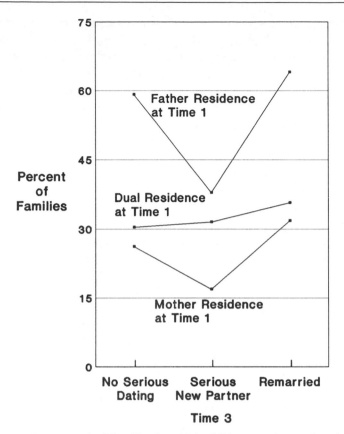

Figure 8.9 Percentage of families in which children are increasing time with mothers from T-1 to T-3, in relation to her remarriage or having a serious new partner at T-3.

the parents. We must ask, then, whether the changes associated with remarriage are reflections of residential moves. For children living with their mothers, who see less of their fathers when the mother remarries, it may be the move, not the remarriage, that causes the decline. This is not the case with children living with their fathers, who see more of their mothers even though the mother has typically moved farther away when she remarries. We examined the independent effects of remarriage and changes in the distance between households, using them jointly to predict changes in contact with the father. We found that distance and mothers' remarriage were both strong factors in their own right, regardless of the connection the two factors had with each other. The exception was that for children in dual residence, the remarriage of the mother or father did not affect the amount of contact the children had with the two parents, while changes in distance did.

About a third of the parents in our study (33 percent of the mothers, 31 percent of the fathers) had not remarried but had formed serious relationships with new partners. In about half these cases the new partner was living in the parent's household. The children's time sharing appeared to be more affected by the *mother's* new relationships than by the father's. As we saw above, her remarriage was associated with the children's spending more time in her household. However, if she had a new partner to whom she was not married, the children spent *less* time with her than if she was either remarried or not involved with a new partner (see Figure 8.9). A father's relationship with a new partner to whom he was not married, however, bore little overall relationship to the children's pattern of residence or visitation, although from comments made by our respondents, we suspect that this null finding masks some countervailing tendencies. Some mothers resisted sending their children to visit the father when he had a new live-in partner, saying, "I don't want another woman to raise my children," or expressing suspicion of the other woman's motives or competence in her dealings with the children. On the other hand, a few felt that the father's household was a *better* environment for the children because another woman was there, and indeed found that it was easier to arrange visits through the father's new partner than it was to talk directly to the father himself. Much depended, of course, on the attitude of the father's new partner, and her willingness to mediate in this way.

The fact that a mother's new partner appears to cause more movement by the children away from her household than a father's new partner does from his calls for explanation. Perhaps parents believe that the presence of a strange man in the mother's household poses greater risks for the children than does a strange woman in the father's household. There is evidence that sexual molestation of stepdaughters by stepfathers occurs more frequently than does similar behavior by natural fathers toward their daughters in intact families (Parker and Parker, 1986). Parents may not be very explicit about these concerns, but they hint at them, as in the following comment by a residential father:

She [mother] is going with someone the family does not approve of. Now she says she is going to get married. She hasn't known the guy for long. It's been me thinking about whether I want Susan [daughter] over there or not. This guy went to jail for a year for writing bad checks. I don't know what's going on.

In addition, a double standard may be operating: some parents may consider it less suitable for children to be exposed to a mother's love affair than to a father's. Possibly, a new relationship interferes more with a mother's normal care of and attention to the children, so that she is willing to relinquish some of their time during the early phases of a love affair. But this is all speculation. For the present, we can only report that remarrying and repartnering of mothers and fathers do not appear to be parallel phenomena in the post-divorce lives of children and families.

Economic Considerations

Are changes in residential arrangements and visitation related to parental affluence or poverty? Under divorce law, arrangements for the children's residence and visitation are not supposed to depend on the relative economic resources of the two parents. It is widely recognized that if money were allowed to control custody, mothers, with their much lower incomes, would be at a great disadvantage in getting physical custody in disputed cases. Nevertheless, as we saw in Chapter 4, the initial arrangements for the division of the children's time between the parents did reflect economic considerations to a limited extent: the dual-residence group included a higher proportion of relatively affluent parents. And parents' unstructured comments during interviews sometimes indicated that in making their decisions about where the children would live initially, some had taken into account which parent was in a better position to support them. We now ask whether the changes in the children's time allocation that occurred between Times 1 and 3 were related to the relative affluence (or poverty) of the two parents.

Our answer is a qualified yes: the *father's* economic resources do matter in the maintenance or change in children's contact with him. For children initially living with their mothers, there was more increase in time with the father—and less loss of father contact—if the father earned more than $40,000 a year than if his earnings were lower. Dual residence was much more likely to be stable over time if the father was a high earner. For children initially living with their fathers, the important thing was not whether he was affluent, but whether he was poor. As we have seen, most of the children initially in father residence increased their contact with their mothers over the three years of the study, but this drift toward the mother was more pronounced if the father earned less than $20,000 per year than if his pay was higher. In contrast, the *mother's* level of earnings bore no significant relationship to changes in the division of the children's time.

Education was also a factor we considered. We found that the father's education was related to his contact with the children—the better educated the father, the better were the chances that he would maintain or increase his contact. However, we found that when education and income were considered jointly (through multiple regression), it was a father's income, not his education, that was important. The mother's education was related to changes in parent contact only for the families initially adopting dual residence: when the mother was a college graduate, the chances were better that a dual-residence arrangement would be maintained.

Perhaps more interesting than the absolute level of a parent's earnings are the changes in earnings that occurred over time. On the average, the earnings of the fathers in our sample increased at about the rate of inflation—5 percent per year was the median increase. For mothers, the percentage increases were somewhat above inflation (their median increase was 8 percent per year), no doubt reflecting their overall moderate increase in working hours. But these modal figures mask great variation: some of the parents in our sample had declining earnings, while others increased considerably beyond inflation levels. When we chart percentage changes in income for the two parents between Times 1 and 3 against changes in the children's contact with each of the parents, we find for the families starting out with mother residence that children saw their fathers more frequently if he had large income increases, and less frequently if his income fell substantially (see Figure 8.10). In our sample of mother-residence families as a whole, changes in the *mother's* earnings were not related to changes in the amount of time the children spent with her. We did have individual cases, however, in which the mother's earning capacity was clearly implicated in residential decisions, as the following example shows:

> Stevie no longer lives with me. He lives with his father. I lost my job and couldn't afford to support them. I was in a real financial bind. He [dad] wouldn't give me any money. The only help he'd give me was if one of the kids would live with him, if one of them would volunteer to go. Stevie did.

In general, however, fathers' income changes had more impact than mothers' income changes on the amount of time the children would spend with each parent, at least for those families with mother resi-

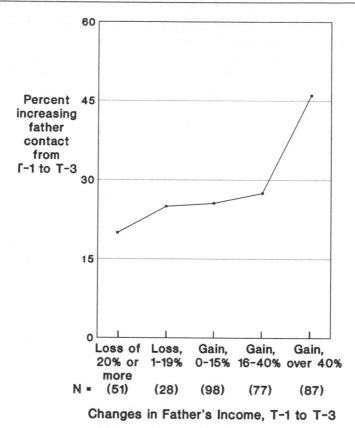

Figure 8.10 Relation of increases in contact with father to changes in father's earnings (for families in which children lived with the mother at T-1;
based on the 340 fathers whose children were living with mothers and for
whom we have income information at both T-1 and T-3).

dence at Time 1. Curiously, for families in which the children initially
lived either with the father or in dual residence, we could not detect
a consistent pattern relating the income changes of either parent to
changes in the distribution of children's time. In particular, the trend
for children initially living with their fathers to spend increasing time
with their mothers did not appear to depend on how much the mother
earned or whether her earnings were increasing or decreasing.

Relationship between the Parents

We tried to determine whether the children's maintenance of contact
with both parents depended significantly on the relationship of the

parents with each other. Divorced parents differ greatly in their attitudes toward their former spouses. Some manage to maintain fairly friendly relationships, despite the fact that there were differences between the spouses sufficient to cause divorce. Others are intensely angry and bitter, feeling betrayed and wronged by the ex-partner. The intensity of such feelings may change over time, but in a considerable number of couples in our sample, anger levels remained high over the three years of the study. It is important to know whether angry parents successfully sabotage visitation to the extent that contact with non-resident parents is broken off. In some couples anger is expressed through intense legal battling, in others it is not; the legal conflict in and of itself may worsen the relationship between the divorcing parents and lead to loss of contact with one of the parents. In families in which the children are spending time in both households, the nature of the co-parental relationship may make a difference in whether contact is maintained (see Koch and Lowery, 1984). (In Chapter 9 we will see that in the process of carrying out their joint parental responsibilities, some divorced parents continue to fight, others cooperate, and others avoid contact with each other.)

We suggested earlier that there might be a self-corrective process at work such that parents who could cooperate would maintain dual residence or frequent visitation, while in families where co-parenting was conflicted, children's contact with one of the parents might decline.

Our findings are surprising: the relationship between the two parents turned out to be only weakly related to our index of change. Families are no less likely to maintain dual residence, or to sustain visitation, when they have had substantial legal conflict than when they have not. For our more general measure of parental hostility at Time 1, the picture is similar, with some exceptions. As mentioned earlier, at the close of each interview, interviewers rated the parent on the level of hostility expressed toward the ex-spouse. The average ratings declined somewhat over the three time periods of our study, so we were able to detect some cooling of hostility, but there was still a wide range of hostility levels at Time 3. As we saw in Chapter 7, in families initially adopting dual residence, when the mother was highly hostile the dual arrangement was often not maintained, and the children typically moved to the mother's household. When the children initially lived with their fathers, high hostility on his part appears to have prevented the increase in contact with mothers that was generally found in father-residence families.[9] However, in our largest group of families— those in which the children lived with their mothers at Time 1—the amount of hostility expressed by mothers or fathers at Time 1 was unrelated to whether the children would see their fathers more or less as time passed. Thus we see that in most cases, neither the mother's hostility nor the father's was related to shifts in the distribution of children's time between the two parents.[10]

What about the nature of the co-parenting relationship that the two parents maintain in families in which the children are spending time in both parental households? We find that for the mother-residence families, there is a modest but significant tendency for families who have higher levels of cooperative communication to maintain or increase the children's contact with their fathers. We see an example of parental cooperation leading to greater contact with the father in the following mother-residence case:

> Originally when we started he was just seeing Deborah every other weekend. I talked to him, he talked to me about it, and he said, "It's too far of a time span between visits. I get out of touch." And I said, "O.K., fine, we'll try Wednesdays, too." If I say I have to work, even if it's my weekend, he'll take her to his house until the time I get back home. Sometimes he comes over here to our house for dinner, too. It's real tough when your kids start getting older to keep in touch. Deborah's father is not involved with anybody, and I think he really felt a void. He didn't interact with her that much when she was younger, but now she's older and can do more things for herself. I like for her to see him because I don't want her to grow up like she hates men, she hates her father. I don't push Deborah on her father. If it's her dad's weekend and she wants to stay home, she stays home. If it's my weekend and he wants to take her to the ballet or whatever, he takes her.

Over the sample as a whole, we found that a cooperative pattern of co-parenting was associated with *stability* in residence and visitation, but not strongly associated with changes in the share of the child's time allocated to mothers as compared to fathers. The amount of co-parental discord prevailing at Time 2 was not related, for any of the residential groups, to an overall shift in parental responsibility from mothers to fathers or vice versa. In families with a conflicted co-parenting style, the children's contact with the non-resident parent might either increase or decrease. A case in which a non-residential mother increased her share of a child's residential time through undermining the other parent is seen in a family in which a teenage boy, who was living with his father, had recently gotten his driver's license. He had been driving his father's car on weekends, but the father had taken away his driving privileges because of a rule infraction. The boy called his mother to complain. Her battle to get physical custody of the boy had been unsuccessful, and she was alert to an opportunity to attract him. She said: "Oh, honey, what you did wasn't *that* bad. I don't see why he grounded you. You can drive my car any time you want." The upshot was that the boy moved to his mother's house.

The major point is that non-residential parents might be somewhat more likely to "drop out" in conflicted families than in families with cooperative or disengaged parents, but they were also more likely to "drop in." In other words, we did not find a self-corrective process that shielded the children in discordant families from continued exposure to parental conflict.

At Time 3, about a third of the non-residential parents said that their ex-spouses had done or threatened to do things to discourage or block visitation. In some cases, this took the form of telling the children derogatory things about the other parent, so that the children became unwilling to visit. There were cases of outright refusal by a custodial parent to allow the visits on weekends and holidays provided by the legal agreement. It is especially surprising, then, to find that in families where parents told us that attempts to block visitation had been made, there was no greater reduction in visitation to the non-residential parent than that which occurred in other families.

In short, the quality of the relationship between the two parents had surprisingly little connection to changes in the arrangements for children's residence and visitation. The level of initial hostility that prevailed between the parents, whether they engaged in legal conflict, whether they were cooperative or conflicted in their co-parenting, or whether they tried to block visitation, seemed to have little to do with the changes that occurred over time to each parent's share of the child's residential time.

Children's Choices

As they grow older, children have more voice in where they live and how much they visit. Not surprisingly, visits to the non-resident parent's house may become less of a treat and more of an interruption, when children are old enough to have their own agendas of activities oriented around their schools or friends. We have already seen that overnight visits decrease as children age. At Time 3 we asked parents how eager their children were to go on scheduled visits to the non-resident parent's house. The answer depended somewhat on which parent was answering the question: fathers believed the children were more eager to visit them than the mothers said they were. Regardless

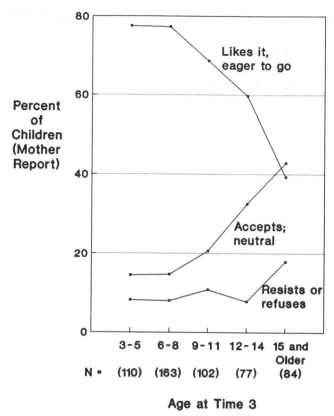

Figure 8.11   Willingness of children in mother-residence families to visit fathers at T-3, by age (based on children who lived with their mothers and visited their fathers at T-3).

of which parent was reporting, however, children who were age 11 or younger were described as eager to go on visits. As the children grew older both parents reported that their attitude shifted from eagerness to matter-of-fact acceptance. For most older children, visits seemed to be regarded as a necessary part of their lives, but not as something they would actively choose (see Figure 8.11, which charts the mothers' reports). The downward drift of visitation for busy older children is described by a mother:

> Their dad sees them less. They have their homework, outside activities they're involved in. They seem to have a tremendous amount of homework projects that they need to work on during the weekends. It just sort

of seemed like on the weekends he wanted them, they had school activities, or he [dad] had something going that weekend. It just worked out that they missed more and more weekend visits.

There were a number of families, however, in which older children actively chose to spend more time at the other parent's house, in some cases moving their primary residence there. In our parent interviews we asked parents about the amount of conflict they were having with their children during the times when the children were in their residence. Over the sample as a whole, we did not find that parent-child conflict, as reported by the parents at Time 1, predicted the amount of change that would occur in the children's residence or visitation over the subsequent three years. Nevertheless, when we asked parents at Time 3 what had been the reasons for change, quite a few did mention that children were sent to the other parent, or chose to go, when relationships with the residential parent (or the parent's new partner) became extremely tense. Commonly, a teenager's move was initiated mainly by the child, but usually with the complicity of the other parent.

Often it is difficult to tell what combination of factors is responsible for a change—parent-child conflict, parental "burnout," and the child's choice may all be involved. Of course, older children are much better able to voice their preferences than are young children, but sometimes even young children convey unmistakable messages. In some cases we were told that a toddler or preschooler cried or hid whenever the non-resident parent came to pick the child up for a visit, and under these conditions the non-custodial parent became discouraged and visitation would drop off.

Although children, especially older ones, are frequently able to influence the residence and visitation arrangements as time goes on, their preferences are not always honored:

He [the father] was not taking care of them and his house was in really incredible disarray. We used to have joint physical custody. I got a court order getting sole physical custody. I know my 14-year-old is having a lot of problems with me right now. He'd rather be living with his father. He told me that's because with his dad he does not have responsibilities, he can just do what he likes. Now with us, he has to do his homework, he has to come home after school—so he's not happy at all.

The Welfare of the Children

We saw in Chapter 4 that parents' concerns about which household would be better for the children played a considerable role in decisions about where the children would live initially. From a statistical stand-point, these concerns did not play nearly as strong a role in triggering *changes* in the division of the children's time between households. Nevertheless, such considerations were mentioned by a minority of parents in their free comments. In a few cases in which parental abuse or neglect was alleged, there was a court order limiting a parent's contact with the child, but more commonly change occurred without court intervention, and most allegations concerned less serious inade-quacies in monitoring, discipline, or child care. While more mothers than fathers expressed concern about their children's care in the other parent's household, some fathers alleged that their former wives were too lax with the children, or too disorganized to maintain a satisfactory home for them, and cited these as reasons for a change in contact.

More commonly, however, changes were based not on the avoid-ance of harm to children but on more positive considerations of what arrangement would be best for the children (as well as manageable for the parents). These quotes from two fathers explain why they sup-ported increasing the children's time with their mothers:

> A father: "If she doesn't see her mom for a while she hurts. I don't like to see her hurting."

> (Father report): "At first her mom was really having problems and she didn't want anything to do with Cathy. So it was Cathy and I against the world. Then Linda [ex-wife] settled down and seemed to get her act together. She wanted, all of a sudden, Cathy back in her life, instead of with me. Like 'Now I'm ready, now I want Cathy.' And I went 'No, sweetheart, you can't do that. For one thing, I won't allow it. For another thing, you've already signed a divorce decree that gave me sole physical custody.' So we discussed it and took it to a counselor, and the agreement we came up with was 50-50. I felt like it was probably better for Cathy to have her mom more involved in her life."

Likewise, a mother who felt that her son needed to spend time with his father applied pressure to increase visitation:

> His father has finally settled down and accepted the responsibility of every single weekend. Before, sometimes he'd call and something would come up and he'd screw up the schedule.

In a number of families, greater parental responsibility had been shifted to the parent whose environment or life style appeared better suited to child-rearing. Some examples are the following: a grandpar-ent lived near one of the parental homes, and could provide after-school supervision; a mother was ill, and could not provide care and supervision while the father could; a father with sole physical custody was in military service and was transferred to a distant post, and he thought the mother and her new spouse could provide a stable home. As noted in the quotes above, one parent might be initially in an emotionally unstable state (usually linked to the divorce) and unable to deal with the children for a period. If this parent was able to reestablish an organized life, the two parents would begin to share parenting to a greater degree.

Summary Comment

Correspondence between the custody decree and de facto residence. When families had been awarded joint physical custody in their divorce decree, the children quite often (approximately half the time) actually lived primarily with one parent or the other, rather than in dual residence. When sole physical custody had been awarded to the mother or father, however, the children's actual residence usually corresponded to the decree.

Continued maternal predominance. More than two-thirds of the families initially adopted maternal residence for their children, and this proportion remained essentially unchanged over the three-year period following our first interview. Furthermore, while many children living with their mothers saw their fathers less as time went on, children living with their fathers tended to see their mothers more. When mothers remarried, the children tended to spend increasing time with her, while a father's remarriage usually did not affect the division of the children's time between the parents. Taken together, these findings point to fairly strong forces pulling children toward the mother's household.

Continued contact with both parents. We have also found that the large majority of children in the panel families maintained contact with both parents over the three years of our study. Although visitation with fathers dropped off somewhat among mother-residence families, rates of visitation with mothers among father-residence families increased, and a substantial minority of families (about a sixth) continued to divide the children's time fairly equally between parental households. Other studies have reported higher rates of father dropout in mother-residence families. Furstenberg, Peterson, Nord, and Zill, reporting results from a national-sample study conducted in 1981, say: "The process of estrangement [of non-resident fathers] from the child appears to be an abrupt one, typically beginning soon after the marriage breaks up . . . Fathers are more likely to see their children at least once a week if their marriage broke up during the past two years, though the rate of frequent contact appears to drop off sharply even sooner than that, after about 12 months'' (1983, p. 664).

By contrast, we have found that, three and a half years after parental separation, there were very few children who had not seen their fathers within the past year, and most children in mother-residence families were visiting on a regular basis. There are many differences between the two studies: theirs was a national sample, while ours was based on two California counties; theirs dealt (for the most part) with divorces occurring in the early 1970s, and ours with divorces in the mid-1980s. Ours included children of all ages, while theirs was confined to children aged 11–16 at the time of study; theirs was a sample of households, ours a sample from court records of divorce filings. Both samples suffered loss (and possible bias) from non-recruited cases. Nevertheless, it is interesting to speculate about what may have brought about the high maintenance of contact with non-residential parents that we have found. The increase in divorce rates occurring over the past several decades must mean that parents who divorce now include different kinds of people than the smaller group who divorced at an earlier time—perhaps, specifically, more committed fathers. Furthermore, there may well have been a change in the public and private attitudes about the continuing responsibilities of *both* parents following divorce. It is clearly possible that the changes in California divorce law that were adopted in 1979 gave substance to this changing ethos, and helped to establish pro-contact assumptions in the minds of divorcing parents and their attorneys, with the result that people began to take it for granted that joint physical custody was a viable option, and that if one parent were to have primary physical custody, visitation with the other parent would be established and taken seriously. However, we cannot make strong inferences about this trend until we have information from families in a different state—families divorcing at about the same time, but making their decisions in different legal and social atmospheres.[11]

Shifts in residence and visitation arrangements. Even though a substantial majority of families maintained the residential arrangement they had adopted initially, many children changed their residential arrangements over the course of our study. In particular, it was surprising to find that only half of the children who were in dual residence or living with their fathers at Time 3 had been living there throughout the three years of the study. For the sample as a whole, more than a quarter of the children (28 percent) had switched residence during the life of the study. In addition, children who remained in either mother or father residence often changed the amount of time they were spending with the non-resident parent. Indeed, nearly half (45 percent) of families in which the children continued to live with their mothers throughout the study substantially changed the amount of contact with their fathers. In about two-thirds of these instances, the father partially or totally dropped out of the children's lives. But in a substantial number of families, children who had not initially been visiting their fathers began to do so, or daytime visits were shifted to overnights. Among the 52 families in which the children lived with their fathers throughout the study, slightly over half changed the amount of their visitation with mothers, with increases in visitation being more common than decreases. In sum, we have found substantial amounts of change in the distribution of children's time between the two parents during a three-year period, and we want to emphasize that both increases and decreases in children's contact with a non-residential parent commonly occurred.

We have not returned to the court records to discover how many of these changes in residence and visitation have been accompanied by court orders. We have the strong impression, however, that in the vast majority of cases, no legal action was involved. Usually, the changes represent informal agreements between parents (with older children having a voice as well) that a different arrangement for the children would be more workable. In some cases, the changes benefit the life situation of one parent more than the other, and changes that leave one parent feeling cheated can leave smoldering resentments in their wake.

Changes in relation to the age and sex of children. Our expectation that children might be shifting toward spending more time with the same-sex parent as time went on was not borne out. Moreover, fathers whose children lived with their mothers were as likely to maintain visitation with sons as with daughters. As far as age is concerned, there has been speculation that fathers might maintain closer contact with older children than with children who were quite young at the time of parental separation. In general, we have not found this to be the case. It is true that among children living with their mothers, those who were infants or toddlers (under age 3) at Time 1 were somewhat less likely to be visiting their fathers at Time 3 (50 percent were not, compared to less than 40 percent for the rest of the sample). However, for children ranging in age from 3 to 15 at Time 1, visitation was maintained at approximately the same rates for all age groups over the life of the study. Throughout, the visits of older children more often took the form of daytime rather than overnight visits.

With respect to residence, we have found that children of different ages were equally likely to be living with their mothers throughout the study. Throughout the three-year period, older children were less likely than younger ones to be in dual residence, and more likely to be living with their fathers. Shifts into father residence became somewhat more common as children grew older; however, our overall conclusion is that children's age had very little bearing on *changes* in where they would live or how often they would visit non-residential parents.

Major reasons for change. The reasons for changes in residence and visitation are bewildering in their variety and complexity. In individual families, there is often no single reason but a cluster of family circumstances that defy easy description. Nevertheless, some identifiable themes are summarized below:

1. Residential moves. The post-divorce period is one of residential instability for at least one parent, and often both. The dual-residence situation appears to be the most vulnerable to residential moves; at least, it is less often maintained in the face of fairly short moves (less than an hour's increase in driving time) than are the visitation arrangements in families having the children's primary residence with one parent.

2. Parents' new relationships. A mother's remarriage is associated with moderate shifts toward children spending more time in her household and less time with the father. A father's remarriage has little effect.

3. Economic circumstances. When children were living with their mothers, fathers were more likely either to maintain their contact with the children or to increase it if their incomes were high or rising. As far as mothers were concerned, neither the mother's absolute level of earnings nor changes in her income over time were related to the share of the children's time that she obtained.

4. Children's choices. At Time 3, most children were described (by their parents) as being not only willing but eager to visit non-residential parents. Their attitude was related to age, however: older children regarded visitation as a fact of life, but for them visits were less often a treat—and more often an interference with their own agendas—than was the case for younger children.

5. The children's best interests. When parents were asked why

changes in residence or visitation had occurred, a common answer (second only to residential moves) had to do with what was deemed best for the children.

It is worth pointing out that some factors which might have been expected to produce change in residence or visitation are *not* on the list. The relationship between the two parents was not related to the dropout of non-residential parents. There was more stability in the arrangements for residence and visitation when parents were cooperative, and discordant parents were somewhat more likely either to increase or decrease the amount of contact with outside parents, with the result that, on average, conflicted co-parenting did not shift the balance of contact one way or the other.

As noted earlier, the age and sex of the children were essentially unrelated to change. How can we compare the factors that produce change with those that do not? We suspect the explanation may have something to do with how perceptible changes are that occur in family circumstances. After all, a child's sex does not change with time, and developmental changes are gradual. Similarly, interparental relationships change only gradually, if at all. There is some inertia in existing arrangements—parents are often reluctant to go through the stress of negotiating new arrangements, and gradual changes usually do not serve to overcome this inertia. Change is usually triggered by some clear event: a residential move, a remarriage, a new partner moving into one of the parental households, a change in a job, a crisis in family functioning. But these trigger events are frequent enough to have precipitated quite a high rate of change among the families we studied.

The frequency of changes in children's residence highlights the importance of parents' not closing off future options for themselves by cutting off the children's access to the other parent. In many families, circumstances will arise that may make a residential change the best solution for all concerned. Such changes can most easily be managed without trauma if the children have maintained a relationship with both parents and if parents have worked out modes of communication that permit them to do business with each other.

The prevalence of informal changes in arrangements for children's residence and visitation raises some important questions for legal policy. Although there has been a great deal of public interest in whether fathers are complying with their court-ordered child-support obligations, there has been little or no attention to the question of whether families "comply" with the agreements concerning custody and visitation that are embodied in their divorce decrees. We suspect this lack of interest reflects two things: first, awareness that post-divorce changes in residence and visitation usually reflect new agreements between parents based on their changing life circumstances; second, a recognition that it would be difficult if not impossible for the legal system to maintain a program of monitoring the day-to-day living arrangements of divorced couples and their children. Many would question whether such monitoring would be desirable, even if it were possible.

Policy issues take on a different aspect for changes in arrangements that are not mutually agreed upon by the two parents. We have seen many different degrees of agreement—ranging from highly cooperative adjustments to highly coercive ones in which one parent is the "loser." True, the law provides recourse, through relitigation, to parents who cannot agree about what changes are necessary or desirable, but few parents take advantage of this option. Furthermore, some issues appear quite intractable even in the courts. Residential moves are a primary example: maintenance of dual residence or biweekly visitation becomes logistically impossible with long-distance moves, and legal doctrine has not yet found a way in which the "rights" of both parents to their agreed-upon share of the child's time can be respected when long-distance moves occur.

A further question is whether monetary agreements can truly be unrelated to the division of the child's time between the parents. In California, child support payments do take into account the division of time, and we have already seen that in families which have been awarded joint physical custody, but in which the children are actually living with the mother, the mother may be paying a modest financial price in terms of lost child support. Parents appear to see a linkage between time and money, and may informally adjust the amount of payments when the children's residence or visitation changes. These difficult issues will be discussed further in Chapter 10 and our concluding chapter.

9

Parenting and Co-parenting Apart

We have identified three residential arrangements in post-divorce families: mother residence, where the children spend most of their time
with the mother, although they may visit the father; father residence,
which is the reverse; and dual residence, where the children spend at
least a third of their time in each household. We begin this chapter by
examining how the day-to-day child-rearing functions are handled in
these three different types of families. In Chapter 2 we suggested that
custodial mothers and custodial fathers might have somewhat different
strengths and weaknesses when they became single parents. Nevertheless, we found it difficult to predict the pattern of child-rearing that
would emerge in each parental household under the conditions of dual
residence—what special difficulties in parenting, if any, are encountered by a parent when the children are spending only from one-third
to one-half of their time in that parent's household.

The second part of this chapter is a study of those families in which
the children were spending time in both households, focusing on the
way in which the parents have divided their parental responsibilities
and how they have handled their co-parental relationship.[1] Although
most children spent more time with one parent than the other, we have
also seen that the majority of the children in our families were spending
some time in *both* parental households. Even at Time 3—three and a
half years after the parents separated—nearly two-thirds of the children who were living with their mothers were still seeing their fathers
during regular portions of the school year. An even larger proportion
of children who were living with their fathers were visiting their mothers. If one adds to these numbers the group of children who were
dividing their time fairly equally between the two households (dual

residence), it is evident that in a substantial majority of our families both parents maintained relationships with their children, and played a role in child-rearing. It is imperative to understand as much as we can about how the co-parental functions are managed between two people who live in separate households and have had enough conflict with each other to break up a marriage. Scholars have examined the effects of parental conflict on children's adjustment (Johnston and Campbell, 1988; Camera and Resnick, 1988). However, previous research provides little information on the way parents and children work out the daily and weekly family management issues that arise in connection with sending the children back and forth between households. In addition, we have seen that divorced couples vary considerably with respect to how much legal conflict they have had and how much hostility each maintains toward the other as time passes. We know little about how the level of conflict between the two parents intersects with interparental dealings concerning the current lives of children when both parents continue to share in the children's lives.

Parenting and Family Management in Each Household

There is evidence that the quality of parenting and family management deteriorates after divorce. Parents are preoccupied with the emotional distress of the spousal divorce, and in addition they often face the stress of residential moves and added working hours. Moreover, most parents begin dating at some point following the separation from the former spouse, searching for or finding new intimate relationships. All these preoccupations make it difficult for the parents to devote as much time and attention to the children as they did before the marital disruption. Under the pressure of these stresses and preoccupations, parents tend to become impatient and peremptory. They do not or cannot so easily devote time to doing joint projects with children, chatting with them about their feelings, interests, and problems, or planning activities and agendas for them. In particular, divorcing parents find it difficult to take the time and trouble required to negotiate with children over task assignments and joint plans. Under these conditions of diminished parenting, children tend to become bored, moody, and restless and to feel misunderstood; these reactions lead to an increase in behaviors that irritate their parents, and mutually coercive cycles ensue. However, longitudinal work in which divorced parents have been compared over time with non-divorced parents has indicated that parental functioning does recover over time, returning nearly to the level found in intact families (Hetherington, Cox, and Cox, 1982).

To date, most of the available information on family process in the post-divorce period comes from intensive study of mother-custody families. Some studies are based on samples of divorced parents who have volunteered for counseling or therapy (for example, those by Wallerstein and colleagues: Wallerstein and Kelly, 1980; McKinnon and Wallerstein, 1986), and the samples are small. Our sample is large and includes a range of "ordinary" divorces. However, because we do not have observations of interactions between parents and children, we must rely on the reports of the parents themselves concerning the difficulties they have faced in carrying out their parental functions after divorce. We suspect that parents may understate their difficulties, but nevertheless their reports yield useful information concerning parenting experiences in the three custodial arrangements.

There are several ways in which the custodial arrangement might affect parenting. In families in which the children's time is divided fairly equally between the two households (dual residence), parents are sharing the burdens of child care, and hence each parent may be experiencing less task overload, finding family management easier even when the children are at his or her residence. On the other hand, it is possible that when children are in dual residence, the gaps in a parent's contact with the children make it more difficult for parents to keep informed about their daily problems and activities, with associated difficulties in maintaining rapport and effective supervision. Such gaps would probably create more difficulties when the parents are conflicted than when they cooperate, a possibility that we examine below.

In Chapter 2 we predicted that because mothers and fathers typically have different parental roles before the separation, custodial mothers and custodial fathers might face somewhat different problems in child-rearing and household management after divorce. Specifically, we thought that custodial mothers, in the absence of paternal backup for their authority, might have difficulty enforcing discipline; in response to children's noncompliance, compounded by the other stresses of single parenting, they might be irritable and impatient. However, we thought they would have little difficulty managing household routines and schedules and supervising the children's daily activities, since these were their accustomed parental activities. We expected that fathers, because they had not interacted as intimately with the children in the past and had not been so accustomed to chatting with them, were likely to know the children less well, and consequently would have more difficulty planning agendas for them and keeping track of their interests, activities, and whereabouts.

Assessing Difficulties in Parenting and Family Management

In our interviews at Times 2 and 3, we asked mothers and fathers how much difficulty they were having with several aspects of family management. The interviewer said: "I'm going to read a list of things parents do and ask you to tell me how easy or difficult it is to do them these days. Use a scale from 1 to 10, where 1 means very easy and 10 means very hard. First, how easy or difficult is it these days to have time just to chat or play with _____ [child's name]." The interviewer then went on to ask how easy or difficult it was to be patient, maintain a schedule for meals and bedtime, supervise health habits, be consistent, enforce discipline, keep track of how the child was doing in school, keep track of the child's whereabouts, and keep track of the child's friends and interests. The last three questions, concerning "keeping track," were asked only about children aged 6 or older. If there was more than one child, parents were asked to make ratings for each of the children, but since their ratings for siblings were highly correlated, we took the average rating across children to represent the level of difficulty the parent was experiencing with the children as a group.

Examination of the correlations among items revealed two separable clusters of items. The first included the parent's difficulty in being patient, enforcing discipline, and being consistent. For the reports that follow, we have combined these items into a score called "difficulty being firm and patient." The second cluster is composed of three items concerned with monitoring, involving the parent's difficulty keeping track of school progress, the child's whereabouts, and the child's interests and friends. We have combined these items into a scale called "monitoring."

Although the questions on family management difficulty were asked of both residential and non-residential parents, they were most relevant for the parents with whom the children spent substantial amounts of time—either the primary residential parent, or both parents for the families whose children were in dual residence. As might be expected, non-residential parents reported more difficulty than residential parents with finding time to play or chat, monitoring, and supervising health habits—presumably because of the limited amount of time the children spent in their households. In the analysis that follows, we focus on the reports of the two kinds of residential parents—dual and primary—who had the children living with them for sufficient amounts of time for the management issues to be focal to them. Table 9.1 shows the mean values on the two composite scores, and on the three single-item scores not included in the two clusters.

Table 9.1 Family management difficulty, by residence and sex of parent[a]

	Children's residence			
	With mother	Dual		With father
	Mother reporting	Mother reporting	Father reporting	Father reporting
Mean difficulty, Time 2				
Monitoring[b]	2.4 (N = 330)	2.6 (N = 75)	3.3 (N = 61)	2.6 (N = 51)
Remaining firm and patient	3.8 (N = 566)	3.5 (N = 145)	3.1 (N = 134)	3.4 (N = 78)
Finding time to play and chat	3.9 (N = 562)	3.7 (N = 145)	3.1 (N = 133)	4.0 (N = 77)
Maintaining routines	3.0 (N = 550)	2.9 (N = 142)	3.1 (N = 130)	3.1 (N = 76)
Supervising health habits	2.6 (N = 545)	2.5 (N = 143)	2.8 (N = 127)	3.3 (N = 71)
Mean difficulty, Time 3				
Monitoring	2.4 (N = 416)	2.4 (N = 99)	3.1 (N = 96)	2.7 (N = 82)
Remaining firm and patient	3.9 (N = 545)	3.4 (N = 129)	3.2 (N = 129)	3.4 (N = 97)
Finding time to play and chat	4.2 (N = 545)	4.0 (N = 129)	3.3 (N = 129)	4.1 (N = 97)
Maintaining routines	3.1 (N = 540)	3.0 (N = 129)	3.0 (N = 129)	3.0 (N = 94)
Supervising health habits	2.6 (N = 535)	2.7 (N = 128)	2.7 (N = 129)	3.1 (N = 92)

	F values		
	Parent	Residence	P × R
Time 2			
Monitoring[b]	5.3*	5.9*	—
Remaining firm and patient	7.5**	5.6*	—
Finding time to play and chat	(1.7)	6.7**	(2.4)
Maintaining routines	—	—	—
Supervising health habits	8.0**	3.3†	(1.7)
Time 3			
Monitoring	11.8***	(2.4)	—
Remaining firm and patient	5.1*	5.1*	—
Finding time to play and chat	4.2*	7.4**	(2.3)
Maintaining routines	—	—	—
Supervising health habits	(2.2)	(1.3)	—

† $p \leq .10$; * $p \leq .05$; ** $p \leq .01$; *** $p \leq .001$.
a. For families with more than one child, scores have been averaged across children to yield a single score for each parent.
b. Monitoring scores are available only for children aged 6 or older.

The first major finding is that parents in general did not report great difficulty with any of the functions examined. Although there was a considerable range of ratings on each question, the most common ratings were 2 or 3 on most of the scales. In view of all the stresses in the lives of divorced parents, and the readjustments they must make in their parental roles, this comes as something of a surprise. Perhaps, as noted earlier, they understated their difficulties. Or perhaps the pre-separation parental alliance was especially problematic for parents whose conflict with each other was serious enough to precipitate divorce, so that the transition to single parenting entailed benefits as well as losses.

Parents reported somewhat greater difficulty in finding time to play or chat with their children than with other management functions, and this is the only one of the five scores that showed a significant increase from Time 2 to Time 3.[2] Remaining patient with children was also reported to be somewhat more difficult than other family-management functions, but for each of the groups shown in Table 9.1, means were still well below the midpoint of the 10-point scale.

Mothers and fathers compared. Table 9.1 reveals a number of differences between mothers and fathers in the nature of their family management difficulties. At both Times 2 and 3, fathers reported more difficulty in keeping track of their children's school progress, whereabouts, and friends and interests than did mothers. (A comparison of non-residential fathers with non-residential mothers indicates that these fathers, too, reported more difficulty with monitoring during the relatively brief periods when their children were visiting them than did non-residential mothers during comparable visitation.) At Time 2, residential fathers reported more difficulty than mothers in supervising their children's health habits. Mothers, on the other hand, at both Times 2 and 3, reported more difficulty in remaining firm and patient. Among non-residential parents, too, mothers reported more of this kind of difficulty than fathers.

We noted earlier that residential parents are not exactly comparable with respect to the amount of time they have with their children. For residential fathers, the children are away (at the mother's house) more often. Can the father's greater difficulty in monitoring, or the mother's greater difficulty in remaining firm and patient, be explained by these differences in residential time? It appears not; when we control for the number of overnights, all the effects shown in Table 9.1 remain significant. Another possibly significant factor is that the children living with fathers are, on the average, older than those living with mothers, and older children are more difficult to monitor.[3] The fathers' greater difficulty in monitoring does not stem from the fact that they are dealing with older children, however. The maternal advantage in monitoring is found for both older and younger children (that is, within age groups). The same conclusion applies when we examine the effects of children's sex: boys are not reported to be any more difficult to monitor than girls, and fathers have more difficulty than mothers monitoring children of both sexes.

Dual versus primary residence. Family management difficulties were modestly related to whether children were in dual residence or lived primarily with one of the parents. Parents whose children were in dual residence reported somewhat less difficulty remaining firm and patient, and said that they were more able to find time for play and chatting. We interpret this as meaning that the continued sharing of parental responsibilities relieves the time pressures on both parents to some extent, perhaps especially for mothers. (We should note that it was only for mothers who were working full time that there was an advantage, with respect to remaining firm and patient, in having dual residence.) On the other hand, at Time 2, dual-residence parents reported somewhat more difficulty keeping track of their children. Getting an uninterrupted flow of information about their children's day-to-day problems and activities when the children are spending substantial amounts of time in a different household is difficult for parents, especially if the parents cannot talk amicably. We believe such information is necessary for successful monitoring.

Later in this chapter we describe the different patterns of co-parenting that parents adopt when their children are spending time in both households. Here it suffices to say that according to mothers' reports, the greater difficulty with monitoring children in dual residence is found only in those families where the parents have a conflicted, rather than a cooperative, co-parenting pattern.[4] We suspect that it is particularly in the situation where children are spending substantial time in both households but where the parents are not exchanging information about the children's activities that children can most easily find opportunities to evade parental surveillance.

Co-parenting after Divorce

Most of the parents in our study are co-parents. At Time 3, in two-thirds of the families in our study, children were still spending time with both parents during ordinary two-week periods of the school year.

In these families divorce has meant severing many, but not all, of the ties that bind married couples together. The sexual union, joint social life, future plans, shared financial transactions, and other aspects of the marital linkage have come to an end. However, the fact that both spouses are continuing to function as parents of the same children presumably means that their relationship to each other in the parental domain is *not* severed, though it has become more ambiguous and more complex.

Beyond the requirement for co-parenting inherent when children are spending time in two households, the fact that the large majority of the families in our study have settlements that stipulate joint *legal* custody must be considered. This element in the divorce decree presumably creates a right and obligation of each parent to be involved in decisions about the child. If such rights and obligations are to have meaning, some degree of communication between the parents is implied. Yet before our study, nothing has been documented concerning the frequency with which parents consult each other about their child-rearing decisions following divorce, or about the nature of the issues that are discussed.

After separation, simply continuing the co-parental relationship that prevailed in the pre-separation period is hardly possible. Even for parents who are willing and able to cooperate in the post-separation period, a new mode of functioning as co-parents needs to be constructed. Parents must negotiate how much time the children will spend in each household. As we saw in Chapters 4 and 8, there is enormous variation in the de facto arrangements for residence and visitation, and a minority of couples experience considerable difficulty arriving at their initial agreement. Furthermore, even after an initial agreement has been reached, it takes considerable effort and experience to work out a *modus vivendi* that permits parents to live separate lives that are joined only where their dealings with the children intersect. Parents must decide who will be responsible for the children's transportation between households. The timing of visits must be arranged, and cannot necessarily remain fixed over long periods of time. Frequently, a parent or a child wants to make a last-minute, one-time change in a visitation arrangement. More important, a parent's residential move or remarriage, or a change of schools for a child, may call for renegotiation of schedules on a longer-term basis. Thus a continuing aspect of co-parenting in the post-divorce period is managing the logistics of the children's movement between households—something that was not an issue in the co-parental relationship before the divorce.

Another aspect of co-parenting that may change considerably after parental separation is the division of child-rearing tasks between the two parents. In intact families, as we and others have noted, the two parents seldom participate equally in all the different aspects of child care. Thus after separation, during times when the children are in a given parent's household, that parent must perform certain tasks previously done by the former spouse, if these tasks are to be done at all. Some parental tasks, such as supervising homework or even seeing that children are bathed, may be done in one household and neglected in the other. Tasks such as feeding and dressing are easily replicated in two households. Other functions, such as shopping for clothes or arranging for medical care, are less so. For the child-rearing functions that are not easily divisible or replicable, a certain amount of parental collaboration would appear to be called for.

The parental alliance, however strong it was during marriage, also must change as the parental relationship is disentangled from the spousal one. Although spousal conflict and conflict in the co-parental roles are often associated, there is considerable variation in the degree to which this is so. In other words, some divorcing parents are better able than others to insulate their co-parental functioning from the anger and hostility that pervades their spousal separation,[5] and when they can manage this the children benefit. Conversely, when the children are exposed to continuing parental conflict, the children clearly suffer (Johnson, Campbell, and Mayes, 1985). As we noted in Chapter 2, the mere fact of parental divorce weakens the parental alliance in important respects, not the least of which is that children become aware that their parents do not love each other. However, it is possible, despite divorce, to convey the feeling that the ex-spouse is worthy of respect. Beyond this, maintaining dispassionate communication about the children so that joint problem-solving about their welfare can occur is probably the most important element in sustaining a parental alliance following divorce.

In Chapter 2 we discussed parental "buffering," noting that parents in intact families can and do protect children from each other's weaknesses, or even sometimes from behavior that might endanger the children. It is difficult for an absent parent to maintain vigilance from a distance. Little is known empirically about how this problem enters into the post-separation co-parenting situation. This is an issue that we have explored in our interviews.

We focus now on families in which the children spent time in both parental households during regular portions of the school year (not including holidays and vacations). We will present information on various specific aspects of co-parenting and use this information to identify three basic patterns or styles of co-parenting: a cooperative pattern, a conflicted pattern, and a disengaged pattern. We will then discuss how stable these patterns are—whether parents shift from one to the other as time goes on—and will also consider the conditions that affect which of these patterns a parental couple is likely to adopt.

The Division of Child-rearing Functions

Certain routine functions (preparing meals, helping young children to bathe and dress, washing clothes) were quite easily replicated in the two parental households, and these routine aspects of child care were carried out in whichever household the children were in at a given time. There was considerable variation, however, in the way the following functions were divided: taking the children to buy everyday clothes; keeping track of shots, checkups, and dental appointments; and supervising homework. Table 9.2 shows how mothers and fathers said these functions were divided in mother-residence, father-residence, and dual-residence families. As the table shows, each parent believed that the other was less involved in these activities than the other claimed to be. For example, for children living with their fathers, half the fathers said that they were the ones responsible for buying the children's clothes; only about a third of the mothers of father-residence children, on the other hand, said that the fathers had major or exclusive responsibility for this task. We assume that these differences in perspective between the two parents reflect the fact that each may be quite poorly informed about what goes on in the other's household vis-à-vis the children.

Apart from these differing viewpoints of mothers and fathers, certain major trends can be seen: first, as might be expected, the parent with whom the child is living takes more responsibility than the non-resident parent for all three functions, and this is true regardless of which parent is reporting. Second, there is a bias toward mothers doing more of the functions when one statistically controls for residence. Thus, mothers do more for children living with their fathers than fathers do for children living with their mothers. Furthermore, both parents agree that in dual-residence families, mothers are more likely than fathers to take major responsibility for each of the functions, although fathers frequently say that *both* parents are involved.

The carry-over of maternal responsibility into the dual-residence situation is pronounced regarding the children's medical regimen. We

Table 9.2 Division of parenting functions at Time 1 (percentage of children, by residential category)

| | Children's residence | | | | | |
| | With mother | | Dual | | With father | |
	Mother report	Father report	Mother report	Father report	Mother report	Father report
Who takes child to buy everyday clothes?						
Mother	91%	71%	65%	38%	40%	10%
Father	1	3	9	12	32	51
Both	8	26	26	50	28	39
	100%	100%	100%	100%	100%	100%
	(N = 670)	(N = 416)	(N = 159)	(N = 159)	(N = 57)	(N = 112)
Who keeps track of shots, checkups, dental appointments?						
Mother	96	85	82	52	36	10
Father	—	4	4	16	30	73
Both	4	11	14	32	34	17
	100%	100%	100%	100%	100%	100%
	(N = 681)	(N = 426)	(N = 163)	(N = 165)	(N = 59)	(N = 116)
Who supervises homework?[a]						
Mother	92	68	48	23	13	—
Father	1	5	6	17	55	79
Both	7	27	46	60	32	21
	100%	100%	100%	100%	100%	100%
	(N = 365)	(N = 228)	(N = 79)	(N = 72)	(N = 38)	(N = 78)

a. This question was asked only for children old enough to have homework.

saw in Chapter 3 that in two-parent households, even when both parents are working, mothers almost always have full responsibility for the "managerial" functions. We suggest that these are the functions most difficult to divide between households after divorce, since so many plans involving children span periods of time that overlap visits or alternation cycles between households. It is simply more efficient for one parent to take primary responsibility for such matters. As Table 9.2 shows, it is usually the parent who has been responsible before the separation—the mother—who continues to arrange for the child's medical regimen. However, in dual and father-residence families, parents often do not agree concerning who is carrying out this function, and in a substantial number of families it appears that both parents attempt to be involved in managing the child's medical care. We have encountered instances where the two parents had different pediatricians (who maintained separate medical records for the child) and where parents did not know whether a treatment (for example, a course of antibiotics for an ear infection) that was supposed to be continued actually was maintained after the child went to the other household. Evidently, this is a function for which coordination is especially important, but for which it does not always occur.

The Logistics of Transitions between Households

How far apart do the parents live? In a few of our families, the parents lived so far apart that children went back and forth for visits by plane. A few lived so close that the children could make the trip by bicycle, or even by walking. In the very large majority of our families, however, transportation was carried out by car. We asked the parents in these families to estimate the usual driving time between households. For children living with their mothers, the median driving distance increased only slightly over the three years of our study—from a 20-minute drive at Time 1 to a 25-minute drive at Time 3. The families with dual residence were even more stable with respect to the distance between households: median driving time remained at 15 minutes for this group. Among the father-residence group, the distance increased from an 18-minute drive to a 29-minute one.

Who does the driving? At Time 1 and Time 2, we inquired about how the transportation chores were divided between the parents. For families in which the children resided primarily with one parent and visited the other, the predominant pattern was for the non-resident parent to do the driving. This was especially true at Time 1 in mother-residence families, where fathers did the driving in more than two-thirds of the families. By Time 2 there was an increase in the frequency with which mothers had taken on a share of the driving, although fathers continued to be the most frequent drivers. Mothers did the major share of driving in father-residence families, although the two parents divided the driving more equally in these families than was the case for mother-residence ones. The most equal division of labor occurred in the dual-residence families, where half the families at Time 1, and three-fifths at Time 2, reported that the driving was shared.

We cannot be sure about the dynamics underlying these driving patterns, but we suspect that a major factor has to do with waiting time. That is, it is more convenient for children to wait to be picked up at their primary residence, where they and the resident parent can carry on normal at-home activities until the visiting parent arrives. Waiting time at the visiting parent's house is probably less comfortable or easily occupied. (Parenthetically, we note that a few residential parents did not want the non-residential parent to know where they lived, so that the non-residential parent drove to a neutral point, such as a shopping center, to pick up the children.)

We did not ask parents how much of a burden the driving routines were; from spontaneous comments, however, it was clear that whichever parent did the driving found it burdensome, and often resented the other parent's lack of participation. There was an implication in some cases that the residential parent was deliberately placing the driving burden on the other parent, as if to say: "If you want to see the children, you have to make the effort to come and get them and bring them back. It would be O.K. with me if you didn't come at all." There were even allegations that some residential parents had deliberately moved farther away so that the driving time would be more than the non-resident parent could manage. In other cases residential parents were eager to see visitation maintained, and cooperated in the transportation tasks.

Logistical problems. Moving children back and forth between households called for some form of understanding between the parents concerning where and when the children would be picked up and returned. While a few families tried to remain so flexible that the outside parent could drop by at any time to see or pick up the children without prior notice, most had a schedule agreed upon in advance. Parents did not always live up to their agreements, however. In our second and third interviews, parents were asked about the frequency with which they encountered problems maintaining agreed-upon arrangements, and how serious such problems were. Although the parent who was doing the driving sometimes complained that the children were not ready to be picked up at the scheduled time (or, what was more irritating, were not at home at all), and some residential parents complained that the children were not brought back on time by the parent whom they were visiting, the most commonly mentioned problem was last-minute schedule changes. Not only was a parent inconvenienced when an ex-spouse called to say that a visit had to be canceled or its time changed, but parents reported that children who had been looking forward to seeing the absent parent felt let down.

Parents were asked to rate their own situation on how serious the logistical problems were (see Table 9.3). Most parents reported that such problems were not serious—the most common ratings at both Times 2 and 3 were 2, 3, or 4 on a 10-point scale, on which 1 was not at all serious and 10 was extremely serious. In general, mothers reported

Table 9.3   Logistical problems at Times 2 and 3, by children's residence at each time

	Time 2 residence		
	With mother	Dual	With father
Mean logistical problems, Time 2 (on a 10-pt. scale)			
Mother report	3.7 (N = 334)	3.1 (N = 133)	3.0 (N = 34)
Father report	2.4 (N = 233)	2.6 (N = 117)	3.0 (N = 52)
	Time 3 residence		
	With mother	Dual	With father
Mean logistical problems, Time 3 (on a 10-pt. scale)			
Mother report	3.3 (N = 313)	2.6 (N = 130)	2.9 (N = 59)
Father report	2.7 (N = 257)	2.5 (N = 126)	3.2 (N = 73)

Note: An analysis of variance based on 564 parents (312 mothers, 252 fathers) in families in which children spent time in both households at both T-2 and T-3, and in which they stayed in the same residential arrangement (with mother, with father, or dual) at both times, yielded the following significance values:

	F	p
Parent	3.96	0.05
Residence	1.83	—
Time	.19	—
Parent × Time	2.42	—
Residence × Time	2.93	0.06
Parent by Residence	3.10	0.05

somewhat more logistical problems than did fathers, probably indicating that fathers were more likely to initiate schedule changes. At Time 3, parents with dual residence reported slightly fewer logistical problems than parents with primary residential custody, despite the fact that the dual-residence children went back and forth between households more frequently.

The seriousness of logistical problems changed very little with time: there was a slight drop in custodial mothers' reports of such problems, but no decline for custodial fathers. The fact that logistical problems did not increase during the two-year period between Time 1 and Time 2 is especially interesting in view of the fact (discussed below) that the frequency with which parents were talking to each other about the children decreased. It appears that parents can manage visitation schedules smoothly with very little communication. We find that the level of logistical problems is very nearly as low among parents who are not speaking to each other as among those who are. We infer that visitation schedules become routinized in most families—indeed, if they do not, they are unlikely to be maintained—and routinized visitation does not necessarily call for much in the way of communication between the parents. In some cases parents exchanged the children at the beginning and end of the day at school or a day-care center, and in these arrangements the parents rarely saw each other.

The Co-parental Relationship

Communication between ex-spouses. At all three interviewing times, parents were asked how frequently they talked to each other about the children. As Table 9.4 shows, there was a considerable decline, over the three and a half years following parental separation, in the frequency with which the parents talked to each other.[6] At Time 1, two-fifths of the couples talked with each other about aspects of the children's lives more than once a week; by Time 2, this proportion had declined to one-sixth. Moreover, the number of families in which one or both parents tried to limit contact between the two former spouses rose somewhat (and significantly) between Times 2 and 3.

When children were returned from a visit to the other household, parents often wanted to be informed about significant experiences the child might have had during the absence—illnesses, upsetting experiences, and so forth. Many parents commented that the ex-spouse provided little such information upon returning the children, and mothers in particular were concerned about the lack of information which they thought it important to have. For example, 42 percent of dual-

Table 9.4 Communication, coordination, and conflict between the divorcing parents, by time since separation[a]

	Time 1	Time 2	Time 3	F (for time)
How often do you and your ex-spouse talk about the children?				
Once a month or less	14.6%	20.0%	27.1%	
2–3 times a month	17.8	29.0	32.4	
Once a week	31.3	24.6	23.7	61.1***
2–3 times a week	30.5	22.8	14.3	
Every day	5.8	3.6	2.5	
	100.0%	100.0%	100.0%	
How often do you argue with your ex-spouse?				
Never	16.0	19.8	24.5	
Rarely	35.7	48.0	43.3	21.3***
Sometimes	35.4	24.6	26.2	
Often	12.9	7.6	6.0	
	100.0%	100.0%	100.0%	
Do you try to coordinate rules between the two households? (% "yes")	48.8%	37.8%	35.3%	14.0***
Does either parent try to limit contact between the two parents? (% "yes")	—	49.6	59.0	10.4**
How much does your ex-spouse try to avoid emotional upsets when negotiating with you? Mean on 10-pt. scale (1 = tries to upset, 10 = tries hard to avoid upsets)	5.8	5.8	6.4	12.3***
How much does your ex-spouse back up your parenting? Mean on 10-pt. scale (1 = undermines severely, 10 = backs up fully)	—	5.5	5.4	n.s.

*** $p \leq .001$.

a. Based on the 374 families in which at least one parent provided a standard interview at all three times, and in which the children spent time in both households at all three times.

residence mothers, but only 19 percent of dual-residence fathers, said that the other parent told them little or nothing about the child's state or experiences at the other household.

At the second and third interviews, parents were asked whether either tried to limit the amount of communication between the parents. As noted above, in quite a few families there were child-exchange arrangements explicitly designed to prevent the parents from having to talk with each other. Other parents tried to avoid telephone conversations, for example, by using an answering machine and not returning messages from the former spouse. A number of parents simply said: "We are not speaking." In cases of little or no communication, when transmission of a message appeared absolutely necessary, teachers, baby-sitters, or the children themselves were called upon to carry messages. At Time 2, one parent or both were reported to be attempting to limit communication between the parents in half of the families, and the proportion had increased to nearly three-fifths by Time 3. These numbers indicate that the avoidance of communication is a widespread phenomenon—one that does not lessen, but instead increases, with the passage of time.

What issues do parents discuss? Within each residential arrangement, divorced parents vary greatly with respect to how much they communicate with each other about the children. We now consider in more detail what kinds of issues are discussed between the parents who do talk to each other, and how the decision-making power is shared or divided. At Time 3, we asked parents in families in which the children were spending time in both households to tell us about what specific child-related issues had come up for discussion between them, and whether or not the decision-making was joint. Table 9.5 shows the percentage of parents in the three residential arrangements who answered "yes" (rather than "occasionally" or "never") when asked whether they currently talked about each of the issues listed. The children's school progress and their emotional states were issues that many parents talked about, and decisions about children's lessons, sports, and other extracurricular activities were also high on the list. Parents of children in dual residence reported the highest rates of discussion of all the issues listed.

Table 9.5 includes all the parents with children spending time in both households, regardless of whether both parents were interviewed. As the table shows, when children were living with their fathers, the reports of the 58 mothers and 78 fathers differed sharply: few of these fathers said that they discussed the listed issues with their ex-wives,

Table 9.5 What issues do parents discuss? (at Time 3, by children's residence)[a]

	Children's residence					
	With mother		Dual		With father	
	Mother report (N = 333)	Father report (N = 267)	Mother report (N = 129)	Father report (N = 128)	Mother report (N = 58)	Father report (N = 78)
Do you and (other parent) talk about (percent "yes"):						
Children's school progress?	51	63	66	66	63	36
Something child is upset about?	49	54	63	65	60	27
Children's lessons, sports, extracurricular activities?	53	58	62	65	53	36
Responsibilities and privileges?	38	42	44	47	50	24
Discipline?	37	38	45	49	50	26
Child-care arrangements?	22	26	40	45	36	13

a. This table includes only families in which children spent time in both households; data obtained at Time 3.

while the majority of non-custodial mothers reported discussing at least some of them with their former husbands. Do these discrepancies reflect sampling differences? That is, do they come about because not all these mothers and fathers were reporting about the same families? A subsidiary analysis was done of only those families in which both parents were interviewed—234 mother-residence families, 105 dual-resident, and 49 father-resident. In the mother-residence families, fathers were more likely than mothers to report discussing these issues; in the father-residence families, mothers were much more likely to report discussions. Thus, it is the non-residential parents who reported the higher rates of discussion, the residential parents the lower. Part of the explanation for this discrepancy undoubtedly lies in the base rate of decisions that each parent knows about. We suspect that residential parents make many routine decisions that the non-residential parent knows nothing about. If they talk over a fraction of these with the other parent, the residential parents will say to an interviewer that they discuss such issues "occasionally," while the non-residential parent, not knowing about the issues that have never been raised, will simply say "yes" if there are *any* instances in which an issue in a given category has been discussed.

A substantial majority of parents whose children spent time in both households reported that they did discuss some of these ongoing issues at least occasionally. Only about a fifth of primary-residence parents, and about one-tenth of dual-residence parents, said that they had not discussed such issues at all.

When asked about how decisions regarding the children were made, some parents said that they usually made decisions jointly. This pattern was much more often reported by parents whose children were in dual residence than by those where the children lived primarily in a single household (40 percent of dual-residence mothers and 61 percent of dual-residence fathers reported joint decision-making). Non-residential parents were considerably more likely than residential parents to claim that the two parents were equally involved in decision-making, and this was true for the subsample of families in which both parents were interviewed as well as for the sample of all parents interviewed. Non-residential fathers were especially likely to claim more involvement than their former wives attributed to them.

In households where the children had one primary residence, it was usually the residential parent who took primary decision-making responsibility. In some cases, issues were discussed with the visiting parent, and then the residential parent decided. In others, the non-residential parent was simply informed after the fact (see Table 9.6).

Parents were also asked about any major issues—concerning religion, or which school the children should attend, or medical care—that had required decisions to be made since the parental separation. Decisions about school attendance were the ones most likely to arise, followed by medical decisions, with religious training being mentioned by only about a quarter of the parents (Table 9.7). With respect to these major decisions, parents were asked about the involvement of the outside parent, and it may be seen (Table 9.8) that the two parents were somewhat more likely to be equally involved in major decisions than they were in the day-to-day issues shown in Tables 9.5 and 9.6.

Table 9.6   How involved is the outside parent in ongoing decisions? (by children's residence and sex of reporting parent, Time 3)

	How involved is father? Mother residence		How involved is mother? Father residence	
	Mother report	Father report	Mother report	Father report
How involved is outside parent in current decisions about children?				
Two parents equally involved	10%	19%	23%	11%
They discuss, then residential parent usually decides	17	22	16	7
Outside parent told after decision is made	32	32	30	37
Outside parent not involved	41	27	31	45
	100%	100%	100%	100%
	(N = 333)	(N = 264)	(N = 57)	(N = 75)

Table 9.7 What major decisions have needed to be made? (by children's residence, Time 3)[a]

	Children's residence					
	With mother		Dual		With father	
	Mother report (N = 332)	Father report (N = 263)	Mother report (N = 125)	Father report (N = 119)	Mother report (N = 56)	Father report (N = 77)
Percent "yes," decisions have needed to be made about:						
Religion	29	26	28	27	19	26
Which school to attend	48	43	62	60	53	49
Medical treatment	36	26	32	30	36	23
Other major issues	26	21	24	23	9	18
Percent none	23	30	18	29	29	23

a. These columns add to more than 100 percent because for some parents more than one kind of major decision needed to be made. The table includes those families in which children were spending time in both households at Time 3.

Table 9.8 How involved is the outside parent in major decisions? (Time 3)[a]

| | How involved is father? Mother residence | | How involved is mother? Father residence | |
	Mother report	Father report	Mother report	Father report
How involved is outside parent in major decisions about children?				
Two parents equally involved	22%	42%	40%	27%
They discuss, then residential parent usually decides	17	15	13	9
Outside parent told after decision is made	35	27	22	49
Outside parent not involved	26	16	25	15
	100%	100%	100%	100%
	(N = 255)	(N = 183)	(N = 40)	(N = 59)

a. This table includes only those families in which parents reported that major decisions had been made.

In general, however, the patterns emerging in the two tables are very similar.

Once again, an especially high incidence of joint decision-making was reported for dual-residence families (51 percent of dual-residence mothers, 74 percent of dual-residence fathers), and visiting parents (compared to residential parents) were more likely to report equal involvement in decision-making.

Does joint legal custody enhance joint decision-making? When California policymakers embodied a preference for joint legal custody in the revised California divorce law, one purpose was to keep non-custodial parents from dropping out of their children's lives. The hope was not only that they would keep up their child support payments more reliably and see the children more often, but that they would involve themselves in decisions concerning the children's lives. We saw in Chapter 8 that when the children were living with their mothers, a joint legal custody award made essentially no difference in whether the children's contact with their fathers would be maintained. There is a similar result with respect to the involvement of non-residential fathers in decision-making: when factors (such as income) that affect whether a family will be awarded joint legal custody are controlled, non-residential fathers who have joint legal custody are no more likely to be involved in either day-to-day decisions or major decisions.[7]

Coordination of rules and standards. In some families, parents attempted to have the same rules in both households. One mother reported, for example, that her former husband phoned during his daughter's visit to him to ask whether the daughter was allowed to wear lipstick to school. The mother's answer was "not till she gets into junior high school"—a decision which the father accepted. In other families, decisions about what the children were allowed to do were made independently in the two households, and the children were expected to conform to two different sets of standards. For example, the child might be required to fasten seat belts by one parent, not by the other; or there might be different rules about television, being present for meals, helping with household chores, or (for older children) curfew hours. As Table 9.4 shows, half the families were attempting to coordinate rules at Time 1, but only about a third were doing so at Time 3.

Some parents talked about the confusion their children experienced when the two households differed in their standards. For example, one father in a dual-residence family said that he allows his 5-year-old son to play on a skateboard, while the mother considers this dangerous and does not allow it:

I just said to him: mom and dad are different, yeah; it's a little weird, but when you're with dad you have one set of behaviors and when you're with mom you have another. And they're different. That makes it a little harder.

In some cases, the two parental households differed considerably with respect to the kinds of rules or demands that were set up for the children, and parents were often fairly critical of the requirements—or lack of them—in the other household. At Time 3, parents whose children were spending time in both households were asked: "When it comes to rules and discipline, do you think that [the other parent] is too strict, just about right, or too lenient?'' Although a few parents said they did not know how strict the other parent was, the large majority thought they did know (Table 9.9). Nearly two-fifths of fathers, and about a third of mothers, approved of their former spouses' level of strictness and demands, and some explicitly provided support for these demands when possible. For example, a father reports:

> Their mother always makes it very clear to the kids that I'm their father; that her boyfriend—possible fiancé—is not their father. If I tell them they have to do something, she reinforces it. Even if they're at her house, she backs me up on it. We pretty much do that both ways. We just let each other know what guidelines we've laid down and back each other up to

Table 9.9　Mothers' and fathers' attitudes about strictness or leniency in the other parent's house, by residence (Time 3)[a]

	Children's residence		
	With mother	Dual	With father
Mothers' attitudes about fathers' strictness:			
Too strict	13.4%	20.9%	20.0%
About right	30.5	30.2	45.0
Too lenient	43.3	39.5	25.0
Inconsistent	4.4	4.7	5.0
Don't know	8.4	4.7	5.0
	100.0%	100.0%	100.0%
	(N = 321)	(N = 129)	(N = 60)
Fathers' attitudes about mothers' strictness:			
Too strict	15.3%	10.8%	4.1%
About right	40.1	40.8	21.0
Too lenient	30.9	39.2	50.0
Inconsistent	7.2	5.4	10.8
Don't know	6.5	3.8	8.1
	100.0%	100.0%	100.0%
	(N = 262)	(N = 130)	(N = 74)

a. Based on 510 mothers and 466 fathers in families where the children spent time in both households at T-3.

make sure they're followed. That's not where we started off, but it's where we are now.

Both mothers and fathers were more likely to complain about lax-ness than about strictness in the other household. Residential parents in particular were likely to feel that the other parent did not sufficiently share in responsibility for maintaining supervision, imposing require-ments, and maintaining disciplinary control. The indulgent practices of "weekend parents," they felt, made it more difficult for the parent who had the children most of the time to maintain needed controls without being seen by the children as too demanding and heavy-handed. As one residential mother put it:

> I'm the one who gets down on her for not cleaning her room or takes her to the doctor when she's sick. I'm the grunt. I think we have a loving relationship. But all she could see was I was the one that was saying: "No, you can't do this"; and it was: "Well, if daddy was here, he would say I could."

A number of residential parents complained about the difficulty of getting children back into orderly, disciplined behavior after they had visited the other parent. An extreme example of rule disparity was reported by a father whose 14-year-old son was in dual residence. The father, a police officer, attempted to provide a structured and disciplined environment when the boy was with him. The mother had a more "laid-back" life style with her live-in boyfriend. The father worried considerably about the situation at the mother's house, where (according to the father) the boy was allowed to drive in downtown traffic without a license, and was allowed to take showers with his girl friend—something the father would never allow.

On the whole, there were relatively few complaints about the other parent being too strict, but when they occurred, they were most likely to come from mothers, especially those whose children were in dual or father residence.

Concerns about the other parent's household. It is evident that the failure to coordinate rules between two parental households may re-flect more than the simple fact that parents do not talk to each other. Sometimes it reflects genuine differences in values, and these differ-ences may mean that one parent is deeply concerned about the kinds of experiences the child is having in the other household. While most parents trust each other to be good parents, some worry about a vari-ety of things that might affect the children's welfare in the other house-hold. When parents are separated, they sometimes feel frustrated over their inability to monitor and counteract what they believe to be the deleterious influence of the other parent. These frustrations can be particularly marked for the primary parent. As we noted in Chapter 4, concerns about these matters appear to affect initial decisions about where the children will live, and in Chapter 7 we saw that they are related to the amount of legal conflict that occurs. Now we consider the role such concerns play in the co-parental process when children spend time in both households.

At both Times 1 and 3, parents were asked whether there was anything upsetting to them about the children spending time in the other parent's household (Table 9.10). At both times, about half the mothers and a third of the fathers (29 percent of fathers interviewed at Time 1, 35 percent of those interviewed at Time 3) said yes.[8] The lower incidence of concerns among fathers reflects in part the fact that many of them are outside parents who see the children only for visits; such parents in general are less likely to express worry about the well-being of the children in the primary household. As Table 9.10 shows, however, even residential fathers (those whose children live with them most of the time, as well as those whose children are in dual residence) were somewhat less likely to express concern than were residential mothers. About 29 percent of residential mothers, and 24 percent of residential fathers, felt that the problems in the other parent's household were either fairly serious or major.

At Time 3, parents who said they were concerned were asked to say what it was they were worried about. Table 9.11 shows that the relatively small group of fathers who detailed their concerns, and the larger group of mothers who did so, had similar complaints about the situation in the other household. Concerns expressed about the values and life styles of the other parents covered a broad range, and included general complaints about poor work habits or manners, living in the "fast lane," having a disorganized or erratic household, mental instability, "kooky" religious beliefs, as well as more specific complaints about the kind of video programs the children were allowed to see, or their exposure to sexual indiscretion. As an example of the latter, one custodial father reported finding a picture of a male stripper in his teenage daughter's wallet. When he phoned the mother to tell her about this and warn her that they needed to monitor the girl's activities more closely, the mother said that she herself had given the picture to the girl. Worries about the influence of the other parent's new partner are also fairly frequently expressed. Sometimes the concern is that this new person will be harsh or unresponsive to the children's needs; in

Table 9.10   Parental concerns about children spending time in other parent's household, Time 3[a]

	Primary residence	Dual residence		Primary residence
	Mothers (N = 333)	Mothers (N = 129)	Fathers (N = 128)	Fathers (N = 78)
Did you find anything upsetting about the child(ren) spending time with other parent? (If yes, how serious a problem?)				
No	52.0%	51.9%	59.4%	62.8%
Yes, minor problem	18.6	18.6	16.4	14.1
Yes, fairly serious	18.6	18.6	13.3	14.1
Yes, major problem	10.8	10.9	10.9	9.0
	100.0%	100.0%	100.0%	100.0%

a. Table includes residential parents whose children are spending time in both households.

other cases the worry is more that this person will be *too* appealing, and work to alienate the children's affections from the natural parent.

We noted earlier that parents were more likely to complain about laxness in the other household than about strictness. Table 9.11 gives more detail. Some parents complained that when the children were at the other parent's household, the other parent did not always stay home but left the children unsupervised. A young child, while on a visit to the non-residential parent, might phone home in a panic in the middle of the night, having discovered that there was no one else in the house. For older children, the concerns were that when unsupervised they were "running wild" at the other parent's house. Sometimes this was reported to happen when the other parent unexpectedly had to work late. Even when the other parent was home, this did not necessarily mean that he or she was spending time with the children—the parent might be doing household maintenance, talking on the phone, watching television, or doing other things which left the children to fend for themselves without an agenda. Some parents had specific complaints about the children returning home from visits in soiled clothes or with unwashed hair; still others mentioned the junk food provided in the other household, and found it difficult to maintain dietary restrictions for children who were overweight.

When asked about problems in the other parent's household, only about 4 percent of mothers and 2 or 3 percent of fathers mentioned problems of drug or alcohol abuse. However, at the end of the interviews, interviewers were asked to provide a summary record as to whether drug or alcohol abuse had been mentioned anywhere in the interview. At Time 2, 9.0 percent of mothers and 4.0 percent of fathers mentioned substance abuse (most often excessive use of alcohol) as something that caused concern about the former spouse's ability to be an effective parent. At Time 3, 9.7 percent of mothers and 3.5 percent of fathers expressed these concerns about the former spouse at some point in the interview.

Many of the concerns parents had about the competence of the former spouse to take child-rearing responsibility undoubtedly antedated the divorce. We asked parents at Time 1 whether the separation had made it easier or harder for them to help their children grow up to be "the kind of person you want them to be." Understandably,

Table 9.11   Specific concerns about other parent's household, by residential parent, Time 3[a]

	Residential mothers (N = 213)	Residential fathers (N = 78)
Concerned about other parent's:		
Life style, general	25.8%	35.9%
New partner	21.1	24.4
Being too lenient	19.2	25.6
Lack of attention to child's diet, exercise, cleanliness	16.0	15.4
Lack of supervision: child's whereabouts, activities	16.4	14.1
Spending too little time with child	16.4	17.9
Alcohol or drug abuse	3.8	2.6

a. This table is based on those residential parents (that is, sole or dual residence mothers, sole or dual residence fathers) who mentioned concerns about child visiting other parent. Columns add to more than 100 percent because some parents mentioned more than one concern.

most non-residential parents said "harder" (see Table 9.12). But among primary residential parents, there were nearly twice as many who said "easier" as there were who said "harder." Perhaps this is not so surprising for primary-residence mothers—for most of them, there is a good deal of continuity in their parenting activities before and after the separation. Furthermore, after separation they are freed from the need to mediate between the children and their father, or to negotiate with him over child-rearing issues. For the smaller group of residential fathers, however, we expected that many more adaptations would be called for, so that at least at Time 1, primary-residence fathers ought to be reporting that raising the children was now harder for them. Nevertheless, the message from both primary mothers and primary fathers appears to be that it is easier to function on one's own as a parent than to co-parent effectively with an incompatible partner.

Mutual backup or undermining. At Times 2 and 3, parents were asked about the degree to which their own parenting was backed up or undermined by the former spouse. They were asked to consider such matters as what the other parent said to the children about them, and whether their disciplinary measures were supported. They were asked to rate their former spouses on a 10-point scale, in which a 10 was "backs up fully," while a 1 was "undermines severely." As Table

Table 9.12 Difficulty of raising children after separation, by residence and sex of parent

| | Children's residence | | | |
| | With Mother | Dual | | With Father |
	Mother report	Mother report	Father report	Father report
Easier or harder to raise children (T-1):				
Easier	60.0%	51.7%	32.1%	58.9%
No change	10.5	7.6	12.5	5.5
Harder	29.5	40.7	55.4	35.6
	100%	100%	100%	100%
	(N = 502)	(N = 118)	(N = 112)	(N = 73)

F values: Parent, 8.54^{**}; Res., 14.12^{***}; P × R, $1.85^{n.s.}$

9.4 shows, there was no change from Time 2 to Time 3 in the average degree of backup reported. At both times, ratings ranged over the full scale from 1 to 10. Mutual support was not more common among dual-residence parents than in families where the children resided primarily with one parent.

Parents were asked to give examples to illustrate their ratings. In extreme cases, children had witnessed physically or verbally abusive interactions between the parents, so that the lack of respect on the part of at least one parent for the other was apparent. Other forms of undermining were less explicit, as for example, when a parent conspires with a child to keep information from the other parent. In one dual-residence family, for example, the father had taken his young son on a fishing trip and the boat had capsized. The mother was very angry over the child's having been exposed to such danger. The father said: "Now the temptation always is to say 'Oh, gee, don't tell mom we're doing this.'" In a few cases, parents alleged that their children were explicitly encouraged to be noncooperative or defiant. For example, a mother reported that the father returned a 4-year-old boy to his mother in a supermarket parking lot; the child showed signs of distress, and the father then goaded him into a full-scale temper tantrum and left the scene laughing while the mother attempted to deal with the screaming child in an embarrassing public situation.

Parents rarely report that they are called on to carry out or continue disciplinary measures instituted by the other parent, though this does occur. For example, one father of a dual-residence 16-year-old boy refused to let the boy drive his car until the boy had improved his grades; the father asked the mother to maintain this ban in her home as well. However, in most cases discipline appears to be handled independently in the two households, and the issue seems to be more a matter of trying to reach some agreement about what children are allowed or required to do in the two households rather than coordination of sanctions when infractions have occurred.

Perhaps the most common form of undermining was talking in derogatory terms about the other parent to the children. Non-custodial parents, in particular, complained about children being turned against them by the primary residential parent. In some cases, this derogation took the form of criticizing the other parent's life style or personality (for example, saying to a child: "Your mom needs to see a shrink"). In other cases, it was a matter of blaming the other parent for the divorce and its aftermath. A remarried father said:

Her whole thing has been to put the finger on me. I'm the one that left home, I'm the one that broke up the marriage. Your father doesn't love you because if he loved you he wouldn't have left us. She wanted Jimmy [age 15 at Time 3] not to come over to my house. She tried the same thing with little Maria, but Maria wouldn't allow it. Maria and my new wife get along just fine. But it's obvious that Maria has to be two different people. She has to show mom that when she's at my house she's not happy, because if she shows she's happy, she's letting her mom down.

In this family, the child was evidently discovering that deceiving one or both parents is one means of protection from the cross-fire between them. In other instances, parents report that children are explicitly encouraged by one parent to lie to the other.

Undermining was associated in some couples with what appeared to be deliberate efforts to upset the former partner emotionally. A mother of a 7-year-old son in dual residence reported:

He called me every day and either baited an argument or he'll start one and jump to some other subject so fast that you're emotionally spent before you can figure out what has happened. You're angry, of course, and upset. By the time you get off the phone and you haven't been able to say anything because your child is standing right there—it affects your own mood, so that your energy—he drains your energy on things that you shouldn't be using your energy on. All of a sudden you have a negativity about you that you didn't have before. Then it's very difficult then to deal with a child who is also demanding.

As Table 9.4 shows, parents were more likely at Time 3 than they had been at Times 1 and 2 to say that their former spouses were trying to avoid emotional upsets during encounters between the two parents. Nevertheless, there were still a substantial number who rated their former spouses at the low end of a 10-point scale on desire to avoid emotional upsets. And although a spouse who escalates the level of conflict may not intend to undermine the other parent's effectiveness, some parents report that it does in fact have that consequence.

Co-parenting Patterns

So far we have been discussing parental responses to a variety of specific questions about co-parenting. There are three basic strategies for dealing with the requirements for post-divorce parenting in families in which the children spend time in both households. Some parents handle their interpersonal conflict by avoidance and practice "parallel" parenting, making little or no effort to coordinate their child-rearing with each other. Other parents stay in contact with each other and their conflicts remain active, spilling over into the parenting domain. Still other parents suppress, mitigate, or insulate their conflicts and cooperate actively in their dealings concerning the children.

We identified families with these different co-parenting strategies in the following way. From among the questions discussed so far, a set of eight questions on co-parenting was selected. These items were those which had been asked at both Times 2 and 3 (seven items had identical wording; the eighth was closely comparable). Our objective in this analysis was to describe the co-parenting pattern that prevailed for a *couple,* rather than for individual mothers and fathers. To this end, it was necessary to merge the answers of the two parents when both had been interviewed.[9] For the items on amount of communication and coordination of rules, the two reports were averaged. For some of the items (such as those on undermining, quarreling, and logistical problems), when parents disagreed, the report of the parent describing the higher level of discord was entered as representing the discord level of the family. (Thus if either parent reported frequent argument, frequent logistical problems, or serious undermining, this was taken as an indication that these situations were indeed occurring, even if the other parent did not report them.)

After examining the intercorrelations among items,[10] we combined five items (by averaging) into a score on "Discord." A high score on this scale indicates that the parents often argued, that they undermined each other's parenting, and had a high incidence of logistical problems (see Table 9.13). In addition, three items were combined into a score on "Cooperative Communication" (see Table 9.13); on this scale, a high score indicates that the parents talked frequently about the children, did not avoid each other, and tried to coordinate rules and standards between the two households.

The two factor scores were then cross-classified.[11] At each time period, the scatter plot indicated that most of the cases were concentrated in three of the four quadrants, with one thinly populated quadrant. The most common patterns were the following three: high cooperative communication and low discord (henceforth labeled "Cooperative"); high discord and low cooperative communication (henceforth labeled "Conflicted"); and low discord with low cooperative communication (henceforth labeled "Disengaged"). The least common pattern was one we call "Mixed": these families had high cooperative communication combined with high discord. The frequency of the four patterns at Times 2 and 3 (for those families providing data at both

Table 9.13   Questions combined for co-parenting scores: Summary

---

FACTOR 1: DISCORD
  *Often argue
  Ex-spouse tries to upset respondent when they disagree
  One or both parents have refused to allow visitation (or threatened to do
    so)
  *High incidence of logistical problems in managing visitation, alternation
  *Ex-spouse undermines respondent's parenting
                    Range: 1–10, Alpha .69 (Time 3)

FACTOR 2: COOPERATIVE COMMUNICATION
  Parents talk frequently about children
  Parents try to coordinate rules in two households
  Neither parent tries to avoid contact with the other
                    Range: 1–10, Alpha .60 (Time 3)

---

*If both parents were interviewed and they differed, the more discordant score was
used.

times) is shown in Table 9.14. We remind the reader that in 26 percent
of the families at Time 2, and 30 percent at Time 3, the children did
not go back and forth between the two households. The figures in this
table, however, are based on the subsample of families whose children
were spending time in both parental households during regular portions
of the school year. Thus, when we use the label "disengaged," we do
not mean that either parent is disengaged from the children; rather,
we mean that the parents are disengaged from *each other,* and are not
maintaining a co-parental relationship except insofar as the children
serve as intermediaries. Table 9.14 shows that about a quarter of the
families whose children spent time in both households maintained a
cooperative pattern, and that there was little change in the incidence
of this pattern in our sample as a whole over the two years between
the Time 2 and Time 3 interviews. The incidence of the conflicted
pattern dropped from about a third to about a fourth, and the frequency
of disengagement increased. These changes reflect the fact that the
divorced parents talked to each other less as the time since their separation lengthened; and, perhaps as a consequence of less frequent contact, the frequency of argument also diminished.[12]

Table 9.14 shows frequencies of the co-parenting patterns at Times
2 and 3. Some change over time can be seen in these frequencies, but
the question still arises concerning how much shifting from one pattern
to another occurred over the two years between Time 2 and Time

3. Were there some parents who were not cooperative in the early post-separation period, but who were nevertheless able to develop a cooperative relationship over time? What happened to the co-parenting of couples who had a conflicted pattern at Time 2? Table 9.15 shows the families classified according to their Time 2 pattern, indicating what kind of pattern they displayed two years later.

We see first of all that the families who were conflicted at Time 2 were somewhat more likely to have had one parent drop out by Time 3. (As we indicated in Chapter 8, p. 193, these were balanced by a group of conflicted families in which visitation with non-residential parents had increased.) The families who had a cooperative pattern at Time 2 were least likely to experience the dropout of a parent. Also notable is the fact that families who had a conflicted pattern at Time 2 were very unlikely to shift to a cooperative pattern; usually, they either continued to be conflicted or became disengaged. Initially cooperative families seldom became conflicted—they either maintained their cooperative pattern, or became disengaged. The couples who were disengaged at Time 2—that is, were low in both conflict and communication—had a better chance of becoming cooperative than those who had been conflicted at Time 2.

Parental satisfaction with residential arrangements. At each interview, parents were asked to rate themselves (on a 10-point scale) with respect to their satisfaction with the amount of time the children were spending in each household. Dissatisfaction was more common among non-residential than residential parents. But regardless of whether they were the residential or the non-residential parent, we find that satisfac-

Table 9.14 Co-parenting patterns (percentage of families)[a]

Co-parenting pattern	Time 2	Time 3
Cooperative	26%	29%
Conflicted	34	26
Disengaged	29	41
Mixed	11	4
	100%	100%
	(N = 580)	(N = 499)

a. In families providing data at both T-2 and T-3 in which children spent time with both parents. The N is smaller at T-3 because there were fewer families at this time in which the children were still going back and forth between households during the school year.

Table 9.15   Changes in co-parenting pattern from Time 2 to Time 3[a]

	Pattern at Time 2			
	Low cooperative communication		High cooperative communication	
	Low discord (Disengaged) ($N = 167$)	High discord (Conflicted) ($N = 199$)	Low discord (Cooperative) ($N = 148$)	High discord (Mixed) ($N = 66$)
Coparenting pattern, T-3				
Cooperative	25.7%	8.5%	48.0%	22.7%
Conflicted	12.0	35.7	11.5	33.3
Disengaged	48.5	32.7	28.4	21.2
Mixed	1.2	4.5	4.0	6.1
No longer visiting	12.6	18.6	8.1	16.7
	100.0%	100.0%	100.0%	100.0%

a. For families in which children spent time in both households at Time 2.

tion levels were highest for both mothers and fathers when the couple were maintaining a cooperative relationship, and lowest when their co-parenting was conflicted. This was true at both Time 2 and Time 3.

What is less clear from these connections, however, is whether parents became more satisfied with their children's residence if they were able to co-parent cooperatively, or whether satisfaction with residential arrangements enabled parents to cooperate in their child-rearing. Multiple regressions predicting Time 3 co-parenting and satisfaction from Time 2 information indicate the following relationships: a cooperative co-parenting arrangement at Time 2 is associated with increases in satisfaction with the residential arrangement over time (between Time 2 and Time 3). However, satisfaction with the children's residence at Time 2 did not increase the chances that co-parenting would become more cooperative during the interval between Time 2 and Time 3. Thus it was successful co-parenting that enhanced satisfaction with residential arrangements, not vice versa.

Factors Associated with the Co-parenting Patterns

Children's residence. It might be expected that the cooperative pattern would be more common in those families in which the children's time was most equally divided between the two households—the dual-residence families. As Table 9.16 shows, the proportion with a cooperative pattern was in fact higher, but the difference was not statistically significant. When we compared the three residential groups on the two measures from which the co-parenting patterns were derived, we found that dual-residence families were indeed higher on cooperative communication, but not lower on discord. It is worth noting, though, that it was only among the dual-residence families with a single child that higher cooperative communication was found.

The primary meaning of Table 9.16 is that the kind of co-parenting pattern that families maintained at Time 3 depended very little on where the children were living. (This was also true at Time 2, for which data are not shown.) There was considerable variation within each residential group with respect to the kind of co-parenting the divorced couple maintained at Time 3. This was true at Time 2 as well. As the table shows, even in dual-residence families, more than a third were disengaged, and approximately the same proportion (one-fourth) were conflicted, in each of the residential arrangements. It is striking that the rate of conflicted parenting is so high among families with dual residence at Time 3, considering that high legal conflict families are less likely to maintain dual residence even if their divorce decrees specify joint physical custody.

Demographic factors. The quality of co-parenting is not related to the socioeconomic level of the family, but it is related to the ages or number of the children. We examined the relation of our co-parenting scores to the education and earnings of the mother and father, and to family size and the ages of the youngest and oldest children. The quality of co-parenting was related neither to the families' economic re-

Table 9.16   Relation of co-parenting patterns to children's residence[a]

	Children's residence at Time 3		
	With mother (N = 367)	With both parents (N = 153)	With father (N = 86)
Co-parenting pattern, T-3			
Cooperative	28.9%	36.6%	25.6%
Conflicted	27.8	24.2	24.4
Disengaged	39.8	35.9	45.4
Mixed	3.5	3.3	4.6
	100.0%	100.0%	100.0%

a. Table based on families in which children spent time in both households at Time 3.

sources, nor to the father's education. There was a tendency for cooperation to be higher, and conflict lower, when the mothers were better educated.[13]

The ages and number of the children were of greater significance. Parents with older children were more likely to be disengaged, even when the children spent time in both households. We suppose that parents find it more necessary to communicate with each other in making arrangements for children when the children are young; for children of grade-school age or older, parents may have found that they could rely on the children to carry messages or to negotiate their own arrangements with the other parent. Also, as we saw earlier, parents of younger children were more often concerned about the child's well-being in the other parent's household; perhaps they did not disengage because of feeling the need to remain vigilant on the child's behalf. Whatever the reason, parents of preschool or kindergarten-aged children do have more frequent negotiations with each other about the children than do the parents of older children, and there is a higher incidence of conflict among them, though not a higher level of cooperation.

The larger the family, the more likely the parents were to be conflicted, and the less likely to be cooperative. Indeed, *half* the families with three or more children were involved in a conflicted co-parenting pattern at Time 2 (this had dropped to a third two years later). The effects of family size and children's age are essentially independent,[14] but they do combine, so that the highest incidence of a conflicted interparental pattern was found in families with three or more children where at least one of the children was still of preschool age. We interpret these findings to mean that co-parental conflict is sparked (at least in part) by the greater amounts of parental investment (effort) required when children are young or families large; the more difficult the total parenting task, the more difficulty separated parents have in allocating the parental responsibilities.

Parental hostility. In our early chapters, we noted that a crucial question for policymakers and practitioners dealing with divorce has been whether couples who have been in sufficient conflict to divorce each other nevertheless can manage to do business together in raising children jointly after they have separated. This inquiry is complicated by the fact that parents differ considerably in how much hostility they harbor (or, at least, express) toward the former spouse. The post-interview hostility ratings made by our interviewers (described in Chapter 7) ranged from very low to very high. So we now ask whether the amount of hostility expressed by either mothers or fathers (or both) is related to their ability to adopt a cooperative co-parenting pattern subsequently.

As Table 9.17 shows, the amount of hostility expressed by mothers and fathers at Time 1 bore a close relationship to their co-parenting pattern at Time 2. Among mothers expressing high levels of hostility at Time 1, only 16 percent were in a cooperative co-parental relationship with their ex-spouses at Time 2, whereas 56 percent were in a conflicted relationship. Very similar results pertain to highly hostile fathers. These figures stand in marked contrast to the situation for parents who expressed little hostility at Time 1: they were much more likely to be in a cooperative rather than a conflicted relationship at Time 2. A highly similar pattern of results may be seen in the prediction of Time 3 co-parenting patterns from Time 2 hostility—a prediction that spans a two-year time period.

The period immediately following parental separation—a time when negotiations over the terms of the divorce are going on for many couples—is well known to be a time when emotions run high. One or both parents may be extremely angry, and feel betrayed or jealous; for many couples violent quarrels, sometimes accompanied by physical abuse, marked the breakup. Over time, there is generally some cooling of these emotions. In our own sample, there was a drop of about one point on the ten-point hostility scale over the three-year period of our interviews, with most of the drop occurring between Time 1 and Time 2. We have seen that couples who are highly conflicted at one time period are unlikely to be cooperative at the next time period. It is of some interest, however, to investigate how long the effect of initial hostility lasts. Mediators and attorneys who work with couples during the immediate post-separation period may wonder whether couples who are highly hostile at that time will be able to co-parent cooperatively at a later time, or whether the parents' initial hostility sets up negative patterns of interaction in their dealings about the children that persist despite changes that may take place in their hostility levels. We had only three time periods to examine this question. We approached it by asking whether Time 1 hostility had any relation to Time 3 co-parenting, after the effects of Time 2 hostility have been controlled. Our answer is a modified "yes." Most of the variance in the amount of co-parental discord at Time 3 is accounted for by Time 2 hostility (which is itself quite strongly related to Time 1 hostility), but there remains a modest contribution[15] of Time 1 hostility to co-parental discord at Time 3, over and above the effect of Time 2 hostility. Thus, even for parents whose anger cooled between Time 1

Table 9.17 Relation between mothers' and fathers' hostility toward each other and their subsequent co-parenting pattern[a]

| | Mother's hostility, Time 1 | | |
	Low (N = 121)	Medium (N = 186)	High (N = 135)
Co-parenting pattern, T-2			
Cooperative	36%	28%	16%
Conflicted	16	31	56
Disengaged	36	29	21
Mixed	12	12	7
	100%	100%	100%

| | Father's hostility, Time 1 | | |
	Low (N = 114)	Medium (N = 128)	High (N = 107)
Co-parenting pattern, T-2			
Cooperative	40%	25%	18%
Conflicted	17	28	56
Disengaged	35	31	17
Mixed	8	16	9
	100%	100%	100%

| | Mother's hostility, Time 2 | | |
	Low (N = 195)	Medium (N = 141)	High (N = 155)
Co-parenting pattern, T-3			
Cooperative	46%	33%	11%
Conflicted	15	23	47
Disengaged	38	40	36
Mixed	1	4	6
	100%	100%	100%

| | Father's hostility, Time 2 | | |
	Low (N = 159)	Medium (N = 135)	High (N = 99)
Co-parenting pattern, T-3			
Cooperative	44%	24%	16%
Conflicted	18	29	40
Disengaged	36	42	39
Mixed	2	5	5
	100%	100%	100%

a. At each time period, interviewers rated each parent on a 10-point scale of hostility toward the former spouse. Ratings 1–4 are in the "low" group; 5–6 are "medium"; 7–10 in the "high" group. There were no interviewer ratings for the respondents who provided only mail information; hence the N is somewhat smaller at T-1 than at T-2.

and Time 2, subsequent support for each other's parenting was not restored to the level found among couples who were initially less angry.

Legal conflict. In Chapter 7, we saw that although parental hostility and legal conflict were related, they were by no means the same thing. We now explore the relationship between legal battling and a couple's ability to cooperate in co-parenting. Figure 9.1 shows that there is a close connection. In investigating whether legal conflict makes an independent contribution to co-parenting conflict, over and above the effects of interparental hostility, we once again used multiple regression. We found that the amount of co-parental discord reported at Time 2 is strongly related to the amount of legal conflict, after the effects of the mother's and father's Time 1 hostility have been controlled. As far as co-parenting at Time 3 is concerned, the effects of legal conflict, though still significant, have diminished somewhat.[16]

Although legal conflict makes an additional contribution to co-parental discord, parental hostility continues to have an effect even after the effects of legal conflict have been accounted for. Thus, even when hostile parents do not carry on their battle in the legal arena, they still find it difficult to do business together as parents. It does not matter which parent harbors the more intense hostility as far as co-parenting at Time 2 is concerned—the hostility of both parents is significant at this time—but two years later there is a difference: the mother's Time-2 hostility is strongly related to the amount of interparental discord at Time 3, whereas the father's Time-2 hostility is not. At first glance, this might appear to mean that mothers hold grudges longer, but this is not the best explanation, since the mean levels of hostility of the two parents at Time 2 are very similar. What appears to be the case is that *if* mothers are hostile, this affects the chances of cooperative parenting, while it matters less if fathers are equally hostile, in terms of co-parenting.

Co-parenting by parents awarded joint physical custody. We saw in Chapter 5 that a substantial group of parents had been awarded joint physical custody despite the fact that this was not the first choice of one or both parents. The 85 families in our study that were awarded joint physical custody and for which we have co-parenting information at Time 2 are divided as follows with respect to what they had wanted:

29 cases: both wanted joint custody

39 cases: one wanted joint, the other wanted sole custody

17 cases: each wanted sole custody

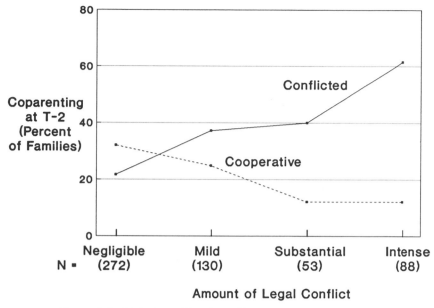

Figure 9.1 Relation of legal conflict to co-parenting styles.

Among the small group in which each parent had wanted sole custody, 65 percent were conflicted in their co-parenting, and only 6 percent were cooperative. By contrast, in the subgroup in which both had wanted joint custody, only 24 percent were conflicted and 45 percent were cooperative. The families in which only one parent had wanted joint custody were intermediate (23 percent cooperative).[17] We can see, then, that an award of joint physical custody in and of itself does not create cooperative co-parenting. Indeed, the prognosis for cooperation is very poor when both parents are initially opposed.

Discrepant perceptions of pre-separation involvement with children. We saw in Chapter 7 that when parents held different views concerning their relative roles in caring for the children before the separation, they were more likely to engage in legal conflict. To a degree, they were also more likely to be in conflict in the co-parenting realm. Although parents who agreed about their pre-separation roles did not differ in their co-parenting patterns from those who had small or moderate discrepancies, the most discrepant group were more likely to be conflicted, and less likely to be cooperative, than other families.

Parents' concerns about each other's households. Earlier we described the kinds of concerns parents had about their children spending

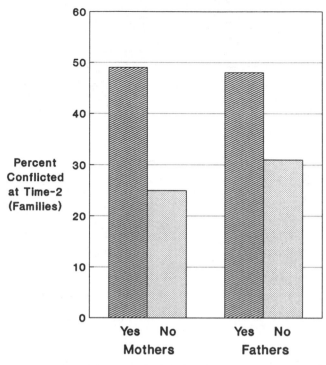

Figure 9.2 Conflicted co-parenting in relation to parents' concerns about the other household.

time in the other parent's household. Figure 9.2 shows that there is a connection between such concerns and a couple's ability to cooperate and co-parent. When parents expressed concerns at Time 1, they were considerably less likely to be co-parenting cooperatively, and more likely to have a conflicted pattern, at Time 2. The Time-1 concerns were also significantly related to co-parenting at Time 3, three and a half years later, though the relation is less strong than that seen in Figure 9.2. Perhaps all we are seeing is that parents who are in conflict at one time are likely to be so at a later time. We have seen that hostility toward the former spouse spills over into the co-parental relationship, and we must ask whether distrusting the former spouse's parenting is simply a reflection of this general hostility, or whether it represents an additional element that disrupts cooperative co-parenting. Multivariate analysis indicates that parental distrust of the other parent's child-rearing environment—in this case particularly the *mother's* distrust—makes an independent contribution to co-parental conflict, over and above the hostility of the two parents. In short, when a mother believes that the father is not an adequate parent, it is difficult for the parents to cooperate in post-separation child-rearing, regardless of how much hostility they harbor toward each other.

Parents' new relationships. Over the three years of our study, many parents were in the process of establishing new relationships. As noted in Chapter 8, at Times 2 and 3 we asked the parents whether they had remarried, and if not, whether they were involved in a serious relationship. Their replies were coded on a four-point scale ranging from not dating, to dating occasionally or casually but not yet committed to any individual, to being seriously involved (including now living with the new partner and/or planning to remarry), to remarriage. As Table 9.18 shows, when either the mother or the father established a new relationship, the parents were more frequently disengaged, even in those families where the children continued to spend time in both households. In addition, cooperation declined and conflict increased when either parent was in the process of acquiring a new partner.

The drop-off in cooperation appears to occur somewhat earlier in the repartnering process for fathers than for mothers. That is, when fathers have begun casual dating, the decline in cooperation and the upswing in conflicted or disengaged co-parenting patterns begins. By contrast, it is only when mothers have developed a serious new relationship that her repartnering appears to affect the co-parenting pattern.

Summary Comment

In Chapter 2 we predicted that fathers and mothers would encounter somewhat different kinds of difficulties if and when they became single parents. This turned out to be true, but only to a moderate extent. Both sole mothers and sole fathers—as well as parents whose children were in joint residence—reported relatively few problems in carrying out the daily functions of parenting and household management. And although a minority did say that the separation had made it harder to raise the children as they would wish to, the majority said (at Time 1) that it was now easier. Fathers were somewhat more likely than mothers to report difficulty with monitoring their children's whereabouts, activities, and school progress. Mothers, for their part, reported more difficulty than fathers in remaining firm and patient. These differences, though small, are significant, and we believe they reflect the different parental roles typically carried out by each parent before the separation.

The primary focus of this chapter has been on the way the co-parental relationship is constructed and managed between the couples whose children are spending time in both households—a substantial majority of the families in our study. This includes the families with nearly equal time-sharing (dual residence) as well as those in which the children live primarily with one parent but visit the other parent during regular portions of the school year. It is clear from the experience of these families that it is not an easy matter for separated parents to do business with each other in carrying out joint parental responsibilities. With the best will in the world, a parent may still find it onerous to

Table 9.18 Relation of Time 3 co-parenting pattern to mothers' and fathers' establishment of new relationships[a]

	Mother's reaffiliation, Time 3			
	Not dating (N = 101)	Casual dating (N = 125)	Serious relationship (N = 204)	Remarried (N = 161)
Co-parenting pattern, T-3				
Cooperative	37.6%	39.2%	25.0%	26.7%
Conflicted	21.8	22.4	28.4	31.1
Disengaged	33.7	34.4	44.1	39.7
Mixed	6.9	4.0	2.5	2.5
	100.0%	100.0%	100.0%	100.0%
	Father's reaffiliation, Time 3			
	Not dating (N = 99)	Casual dating (N = 163)	Serious relationship (N = 171)	Remarried (N = 157)
Co-parenting pattern, T-3				
Cooperative	46.5%	29.5%	31.0%	20.4%
Conflicted	16.2	27.6	26.3	32.5
Disengaged	33.3	38.6	39.2	44.6
Mixed	4.0	4.3	3.5	2.5
	100.0%	100.0%	100.0%	100.0%

Chi^2 for mothers: 18.0, $p \leq .05$; for fathers: 22.6, $p \leq .01$.
a. Based on families in which children were spending time in both households at Time 3.

drive children back and forth between households, to negotiate with the other parent about schedules or child-related decisions, or to adapt his or her own schedule to the comings and goings of the children.

Only about a quarter of our families appeared to be able to cooperate effectively. These parents were able to subordinate their spousal conflict and to cooperate in managing the children's lives and protecting their welfare. Another substantial group of parents were not able to insulate the parental realm from their general state of conflict. They fought over the management of the children's lives and undermined each other's parenting. The third most common strategy for dealing with post-separation parental responsibilities was disengagement, with the parents avoiding contact with each other and practicing "parallel," uncoordinated parenting in the two households. A small group of parents attempted initially to maintain coordination while at the same time engaging in conflict and undermining, but this pattern tended to disappear with time. Our data indicate that it is more difficult for parents to sustain a cooperative relationship—and more likely that they will be in conflict over the children—if their children are quite young, or if they have more than one child. We infer that whatever family circumstances make child-rearing more difficult will exacerbate parental conflict and reduce the chances of successful post-divorce cooperation. We do not know how far this principle extends, however, since we have found that low income—surely a stressful condition for child-rearing—does *not* in and of itself increase post-separation conflict between parents.

Predictably, parents who expressed intense hostility toward each other seldom proved to be able to cooperate as co-parents as time went on. If they had been involved in a legal struggle over custody or visitation, their chances of cooperation were further reduced. When joint physical custody had been awarded contrary to the wishes of one or both parents, cooperation was also unlikely.

Many parents cited worries about their children's welfare in the other parent's household, and expressed frustration over not being able to do anything about what they perceived as potentially harmful conditions. As we listened to these parental complaints, they sometimes seemed to reflect incompatible values, where it was not clear which parent would be providing the more beneficial environment. In other cases, parents provided convincing details that made us believe that their worries were well founded. Earlier we noted that in two-parent families, parents act as "buffers" for each other, shielding the children from the other parent's inadequacies (whether short-term or long-term). It is hardly possible for divorced parents to provide this buffering while the child is at the other parent's household.

We assessed co-parenting at both Time 2 and Time 3. During the two-year time span between the assessments, we found that the frequency of cooperative parenting increased slightly, while conflicting parenting diminished and disengagement increased. As time went on, parents tended to reduce their efforts to coordinate child-rearing standards between the two households. They also talked to each other less, especially if either had remarried. In families where the children were spending time in both households, no increase in the difficulty of maintaining visitation schedules was reported, despite the clear drop in communication between parents that occurred over time. It would appear that parents can maintain their children's contact with the other parent without having to talk to each other. However, certain aspects of active cooperation in parenting do require communication (for example, coordination of rules and standards), and these are the functions that tend to diminish with time.

We regard it as good news that conflicted co-parenting gives way to disengaged parallel parenting. The follow-up study of the adolescent children of our sample families indicates that when parents maintained a cooperative co-parental relationship at Time 3, their children were relatively unlikely to experience the distress of being caught up in the parental conflict a year later (Buchanan, Maccoby, and Dornbusch, 1991). The families in the disengaged group were intermediate between the cooperative and conflicted co-parenting groups in the likelihood of the adolescents' being caught in the middle between parents. Predictably, the children of conflicted parents were most at risk of being caught in the conflict. It is significant that those adolescents who did feel caught in parental conflict showed more symptoms of maladjustment (for example, depression, deviant behavior) than those who did not. Thus, if initially conflicted parents became disengaged over time, this was probably beneficial for the children.

If parents were initially conflicted, there was little chance that they would become cooperative with time. On the other hand, if they were initially disengaged, they stood a good chance of becoming cooperative. We conclude that the existence of initial overt conflict and angry communication weakens or wipes out the chances that parents will be able to do business together effectively at a later time when anger has cooled. Our findings suggest that if parents cannot initially cooperate, they can keep the door open for later improvements in co-parenting by initially reducing communication.

10

Economic Changes over Time

We demonstrated earlier that the initial pattern of child and spousal support awards is highly gendered. The vast majority of custodial mothers in our study received child support, while fewer than half of custodial fathers did so. Similarly, 30 percent of mothers but only one father in our sample received a spousal support award. These discrepancies, in the main, reflect fathers' much higher incomes. We saw that while most custodial mothers received support, the amounts awarded constituted only a minor fraction of their post-divorce family income, and the standard of living for these mothers and their children dropped sharply immediately after divorce.

This chapter examines changes in the economic status of divorced spouses during the several years following their separation. In particular, we investigate whether and how compliance with support obligations varies over time. Much recent literature has focused on the problem of fathers' noncompliance with support orders.[1] How many fathers fail to pay support—or pay only part of the support awarded? What factors affect compliance behavior? As discussed in Chapter 8, residence and visitation patterns in many families change substantially in the years after the divorce has become final. Do support payment patterns bear any relationship to these changes? If so, does partial compliance reflect informal, amicable agreements between divorced spouses, or unilateral strategic behavior by fathers in high-conflict families?

We also investigate whether the economic position of custodial mothers improves in the years following the divorce. How do the employment status and the earnings of divorced women change over time? When divorced mothers remarry, how does this affect their economic position? Most important, how do custodial mothers fare relative to non-custodial fathers? Does the gap between the post-divorce household incomes of the two groups narrow?

Patterns of Child Support Compliance

In our analysis of child support compliance, we included only those families with child support awarded to the mother. As discussed in Chapter 6, 89 percent of mothers in mother physical/mother legal custody families, 96 percent of mothers in mother physical/joint legal custody families, and 67 percent of mothers in joint physical custody families—a total of 88 percent of these families—received such awards. In our Time 2 and Time 3 interviews, we asked these mothers how much child support per month their decrees awarded and how much they actually received.

We found that, on average, fathers pay between two-thirds and three-quarters of the child support awarded. Moreover, our data suggest that compliance with child support obligations falls over time. At Time 2, the mean compliance rate (defined as the ratio of support paid to support awarded) for families with final divorce decrees at that time was .81; by Time 3, their compliance rate had dropped to .69.[2] The group who completed their divorces between Times 2 and 3 had a compliance rate of .72 at Time 3, and we may surmise that their rate, too, would drop during the ensuing year. Table 10.1 shows that at Time 3 somewhat more than half of the fathers who owed child support

Table 10.1 Child support compliance status at Time 2 and Time 3 by date of divorce[a]

	Divorced by Time 2		Divorced by Time 3
	Compliance at Time 2	Compliance at Time 3	Compliance at Time 3
Zero (%)	14.7	23.0	17.6
Partial (%)	15.7	19.8	25.9
Full (%)	69.6	57.1	56.5
Mean compliance ratio	.807	.692	.724
	($N = 217$)	($N = 217$)	($N = 108$)

a. Sample includes only one-child families with positive child support awarded to the mother.

Table 10.2 Cross-frequency of child support compliance status at Time 2 by compliance status at Time 3[a]

	Compliance status at Time 3			
	Zero (%)	Partial (%)	Full (%)	Sample size
Compliance status at Time 2				
Zero (%)	53.1	25.0	21.9	32
Partial (%)	20.6	26.5	52.9	34
Full (%)	17.2	17.2	65.6	151

Note: Rows may not sum to 100 because of rounding.

a. Sample consists of one-child families with positive child support awarded to the mothers who were divorced by Time 2.

were paying the full amount; about a quarter were paying part of what they owed, and the remainder paid no support at all.

We also examined whether individual fathers exhibit consistent levels of compliance over time, or whether their levels of compliance vary. It appears that there is considerable mobility in compliance status. As Table 10.2 demonstrates, nearly half of those fathers who were noncompliant at Time 2 became partially or fully compliant by Time 3. Conversely, about 35 percent of those who were fully compliant at Time 2 were only partially compliant or noncompliant by Time 3.

Factors Related to Support Compliance

Child support. There are two categories of reasons for noncompliance or partial compliance with child support obligations: the father might be *unable* to pay all or part of the award specified in the decree, or he might simply be *unwilling* to comply with the award. Clearly, unwillingness to pay might stem from a lack of involvement with the children; some researchers have also hypothesized that noncompliance occurs when the father feels that he lacks sufficient information or control concerning how the child support payments will be spent (Weiss and Willis, 1985). Both points of view suggest that compliance behavior is related to the amount of contact between the father and his children. Finally, still others have suggested that compliance with support obligations represents the result of ongoing bargaining between the parent who controls access to the children and the parent who controls support (Mnookin and Kornhauser, 1979). According to this theory, compliance behavior should be correlated with the degree of conflict between divorced parents.

To assess the extent to which noncompliance with child support obligations is a function of inability to pay, we examined compliance rates in conjunction with the employment status of the fathers in our sample. Figure 10.1 shows that unemployed fathers were three times more likely than employed fathers to pay no child support. More than half of employed fathers but fewer than one-third of unemployed fathers were in full compliance with child support obligations. It seems clear, then, that unemployment lowers compliance.

Figure 10.2 depicts mean compliance rates according to the level of contact between fathers and children in families which have been awarded either mother or joint physical custody. Fathers who had no regular contact with their children had a mean compliance rate of just

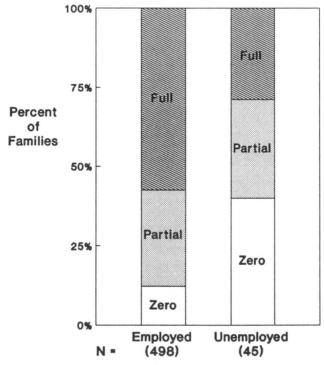

Figure 10.1   Child support compliance at Time 3, by father's employment status (includes families with either mother or joint physical custody in which fathers were ordered to pay child support to the mother; $N = 543$).

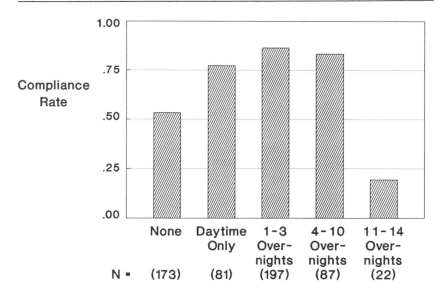

Figure 10.2   Child support compliance at Time 3 by father's contact with children.

under 52 percent. Compliance levels increased sharply for fathers who had daytime visits with their children, and rates for fathers with overnight visits or dual residence were slightly higher (but not significantly so) than for fathers who had only daytime visits. In the 22 families in which physical custody had been awarded to the mother or to both parents jointly but in which the children were actually living with the father, the father seldom paid the child support that had been ordered.

This finding draws our attention to the fact that some of the changes in children's residence documented in Chapter 8 must have been accompanied by changes in the arrangements for financial support. We compared compliance rates for families that reported no change in the custodial arrangement originally specified, families in which the children spent more time with their father than originally agreed, and families in which the children spent less time with their father than originally agreed. As Figure 10.3 shows, zero or partial compliance is most likely to occur when the custodial arrangement has been changed so that the children spend more time living in the father's household. Thus it seems that when fathers incur additional costs because their

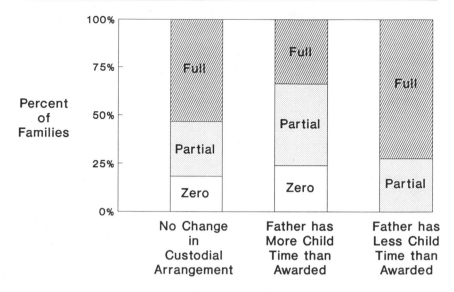

Changes in Custodial Arrangement

Figure 10.3   Child support compliance at Time 3 by changes in the custodial arrangement.

children are spending more time in their households, they may arrange to contribute less child support to the mother's household than originally specified. Conversely, when the children spend less time with their father than originally agreed, fathers are more likely (or more willing?) to pay the full amount of child support.

We conducted regression analysis of child support compliance levels to examine the joint impact of a number of potential explanatory factors (see Table 10.3). As a first step, we measured compliance as the ratio of the amount paid to the amount specified in the divorce decree. We found that the most important predictor of child support compliance was the father's employment status; unemployment decreased the percentage of child support paid by almost 25 percentage points. The father's education was also a strong predictor of child support compliance: a college education increased the compliance rate by nearly 11 percentage points. The father's earnings, on the other hand, had no significant effect on compliance independent of education and employment status, and therefore we did not include the father's earnings in the regression.

Table 10.3 OLS regressions of child support compliance at Time 3[a]

	Compliance with legal agreement[b]	Compliance with informal agreement[c]
Constant	0.790*	0.925*
(*t*-statistic)	(16.50)	(15.41)
Father unemployed[d]	−0.247*	−0.165*
	(3.84)	(2.05)
Father college graduate[d]	0.108*	0.105*
	(3.03)	(2.34)
High conflict during negotiation[d]	−0.066†	−0.057
	(1.70)	(1.17)
Joint legal custody[d]	0.045	0.011
	(0.98)	(0.20)
Father has less time than court award[d]	0.123*	−0.087
	(2.14)	(1.21)
Father has more time than court award[d]	−0.162*	−0.110
	(3.03)	(1.63)
Father without contact[d]	−0.163*	−0.188*
	(3.97)	(3.65)
Father remarried[d]	−0.049	−0.053
	(1.36)	(1.16)
Mother remarried[d]	−0.013	−0.035
	(0.37)	(0.76)
R^2	0.17	0.10
	(N = 400)	(N = 400)

† $p \leq .10$.
* $p \leq .05$.

a. Samples are restricted to families where the mother has either joint or sole physical custody and the divorce is final by the third interview. The child support award is taken from the court record. Cases where the mother is required to pay child support are dropped from this analysis. Unless indicated, all time-varying variables are measured as of the Time 3 interview.

b. Compliance is defined as the amount of child support received divided by the amount of the court award. Mother's and father's reports are averaged if they report different amounts.

c. The informal compliance rate reflects formal and informal changes in the agreement about child support payments. Parents were asked if a change in child support was agreed upon. If so, we adjust the legal compliance ratio to reflect full compliance (that is, the informal compliance ratio = 1).

d. Defined as a dichotomous variable equal to 1 if the individual has the characteristic, otherwise equal to 0.

As expected, the level of contact between the father and his children was also a strong predictor of child support compliance, even after other factors were accounted for. Compliance rates for fathers who had no regular contact with their children were lower by approximately 16 percentage points. Fathers who had *more* custodial responsibility for the children than originally specified in the divorce decree also had significantly lower compliance rates (reflecting mainly the small group of families with mother or joint custody decrees in which children were actually living with the father). In families in which the mother had more custodial responsibility than originally specified, but in which the fathers were maintaining contact, fathers had somewhat higher compliance rates.

If fathers are paying less than the amount specified in the divorce decree because of a change in the agreement, however, the ratio of support paid to support awarded would be an inaccurate measure of compliance. In our Time 3 interviews, we asked parents if there had been any modifications to the initial terms of the divorce agreement. We determined that divorced spouses had made post-divorce modifications in between 15 and 30 percent of our sample families, and that more than 80 percent of these modifications were negotiated and adopted informally rather than through the legal system. Accordingly, we estimated a second regression of child support compliance, taking into account reported modifications.[3] Significantly, the mean adjusted compliance rate for the fathers in our sample was 76 percent, compared with an unadjusted compliance rate of 71 percent.

When compliance rates were adjusted to reflect modifications of the agreement, the father's unemployment decreased the level of compliance by only 16 percentage points. This result suggests that prolonged unemployment leads some families to adopt informal changes in their child support agreements. The father's education remained a significant predictor of child support compliance in the adjusted regression; a college degree increased the level of compliance by 10 percentage points.

As in the unadjusted regression, fathers who had no regular contact with their children had lower compliance rates, approximately 19 percent lower than fathers who did have regular contact. However, the impact of the variables measuring change from the original custody and visitation arrangement dropped sharply. Fathers who had had a change in the custodial arrangement no longer differed significantly from other fathers in their compliance patterns. These results indicate that while reduced support payments in some cases reflect an informal

modification of the agreement between the parties, increases in a father's contact with his children are likely to help sustain his support
payments even in the absence of such an agreement.

Other variables that might affect contact—the remarriage of either
parent, the existence of a joint legal custody arrangement, and the
distance between the two parents' households—had no significant impact on either adjusted or unadjusted levels of compliance. Compliance
with child support obligations was also unrelated to the duration of the
marriage. Most important, we found no relationship between conflict
over custody during negotiation of the divorce agreement and subsequent compliance with child support obligations.

Spousal support. We conducted similar regression analyses of spousal support compliance patterns. As with child support, the father's
unemployment was a strong predictor of decreased spousal support
compliance; however, the correlation became smaller and less significant when we adjusted compliance rates to reflect reported modifications in the spousal support agreement. The duration of the marriage,
which may affect willingness to pay, was a significant predictor of
spousal support compliance in both unadjusted and adjusted regressions: compliance increased by almost 1.5 percent for each year of
marriage. Finally, both regressions revealed a strong correlation between compliance with child support obligations and compliance with
spousal support obligations.

Changes in Economic Well-being

After separation, each parent's earnings were, of course, lower than
their combined earnings had been before the separation. However, as
we saw in Chapter 6, the drop was much sharper for women than men.
Indeed, if one takes into account the fact that most fathers had only
themselves to support, while the mothers' households usually included
both themselves and the children, fathers could be said to be better
off following the separation than they were before, while mothers were
much worse off. Does this disparity persist, or do the economic situations of divorced mothers and fathers converge over time? In our Time
2 and Time 3 interviews, we explored the effects of changes in employment status and earnings, child support paid or received, and remarriage on divorced spouses' economic well-being.

Employment status. Table 10.4 shows that among divorced and separated women, both employment rates and earnings increased. Nearly
three-fourths of the women in the sample were already working before

Table 10.4 Changes in economic circumstances over time

	Mother				Father			
	Before separation	Time 1	Time 2	Time 3	Before separation	Time 1	Time 2	Time 3
Employed (%)								
All women/men	72.9	80.1	85.0	82.2	94.6	90.0	90.4	92.1
Remarried[a]	—	—	75.5	73.1				
Not remarried	—	—	87.0	85.4				
Yearly earnings, if employed[b]								
All women/men	$15,535	$18,000	$19,456	$21,596	$32,106	$34,800	$37,307	$37,887
Remarried	—	—	18,378	20,838				
Not remarried	—	—	19,635	22,066				
Earnings, all women/men	$10,357	$15,600	$16,690	$18,944	$31,070	$32,000	$34,361	$36,940
Hours per week, if employed								
All women/men	41.5	42.5	42.5	40.0	45.0	45.0	45.0	45.0
Remarried	—	—	42.5	40.0				
Not remarried	—	—	42.5	40.0				
Any welfare received (%)[c]								
All women/men	—	8.8	7.2		—	4.5	7.0	—
Remarried	—	—	—					
Not remarried	—	—	7.9					
Remarried (%)	—	—	8.2	27.3	—	—	7.8	28.2

Note: This table is based on the 705 families in which either the father or the mother was interviewed at 3 time periods. Sample size varies for each cell.

a. Figures at Time 2 reflect the group who were remarried at Time 2. Time 3 figures are based on the group who were remarried at Time 3.

b. Earnings are expressed in 1985 dollars. Median earnings and hours are reported.

c. Time 1 and Time 2 indicate receipt of government assistance at the time of the survey. The definition of welfare receipt was changed in the Time 3 interview, and therefore is not reported in this table.

the separation, but by Time 3 an additional group had gone to work, increasing the proportion working from 73 percent to 82 percent approximately four years later. Median working hours changed very little, however.[4] Median yearly earnings for those mothers who were working increased (in 1985 dollars) by more than a third—from $15,535 just before separation to $21,596 by Time 3. By contrast, the divorced fathers in our sample initially decreased their employment rates slightly. Prior to divorce, almost 95 percent of the fathers in the sample were employed; by Time 1, approximately six months after the initial separation, the employment rate for fathers was 90 percent. By Time 3, however, the employment rate for our sample fathers had partially recovered—to 92 percent. The median yearly earnings of employed fathers increased by about 20 percent following the divorce.

Table 10.4 further reveals that although divorced mothers on average substantially increased their annual earnings, by Time 3 the median annual earnings of employed mothers in our sample ($21,596) were still only about 60 percent of the median annual earnings of fathers ($37,887), and if one takes into account the fact that fewer mothers were employed, the discrepancy is even greater.

Comparison of earnings, however, does not take into account the fact that money was being transferred from one household to the other. In most families, the father was ordered to pay support to the mother; in a few families with father custody, it was the other way around. We added to each parent's earnings the amount of any support awarded to that parent, and subtracted the amount of any support the parent was required to pay. The results may be seen in Figure 10.4. When support payments were factored in (even with the assumption that the amounts of support awarded would be paid in full), the gap between the economic well-being of mothers and that of fathers narrowed only slightly. The drop in income from pre-separation levels was nearly twice as great for mothers as for fathers, and the discrepancy remained nearly this great through the three-year period following our first interview.

To obtain a clearer picture of how the economic well-being of each parent compared to the pre-separation situation, we first calculated the income of each (defined as earnings plus or minus support awards). We also needed to take account of the differences in family size between the two parental households, since the fathers had fewer people to support, on average, than did the mothers.[5] Figure 10.5 shows the adjusted ratios; we can now see that at Time 1, fathers were significantly better off than they had been before the divorce, and remained

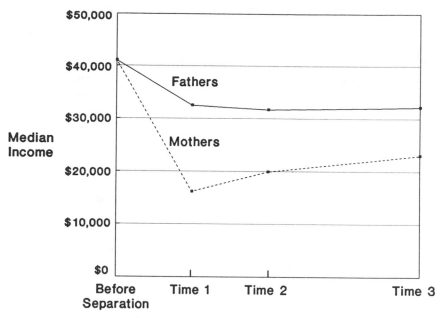

Figure 10.4 Changes in median family income over time: mother versus father. (Income consists of earnings plus or minus court awards.)

so through the following three years. Mothers, on the other hand, had only about half the resources of their former family, and increased their relative standing only gradually, so that by Time 3 they still had only about two-thirds of the resources they had had before the separation.

It is important to note that these calculations do not take into account several potentially significant factors. First, we do not have information on possible sources of income other than earnings. In particular, we did not include welfare payments, non-earned income, and income from other household members—the children or a new live-in partner. Our calculations thus overestimate the decline in well-being for mothers and underestimate the increase in well-being for fathers. Second, Figure 10.5 is based on the amounts of child and spousal support awarded, not the amount actually paid, and this would lead to some overstatement of the well-being of mothers (and some understatement for fathers), since we know that many fathers do not comply fully with the awards. Finally, the amount added to mothers' income for money received as support payments from the fathers is somewhat too low at Time 1. At that time, few divorces were final; however, some money was no doubt paid by fathers on an informal, interim basis pending the divorce.

Components of the economic well-being of custodial mothers. Figure 10.6 gives a more detailed picture of the mothers' situation relative to their pre-separation family income, and shows the components of their economic situation at each of the three time periods of our study. In this figure we consider the unadjusted earnings of mothers (all mothers, regardless of whether they have custody of the children) and the money actually received in child and spousal support. We also show the magnitude of the adjustment for family size. (This adjustment makes the mother better off, since her income does not have to cover as large a household as the couple's joint income covered before the

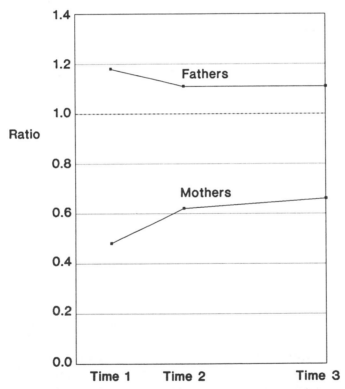

Figure 10.5   Ratio of current income to family income before separation, adjusted for family size. (Family income before separation is father's earnings plus mother's earnings. Each parent's income is own earnings plus or minus support payments received from or made to former spouse. Ratios are calculated using 1985 dollars, adjusted for family size.)

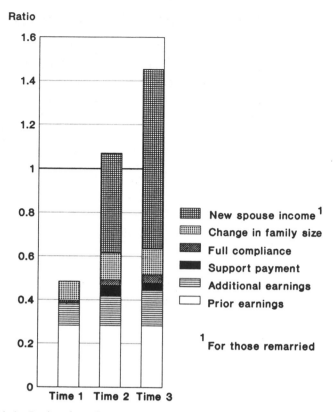

Figure 10.6   Ratio of mothers' current income to family income before separation.

separation.) It may be seen that even though the amount of support being received by mothers from fathers at Time 1 may be understated, this would make little difference in the overall picture, since even at Times 2 and 3, when most divorces were completed and awards had been made, money from this source (if paid in full) constitutes only 8 to 10 percent of total family income prior to separation, and about 15 percent of custodial mothers' post-divorce incomes. Furthermore, the support actually received is lower by several percentage points because of noncompliance. Unless mothers remarry, then, their economic well-being (and that of the children who are living with them) depends primarily on the mothers' own earnings rather than on payments from fathers, welcome though these may be.

Remarriage. Remarriage rates for divorced mothers and divorced fathers in our sample were approximately equal. By Time 2, 8 percent of mothers and fathers had remarried; by Time 3, remarriage rates for mothers and fathers were 27 percent and 28 percent respectively. Table 10.4 shows that after remarriage the employment rate for women drops back to its pre-divorce level. At Time 3, 85 percent of single divorced mothers but only 73 percent of mothers who had remarried were employed. Those mothers who had remarried and remained in the labor force earned slightly less per year than working mothers who remained single.

Remarriage has a substantial effect on post-divorce financial well-being. As Figure 10.6 shows, this effect is dramatic for women. For women who remain single, the ratio of current family income (including child and spousal support received) to family income before the divorce is 66 percent at Time 3, whereas for women who remarry, current family income including the new spouse's income is 48 percent greater than family income before the divorce. The increase in standard of living for the remarried women is not quite so dramatic as Figure 10.6 indicates, because the increased family income in these newly expanded families now must cover an additional adult. But even when this factor is taken into account (data not shown), the incomes of remarried women rebound to higher than the pre-divorce level. Fathers, too, benefit from remarriage, though less so. In Figure 10.5 we saw that considering only the father's own earnings (minus money paid to the former spouse in the form of child or spousal support), and after adjustment for family size, fathers were approximately 25 percent better off at Time 3 than they had been before the separation. With remarriage they gain the income of their new partner, although, of course, this will be somewhat offset by the increased family size at remarriage.

Summary Comment

Our data indicate that at least half of fathers who were ordered to pay child support complied fully with the terms of the support order, but a substantial minority did not. When fathers did not comply, in some cases this was a function of inability rather than unwillingness to pay. However, only a small fraction of the fathers in our sample were unemployed at any of the interview times. Thus, inability to pay does not explain most of the cases of partial or complete noncompliance that we observed.

In accordance with theoretical accounts of noncompliance, we found a strong relationship between compliance behavior and a father's having some contact with his children. Frequency of contact did not matter as much as the fact that contact was continuing to occur. For children living with their mothers, compliance rates were relatively high unless the father was not seeing the children on a regular basis.

A sizable fraction of our sample families reported some informal modification of the divorce agreement, and when we adjusted our analysis to reflect reported modifications, we observed an increase in the mean compliance rate. Thus it appears that in some families, fathers pay less than the amount specified in the divorce decree because the parents have modified their agreement to reflect costs incurred by the father while the children are in his household. If the children had moved in with their fathers after the time when support awards were made, the father was unlikely to be making the support payments that had been ordered to accord with a different custodial arrangement, but this hardly reflects "noncompliance" for policy purposes. The fact that some parents increased the amount of child support paid as family circumstances changed, while others decreased the amount, indicates that some proportion of divorced couples regard their agreement as a flexible one.

We demonstrated in Chapter 7 that, in general, the level of conflict between divorcing parents does not affect the amount of child support awarded except for a few mothers with joint custody decrees. Similarly, data presented in this chapter suggest that conflict between divorced spouses affects support *compliance* behavior in only a small group of cases. Our finding that fathers who have no regular contact with their children are less likely to comply with support obligations is evidence that a breakdown of communication between noncooperative parents may affect compliance; however, this group of fathers represents a minority of our sample. Moreover, we found only a slight relationship between compliance behavior and our measures of reported conflict over the terms of the formal decree, and this was not significant in terms of compliance with the informal agreement.

Our findings concerning the sharp disparity in economic well-being between divorced mothers and fathers in the years following the divorce place this account of fathers' compliance behavior in broader perspective. Although the economic well-being of divorced mothers and their children increases over time, the well-being of those mothers who do not remarry remains substantially below pre-separation levels. By contrast, the economic well-being of divorced fathers remains substantially above pre-separation levels. Despite this significant discrepancy in the economic status of the two parents, custodial mothers remain the primary source of support for their children in the years following the divorce. Even if paid in full, child and spousal support represents only a fraction of the mothers' post-divorce household income. Moreover, even if fathers comply fully with their support obligations, their post-divorce household income remains 11 percent higher than the family income prior to separation, once the change in family size is taken into account. In sum, not only could most fathers in our sample afford to pay the full amount of support awarded; they could afford to pay more. Although our data suggest that variable compliance behavior in some families reflects cooperation rather than conflict, the agreed-upon amounts are low in relation to what might be considered both possible and appropriate.

11

Facing the Dilemmas of Child Custody

There is no easy solution to the question of how the care of children and responsibility for their upbringing should be shared between parents after they have separated. Usually both parents are strongly attached to the children, strongly committed to their welfare, and have a clear record of having been responsible, fit parents before the separation. Yet a new division of responsibilities must be made—inevitably different in some ways from the division of labor between the parents that prevailed when they still shared a household. Our study has been concerned with how parents actually make arrangements for their children, and what kinds of adaptations they make to changing circumstances as time passes. Four clusters of questions have been central to our inquiry: (1) gender differentiation in parental roles, (2) legal conflict, (3) children's contact with both parents over time, and (4) the nature of the co-parenting relationship.

We have not sought in this book to measure the impact of legal change on the behavior of divorcing spouses; nor was our purpose to evaluate or formulate specific legal reforms. Nevertheless, in this final chapter we wish to step back and consider more broadly the implications of what we have learned for those concerned with the well-being of children whose parents divorce.

We proceed as follows. First, using our four central organizing themes listed above, we will compare what we have found with what might be seen as the aspirations underlying the legal reforms adopted in California and emulated in a number of other states. In California, as elsewhere, reformers sought to eliminate gender stereotypes, to encourage divorced fathers to remain more involved in their children's lives, and to create greater gender equity for mothers and fathers alike. Various substantive and procedural changes were adopted in the hope of dampening legal conflict and diminishing the adversarial nature of divorce. California sought to encourage "frequent and continuing contact with both parents," and to authorize explicitly joint physical custody and joint legal custody so that parents might choose to share responsibility more equally. Cooperative co-parenting, not conflict, was the goal. On the basis of what we have found about the way the legal system works and the way post-divorce families function, we will consider how much impact family law may reasonably be expected to have on the parental roles of men and women and on their level of cooperation. Next we will assess the implications of our principal findings for policymakers concerned with divorce. We will then comment on current debates regarding the legal standards for custody, visitation, and child support. Finally, we will discuss the implications of our findings for divorcing parents themselves, and for those professionals concerned with divorce.

The Persistence of Gender Role Differentiation

The first and perhaps most basic finding of our study involves the extent to which the roles of mothers and fathers differ after divorce. Obviously parental role differentiation is very much a matter of degree. But consider three possible allocations which we will call "traditional," "undifferentiated," and "reversed." During marriage, a traditional household would be one in which the mother was a full-time homemaker primarily responsible for child care and the father was the exclusive breadwinner. An "undifferentiated" household would be one in which the mother and father had roughly equal earnings and equally shared day-to-day child-rearing responsibilities. "Reversed" would be the mirror image of "traditional": the father would be the homemaker, the mother the breadwinner.

After divorce, a traditional allocation would mean that the children would live with the mother, who would have physical custody; the father would have a right of reasonable visitation and would remain responsible for the primary support of the children. An undifferentiated allocation would mean that the children would divide their time in roughly equal proportions between the households of the mother and the father, who would share equally the responsibility for supporting the children. A reversed allocation would mean that the father had custody, with the mother having visitation rights and providing child support. Families differ, of course, and we have seen that there is an enormous variety of ways in which parents allocate responsibility for children after divorce. Nevertheless, these three simple templates provide a useful shorthand to describe what we have found.

As we described in Chapter 3, before the separation the distribution of families in our study was heavily weighted toward the traditional end of the spectrum. Although only 30 percent of the mothers were full-time homemakers before the breakdown of the marriage, most mothers who worked outside the home were typically employed either part time or for substantially fewer hours than the father. And even then, mothers who worked 35 hours or more per week earned on average only 60 percent of what their husbands earned. In only about a quarter of our sample were the earnings of the two spouses roughly equal. (We should note that in quite a few of these families, the mothers were doing more of the child-rearing—a "second shift" pattern that is traditional in terms of parental involvement with children, but not with respect to the provider role.) In a small minority of the families (about 10 percent), the mother was the primary breadwinner, but this was almost always because the father was unemployed (perhaps temporarily), not because he was the children's primary caretaker. In a substantial majority of our families, we believe the mother had primary managerial responsibility for the child-rearing functions before the divorce. Although fathers were often involved in the day-to-day lives of their children, we judge (on the basis of other studies as well as our own) that on average they usually spent much less time alone with the children and did not normally share equally in the responsibility of child care on an everyday basis. It is important to recall, however, that often the divorcing mother and father had divergent perceptions of how involved each had been with the children before separation. The fathers we interviewed tended to claim that they had been much more involved than mothers as a group gave them credit for, while the large majority of mothers saw the pre-separation child-rearing roles as having been largely traditional, and almost none of them believed that the father had been more involved than they themselves were.

In considering the arrangements parents made for their children following divorce, we found that the distribution of outcomes was again heavily weighted toward a traditional pattern of child care. At each of the three times following separation when we interviewed parents, we found that in about 70 percent of the families we studied, the children resided with the mother. Typically the father maintained some contact with the children, often by having them spend one or two nights in his household during a two-week period but sometimes having daytime visits. In about one out of six families the residential arrangements were more evenly balanced: in these "dual residence" families, the children spent between one-third and one-half of their residential time (defined as overnight stays) with each parent in a typical two-week period. In about 10 percent of the households, there was some reversal of the traditional roles in that the children lived with the father, with the mother typically visiting but usually not paying child support.

We suspect that dual residence was much more common in the late 1980s in California than elsewhere in the country or in California twenty years ago, but we cannot know for certain because comparable data are unavailable. In any event, this probable increase in dual residence does not suggest that undifferentiated arrangements are likely to become the norm. Even in these dual-residential families, the division of child-rearing responsibilities was not typically 50-50. More often than not, the mother was responsible for doctor's appointments and for buying everyday clothes. And in two-thirds of the dual-resident families, the children stayed overnight with their mothers somewhat more frequently than with their fathers.

In a curious way, the father-residence families illustrate our gender theme as well. Custodial fathers were not unemployed house-husbands married to high-earning mothers who paid child support. Instead, children resided with the father most commonly because circumstances encouraged or required a father who had been a secondary parent before the divorce to assume the primary role after separation. Over the three and a half years of our study, the proportion of children—especially teenagers—living with their fathers went up slightly, a shift that appeared to reflect the fact that the children in our sample families were growing older, and reaching an age when residence with the father was deemed more practicable. We found nothing to suggest, however, that there is an underlying trend toward father custody. Our findings essentially confirm that father residence, like dual residence, remains the exception, not the rule. We expect that the more traditional allocation of responsibility—where most divorced children live with their mothers—will remain the common arrangement for the foreseeable future.

In a number of ways, large and small, we saw significant differences in the preferences and behavioral patterns of mothers and fathers. The overwhelming majority of mothers indicated that they wished and expected to be the children's primary custodian, and most mothers acted on that desire. Although a surprisingly high percentage of the fathers we interviewed indicated a preference for some physical custodial arrangement other than mother custody (with or without visitation), few of these fathers actually sought custody through the formal legal process. When we compared mother-residence households with father-residence households with respect to how well contact was maintained with the secondary parent, we discovered that non-residential mothers tended to increase the amount of visitation over time while the fathers dropped off somewhat. Moreover, although the proportions of each of the three residential arrangements remained surprisingly stable over the period of our study, on average the mother-residential households were much more stable, with a much smaller proportion of residential changes, than was true for dual-residence or father-residence households. When we compared the custodial provisions of the legal decree with the actual residence of the children, we found that the decree can function to confirm mother residence if it exists initially and to bring it about if it does not exist initially, but that the decree was much less powerful in moving children out of maternal residence once it was established. Moreover, we found that when a residential move of either the mother or the father triggered a change in the children's residence, they almost always moved into the mother's household rather than the father's. All of these subsidiary findings suggest to us that there is a strong inertial pull—based on social custom rather than law—toward mother residence.

Like custody awards, the pattern of child support awards is also heavily gendered. In 90 percent of the mother physical custody cases in our study, the father was ordered to pay child support. When the children lived with the father, the mother was ordered to pay support in only one-third of the cases. In cases where the decree provided for joint physical custody, fathers were ordered to pay child support to mothers 68 percent of the time, while mothers were ordered to pay support to fathers in only 1 percent of the cases. These results are hardly surprising given that in most families, the father earns substantially more than the mother. The importance of the father's economic role is further indicated by the fact that if fathers had high or increasing incomes they were more likely to maintain or increase their time with the children; it was the fathers whose economic resources were low or falling who tended to lose contact. By contrast, mothers' earnings bore essentially no relationship to the amount of time the children spent with them.

Because of the great differences in earnings between mothers and fathers, we, like other researchers, have found a sharp disparity in the economic well-being of divorced mothers and fathers. Although the economic circumstances of divorced mothers and their children improve over time, the well-being of those mothers who do not remarry remains substantially below pre-separation levels. By contrast, the economic well-being of divorced fathers remains substantially above pre-separation levels.

Our analysis suggests that in one important respect, for most of the families in the study, divorce imposed a significant reallocation of gender roles. Before separation, in most families, the father had assumed primary responsibility for the financial support of the children. After divorce, this is no longer the case. An important shift in the allocation of economic responsibility occurs: following a divorce, custodial mothers become the primary source of support for their children. Although these mothers are typically awarded child support, the amounts involved usually represent only a small fraction of their total post-divorce household income, even in those households where child support is paid in full.

In short, despite some revolutionary changes in the law to eliminate gender stereotypes and to encourage greater gender equity, the characteristic roles of mothers and fathers remain fundamentally different. In a sense, there is less gender equity after divorce than before, since mothers continue to carry the major responsibilities for child care and also take over from fathers some of the responsibility for economic support, even though fathers characteristically continue to have far greater earning power than mothers. Reforms in divorce law appear to have done little to change this picture. In most of the divorcing families we studied, each parent continued to play a role in the child's life. But in very few families were the parenting roles of mothers and fathers equivalent.

Legal Conflict

Using various measures of legal conflict, based on both court records and parental interviews, we have demonstrated that most divorcing families have little legal conflict over the custodial or financial terms of the divorce decree. For each of the issues relating to custody or money, a substantial majority of parents indicated in their interviews that they experienced little legal conflict. The court record information revealed a conflict pyramid, with a smaller and smaller percentage of cases resolved at each successive stage of the legal process. We estimate that nearly three-fourths of the families in our sample experienced little, if any, conflict over the custody and visitation terms.

For those families with high legal conflict, nearly all of these disputes were resolved through negotiation, some of which were stimulated by court-annexed mediation or a court-ordered evaluation. Only a trivial number of cases (less than 2 percent of our sample) required formal adjudication. Our findings suggest that the procedural innovations adopted in California to reduce reliance on adversarial proceedings and promote resolution through negotiation may have proved successful in reducing the number of adjudicated custody cases. Even before the California procedural reforms, we suspect only a small proportion— perhaps 10 percent—of divorces required adjudication of custody. Nevertheless, it would appear that the legal changes have increased the number of families who settle during mediation, and reduced the number for whom a formal evaluation or adjudication is required. Our study points to the important role that mandatory court-annexed mediation now plays in resolving conflicted cases.[1]

How are high-conflict families different? Demographic variables do not differentiate them from lower-conflict families. Parents involved in high legal conflict often express serious concerns about the adequacy of the other spouse's parenting capacity and the quality of the child-rearing environment that would be provided in the other household. We do not know how justified these accusations were, and can only report that they were part of the psychological profile of high-conflict families. It may well be that the attitudes and behavior of fathers, more than those of mothers, will provide the key to understanding better how families with high legal conflict differ. We saw that the two variables most significantly related to legal conflict were the father's concern over the child's well-being in the mother's household and the father's hostility toward the mother. In addition, parents involved in high levels of legal conflict often had very different perceptions of how much each had been involved in the children's lives before the separation. When fathers believed they had been substantially involved, they were more likely to press for their rights to time with the child, while mothers who thought that fathers had not been substantially involved were more likely to resist such demands. The roots of legal conflict may often lie in psychological aspects of the spousal relationship that existed long before the separation—factors which we made no attempt to assess. Nevertheless, there is much more variability in the behavior of fathers than of mothers. Most mothers want custody and will act to secure their preferred custodial arrangement. Intense legal conflict is very much the exception, and it arises most frequently when a father chooses to act and presses for more custody.

When there is legal conflict, and the parents ask for different custodial arrangements, the mother secures her preferred arrangement twice as often as the father. Nevertheless, the proportion approaches 50-50 at the top of the conflict pyramid—where conflict is resolved after a court-appointed evaluation, through negotiations on the courthouse steps, or through adjudication. While advocates on both sides of the gender debate may claim that our findings demonstrate the possible bias of the legal system, we have noted a 50-50 division of custody between mothers and fathers would be gender-neutral—that is, unbiased—only in a statistical sense. Considering that families who agree on custody without dispute allocate physical custody to the mother more than two-thirds of the time, we could regard this ratio as "normative neutrality." We have suggested that the fact that the gender ratio shifts toward a 50-50 balance as one moves up the pyramid most likely reflects a selection bias built into the divorce process: fathers without strong claims are likely to settle earlier in the process, and therefore it is not surprising that a higher proportion of fathers at the top of the pyramid "win."

One of our most surprising conclusions relates to what we did not find: advocates and academics alike fear that fathers commonly persuade mothers to accept less financial support by using custody as a bargaining chip. In fact, we found no statistically persuasive evidence that mothers who experienced more legal conflict had to give up support to win the custody they wanted. We credit the use of support schedules and community property rules for this result, for these should make it easier for women to resist any attempts to link money and custody. We also believe that under the best interests standard—despite its ostensible gender neutrality—parents and lawyers alike perceive the system as giving a substantial weight to continuity of care. That is, if a competent mother has in fact provided the greater share of day-to-day care for the children before separation, she receives "credit" for this fact in the negotiation process.

Our most disturbing finding with respect to legal conflict concerns the frequency with which joint physical custody decrees are being used by high-conflict families to resolve disputes. About a third of the 166 cases in our study in which the decree provided for joint custody involved substantial or intense legal conflict. In about half of these cases, the children in fact resided with the mother—the legal label did not reflect the social reality. Nevertheless, we did find some 25 joint physical custody cases in which the children were in fact dividing their residential time fairly equally between parents who had substantial legal conflict. Moreover, we found a strong relationship between the intensity of legal conflict and the ability of parents to develop cooperative co-parental relations following the divorce: a much higher proportion of those families with substantial or intense legal conflict had conflicted co-parenting styles, and many fewer were able to develop cooperative co-parenting relationships. Legal conflict was not related, however, to how well the father subsequently abided by his support obligations.

Contact: Maintenance and Change

An important goal of California lawmakers was to assure children "frequent and continuing contact with *both*" divorcing parents. This has never been a problem for mothers. Previous researchers have suggested, however, that many if not most fathers essentially divorce their children as well as their former spouse; after the passage of some time, others have found that fathers typically no longer regularly see their children and often fail to maintain their support obligations.

How do our findings compare with these earlier studies? For a substantial majority of the families in our study, fathers as well as mothers have remained in regular contact with the children. For those families with dual residence, obviously both parents are deeply involved. For the small minority with father residence, mothers have maintained contact very well indeed. Our most significant finding is that in a majority of families where the children lived with the mother, visitation with the non-residential father was maintained over the period of our study, and the visits most commonly involved overnight stays. At Time 3, only 14 percent of the children living with their mothers had not seen their fathers within the past year.

The proportion of mother-resident families in which the children had overnight visits with their father remained remarkably constant over three and a half years. On the other hand, when the father had only daytime visits at Time 1, with no overnights, this arrangement proved quite unstable: it often evolved either to no regular visitation at all, or (less commonly) to overnight visitation. Because of this decline in visitation by fathers with only daytime visits, the proportion of mother-resident families having no visits with the father increased from 23 percent at Time 1 to 39 percent at Time 3. On the other hand, almost a quarter of the families who initially had no visitation had established some by Time 3. Thus, within the overall picture of declining visitation with fathers—particularly for those who only had day-time visits—there was a substantial minority of mother-resident families in which visitation was increasing over time.

What factors affect whether children living with their mother maintain contact with the father? A mother's conviction that it is good for the children to sustain their relationship with their father is strongly associated with sustaining contact. Remarriage of the mother has a slight effect; it tends to diminish the amount of time children spend with their father. A residential move of one or both parents has a more powerful effect: when the distance between the two households increases, the children, not surprisingly, see their fathers less.

It is possible, of course, that the amount of contact between children and their fathers will continue to erode, and perhaps at a faster rate, as more time passes.[2] However, we should note that in the follow-up of adolescent children conducted a year after the present study, the large majority of the children in the sample were still seeing their fathers on a fairly regular basis, and very few had not seen him during the past year. In short, during the more than four years following the initial separation, a high proportion of the children in our study maintained "frequent and continuing contact" with both parents.

A second way in which fathers remain involved with their children has to do with economic support. We found that a majority of fathers maintained some economic relationship with their children, although the father's role in providing economically for the family was much reduced compared to what it had been before the divorce. At Time 3, half of the fathers who owed child support were paying the full amount; another 25 percent were paying part of what they owed. The remaining quarter paid no support at all. When we examined individual fathers to track compliance over time, we found that there was considerable mobility in compliance status. Like other researchers, we found a strong relationship between compliance behavior and the amount of contact between the father and the children.[3] For children living with their mothers, the likelihood that a father would comply with child support awards was much reduced if he did not see the children on a regular basis.

Our study shows that many families change the residential living arrangements and visitation patterns during the first several years following the separation. This is especially true for families with dual residence or father residence. Although the overall proportion of families with mother, dual, or father residence remained remarkably steady in all three time periods, arrangements involving dual or father residence are plainly less stable than mother residence. Indeed, only half those children who were living with their fathers or in a dual arrangement at Time 3 had lived there continuously since Time 1. In contrast, five-sixths of the children in mother residence at Time 3 had maintained a stable residence with her over the three years of our study.

In sum, we found that at the end of three and a half years, most of the children in our study had contact with both their mother and their father, and typically each parent was providing for part of their support. We also found a great deal of change in residence, visitation patterns, and support compliance.

Co-parenting Relationships

We have argued that the co-parental relationship between divorced parents is something that needs to be constructed, not something that can simply be carried over from pre-separation patterns. It takes time and effort on the part of both parents to arrange their lives in such a way that the children can spend time in both parental households. The dual-residence arrangement, although it offers parents some benefits in terms of time off from parental duties, is nevertheless particularly demanding—the need to negotiate with the other parent over schedules arises frequently, more trips must be made to take the children back and forth, and it is especially difficult to maintain the arrangement if a parent moves and the driving distance increases. We have found that parents are less likely to adopt a dual arrangement if they have more than one child, or if one of the children is very young; in addition, they are less likely to maintain such an arrangement in the face of intense hostility between the former spouses. We believe these facts imply that any factor that increases the overall time and effort involved in parenting will make it less likely that parents will take on the additional demands of a dual-residence arrangement.

Most of our parents did not adopt dual residence, but they did maintain a visitation schedule. Although some complained about the other parent's making last-minute changes in the arrangements for visits, or being late to pick up or drop off the children, most felt that these problems were not serious. More difficult for some parents was the knowledge that their children were spending time in settings they did not fully trust. They worried about the children not being adequately supervised, or being exposed to undesirable influences, in the other parent's home. Such concerns serve as an impediment to the development of an effective co-parental relationship.

Because both mothers and fathers commonly maintained contact with their children following divorce, the quality of co-parenting relationships emerged as a central issue in our study. Among the families in which the children were spending time in both parental households, we identified three common patterns; cooperative, conflictual, and disengaged. Only a minority of our families—about 30 percent by Time 3—were able to establish cooperative co-parenting relationships. Spousal disengagement, which essentially involved parallel parenting with little communication, had become the most common pattern by that time. It is interesting that disengagement was less common—we believe, less possible—when the children were young. Parents of infants, toddlers, or preschoolers found that there was more they needed to communicate about if the children were to spend time in both households, and, probably in consequence, they had more conflict as well as more communication. When the children were of school age, they could manage themselves more of the arrangements needed for transition between households.

Although the proportion of families with conflicted co-parenting relationships declined over time, nevertheless about a quarter of our families remained conflicted at the end of three and a half years. We also saw a common migratory pattern. Many families that were conflicted at Time 1 became disengaged by Time 3, while some spouses who started out as disengaged were later able to establish cooperative co-parenting relationships.

While our study did not attempt to measure the impact of co-parenting relations on the well-being of children, the results of the follow-up study of the adolescents in our sample families, as well as the research of others, make us confident that there are important effects. Children derive real benefits—psychological, social, and economic—when divorced parents can have cooperative co-parenting relationships. With conflicted co-parental relationships, on the other hand, children are more likely to be caught in the middle, with real adverse effects on the child. Where there is spousal disengagement, the effects on children are intermediate: better than conflicted but less good than cooperative (Buchanan, Maccoby, and Dornbusch, 1991).

Contrary to what might have been expected, we found roughly equal proportions of the three types of co-parental relationships in each of the residential arrangements. In other words, the proportion of families with conflicted co-parental relations was as high with dual residence as with mother residence or father residence. We believe that conflicted co-parental relations are a function of anger arising from the spousal

divorce and from the extent of legal conflict. It does not appear to be
the case that parents with cooperative relationships will more frequently choose dual residence; nor is it true that once dual arrangements are adopted, conflicted parents become cooperative.

In sum, we found that former spouses obviously have a great deal
of difficulty doing business together with respect to the children. Although conflict declines over time, avoidance is commonplace. Many
parents would prefer not having to deal with the other, and mothers
and fathers with sole residence both indicate that in some ways it is
easier for them, now that they are separated, to raise the children
according to their own values, with less need to consider those of the
other parent.

The Impact of the Law and Legal Change

Two cornerstones of divorce law, in California and elsewhere, have
been that (1) a custodial parent must allow the other parent reasonable
visitation with the children, unless the outside parent has been shown
to be unfit; and (2) a non-custodial parent must pay child support,
within the limits imposed by the respective incomes of the two
spouses. We believe, though we cannot demonstrate, that these two
components of divorce law have had a deep and continuing influence
on the agreements parents arrive at in negotiating their settlement of
custody, visitation, and financial issues. We did not ask primary custodial parents: "Would you have agreed to allow visitation if you did
not have to under the law?" Nor did we ask fathers whether they
would pay child support if there were no court order requiring it. Such
questions would have been hypothetical, and we doubt that parents
could have answered them meaningfully. Nevertheless, we take note
of the fairly large number of custodial parents who expressed concerns
about the child's well-being in the other parent's household, and infer
that given the choice, such parents might well choose to block visitation if they were free to do so. The existence of legal obligations and
the threat of legal sanctions hardly results in full compliance. Like
others, we have documented the difficulty of getting many fathers to
comply with their support orders. This strongly suggests that even less
would be paid if there were not a legal obligation to pay child support.
Self-help remedies and reciprocity might well lead some reluctant parents to "trade" support payments of some sort for visitation even if
there were not legally enforceable rights. Nevertheless, we are per-

suaded that parents tend to negotiate in the shadow of the legal standards for support and for visitation.

We suspect, too, that the reforms enacted in California divorce law, explicitly authorizing joint custody and encouraging frequent and continuing contact with both parents, have had something to do with our finding of relatively high frequencies of joint physical custody awards and sustained visitation. Once again, however, we cannot be sure, and we find it plausible that the California legal reforms may reflect social change more than create it. Comparative data are needed from other jurisdictions in which legal reform has proceeded at a slower pace. When it comes to the broader aspirations underlying the California reforms, however—to foster greater gender equity and support cooperative co-parenting—our findings suggest a mixed picture. First, and most fundamentally, the gender roles of divorced parents remain substantially differentiated. While there is apparently little legal conflict, and legal conflict usually does not require formal adversarial proceedings in court for resolution, most divorcing parents are unable to develop cooperative co-parental relations, despite the policy changes.

These basic findings clearly point to limits in how far the reach of the law can extend when it comes to creating fundamental change in gender roles or influencing co-parental relations. Gender roles, and issues of gender equality and gender equity, have been central to family law policy reform during the last generation. Equality and equity are hardly self-defining, but many in our society are understandably troubled by the extent to which gender role differentiation persists in our society. For women, roles within the household—especially with regard to parenting—and opportunities in the labor market are closely connected. Long before our study, it was well known that mothers typically cared for children both before and after divorce and were often at a substantial economic disadvantage compared to fathers.

Using family law to modify gender role differentiation may be a worthy aspiration, but is it realistic to believe that law can have a substantial impact in this regard? We have argued that the gender differentiation that follows divorce rests largely on the differential roles that parents occupied before the separation. Unless family law can modify the pre-divorce roles, then, it is doubtful that it can have a much greater impact on the post-divorce division of parental responsibilities; most divorcing couples would still typically end up allocating primary child-rearing responsibility to mothers. This is not to say that a change in the standard might not affect residence in a few cases, and perhaps the legal label in many more. And it might well affect the mother's bargaining power with respect to the economic issues, although we are not even sure of that, provided the support schedules established child support on the basis of where the child actually spent time.

Law can be used to create enforceable support obligations and to divide property. We very much applaud efforts to improve support schedules and enforcement mechanisms in order to require non-custodial fathers to pay more for the support of their children. Even though law may have limited impact on which parent the children live with, this does not mean that it is unimportant at the time of divorce. It can also make an important difference in stabilizing the residential arrangements of the custodial parent and protecting them from interference by the secondary parent. Moreover, as we have noted, it can provide important visitation rights to the secondary parent. But we doubt that changing divorce custody standards alone is likely to have significant effects on the way most parents allocate basic responsibility for day-to-day care, either before or after separation.

We are not suggesting that gender roles are fixed now and forever. Indeed, our study suggests some modest social change. Instead, we are expressing skepticism about the power of family law. The function of law as an agent of behavioral change is a complex issue about which others have written thoughtfully (Gusfield, 1963). As we see it, family law may reflect and reinforce some tendencies, but its effects will be mainly at the margins, affecting mainly those cases in which the preexisting parental roles are unclear or in which parents are ambivalent about what they want. It can hardly bring about fundamental change in gender roles. Deeper forces—cultural, economic, and, some would claim, biological—limit the power of law in this domain.

If gender role differentiation poses "macro" questions that in some respects are too large for law to affect substantially, the failure of parents to achieve cooperative co-parenting poses "micro" questions that are too small. The law is simply too crude an instrument to regulate and control day-to-day interpersonal relations; its net is not fine enough to deal with the sorts of everyday issues that cause difficulties in co-parental relations. As we have seen, parental anger and hostility often erupt because a father shows up late for visitation, or because a mother is seen as bad-mouthing or undercutting a father's relationship with his children. Divorced parents have conflicts over value issues relating to the importance of homework, how much supervision a young child requires, what food children should eat, whether a parent should smoke in the children's presence, and what reasonable bedtime hours are. Obviously such issues are not easily subject to judicial control.[4]

This does not mean that the legal system cannot make parental relations worse. The adversarial nature of traditional divorce proceedings may in fact make cooperation more difficult. Lawyers who negotiate in a highly competitive way and who urge parents to stop all communication during the proceedings may disrupt communication not only during the pendency of the legal divorce, but thereafter. We are quite sympathetic to reformers who have sought to dampen the adversarial nature of traditional divorce proceedings.

Professionals who are divorce mediators and family therapists may well be able to help parents improve their co-parental relationship so that they can more easily do business together. Many divorce mediators are committed not simply to facilitating dispute resolution during the legal divorce itself, but also to helping parents develop the skills to deal with each other more constructively thereafter. This is a worthy aspiration. It is true that research to date has not demonstrated that intervention through mediation during the legal divorce has much effect on co-parental relations during the years that follow (Kelly, 1990).[5] Indeed, there are some who argue strongly that mediation—especially mandatory mediation—more often than not puts women at a disadvantage (Shaffer, 1988; Grillo, 1991). On the basis of what we know now, it is unrealistic to expect statutory language about cooperation—or even mandatory mediation—to have much impact on the degree of co-parental cooperation. However, court-annexed mediation is currently geared mainly to moderating immediate interparental conflict so that parents can reach an agreement about custody and money; it has usually been less concerned with helping parents to establish a workable long-term *modus operandi* for arranging the children's lives. Existing research, too, has been narrow: it has examined the satisfaction of the two parents with the agreements achieved through the mediation process rather than the success with which they handle co-parental responsibilities once the divorce process has been completed. It remains to be seen whether mandatory mediation can have a significant influence on post-divorce family functioning.

In the following sections we analyze some of the implications of our findings for policy, while keeping in mind the complexity of the issues and the limits of our data. Policy changes concerning the legal rules are not unimportant; some alternatives may be much worse than others. Nevertheless, our experience in this study leaves us both with a strong sense that advocates and academics often expect too much from divorce law and policy. As we proceed, we therefore keep in mind the basic notion that there may well be critically important concerns that are either too big or too small to be substantially affected by legal policy changes.

Physical Custody Standard

What should the legal standard be for physical custody determinations? This question has dominated policy debates during the last twenty years.[6] Most states, like California during our study, use a "best interests of the child" standard with no preference given to either parent simply on the basis of gender.

One criticism of the best interests standard is that it gives substantial discretion to a judge to make his own implicit predictions and impose his own value judgments about which parent might better serve the child's needs or interests.[7] One striking finding of our study, however, is that very few cases in fact ever get to a judge. While the best interests standard does potentially confer a great deal of judicial discretion, that discretion is rarely being exercised directly by a state official. Instead, the more basic criticism is that the best interests standard provides an uncertain backdrop for out-of-court negotiations.

Because of the strength of the social norm that mothers are the primary custodians for children, it may well be that parents see this best interests standard as much less uncertain than theoretical analysis would suggest. It certainly seems that in actual operation the best interests standard—even with its insistence on gender neutrality—is in no sense equivalent to a coin flip between two fit parents. With a coin flip, a fit mother and a fit father each have a 50 percent chance of becoming the primary custodian even though their pre-divorce roles may have been fundamentally different. In actual operation, there is no reason to think that the best interests standard operates in this way. While the formal legal standard may reject gender role stereotypes and presumptions, it in no sense insists that the reality of the pre-divorce roles be ignored either by parents or by judicial decision makers.[8]

As we and others know well, there is little equivalency of parental roles prior to divorce in most families. Typically, mothers carry more of the day-to-day burden of child-rearing and fathers provide substantially more than half of the household income. This is not to say that today most married women with children do not have earnings themselves—they do, but characteristically these are much smaller than the father's. Nor do we suggest that most fathers are uninvolved with their children prior to divorce. On the contrary, most have significant relationships with their children, but their parental role characteristically differs from that of the children's mother.

In California, until the early 1970s, the differential roles of fathers and mothers—particularly with respect to young children—were incorporated in a legal presumption that favored maternal custody. In terms of the law on the books, this presumption has disappeared, but our study suggests that as a social norm—if not a legal norm—it still persists. When two competent parents—a fit mother and a fit father— each want to be primarily responsible for the child following divorce, mothers usually end up with the children.

How much should the pre-divorce roles of the mother and father influence custody and visitation standards? Some commentators suggest that the formal legal standard should provide that custody goes to the "primary parent" in a contested case (Neely, 1984). Proponents of this standard point out that this would have the advantage of reducing the uncertainty of the best interests standard, and would protect the child's relationship with that parent who prior to divorce had been more substantially responsible for the child's day-to-day care. For most families, this standard would essentially operate like a maternal presumption. Indeed, a cynic might claim that the primary care standard is nothing more than a maternal presumption in disguise. There are differences, however. For one thing, in the unusual case in which the father had been the primary parent before divorce, the presumption might operate in his favor as well. More fundamentally, in cases where the court was persuaded that both parents had been equally involved prior to the divorce, the standard presumably would imply that there had been two primary parents, and other criteria would be controlling.

David Chambers' (1984) thoughtful analysis of the advantages and disadvantages of the primary parent standard concludes on the basis of an evaluation of existing developmental psychological literature that there is no evidence—other than for the very young—that after a divorce a fit father could not learn to be the primary parent as well as a mother who previously had occupied that role. Although we agree with his reading of existing research, we do not think this necessarily implies that as a matter of policy the father and mother of a child beyond the toddler stage should have the same opportunity for custody where the mother in fact was the primary parent before separation. A woman who has served as the primary parent, after all, has already largely developed and demonstrated the skills to care for the child on an everyday basis. While her post-divorce role as custodial parent would require change, she has much less to learn in most cases than the father. Her experience as well as his inexperience strike us as relevant to the custodial decision.

Another justification for the primary parent standard is that it would increase the bargaining position of women and decrease the risk that fathers can use a custody claim under the vague best interests standard as a bargaining chip to reduce economic support. We think it plausible that a primary parent standard might improve the bargaining endowment for women in the divorce process. On the other hand, our research demonstrates that even under the best interests standard, at least where there are reasonably precise support guidelines, there is no evidence that the strategic use of custody conflict is leading to less financial support for women. We find it hard to predict what kind of effect a primary parent standard might have on the amount of legal conflict between parents. On the one hand, it should be easier for families and courts to identify which parent has had the primary caretaking role than to apply the vague "best interests" standard. The reduction of uncertainty might reduce conflict. On the other hand, there might be more disputes over who was in fact the primary parent if this factor became determinative (see Crippen, 1990). On balance, we lean toward favoring a primary parent standard over the present use of the best interests standard. Nevertheless, our research findings suggest that the difference between the two standards has probably been substantially exaggerated, and that in actual operation the best interests standard is not fundamentally different.

A more radical alternative to the present best interests custody standard is a presumption in favor of joint physical custody.[9] We oppose such a presumption. First, as we have seen, fathers and mothers before divorce characteristically play differentiated roles. Some commentators have suggested that a joint physical custody presumption might encourage greater sharing during marriage, but for reasons already described, we are skeptical that the law would have much impact. Our second and more basic objection is that we are deeply concerned about the use of joint physical custody in cases where there is substantial parental conflict.[10] Although our study has not examined the impact of co-parental conflict on children, follow-up work in the context of the Stanford Child Custody Study as well as the research of others strongly suggests that such conflict can create grave risks for children. True, some intensely hostile parents manage not to draw the children into their conflict. But many do. We do not think it good for children to feel caught in the middle of parental conflict, and in those cases where the parents are involved in bitter dispute, we believe a presumption for joint custody would do harm. Our study suggests that in a number of cases in which families today adopt joint physical custody, there has been substantial legal conflict. To the extent that this custody arrangement is the result of encouragement by mediators, or judges for that matter, we think it is unwise. We wish to note, however, that joint custody can work very well when parents are able to cooperate. Thus we are by no means recommending that joint custody be denied to parents who want to try it.

Visitation Standard

A second policy issue concerns whether *both* parents after a divorce should have a legal right to maintain some regular contact with the child, short of dual residence. Should a non-custodial parent have a legally enforceable right of access to the child? From the children's perspective, the risks relate to co-parental conflict. If a child lives with her mother, for example, and the child's parents remain enmeshed in disputes that put the child very much in the middle, a powerful argument can be made that it would be better from the child's perspective for the custodial parent (here the mother) to be able to end the father's visitation rights. In *Beyond the Best Interests of the Child,* Goldstein, Freud, and Solnit suggest that the custodial parent be given this legal power.

Some children would no doubt benefit from a rule that gave the custodial parent control over the other parent's access. What concerns us, however, is the risk that many other children might well be harmed by such a rule. Our research suggests that a significant if declining portion of parents do remain enmeshed in conflict. For some of these conflicted families, ending visitation might benefit the children. But among the families in our study, the conflicted pattern of co-parenting was not the most common pattern several years after parental separation. Rather, spousal disengagement became the norm as time passed. The Stanford follow-up study suggests that spousal disengagement does not benefit children as much as cooperative co-parental relations do, but it also poses less risk for children than conflicted co-parenting (Buchanan, Maccoby, and Dornbusch, 1991). Spousal disengagement is common because many parents find it extremely difficult and painful to remain in contact with their former spouse. Our concern is that because of difficulties related to the spousal divorce, a significant number of custodial mothers might put an end to paternal visitation in circumstances where the children would not in fact suffer long-run harm by reason of parental conflict, and where they would receive important long-run benefits from a continuing relationship with their father.

We suggested earlier that children who are primarily residing with their mother can nevertheless receive a variety of benefits—psychological, social, and economic—from a continuing relationship with their father.[11] In our view the father's support obligation should in no sense be contingent upon his willingness to remain in contact with his children. Nevertheless, the evidence in both our study and others makes it clear that there is better compliance with support obligations by fathers who maintain contact with their children. In many states, a father's legal obligation to support his children ends when the child reaches age 18. We think it quite plausible that fathers who remain in contact are more likely to help a child with college expenses after this age. Moreover, in addition to possible economic benefits, we think children can benefit in other ways from a continuing relationship. We have seen that a significant minority of children who start out living with one parent go to live with the other at a later time, at least temporarily. We think it important that this option be kept open for the benefit of cases in which the initial residence becomes a less supportive environment as time passes. And in cases where the children continue to live with the mother, the relationship with the father—although not nearly so important to a child's development as the relationship with the custodial mother—can nevertheless provide emotional support in times of crisis and possible guidance for the child over the years. A father who has remained in contact is also more likely to provide substitute care should something happen to the custodial mother or to the child's relationship with the mother.

Another possibility is a legal rule that would permit the termination of visitation if a court found that there was in fact a continuing conflict between the parents. Although this is more narrowly focused than the Goldstein, Freud, and Solnit alternative, we could not support this change either. This standard might have unfortunate incentive effects, in that a disengaged custodial parent might choose to create conflict so that she could create the factual grounds for the termination of visitation.

In recent years, there has been considerable debate concerning the wisdom of children's having continuing contact with a non-custodial parent in families where there is a history of domestic violence (Cahn, 1991; Ellis, 1990). We do not doubt that when the *child* has been abused by the non-custodial parent, the court is justified in denying visitation or limiting it to supervised situations. However, in cases of violence between the spouses, the issue is more complex. Incidents of violence (for example, hitting, throwing objects) are quite common at the time a marriage breaks up, and husbands and wives are almost equally likely to engage in violent acts, though women are much more likely to get hurt (Johnston, in press; Straus, Gelles, and Steinmetz, 1981). Furthermore, allegations of physical abuse are common during divorce negotiations (Depner, Cannata, and Simon, in press), and verifying their frequency or severity is difficult indeed. We believe that allegations of violent acts should not be automatic grounds for denying visitation. A history of chronic physical abuse must be taken very seriously, however. While it may not be possible to devise a blanket statutory rule that would be applicable to all cases, we certainly believe that courts should retain the power to eliminate visitation in order to protect mother and children from a physically abusive father.

In families where no abuse has occurred, there are nevertheless some potential risks of maintaining visitation in families in which the parents have disengaged. The child may become the carrier of necessary messages, and may get caught up in parental conflict in the process. Beyond this, children—particularly teenagers—may well be able to weaken the authority of the custodial parent by playing off the two parents against each other. In some cases such manipulation may well have detrimental long-run consequences for the child. It is of course possible that even where spouses are not communicating with each other, the non-custodial spouse will nevertheless back up the authority of the custodial parent and will not allow the manipulation to take place. However, our interviews with parents suggest to us that this is not the common pattern, and that disengaged parents are not typically so mutually supportive.

Despite these potential disadvantages, we are not persuaded that on balance the potential benefits of a general policy giving the custodial parent the legal right to terminate visitation would outweigh the potential costs. Of course, we are constrained by the existing research, which does not allow precise quantification and comparison of the benefits and costs of a legal rule that would give a custodial parent the legal power to end visitation. It is certainly conceivable that research in the future might suggest that on balance the benefits of such a rule would outweigh the costs. But on the basis of existing evidence, and in the absence of a showing of abuse, we are not persuaded this would be so.

Our conclusion is influenced by a value judgment that is quite independent of social science evidence. Because most divorced fathers have established a substantial relationship with their children before the breakup, we are sympathetic to the view that the father should ordinarily have the legal right to maintain some sort of ongoing relationship with the children after divorce, even though he was not the primary parent and no longer gets along with the mother. This is not to say that the father should have the right to maintain the same sort of relationship with the children as he had before the separation—that is impossible. But to give the custodial parent the power to end visitation would mean that the legal system would be giving no recognition or protection to a relationship that many—probably most—divorced fathers cherish.

In short, we would not change existing legal standards which give a non-custodial parent the legal right to reasonable visitation. We obviously do not believe that "reasonable visitation" should be construed to require anything equivalent to dual residence. But that is hardly the legal norm today. Instead, reasonable visitation ordinarily implies the opportunity to have the child spend one or two overnights during a two-week period with a non-custodial parent. Because our evidence suggests that the probability of a father maintaining a connection with the child over time is greater if there are overnight visits, we believe that visitation should ordinarily be construed to permit overnight stays if that is what the secondary parent desires.

One last word on visitation. Should it be a *duty* as well as a legal right? Should the law be used to create a legal obligation on the part of a non-custodial parent to stay in contact with the children? Although some commentators have argued for such a legal obligation, we are very skeptical. For reasons previously stated, we doubt whether law can effectively sustain a relationship when the parent himself is not motivated to do so. Therefore, although we would certainly support the use of law to enforce a father's duty to support his minor children financially, we think it unwise to attempt to use law to create a legal duty on the part of the non-custodial parent to maintain contact.

Legal Custody Standard

Among California's other innovations was its statutory differentiation between legal custody and physical custody. We have found that for most of the families in our study—nearly 80 percent—the divorce decree provided for joint legal custody, which is defined by statute to mean that "both parents shall share the right and responsibility to make decisions relating to the health, education and welfare of the child."[12] Today the most common custodial arrangement following California divorces is mother physical custody with joint legal custody.

Does joint legal custody matter?[13] We were especially interested in exploring whether joint legal custody strengthens or maintains a non-residential father's commitment to his children in a way that results in increased contact, better support compliance, or more communication between the parents and more involvement by both parents in decisions affecting the children. We found that joint legal custody had no significant effects on contact or support, once the initial income differences between custodial groups had been taken into account. Furthermore, it did not increase non-resident fathers' involvement in decision-making. It also had little bearing on parental relations.

What are the implications of these findings for policy concerning joint legal custody? Although in the aggregate data we found no evidence to support claims for the positive or negative effects of joint legal custody, it is important to emphasize that this does not preclude such effects in some families over the longer term. Nevertheless, it appears that joint legal custody is neither the solution to the problem of maintaining the involvement of divorced fathers, nor a catalyst for either increasing or softening conflict in divorcing families. Broad claims either advocating or condemning joint legal custody, therefore, seem unwarranted.

Nevertheless, we would cautiously support a presumption in favor of joint legal custody largely on symbolic grounds: we like the affirmation that both mothers and fathers have rights and responsibilities with respect to their children after divorce. Joint legal custody will not make divorced parents equal partners in the lives of their children, but it does affirm the idea that in the eyes of the law fathers should play a continuing role in their children's lives despite the divorce.

Procedures for the Resolution of Legal Disputes

A worthy policy goal is to minimize parental conflict over the terms of the legal divorce. It is good news that most divorcing families have little legal conflict. In our study, for those who did, California's system of mandatory mediation followed by evaluation nearly eliminated the need for contested adversarial hearings to determine the custody and visitation provisions in the final decree. More needs to be known about the effects of divorce mediation, but our study certainly supports the notion that mandatory mediation is a useful if imperfect means for resolving legal conflict during divorce. It obviously will not work in all cases, but court-annexed mediation in the two counties we studied plainly led to the resolution of many disputes without the need for a trial.

Mediation needs to be studied further. We are concerned that on occasion a divorce mediator may push reluctant parents to accept joint physical custody as a compromise. We note, however, that the proportion of joint physical custody outcomes in mediated cases was only slightly higher than for our sample as a whole. Cases resolved after evaluation and on the eve of trial had a significantly higher proportion of joint physical custody outcomes. Although we did not have access to the evaluation reports, we suspect that many recommend joint physical custody. For reasons already described, if this is so, it is a matter of genuine concern.

We found no evidence to suggest that mandatory mediation affects the ability of parents to create and sustain a cooperative co-parental relationship after the decree is issued. Although more research needs to be done on this issue, we do not hold out great hope in this regard. Court-annexed mediation characteristically involves a brief intervention by a neutral party—no more than ten or twenty hours, and usually far less. It would be remarkable indeed if an intervention of this sort had powerful long-term effects on co-parental relations after the divorce.

Economic Obligations

Although there may well be limits to the effectiveness of the law, our research also suggests that legal distinctions are important and that in some areas a change in the legal standards can have a significant impact. The most important of these concerns the economic relations between spouses. A non-custodial parent's support obligations, in our view, can be substantially affected by legal standards and available enforcement mechanisms. Our research along with that of others plainly suggests that support guidelines and more precise support standards can have an impact on the amount of support ordered, and that the amount ordered can significantly influence the amount of money actually transferred if enforcement mechanisms are available. Therefore, our own concerns about the limits of law to shape gender role specialization, or the details of co-parental relations, should not be understood to extend to the economic sphere.

We applaud the use of support schedules, which provide greater clarity and certainty for parents in establishing their respective obligations as they go through the process of securing their divorce. Indeed, the use of schedules was pioneered in the two California counties where our study took place, and it is noteworthy that federal legislation now requires every state to adopt schedules of some sort, at least as guidelines.

Because the economic aspects of divorce have not been the primary focus of our study, and others are now evaluating the advantages and disadvantages of different ways in which support schedules can be formulated, we offer here only one very basic observation: at the time of our study, custodial mothers typically received too little support from non-custodial fathers, given the disparity in their incomes. Under the support schedule then in effect, the amount of support depended on (1) the total joint income of the two parents; (2) the relative income of each parent; (3) the number of children of the marriage; and (4) the amount of time the children spent in each household. Our basic concern with these schedules is not so much with any of these underlying premises as with the basic levels of support required. Even if the basic structure of the California schedule were left unchanged, increases in basic support levels are needed and justifiable.[14]

Implications for Parents

Our study's primary relevance for parents is to remind them of the important benefits for their children, and potentially for themselves as well, of cooperative co-parental relationships. We do not suggest that this is an easy task. But nothing we have found diminishes the importance of this goal. No matter how strongly parents might wish to have the other parent completely out of their lives, the fact is that if the children are to continue seeing both parents—as most children do—some connection between the divorced couple necessarily remains. The fact that a significant number of parents after divorce *are* able to create and sustain cooperative co-parenting demonstrates that it is not an impossible task. Our second message to parents is to avoid putting children in the middle of parental conflict. The follow-up study of the adolescent children in our sample of divorced families (Buchanan, Maccoby, and Dornbusch, 1991), as well as other studies of children whose parents have divorced (Camera and Resnick, 1988; Johnston, Campbell and Mayes, 1985), clearly points to the harm that can be done when parents draw the children into their conflict. We have found that in the case of parents who are not able to have cooperative relationships, it may nonetheless be possible to avoid conflict. One way to do this is through spousal disengagement, and, as we have seen, this pattern of co-parenting is in fact quite common. It appears that parents can manage to share the residential time of their children even though they are not talking to each other or trying to coordinate the child-rearing environments of the two households. Although this is not the "first best" alternative, it is far better for children than open conflict. Spousal disengagement during one period of time also leaves open the possibility that in the future parents may be able to establish cooperative co-parenting relations. Our evidence suggests that for some number of parents this sequence does occur. Cooperation is far more likely to emerge from disengagement than from conflicted co-parenting.

Our study also suggests the importance of overnight visits for the purpose of sustaining over time a child's relationship with the non-custodial father. The dropout rate for fathers who have only daytime visits is far greater than for those with overnights. In making arrangements for children after divorce, parents may wish to keep in mind this potential benefit of overnight visitation.

Finally, we would advise parents to be prepared for change. We were surprised that the developmental changes occurring in children over a three-year period did not appear to have much impact on the arrangements made for children's residence and visitation schedules. But other things do trigger change. When mothers and fathers establish new spousal relationships, or move to a different location, many families discover the need to renegotiate their original arrangements. There is every reason to think that this should be easier to manage when parents have previously established a cooperative co-parenting relationship. Moreover, modifications and changes seem particularly common for those families who choose to adopt joint custodial arrangements or where the children reside primarily with the father. These families in particular should be prepared to deal with change.

Implications for Professionals

Undoubtedly, most professionals already recognize the potential benefits arising from cooperative co-parental relations after divorce. We can only applaud those who advise parents in this regard and who do what they can during the process of divorce to avoid making the conflict worse. In every case in which both parents maintain contact with the child, divorced spouses have a relationship that extends over time. This reality needs to be kept in mind by all parties involved in divorce negotiations. When there are children involved, lawyers who adopt extremely adversarial postures often disserve their clients' long-run interests.

The second point we would like to bring to the attention of professionals concerns the use of joint physical custody in circumstances where there is a great degree of conflict between the parents. Our finding that more than a third of those families with joint physical custody decrees had substantial legal conflict gives us pause. We think professionals involved in this process have a responsibility to caution parents about such arrangements. Without additional research, we are not prepared to recommend a rule that would legally prohibit the use of joint physical custody in all cases where there is parental conflict. But we believe that professionals involved in the divorce process should proceed with extreme caution.

Our research also supports the idea—often put forward by divorce mediators—that detailed planning and some regularity can help parents manage co-parental relationships after divorce. When parents are helped to develop specific and detailed plans, there is reason to think that co-parental relations can be better managed. We saw that more fathers drop out when visitation is irregular rather than regular. We also saw that overnight visits by the children offer a better chance for sustaining a relationship. These findings imply to us that parents would often benefit if their advisers helped them work out reasonably detailed and regular visitation arrangements.

Some Final Reflections

The overall picture of the divorcing families in our study differs somewhat from the dark scenario that has been portrayed by others studying divorce. Three and a half years after their separation, most of the parents were coping with their daily lives in ways that did not appear to indicate pathology or deep distress. Many continued to harbor strong resentment toward the former spouse, but they were in the process of forming new relationships, they were managing reasonably well in their jobs (as indicated by rising earnings), and they were not finding the burdens of household management to be unduly great. Most were coping adequately with managing their own schedules and those of the children so as to allow the children to spend time in both households. Most expressed satisfaction with the division of the children's time they had worked out. Although we did not assess the psychological well-being of the children directly in the present study, the follow-up study of the adolescent children in these families appears to indicate that the majority are functioning well within the normal range.

Perhaps the most striking thing about these families, however, was their diversity. Among this fairly representative group of divorces could be found almost all the kinds of distressing events that regularly capture headlines. There were several cases of kidnappings; there were cruel stepparents; some parents had threatened each other with knives or guns, and some had been beaten by the former spouse and told us they went in fear of their lives; some had tried to get the former spouse arrested; there were allegations of child abuse; in some cases, a parent's drunk driving had endangered the lives of children; there were families so disorganized that young children were being left essentially unsupervised and unprotected; some couples had had irreconcilable differences over their children's religious training. These cases are real, but they are uncommon. The images of such cases are so vivid that it is difficult to keep in mind the ordinary lives that most divorced parents lead. In particular, it is hard to remember that many divorced people, even though they harbor strong resentment toward the former spouse and try to avoid contact, nevertheless are capable of civilized and even considerate behavior when they do need to interact.

Of course, the law must take account of exceptional cases; indeed, in its reliance on cases heard in appeals courts, the law gives considerable weight to exceptional cases. Nevertheless, we believe it important for policymakers to maintain awareness of the great bulk of ordinary divorces. Social science can help by providing information based on a large, diverse, and reasonably representative sample of families rather than relying, as some researchers have done in the past, on small samples drawn from families who are seeking clinical help or who are involved in legal conflict.

We have presented a fairly optimistic picture about the bulk of divorcing families. Nevertheless, divorce creates certain problems that are essentially intractable. This means, we believe, that life with divorced parents is seldom as supportive for children as life in a well-functioning non-divorced family. The simple fact that the child cannot spend as much day-to-day time with both parents threatens the closeness of the relationship with at least one of the parents. Of course, even in intact families, during much of the time when parents and children are under the same roof, they are not interacting with each other one-on-one. But there is a frequent occurrence of what we might call important "parenting moments"—opportunities for a parent to enforce standards of behavior, provide guidance, or convey warm support. After divorce, one of the parents is absent when such moments occur, and as a result both influence and emotional ties diminish. When a parent moves to a more distant location, this poses an especially great problem, in that such moves necessarily reduce the frequency of contact. We believe that both parents should have the right to reorganize their lives, through remarriage and the pursuit of career opportunities, even if this entails moving some distance from the former partner. We have also argued that it is desirable for children to have regular contact with both parents, at least if the parents do not continue to have high overt conflict. These two values clash when a parent needs to move beyond commuting distance. It becomes important to know how much contact with non-residential parents is needed for those parents to sustain a close, committed relationship with their children. Is a month in the summer, plus a Christmas holiday, enough? If so, long-distance moves are not as threatening to a non-custodial parent as they would otherwise be. We do not yet know the answer to the question of how much difference the frequency of contact makes, and the answer will surely vary, depending on many things such as the children's age and the degree of support each parent gives to the other's tie with the children. In any case, long-distance moves clearly do undermine the possibility of joint physical custody (except for yearly alternation). It is clear that when the two values clash, compromise will be necessary, and not all objectives can be fully served.

There is another intractable outcome of divorce: individual parents are no longer able to feel (or be) fully responsible for a child's welfare when that child is spending time with the other parent. When the two parents were under the same roof, although of course most had some value differences about how the children should be dealt with, they were able to spell each other, to mediate between the other parent and the children when necessary, and to work out value compromises. After separation, there appears to be no way in which a parent can truly have a voice in what is happening to the children in the other household. This being so, parents must reconcile themselves to their lack of power to be responsible when the children are away—a form of lowered commitment that we see as regrettable.

Clearly, then, from the standpoint of arranging for the care of children, divorce creates problems that are difficult to solve. We have documented a wide variety of ways in which parents have attempted to sustain their involvement with the children while developing coherent patterns of daily life in two separate households. Their solutions for ways to divide the children's time are not always satisfactory to both parents, but more often than not, the parents are well reconciled to the pattern they have established. Are the children reconciled as well? Our second-hand evidence, derived from what the parents have told us, indicates that they are. But we do need to know more, from the children's own perspective, about what it means to sustain relationships with two parents who do not live together and who do not attempt to speak with one voice when it comes to the standards they set for their children.

Meanwhile, what we have seen is that life goes on in a fairly normal fashion in the households of divorced families. The families we have studied are, in a sense, part of a wave of social change. Whether aware of it or not, these parents have been engaged in the process of developing a new set of social norms concerning the ways in which children's residential time can be divided between the households of divorced parents. They have been experimenting with a variety of arrangements, and have met with varying degrees of success. Clearly the newer forms of custodial arrangements work well for some families, poorly for others. No one can write a cookbook recipe for an ideal arrangement applicable to all, or even most, families. In our view, the developing social norms can and should embody diversity. And, we believe, social norms about custody will continue to evolve. We hope that the information we have gathered from parents going through the process of custody decisions will prove to be relevant as this evolution occurs.

Appendixes
Notes
References
Index

Supplementary Tables

Table 5.A1 Outcome for physical custody when parents' requests do not conflict

	Request[a]		
	Mother ($N = 508$)	Joint ($N = 150$)	Father ($N = 47$)
Outcome:			
Mother	89.4%	30.7%	12.3%
Joint	6.5	54.0	6.1
Father	2.8	8.0	75.5
Split	1.3	7.3	6.1
	100.0%	100.0%	100.0%

a. Excludes two families with petitions requesting split or non-parental custody.

Table 5.A2 Percentage of cases that resulted in joint legal custody as a function of attorney involvement[a]

	N	Percentage joint legal custody
Who has a lawyer:		
Neither parent	182	51%
Mother only	225	73
Father only	81	88
Both parents	435	92

a. Includes only those cases for which we have information regarding employment of a lawyer. No information exists for 10 cases.

Table 7.A1   Matrix for determining overall legal conflict over custody and visitation

Parent rating on difficulty of reaching agreement on custody and visitation	Uncontested	Settled but not uncontested	Settled with mediation	Settled after evaluation during trial or with judge
1.0–3.25	I (N = 297)	I (N = 121)	II (N = 22)	III (N = 5)
3.25–5.5	II (N = 87)	II (N = 52)	III (N = 19)	III (N = 10)
5.51–7.75	II (N = 31)	III (N = 17)	III (N = 17)	IV (N = 10)
7.76–10.0	III (N = 16)	IV (N = 30)	IV (N = 27)	IV (N = 54)
Total (N = 815)				

Table 7.A2   Comparison of conflict levels: Demographic measures

	Levels I–III	Level IV	t-statistic
Mother's age at petition	32.6	31.9	0.91
	(N = 542)	(N = 90)	(n.s.)
Father's age at petition	35.1	35.3	−0.27
	(N = 543)	(N = 90)	(n.s.)
Mother is Anglo	81.5%	80.3%	0.29
	(N = 680)	(N = 117)	(n.s.)
Father is Anglo	79.3%	73.5%	1.41
	(N = 681)	(N = 117)	(n.s.)
Mother has a college degree	22.2%	24.8%	−0.62
	(N = 681)	(N = 117)	(n.s.)
Father has a college degree	34.9%	31.0%	0.82
	(N = 681)	(N = 116)	(n.s.)
Mother unemployed at Time 1	17.9%	28.0%	2.04*
	(N = 543)	(N = 93)	
Father unemployed at Time 1	11.1%	4.4%	−2.68**
	(N = 92)	(N = 539)	
Mother's annual income at Time 1	$16,399	$15,611	0.47
	(N = 510)	(N = 86)	(n.s.)
Father's annual income at Time 1	$34,256	$36,636	−0.72
	(N = 472)	(N = 78)	(n.s.)

*$p \leq$ .05.
**$p \leq$ .01.

Table 7.A3   Indication of possible substance abuse, child abuse, and
               inadequate parenting

	Levels I–III	Level IV	*t*-statistic
Fathers' reports of	0.8%	10.0%	−2.86**
mothers' child abuse	(*N* = 488)	(*N* = 90)	
Mothers' reports of	3.0%	8.5%	−1.83†
fathers' child abuse	(*N* = 591)	(*N* = 94)	
Fathers' reports of	3.2%	8.9%	−1.80†
mothers' substance abuse	(*N* = 490)	(*N* = 90)	
Mothers' reports of	10.8%	11.7%	−0.23 (n.s.)
fathers' substance abuse	(*N* = 593)	(*N* = 95)	
Fathers' reports that			
mother's residence is poor			
environment for	19.0%	41.0%	−3.98****
child-rearing	(*N* = 475)	(*N* = 88)	
Mothers' reports that			
father's residence is poor			
environment for	29.0%	52.0%	−4.33****
child-rearing	(*N* = 574)	(*N* = 93)	

†$p \leq .10$.
**$p \leq .01$.
***$p < .001$.
****$p < .0001$.

Table 8.A1 Residence of children by sex of child at each of three time periods (percentage of children)[a]

	Time 1		Time 2		Time 3	
	Boys (N = 725)	Girls (N = 691)	Boys (N = 725)	Girls (N = 691)	Boys (N = 725)	Girls (N = 691)
Residence:						
With mother	66.2%	72.3%	65.1%	73.9%	65.2%	72.2%
Dual residence	15.6	13.3	19.6	13.2	15.2	14.0
With father	13.9	8.5	13.8	10.0	17.0	11.3
Other	4.3	5.9	1.5	2.9	2.6	2.5
	100.0%	100.0%	100.0%	100.0%	100.0%	100.0%

a. This table is based on the 1,416 children for whom residential data are available at all three time periods.

F table

	Sex	Time	S × T
For % in mother residence	12.1***	.72 (n.s.)	.98 (n.s.)
For % in father residence	10.7**	2.2 (n.s.)	1.09 (n.s.)

Table 8.A2   Visitation with father by mother-resident children at three time periods, by sex of child (percentage of children)[a]

	Time 1		Time 2		Time 3	
	Boys	Girls	Boys	Girls	Boys	Girls
Usual visitation with father during the school year:						
None	24.5%	27.4%	33.9%	33.5%	39.2%	41.7%
Daytime	33.1	28.9	20.8	23.1	15.2	19.7
Overnights	42.4	43.7	45.3	43.4	45.6	38.6
	100.0%	100.0%	100.0%	100.0%	100.0%	100.0%
Chi^2	n.s.		n.s.		*	

a. This table is based on the 787 children (375 boys, 412 girls) who remained in the mother's residence at all three time periods.

	F values		
	Sex	Time	S × T
No visitation	.39	4.1*	.64
Daytime only	.15	9.35***	2.64†
Overnights	.76	1.73	2.42†

Table 8.A3   Visitation with mother by father-resident children at three time periods, by sex of child (percentage of children)[a]

	Time 1		Time 2		Time 3	
	Boys	Girls	Boys	Girls	Boys	Girls
Usual visitation with mother during the school year:						
None	34.4%	32.4%	26.2%	21.6%	32.8%	21.6%
Daytime	21.3	24.3	42.6	29.7	39.3	29.7
Overnight	44.3	43.3	31.2	48.7	27.9	48.7
	100.0%	100.0%	100.0%	100.0%	100.0%	100.0%

a. This table is based on the 98 children (61 boys, 37 girls) who remained in the father's residence at all three time periods.

	F values		
	Sex	Time	S × T
No visitation	.71	1.37	.39
Daytime only	1.04	2.93†	.97
Overnights	2.63	.47	1.96

Table 8.A4   Residence of children at three time periods, by age of child at Time 1 (percentage of children)

	Age at Time 1				
	Less than 3 years (N = 289)	3–5 years (N = 424)	6–8 years (N = 280)	9–11 years (N = 192)	12–14 years (N = 201)
Residence at Time 1					
With mother	70.9%	68.9%	68.9%	67.2%	69.1%
Dual residence	16.6	17.2	15.7	10.9	9.0
With father	8.0	9.7	11.5	14.6	15.4
Other	4.5	4.2	3.9	7.3	6.5
	100.0%	100.0%	100.0%	100.0%	100.0%
Residence at Time 2					
With mother	67.5%	67.2%	68.2%	72.4%	75.6%
Dual residence	21.1	18.2	17.1	12.5	9.5
With father	9.0	11.3	12.6	14.1	13.9
Other	2.4	3.3	2.1	1.0	1.0
	100.0%	100.0%	100.0%	100.0%	100.0%
Residence at Time 3					
With mother	70.6%	69.6%	66.4%	67.2%	69.6%
Dual residence	17.3	17.2	17.2	9.9	8.5
With father	10.0	11.3	13.9	19.8	17.9
Other	2.1	1.9	2.5	3.1	4.0
	100.0%	100.0%	100.0%	100.0%	100.0%

Note: This table is based on the 1,386 children for whom residential data are available at all three time periods.

	F values		
	Time	Age	T × A
% in dual residence	5.41**	4.43***	0.83 (n.s.)
% in father residence	14.01***	3.20**	2.06*

Table 8.A5 Visitation with father by mother-resident children at three time periods, by age of child (percentage of children)

Usual visitation with father during the school year	Age at Time 1				
	Less than 3 years ($N = 163$)	3–5 years ($N = 235$)	6–8 years ($N = 157$)	9–11 years ($N = 107$)	12–14 years ($N = 110$)
At Time 1					
None	33.1%	26.4%	18.5%	20.6%	28.2%
Daytime only	29.5	24.2	29.9	43.6	46.4
Overnights	37.4	49.4	51.6	45.8	25.4
	100.0%	100.0%	100.0%	100.0%	100.0%
At Time 2					
None	42.3%	38.7%	26.1%	23.4%	30.0%
Daytime only	19.0	19.2	16.6	21.5	38.2
Overnights	38.7	42.1	57.3	55.1	31.8
	100.0%	100.0%	100.0%	100.0%	100.0%
At Time 3					
None	50.3%	42.1%	33.8%	33.7%	39.1%
Daytime only	12.9	12.4	12.7	19.6	35.5
Overnights	36.8	45.5	53.5	46.7	25.4
	100.0%	100.0%	100.0%	100.0%	100.0%

Note: This table is based on the 772 children who lived with their mothers at all three time periods, and who were less than 15 at Time 1.

	F values		
	Age	Time	A × T
None	4.9***	29.0***	0.80
Daytime only	11.7***	24.6***	0.53
Overnights	8.8***	2.65†	2.0*

Methods

by Charlene E. Depner

In this appendix we review the research methods that we adopted to study the family processes involved in developing arrangements for money and custody, reorganizing household routines, redefining family relationships, negotiating the legal terms of the divorce, and complying with agreements. Because the study of divorcing families is a relatively new and burgeoning field, research practices are far from standardized. This appendix explains the methodological approach that we developed. First, we review the research strategies that we chose and the reasoning underlying their selection. Next, we describe the structure of the data set that was generated using these methods. Finally, we explain the guidelines that we developed to work with recurring issues in analysis and interpretation that were presented by this data set.

Research Design

Some elements of our research design were dictated by special considerations governing the study of family processes over time. In addition, we hoped to avoid some of the methodological problems that have rendered findings from earlier investigations equivocal or difficult to interpret. (For reviews, see Clingempeel and Reppucci, 1982; Emery, 1982; Furstenberg et al., 1983.) Among the most serious charges leveled against the existing body of research on divorcing families is that it is limited in scope. Well-educated white families dominate the literature. Few studies include father-custody or joint-custody families. Investigations are not comparable with respect to the age range of children involved, the family members studied, or the measures used to study them. As a result, it is difficult to evaluate conflicting findings or to determine the kinds of families to whom the conclusions apply.

No one study can remedy this situation, but we felt that a useful step toward advancing our understanding about divorce-related processes would be an investigation that combined four key design features, as described below.

First, we wanted a longitudinal approach that would measure critical events as they transpired. The second important feature of our design was that it involved following a cohort of families who were all initiating the divorce process at about the same time. Collection of data from both mothers and fathers was the third key aspect of the design. Finally, we wanted sufficient breadth and heterogeneity in the sample to permit comparison of crucial subgroups of families (for example, those with different forms of custody, the full range of children's ages, varying economic circumstances, and diverse cultural backgrounds).

Prospective Longitudinal Measurement

Our longitudinal design is informed by a body of research (see Hetherington, 1989) that characterizes marital dissolution as a dynamic process that transpires through a series of stages. Factors that drive the process co-vary over time. Individuals adapt at different rates. Therefore, in order to study the process, it is useful to conduct repeated data collections over the course of time. We scheduled our contact with parents to coincide with key events identified in the literature. Three interviews were planned: the first (T-1) occurred shortly after a petition for divorce had been filed; the second (T-2) took place one year after the petition, when many of the early divorces were completed; the third (T-3) took place three years after the petition, when protracted divorces were ending and when families had had time to establish new routines and relationships. Using this useful schedule of interviews, we hoped to optimize the chances of obtaining prospective data. Events would be fresh in the minds of respondents, and bias introduced by intervening events and post hoc reconstruction would be minimized. Retrospective questions would be used to fill in information on events occurring between or before the measurement periods.

Cohort Design

Another important feature of this research is that it employs a "cohort design" (Kessler, 1983). That is, all participants begin the study at an equivalent point in time (the onset of divorce) and engage in successive interviews conducted on the same timetable. This approach offers several advantages over the more common practice of including participants who vary considerably with respect to the time since divorce.

First, the cohort design allows us to observe the status of families across a comparable set of marker points. In addition, we can be assured that differences observed between groups are not attributable to variation in the time since divorce. For example, if we compare the nature of legal conflict found among families, the results are easier to interpret if all families have had the same amount of time to work through the court system. Otherwise, those who separated earlier would have had more time to take legal action and also to resolve disputes.

Despite the considerable advantages of a cohort design, it introduces certain limitations to causal inferences. Because the population of interest is a cohort created by the onset of an event (divorce), the design does not permit collection of information prior to the onset of the event. For example, although we can assess the nature of post-divorce parental interactions, this design does not allow us to measure the parent-child relationship that existed when the family was intact. The absence of antecedent measures of course prevents us from evaluating the relative impact of preexisting characteristics of families or their situations. For example, suppose we observe that fathers who have joint custody feel a stronger emotional bond with their children than other fathers. Is the emotional bond attributable to joint custody, or did the prior emotional bond affect both the custodial choice and the post-divorce relationship? Given the realistic constraints on our research design, how can we evaluate the two different explanations? Like other researchers, we must resort to the use of retrospective measures to complete the picture.

Interviews with Both Parents

Every effort was made to locate and recruit both parents; however, the participation of just one parent was sufficient to include a family in our study. This approach was dictated by the potential advantages of interviewing both parents as well as by the practical constraints associated with recruiting two family members.

It is estimated that only about one family study in seven collects data from more than one parent (Hodgson and Lewis, 1979). The traditional practice of relying exclusively on mothers' reports of family events has recently been severely criticized by family researchers who call for a more balanced perspective. Safilios-Rothschild (1969) argues that only by sampling the points of view of all family members can we gain a clear understanding of the dynamic interactions within the family. Specifically within the field of divorce, researchers insist that the perspectives of both mothers and fathers must be represented. Many previous studies have failed to include the father's viewpoint on visitation, support, and other key issues in the divorce literature (Bowman and Ahrons, 1985; Kelly, 1982; Braver, 1988).

Despite the potential advantages of including both parents, it was deemed inadvisable to restrict the sample to those families in which both parents agreed to participate. Other researchers have reported that dual-participation sampling constraints rule out so many families that the resulting sample is severely biased. Scanzoni (1965) questions whether the findings from such a selective group can be legitimately generalized to the full population. Hiller and Philliber (1985) conclude that restricting a sample to dual participation usually results in a response rate so low that the use of inferential statistics cannot be justified.

A review of existing evidence did not support a high projected rate of dual participation in our own study. For general family research, Scanzoni estimated that only in about half of the eligible families would both parents agree to participate. In divorce-related research, Hetherington, Cox, and Cox (1982) reported that it is particularly difficult to recruit non-custodial parents who do not visit their children. In our study, we faced the added challenge of locating parents. There was a low probability that current address information for both parents would be found in court records, and it was impossible to project how many addresses could be added using supplementary search methods. With these considerations in mind, we sought but did not require the participation of both parents in our study. We expected that when only one parent was interviewed, that parent could give us valid "proxy" information about the other parent with respect to *some* needed items, and this has proved to be the case.

Of the families in the T-1 data collection, 44 percent of the families had both parents participating, 39 percent had the mother only, and 17 percent had the father only. The most common reason for one-parent participation was that the second parent could not be located. Many parents had not yet established their own households at the time when the legal divorce began; often they resided temporarily with family or friends and did not have addresses or telephones in their own names. Because of such transitions and also because of tension between the divorcing couple, it was sometimes the case that one parent did not know (or would not reveal) the whereabouts of the other.

At the time of the final interview, we speculated that things might have stabilized sufficiently so that some second parents could be located. In the final year of the study, we made a concerted effort to establish addresses and telephone numbers for second parents whom we had been unable to locate previously. This effort added 153 second parents (43 mothers and 110 fathers) to the final wave of the study.

Breadth and Heterogeneity

The final key objective of our research design was to develop a sample diverse enough to permit sorely needed comparisons of key population subgroups. Specifically, there is a compelling need to describe different custodial arrangements on comparable dimensions and to make provisions in such comparisons for variations in childrens' ages and family circumstances. It is surprising to find that, although the relative merits of alternative forms of custody are fiercely debated in the literature, few investigations actually provide comparative data about two or more custody arrangements.

Comparisons within and across studies are further limited by constraints imposed on the range of family characteristics represented. For example, studies of divorce are often limited to children within a specific age range, and studies have focused on dissimilar age ranges. Most research evidence about divorce is also confined to the white middle-class population. What is perhaps more serious, a number of studies have limited their samples to people who have volunteered to be studied in return for free counseling or therapy. Our objective was to achieve good dispersion across these family characteristics and to avoid the "volunteer" bias as far as possible, in order to permit an initial glimpse at comparative material.

Nonetheless, the comparison of custodial groups introduces the classic problem of quasi-experimental design. How does one make valid comparisons in the absence of randomization? That is, we know that families are not randomly assigned to custodial groups; these arrangements are very much a reflection of the inclinations and options of each family. For these reasons, preexisting differences in the custodial groups must be considered in any comparison. Any analysis should be sensitive to personal and situational factors that could, over and above the custodial arrangements, affect the course of post-divorce circumstances. It would be misleading to conclude, as some investigations have, that outcomes associated with a particular arrangement can be attributed exclusively to the nature of that arrangement.

Using methods described in the next section, we obtained a good dispersion of family characteristics, including the age, number, and sex of children and the socio-demographic status of parents. The sample includes families from a wide range of backgrounds and circumstances. The average age of mothers at the onset of the study was 33 years, ranging from 19 to 58 years. The average age of fathers was 35 years, ranging from 20 to 63 years. The educational background of parents was quite varied as well: 31 percent of the parents interviewed had a high school education or less; 41 percent had some college or training beyond high school; and 28 percent had completed college or gone on to graduate work.

The mean earnings for mothers at the time of the first interview were $16,049 per year; for fathers, the figure was $34,923. The range is very wide—from those currently unemployed to one respondent with an annual income of $250,000. The sum of parental earnings was somewhat higher at T-1 than it was at the time of parental separation (see Chapter 10).

The ethnic composition of the sample is similar to that of the counties from which it was drawn. Blacks, Asians, and Native Americans are included in small proportions. Only one minority group, Hispanics, was large enough for comparative analysis at 12 percent.

Children of all ages are included in the sample families, ranging from one not yet born at the time of separation to those approaching the legal age of majority. Family size varied from one child to more than six; 47 percent of the children in the study were in one-child families, 41 percent in two-child families, and 12 percent in families with three or more children.

Methodology
Sampling

In order to meet the four central design objectives for our research, we first identified criteria for target families. We needed families with children who would remain minors throughout the course of the study. In addition, we decided to exclude families who had been separated for a lengthy period at the time the divorce was initiated. We reasoned that such families would have completed some of the early decision-making processes of interest to us. Therefore, we excluded these extreme cases and defined our sample to include families with a separation period of no longer than fourteen months prior to the initiation of divorce proceedings.

How does one draw a sample of families who meet our target criteria? The majority of studies of divorcing families have resorted to convenience samples of clients, volunteers for free counseling, or members of parent organizations. We rejected these strategies. Unless a study begins with a listing from the population to which inferences will be made (for example, all divorcing families), it is not possible to determine how well the sample matches that population. Therefore, it is difficult to extrapolate frequencies observed in the sample (such as rates of visitation) to the divorcing population at large.

For example, a convenience sample of families seeking counseling is likely to overrepresent families experiencing adjustment problems or those who use mental health professionals as a coping strategy. It may exclude those who are not experiencing problems, or who deal with family problems in a different way. In the absence of a listing of families from the full population, the extent of such potential bias cannot be evaluated. Therefore, it cannot be determined whether frequencies observed in the sample may be inflated or deflated estimates of those in the full divorcing population.

How could we move closer to making inferences about a wider spectrum of divorcing families? Two challenges are involved: identifying a pool of eligible participants and locating them. Conventional household sampling techniques are not efficient methods of identifying eligible participants. Alternative sampling methods identify eligibles but introduce the new problem of locating them.

The currently divorcing population fits the criteria for what sampling experts define as a "special population" (Sudman and Kalton, 1986). That is, it constitutes such a small segment of the general population that it is difficult and costly to identify this population through conventional screening of households or telephone numbers. For this reason, few nationwide data collections have focused on the divorced population and none on the currently divorcing population. As a matter of practical necessity, the few national data sets (Sweet and Bumpass, 1987; Furstenberg et al., 1983; Zill and Peterson, 1982) target the full population of ever-divorced families (pooling the currently divorcing with those who have been divorced for many years). For example, Furstenberg and colleagues (1983) studied a national sample of families ranging from those who had separated recently to those who had separated more than ten years prior to the data collection. This sample yielded just 28 families who had been separated for two years or less.

In order to obtain a cohort of currently divorcing families, we drew names from court records of divorce petitions. This strategy gave us access to the full range of divorcing families; but it introduced alternative methodological constraints.

The necessity to examine records in order to establish a list of eligibles imposed practical constraints on the geographic scope of our study. Thus we restricted our work to two counties in California: Santa Clara County and San Mateo County. Table B.1 provides a comparative breakdown of age, education, earnings, and ethnicity in the counties studied. Examination of the demographic characteristics of the populations of these two counties reveals a good dispersion of age and education. Direct comparisons are not possible, since the geographic breakdowns reflect the population at large and are not restricted to currently divorcing individuals. Nonetheless, comparison of county, state, and national data on the 1980 Census reveal no striking dissimilarities between the counties chosen for investigation and other regions. Most deviations are probably explained by the fact that our sample is limited to individuals in the child-rearing years. This factor, along with five years of inflation, contributes to the relatively high level of joint parental earnings at Time 1, compared to the norms for our two counties in 1980.

We inspected court records to identify a cohort of families initiating their divorces within a specific time frame (September 1984 to March 1985). Although we were able to identify a list of eligibles, the task of locating them still remained. The difficulty of the task was heightened because a court record sampling frame is comprehensive, including the following groups of difficult-to-locate individuals who would be overlooked in a conventional sampling of households: (1) people without a permanent residence (as a result of the temporary dislocation associated with divorce); and (2) individuals who are incapacitated, incarcerated, or in the armed services (these subpopulations are conventionally excluded from household listings).

Table B.2 summarizes the results of our location and recruitment efforts. Of the 6,685 petitions for divorce that were screened for eligibility, 2,286 met the sampling criteria. Locating mothers and fathers in the eligible families proved to be a difficult task. Court records typically contain the address of the parent with whom the children reside. Additional address information is required only when a parent files forms without the assistance of an attorney. Because of the mobility of divorcing parties, addresses found in the records are not always current (Furstenberg and Spanier, 1984). Information about telephone listings is not required in the court record. When the court records did not yield a current address, we resorted to a battery of standard search techniques used in survey research (such as telephone listings, reverse directories, calls to neighbors, or other referrals).

At the point when families were contacted, we found that some were

Table B.1   Comparisons with full-population demographic statistics

	Age distribution				
	United States[a]	California[b]	Santa Clara County[c]	San Mateo County[c]	Study respondents
19 and under	31.98%	30.78%	31.62%	28.86%	.26%
20–24	9.41	9.95	10.28	8.70	9.31
25–29	8.59	9.43	9.76	9.21	21.98
30–34	7.82	8.49	9.05	8.91	25.02
35–44	11.32	11.89	13.36	13.15	37.29
45–54	10.03	9.97	10.32	11.55	5.61
55–59	5.14	5.08	4.70	6.17	.46
60–64	4.47	4.19	3.46	4.89	.07
65 and older	11.26	10.2	7.47	10.57	0

Mean annual earnings

Families with children under age 18 in:

United States	$23,092
California	$25,540
Santa Clara County	$29,750
San Mateo County	$31,740

Sample families (at T-1, 1985–1986)

Mothers only	$16,049
Fathers only	$34,923
Family total	$51,024

not eligible for inclusion in the study. Some couples had reconciled. In other cases, information on the record, such as the birth date of the child or the date of separation, was incorrect, and the true information changed the eligibility status of the family. Of the 2,286 families that appeared to be eligible from the records, an estimated 1,966 fit the criteria for target families.

By the conclusion of the initial data collection period (August 1985), we had located at least one parent in 61 percent of the eligible families. Location rates for court records sampling frames are usually low and seldom reported. Our location rate compares favorably to those that have been disclosed; for example, Weitzman (1985) reported a location rate of 50 percent, and Spanier and Thompson (1984) one of 37 percent.

Table B.1 (cont.)

	Ethnic identification			
	United States[a]	California[b]	Santa Clara County[c]	San Mateo County[c]	Sample families
Anglo	79.6%	67.0%	71.0%	71.6%	78.7%
Black	11.5	7.5	3.2	5.9	2.7
Hispanic	5.1	19.2	17.5	12.4	11.7
Native American	1.3	.8	.6	.3	.8
Filipino	.6	—	—	—	1.2
Asian	1.5	5.2	7.4	9.5	4.3
Other/mixed	.3	.2	.3	.3	.8
Refused/missing data					.97

	Highest level of education attained: persons 25 years and over				
	United States[a]	California[b]	Santa Clara County[c]	San Mateo County[c]	Study respondents
Elementary school					
0–8 years	18.26%	14.21%	10.52%	8.97%	.59%
High school					
1–3 years	15.27	12.31	9.98	9.45	4.77
4 years	34.59	31.44	28.87	31.46	23.16
College	15.65	22.43	24.27	24.67	40.88
4 or more years	16.23	19.60	26.37	25.45	29.94

a. U.S. Department of Commerce, Bureau of the Census. *1980 Characteristics of the Population: General Population Characteristics: United States Summary.*
b. U.S. Department of Commerce, Bureau of the Census. *1980 Characteristics of the Population: General Population Characteristics: California.*
c. U.S. Department of Commerce, Bureau of the Census. *1980 General Social and Economic Characteristics: California.*

Like other divorce researchers (Wallerstein and Kelly, 1980; Weitzman, 1985), we found that the vast majority of those located were willing to be interviewed. Of the 1,395 eligible families who were located, we recruited 1,124 into the study. In 41 families both parents refused to participate. This refusal rate (3 percent) compares favorably to those reported in other court-records-based research. In Weitzman's (1985) research, 17 percent of those located refused to participate; in Spanier and Thompson's (1984) study, 39 percent refused.

Table B.2   Sample structure

	Time 1		Time 2		Time 3	
Records reviewed	6,685					
Cases pursued	2,286		1,124		1,075	
Estimated eligible	1,966		1,915		1,798	
T-1 families eligible			1,072		1,002	
Not located	891		61		78	
Est. eligible		801		58		70
Est. not eligible		90		3		8
Located						
Not eligible	230		49		114	
Not recruited	41		36		15	
Recruited	1,124		978		917	
Parents	1,615		1,398		1,444	
Mothers		936		799		783
Fathers		679		599		661
Both parents interviewed	491		420		527	
Children		1,875		1,613		1,487
Percentage of pursued cases located	61.02%		94.57%		97.30%	
Percentage of estimated eligible families recruited	57.16%		51.08%		51.00%	
Percentage of pursued cases recruited	54.67%					
Loss due to location	43.34					
Loss due to refusal	1.99					
Percentage of pursued cases maintained			90.98%			
Loss due to location			9.02			
Loss due to refusal			3.35			

At Time 2, we followed only those families who had participated at Time 1. No further attempts were made to locate or to recruit other families eligible at Time 1. The remainder of Table B.2 summarizes sample maintenance over time. The fate of the sample at Time 2 is presented in the next column. An estimated 4.63 percent of the families in the Time 1 sample were no longer eligible at Time 2. This was primarily a result of reconciliation. Of the 1,072 families remaining eligible, 5.41 percent could not be located at Time 2. An additional 3.36 percent refused to participate. The remaining 91.23 percent were interviewed.

The results of the final round of interviewing are shown in the last column. At this point, an estimated 1,002 families remained eligible to be interviewed. Of these, 6.98 percent could not be located. An additional 1.50 percent refused to be interviewed. The remaining 91.52 percent were interviewed.

Table B.2 shows that failure to locate eligible families at Time 1 resulted in the greatest loss to our sample. By exhausting all possible leads, we located 61 percent of the families on the court dockets. Families remaining eligible at subsequent interviews were recruited at a rate of over 90 percent. Even so, location difficulties were the primary source of loss of eligible families. The following tables assess the impact of attrition on the nature of the sample recruited.

Comparison of Recruited and Nonrecruited Cases

Table B.3 uses data from the court records to compare the 1,124 families who were recruited to complete Time 1 interviews with eligible families who did not participate. Recruited and nonrecruited families are similar in family size and the gender of the children. On average, the oldest child was about 5 months older in families not recruited. This difference is not statistically significant.

We also analyzed what the petitioner reported about the residence of the child. In 14.86 percent of the recruited families, the petitioner reported that the children lived with each parent part of the time. This was true in 9.87 percent of the families not recruited. Thus, we were more likely to recruit families in which children were alternating between households. The difference is plausible, since parents who had not established permanent households would be difficult to locate for an interview. Residential instability would also reduce the feasibility of alternating children. The proportion of families in which children lived with their mothers was virtually identical in the nonrecruited and recruited groups. Recruited families were slightly less likely to include families in which children resided with fathers, but this difference is not significant. Families in which there were other arrangements for the child's residence or in which the residence was not given on the petition ($N = 67$) were more likely to be found among those not recruited; this difference is not significant.

We also used court records to compare the petitioners' initial requests for custody. Such preferences were not always borne out in the

Table B.3   Initial comparison of families recruited and not recruited[a]

	Recruited ($N = 1{,}124$)	Not recruited ($N = 932$)	*t*-statistic
Average age of oldest child	6.83	7.23	− 1.85 (n.s.)
Family has a male child	729 (64.86%)	600 (64.38%)	− 0.23 (n.s.)
Family has only one child	531 (47.24%)	473 (50.75%)	− 1.63 (n.s.)
Dual residence at petition	167 (14.86%)	92 (9.87%)	− 3.50 ($p \leq .01$)
Mother residence at petition	825 (73.40%)	687 (73.71%)	0.16 (n.s.)
Father residence at petition	110 (9.79%)	103 (11.05%)	0.93 (n.s.)
Petitioner requests joint physical custody	233 (20.73%)	147 (15.77%)	− 2.79 ($p \leq .01$)
Petitioner requests mother physical custody	768 (68.33%)	651 (69.85%)	− 1.22 (n.s.)
Petitioner requests father physical custody	87 (7.74%)	92 (9.87%)	− 1.78 ($p \leq .10$)
Petitioner requests joint legal custody	777 (69.13%)	541 (58.05%)	− 4.82 ($p \leq .01$)
Petitioner requests mother legal custody	292 (26.07%)	317 (34.01%)	− 4.09 ($p \leq .01$)
Petitioner requests father legal custody	32 (2.85%)	42 (4.51%)	− 2.03 ($p \leq .05$)

a. Based on court records of filings for divorce, 1984–1985.

final judgment; but they do allow us to determine whether the families started out with different objectives. Recruited families were more likely to request joint physical custody by a 5 percent margin. Requests for mother physical custody were equivalent, while there was a tendency (not statistically significant) for father physical custody to be requested less frequently among those recruited. Families not recruited were more likely to be those in which the petitioner's request was not specified; this difference was not significant.

When requests for legal custody are compared, those recruited were more likely to request joint custody by an 11 percent margin, less likely to desire mother legal custody by a 12 percent margin, and less likely to request father custody by a 2 percent margin. All of these differences are statistically significant. In recruited families, the petitioners were also less likely to leave legal custody requests unspecified.

Taken together, these findings suggest that our sample includes a somewhat higher proportion of families who prefer to share child-rearing responsibilities than would be found among all divorcing families. Equivalent proportions of recruited and nonrecruited families had children residing with the mother at the time of petition, and similar proportions requested physical custody for the mother in the divorce petition. The sample does include a smaller number of families in which the petitioner requested mother legal custody. Families in which father was the primary caretaker at the time of the petition are equally present in the recruited and nonrecruited group. In the recruited group, there is a slight tendency for petitioners to be less likely to request father custody; but this is statistically significant for legal custody only. Put another way, we were slightly more successful in recruiting families who preferred child-sharing arrangements and somewhat less successful in recruiting families electing sole legal custody.

At the conclusion of the study, we returned to the court records to make further comparisons between the recruited families and a random sample of eligible families not recruited (Table B.4). We found that the two groups were similar in many respects: they did not differ in the length of their divorce proceedings, the physical custody dispositions, the likelihood that child support would be awarded, or the amount of the awards. This last is especially encouraging in that it points to income similarity between the recruited and nonrecruited families.

Certain differences were found, however. A higher proportion of those not recruited lacked a final divorce judgment in the file. This could be attributable to several factors: if the couple decided not to pursue the divorce but did not formally withdraw the action, no judgment would appear in the file. On the other end of the spectrum, there would also be no judgment if the case was embroiled in protracted legal conflict. When we examined specifically those cases with no final judgment, we found that only a relatively small number (40 in recruited families, 45 in the sample of nonrecruited families) were incomplete and contested, but the proportion was higher among the nonrecruited families. We did not measure the intensity or duration of the disputes, and know little about the nature of these contested matters. The contested cases could range from families who had engaged in heated legal

Table B.4 Later comparison of families recruited and random sample of
not recruited[a]

	Recruited (N = 1,124)	Not recruited (N = 300)[b]	Significance test[c]
Length of divorce pro-ceedings (mean days)	366	393	(n.s.)
Divorce is final	954 (90.6%)	212 (75.7%)	44.71 ($p \leq .01$)
Delay: contested	40 (38.8%)	45 (56.3%)	5.49 ($p \leq .05$)
Contested matters	468 (45.2%)	157 (55.7%)	9.8 ($p \leq .01$)
Joint physical custody	189 (19.8%)	36 (17.0%)	0.89 (n.s.)
Mother physical custody	628 (65.8%)	144 (67.9%)	0.34 (n.s.)
Father physical custody	80 (8.4%)	21 (9.9%)	0.51 (n.s.)
Joint legal custody	743 (77.9%)	140 (66.0%)	13.24 ($p \leq .01$)
Mother legal custody	175 (18.3%)	53 (25.0%)	4.89 ($p \leq .05$)
Father legal custody	17 (1.78%)	9 (4.25%)	4.83 ($p \leq .05$)
Father ordered to pay child support[d]	748 (95.2%)	140 (95.9%)	0.14 (n.s.)
Monthly award per child	$237.30	$223.00	$F = 1.13$ (n.s.)

a. Based on a search of court records conducted in 1989.
b. Random sample of the 932 cases not recruited.
c. The test is Chi square unless otherwise indicated.
d. Includes two cases in which a specified portion of family support was allocated to the child support.

battling for several years, to those who "agreed to disagree" and left a single unresolved matter open in the legal file. Whatever the case, it is clear that the sample we recruited underrepresents the relatively rare cases that have contested matters that persist over time.

Attrition during the Study

Table B.5 compares the families who completed both Time 1 and Time 3 with those who dropped out in the course of the study. Here our sources of comparative data are not limited to the court record; information from the Time 1 interview is used.

The table shows that we did not suffer disproportionate sample loss on the basis of the age or gender of children. Families with multiple children were somewhat more likely to remain in the study.

Mothers and fathers who lacked college degrees were less likely to remain in the study through all data collections. Parental earnings did not influence the probability that the family continued in the study.

At Time 3, we were more likely to retain parents who identified themselves as Anglos. This difference is significant for mothers only. It may be attributable to our loss of funding to maintain the Hispanic version of the interview.

When we compare those who remained in the sample at Time 3 with those who did not, we find no significant differences in the Time 1 residential status of the children nor in the number of overnights that children spent with the father at Time 1.

Those who remained in the sample at the end of the study were significantly more likely to elect the three most prominent forms of physical custody (mother, father, and joint), particularly joint. Joint legal custody was also more prevalent among those who remained in the study.

Rates of sample retention were very high for a survey of this nature. Nonetheless, inferences based on over-time data should take into account that the sample losses that did occur were more pronounced among the less educated, ethnic minorities, families with just one child, and those who did not elect joint legal custody. (In fact, such characteristics are not necessarily independent.)

To summarize, the use of a court records sampling frame restricted our ability to locate substantial portions of families who met our sampling criteria. Although our sample loss holds up favorably to comparable studies of the divorcing population, subsequent attrition analyses point out areas in which our inferences should be cautious. The most severe losses were at the initial recruitment phase. This resulted in a sample with a slightly higher proportion of formal and informal arrangements for child sharing. The proportion of petitioners requesting joint physical custody was about 2 percent higher among those recruited than in the sampling frame as a whole. The proportion of joint legal requests was about 6 percent higher in the recruited sample than in the total. Attrition after initial recruitment was very low. Nonetheless, sample loss served to accentuate the joint-custody bias. Joint physical custody was a little over 2 percent higher among those who

Table B.5 Comparison of families who completed Time 3 with those who
did not

	Time 3 completed (N = 917)	Time 3 not completed (N = 207)	t-statistic
Average age of oldest child	7.20	7.52	0.77 (n.s.)
Family has a male child	606 (66.09%)	124 (59.90%)	1.68 (n.s.)
Family has only one child	409 (44.60%)	124 (59.90%)	4.00 ($p \le .01$)
Mother has a college degree	204 (22.25%)	30 (14.49%)	−2.76 ($p \le .01$)
Father has a college degree	310 (33.81%)	34 (16.43%)	−5.76 ($p \le .01$)
Mother's earnings 1 year prior to separation	$11,374	$12,060	0.60 (n.s.)
Mother's earnings when petition filed	$15,400	$16,217	0.66 (n.s.)
Father's earnings 1 year prior to separation	$32,389	$36,729	1.03 (n.s.)
Father's earnings when petition filed	$34,261	$36,385	0.71 (n.s.)

completed the study and joint legal custody a little less than 5 percent
higher. We were slightly more successful in locating families who were
inclined to share child-rearing responsibilities, presumably because of
the fact that they maintained more stable living arrangements. This
upward bias in shared arrangements should be considered in the interpretation of all statistics based on the sample as a whole. Conversely,
the advantage of over-sampling shared arrangements is realized in the
extra cases available for the study of this innovative arrangement.

Measures

For each of the families included in the study, we attempted to conduct
three interviews with each parent and to complete a content analysis
of the court record of the divorce proceedings. The research was de-

Table B.5 (cont.)

	Time 3 completed (N = 917)	Time 3 not completed (N = 207)	t-statistic
Mother is Anglo	740 (81.23%)	68 (66.02%)	−3.03 (p ≤ .01)
Father is Anglo	714 (79.16%)	42 (73.68%)	−0.78 (n.s.)
Average overnights with child in a two-week span	3.10	2.58	−1.55 (n.s.)
Dual residence at Time 1	146 (15.92%)	22 (10.63%)	−1.77 (n.s.)
Mother residence at Time 1	620 (67.61%)	140 (67.63%)	−0.01 (n.s.)
Father residence at Time 1	90 (9.81%)	17 (8.21%)	−0.71 (n.s.)
Joint physical custody	175 (19.08%)	14 (6.76%)	−3.51 (p ≤ .01)
Mother physical custody	527 (57.47%)	101 (48.79%)	2.80 (p ≤ .01)
Father physical custody	72 (7.85%)	8 (3.86%)	−1.17 (n.s.)
Joint legal custody	651 (70.99%)	92 (44.44%)	−2.23 (p ≤ .05)
Mother legal custody	142 (15.49%)	33 (15.94%)	1.93 (n.s.)
Father legal custody	14 (1.53%)	3 (1.45%)	0.41 (n.s.)

signed to measure key events in the divorce process and to monitor progress toward adaptation and factors assumed to be crucial to that adaptation.

Data were taken from survey interviews. The study does not provide clinical assessment. Each interview lasted approximately one hour, with the duration varying with the number of children, the complexity of the dissolution process, and the verbal fluency of the respondent.

Telephone interviewing was the primary mode of data collection used in the study. Nonetheless, face-to-face interviews and mail questionnaires were available to respondents in order to maximize participation in the study (see Freedman, Thornton, and Camburn, 1980).

Telephone interviewing is rapidly becoming a prominent mode of survey interviewing. Although the technique was initially viewed with skepticism, initial reservations have proven unfounded (see Cannell, Miller, and Oksenberg, 1981; Groves and Kahn, 1979). Conversely, the costs of face-to-face interviewing have increased with the number of visits necessary to recruit subjects. Each method has inherent limitations in sample coverage: face-to-face interviewing is difficult for households with security provisions or in high-risk neighborhoods; telephone interviewing is limited to those with telephones.

It was our judgment that a mixed-mode strategy that emphasized telephone interviewing would yield the best sample coverage. One clear advantage of telephone interviewing is that it minimizes the amount of interviewer time relegated to establishing contact and following up on subjects who break appointments. Indeed, since the number of respondents who were not available for scheduled appointments ranged from 30 percent to 50 percent during the field period, the ability to fill in alternative appointments quickly had a marked effect on the number of interviews that we were able to complete. Another benefit of telephone interviewing is that it permits the researcher to follow subjects who move outside the geographic area in which interviewing is initiated. The disadvantages of the telephone method were balanced by the option of using alternative methods. For example, when a telephone number was not obtained, we were able to resort to a mail questionnaire. If a respondent preferred personal contact, it was possible to schedule a face-to-face interview. It should be noted, however, that requests for personal interviews were quite rare. Respondents seemed to prefer the flexibility, and perhaps the anonymity, of telephone conversations.

In situations in which we were unable to reach the prospective subject by telephone (either because repeated attempts had failed or because we were unable to establish a telephone number), we mailed a brief, self-administered version of the questionnaire to the respondent. At T-1, 1,231 parents were interviewed by telephone or in person, and 384 completed a shorter version of the form by mail. Once we had established telephone information for a participant, we were able to conduct subsequent interviews by telephone or in person. Therefore, at T-2 only 28 interviews were conducted by mail, and at T-3 no mail interviews were conducted.

Interviews administered face-to-face or by telephone were identical and included the full range of questions. We use the label "standard interview" to refer to this form. What we refer to as the "mail interview" includes a smaller number of questions that were suitable for a self-administered format.

For the initial two data collections, the interview was translated into Spanish and conducted by a bilingual interviewer with respondents who preferred to complete all or part of the interview in Spanish. At T-1, this added 31 families to the sample. These families were followed at T-2; but funding constraints at T-3 made it impossible to maintain the bilingual component of the study.

In addition to interviews, we conducted content analysis of the court records themselves. At regular intervals, we scanned records for the sample families. When the final divorce was completed, we coded information from the files about the duration of the process; the involvement of third parties, such as attorneys and mediators; contested issues and their resolution; and the terms of the final judgment. At our final data sweep in the summer of 1989, 170 families still had not completed the legal divorce.

The Data Set

One overriding principle guided the methodological choices described in this appendix: maximization of the information for each family. Following this principle, we interviewed all available parents at all possible time points using whatever mode of interviewing was necessary. From the perspective of sample coverage, this was a wise decision. Had we confined our sample to those families in which standard interviews could be obtained from both parties over all time periods, the number of families included would have been reduced from 1,124 to 289. Obviously, such a stringent sample constraint would have resulted in a very selective sample.

Nonetheless, the complexities of the sample's structure and the mixed interviewing modes introduce a high level of variability in the amount of material available from sample families. A family with the minimal amount of information would be one in which one parent was interviewed by mail at Time 1 only. A family with the maximum amount of information would be one in which both parents completed standard interviews for all three waves and for whom court record analysis was completed. In all, we find 86 different combinations of data sources and interview modes. Therefore, any data analysis strategy that confines itself to a specific pattern or set of patterns is apt to rule out large segments of the sample. Our approach was designed to permit maximum utilization of available information.

Table B.6 describes the number of cases that would be available under different measurement contingencies. By combining categories,

Table B.6 Number of standard interviews, mail questionnaires, and supplemental cases at Time 3

Time 1		Time 2		Time 3		
Mother	Father	Mother	Father	Mother	Father	N
Standard	Standard	Standard	Standard	Standard	Standard	289
Standard	Standard	Standard	Mail	Standard	Standard	2
Standard	Standard	Mail	Standard	Standard	Standard	1
Standard	Mail	Standard	Standard	Standard	Standard	42
Mail	Standard	Standard	Standard	Standard	Standard	16
Mail	Mail	Standard	Standard	Standard	Standard	15
Mail	Mail	Standard	Mail	Standard	Standard	1
Mail	Mail	Mail	Mail	Standard	Standard	1
Standard	Standard	Standard		Standard	Standard	3
Standard	Standard		Standard	Standard	Standard	2
Standard	Standard	Mail		Standard	Standard	1
Standard	Mail	Standard		Standard	Standard	3
Mail	Standard		Standard	Standard	Standard	2
Mail	Standard	Standard		Standard	Standard	1
Standard	Standard	Standard	Standard	Standard		14
Standard	Standard	Standard	Mail	Standard		1
Standard	Mail	Standard	Standard	Standard		3
Standard	Mail	Standard	Mail	Standard		1
Standard	Standard	Standard	Standard		Standard	5
Standard	Standard	Standard	Mail		Standard	1
Standard	Mail	Standard	Standard		Standard	1
Mail	Standard	Standard	Standard	Standard		1
Mail	Standard	Standard	Standard		Standard	2
Mail	Mail	Standard	Standard	Standard		1
Standard		Standard	Mail	Standard	Standard	1
Standard	Standard	Standard		Standard		7
Standard	Standard		Standard		Standard	9
Standard	Standard		Standard	Standard		1
Standard	Mail	Standard		Standard		4
Standard	Mail		Standard		Standard	1
Standard	Mail		Standard	Standard		1
Mail	Standard		Standard		Standard	2
Mail	Standard		Standard	Standard		1
Mail	Mail	Standard		Standard		2
Mail	Mail		Standard		Standard	1
Mail	Mail		Standard	Standard		1
Standard		Standard		Standard	Supplement	51
Standard		Mail		Standard	Supplement	2
Mail		Standard		Standard	Supplement	48
	Standard		Standard	Supplement	Standard	17
	Mail		Standard	Supplement	Standard	20
	Mail		Mail	Supplement	Standard	2
Standard		Standard		Standard		147

Table B.6 (cont.)

Time 1		Time 2		Time 3		
Mother	Father	Mother	Father	Mother	Father	N
	Standard		Standard		Standard	67
	Standard		Standard	Supplement		1
Standard		Mail		Standard		1
Standard		Standard			Supplement	5
	Standard		Mail		Standard	1
Mail		Standard		Standard		45
Mail		Mail		Standard		4
	Mail		Standard		Standard	29
Standard	Standard	Standard	Standard			18
Standard	Mail	Standard	Standard			2
Mail	Standard	Standard	Standard			1
Mail	Mail	Standard	Standard			1
Standard	Standard			Standard		1
Standard	Standard	Standard				1
Standard	Standard			Standard		3
Standard	Standard	Mail				1
Standard	Mail	Standard				2
Mail	Standard	Standard				1
Mail	Standard		Standard			1
Mail	Mail		Standard			1
Mail	Mail		Mail			1
Standard				Standard	Supplement	1
	Standard			Supplement	Standard	2
Mail				Standard	Supplement	3
	Mail			Supplement	Standard	1
Standard				Standard		7
	Standard				Standard	4
	Mail				Standard	6
Standard		Standard				31
	Standard		Standard			7
Standard		Mail				2
Mail				Standard		12
Mail		Standard				14
	Mail		Standard			8
Mail		Mail				3
Standard	Standard					15
Standard	Mail					1
Mail	Standard					1
Mail	Mail					1
Standard						32
	Standard					12
Mail						36
	Mail					11
Total						1,124

we see that of the 1,124 families who started the study, 880 have data for all three waves of the study, 135 for at least two waves, and 109 for one wave only (see Table B.7).

Working with the Data Set: Conventions

The intricacy of the sample structure posed special problems for variable construction and for the analysis and interpretation of research findings. In this section we discuss our approach to two related problems, aggregation and missing data, and describe the construction of our measure of de facto residence in light of the rules that we established for the analysis of this data set.

Rules of Aggregation

The structure of our data set is complex. Both parents were interviewed whenever possible; each answered some questions about each child individually. Therefore, some of our variables can be constructed at the child level, at the parent level, or at the family level. For example, we can conduct an analysis in which each of the 1,879 children in the study is one unit. Alternatively, we can base an analysis on the 1,615 parents in the study. Finally, information can be combined across children and from each parent reporting to conduct analyses on the 1,124 families in the study.

Table B.7 Summary

At least one parent for all three waves		880
Both parents, all waves	367	
At least one parent per wave		
Both parents, waves 1 and 3	12	
Both parents, waves 1 and 2	30	
Both parents, waves 2 and 3	1	
Both parents, one wave	170	
One parent per wave	300	
At least one parent for 2 out of 3 waves		135
Both parents, waves 1 and 2	22	
Both parents, wave 1 only	12	
Both parents, wave 3 only	7	
One parent per wave	94	
At least one parent for one wave only		109

There is increased recognition of the benefits of collecting information from and about multiple family members (Ransom et al., in press), but no consensus exists in the field of family research as to how to combine multi-source information to form variables that describe the family. How are multiple responses from two parents appropriately used in conjunction? A common approach is to measure the "response sufficiency" of reports from one family member (Monroe et al., 1985). That is, by comparison of reports from the mother and the father, the researcher determines how well one report would constitute a valid measurement of the family attribute. Such an analysis may advise the use of one report to represent the family (thus alleviating the sampling restrictions imposed by recruiting multiple family members). When the congruence between mother and father reports is low, a single report is biased. Collection of additional interviews may be required to balance the perspective of a single reporter.

Our goal was to use any and all data available from the families in the study. Two fundamental issues were addressed in each analysis: (1) how, if at all, to summarize information across children; and (2) how, if at all, to merge the reports of two parents.

Combining information across children. In this research we are dealing exclusively with parent reports about the children. No information was collected directly from the children.

Numerous questions in the interview require answers for each child individually. For many purposes it is useful to report the full range of answers to these questions. For example, in examining the amount of contact that children who live with one parent have with the non-custodial parent, we might want to compare boys with girls, or children in different age groups; for this purpose, it would be appropriate to take each of the 1,879 children in the sample as one unit of analysis. However, if we want to see whether the amount of contact is related to the amount of legal conflict that has occurred between the parents since divorce papers were filed, the appropriate unit of analysis is the family ($N = 1,124$ at Time 1). (Otherwise, families with more than one child would be represented more than once in the analysis.)

There are several alternative strategies for developing a measure that summarizes properties of the children collectively. For example, depending on the purpose of the analysis, it is legitimate to create a sum, an average, or a deviation score. Single indicators could be constructed to capture the variation in family composition (for example, the family has boys only, girls only, or children of both sexes). In other cases it is useful to select a target child to represent the family.

Despite the wide range of choices for variable construction, a consistent strategy was preferable. This would ensure that differences observed in two variables were not attributable to artifactual variation in the creation of a summary measure. We were interested in an aggregation strategy that would be easy to interpret and that could be used consistently across the broadest possible range of analyses included in this book. Therefore, we rely most frequently on averages to summarize answers across children. Exceptions to this rule occur only when the use of an average is not advisable for a specific analysis. These instances are noted and described.

Combining information across parents. Various methods exist for combining information across parents to form a measure of a property of the couple or of the family. Again, the specific approach must be guided by the theoretical objectives. In our own research, we considered the report of one parent to be a sufficient representation of the family for some variables but not for others. Either parent could tell us, for example, about family demographics, the current residence of the children, and what each parent was asking for in the bargaining over custody. Parents frequently differed, however, in their perceptions of family dynamics, and we did not use proxy information to fill in data for noninterviewed parents for such variables. For some variables where we could use the report of only one parent, we nevertheless wished to use information from both parents.

How do we combine the two-parent observations? Several strategies are possible. For example, we could sum answers, present patterns of responses, or measure the consistency in parental perspectives. All such strategies would, however, be limited to families in which both parents were interviewed, precluding the use of more than half of the families in the sample. We needed an approach that would allow us to use data from families in which just one parent reported but that would also allow us to augment the variable with information from a second parent when available.

Our aggregation rules needed to take the fullest possible advantage of the data we had been able to collect. For example, having invested in the collection of information from both parents, we were opposed to strategies that would ignore huge segments of data (such as random selection of one parent from each family). Nonetheless, we needed to be sensitive to the fact that the families in our study were not equivalent with respect to the number of family data points available (such as number of parents interviewed, mode of interview, participation over time). Throughout the analysis-inference process, we needed to consider the impact of this lack of equivalence.

Averaging was the most useful aggregation strategy for our purposes. As with aggregation across children, the technique had widespread utility and easy interpretability. In addition, it permitted us to use second-parent data when available and in a metric that was comparable to the answers derived from sole-parent data. Nonetheless, we are aware of the limitations and potential abuses of averaged data (see Ransom et al., in press; Townsend and Deimling, 1983), and we adopt this technique with caution. For example, averages are influenced by, yet conceal, extreme individual scores. Therefore, we cannot assume that two families with the same average family score have the same underlying configuration of parent scores.

Throughout the book, there are instances when simple averaging strategies were not sufficient. Most prominent is the construction of the variable indicating the residence of a child. Later in this section we describe our strategy for constructing this variable. Our rules for combining information from two parents about multiple children were governed by two considerations: consistently resolving legitimate sources of discrepancies (intervening changes between the parents' interviews), and assigning preference to the data of best quality (for example, giving priority to interview modes that permitted probing and clarification).

Missing Data Conventions

All longitudinal research faces the problem of missing data. Invariably, some cases in the sample have missing data at certain points in the data base. The classic trade-off is whether to delete the case missing the information or to estimate the information from other data about the individual. The danger associated with case deletion is that it limits sample representation and reduces statistical power; the danger inherent in imputation is that it does not provide an accurate estimate of the missing information. For example, in analyses that require that all included cases have answers to all variables included, our choice is to drop the sample data base down to the subset of cases with full data or to find a suitable approximation to the missing information. If a potential proxy measure is identified, it is possible to compare results of analyses including proxy cases with analyses confined to extant data. This procedure identifies the effects of case deletion versus estimation.

   The worst-case scenario in our own data set is the income variable.
We know that, at Time 1, 220 mothers and 164 fathers completed mail
interviews. Since the mail interview did not include income information, we are missing self-reported income from one parent in five.
Certainly, such a large gap could influence findings involving this crucial variable. Our approach to this egregious missing data problem was
first to seek potential variables for imputation and then to test how
well they estimated the missing information. Guiding this process is
the degree of precision required for the income measure. That is, if
our inferences require precise estimation of dollar amounts, any imputation strategy will have difficulty meeting that requirement. However,
if we are interested in assigning individuals to fairly broad income
categories, it may be possible to identify a proxy measure that is satisfactory.
   Fortunately, we have several alternative items to use in imputing
missing income information. Because most mail respondents completed standard interviews in subsequent waves, we have their self-
reports at Time 2 and Time 3. Another source of income information
is the court record itself, since income information is usually collected
as a basis for child support awards. Finally, since the standard interview asked for income of spouse as well as self, the proxy report of
the other parent is another source of information for imputation. Thus,
it is possible to run a regression using cases that have all sources of
information and to learn which of the alternative income measures is
the best estimator of Time 1 self-reported income.
   In addition to the statistical test, two other considerations must
guide the selection of a proxy measure: simplicity and consistency. In
order to preserve the original data as much as possible, we tried to
minimize the number of manipulations to the raw data. In addition, we
were interested in a missing data strategy that had the most widespread
utility for the greatest number of situations.
   Using the second parent's report to estimate missing income information met the tests of simplicity, consistency, and accuracy. This
convention was used as much as possible to form a general approach
to missing data problems. In each case, before using one parent's
report as a proxy for the other's, we first examined the degree of
relationship between existing self-reports and spouse reports. If congruence was low, spouse reports were not used as proxy measures. In
the case of income, there is no significant difference between spouse
report and self-report on the income measure. A final test of the effects

of case deletion versus imputation is to repeat the analysis, first excluding and then including the cases with proxy data.

To summarize, our objective once again is to make use of the maximum amount of data collected. Our conventions for the treatment of missing data attempt to avoid situations in which the analysis is confined to the families with perfect representation throughout the study. Instead, we have attempted to develop simple and consistent strategies that permit additional cases to be added without introducing new error. Our augmentation strategies are routinely tested to ascertain how they have affected the results.

Frequently Used Subgroups

Our approach to the analyses presented in this book is to regard the three interviewing times as snapshots in the progression of the divorce. At each time, we use all available information. In analyses that compare families over time, we include all available cases at each time period. This would include proxy information, if it passed tests of sufficiency. Obviously, this approach requires a system of subsidiary checks to verify that alternative forms of error are not introduced by the strategy of allowing cases to appear in some waves but not others.

For example, in some of our analyses, we include all families with information at a particular wave. A more conservative strategy might require deletion of families that do not have information for every wave. In such instances, we first conduct the analysis using all available cases. Then we repeat the analysis, restricting it to those with data at each time point. If the outcome of each analysis is equivalent, then we can be assured that the use of all available cases is justified. When the results deviate, then our inferences must be tempered by the possible effect of sample loss on the analysis.

A similar problem encountered in other analyses is the use of all parents to compare perspectives of mothers and fathers. If such analyses are confined to families with both mothers and fathers represented, then we could be assured that the results suggested differences in perspective in the same family. When families with only one parent reporting are included, the results may be affected by the kinds of families with sole-mother or sole-father reports. In order to assess the effects of the case inclusion strategy, we conduct the analyses first using all available parents; then the analysis is repeated on the families with two-parent reports. If the results are the same, we know that the inclusion of families with one parent reporting has not distorted the results, and we can be assured that the use of additional families better represents the full spectrum of families. When the results differ, our inferences must be adjusted accordingly.

Some sample restrictions are dictated by specific analyses. For example, in cases comparing the parenting activities of each parent, it is necessary to confine the sample to those families in which each parent has sufficient contact with the child. Similarly, an analysis of change over time requires a subsample of those families with data at all three time periods. The maximum N from one variable to another varies for a number of reasons. Some measures were available on both mail and standard forms of the questionnaire; others were not. For some variables, reports from the ex-spouse were available; for others, they were not. Different levels of analysis also yielded different Ns.

Determining Time 1 De Facto Residential Custody

The pivotal measure in the analyses used in this book is the de facto residence of the child. This section describes the construction of this complex measure and illustrates the principles for measurement and analysis described above.

Our measure of residence was based on the number of overnights that a child spent in each parent's household. Following the convention in the literature (Steinman, 1981; Kelly, 1980), we defined an arrangement as "dual" if the child spent a minimum of one-third of the time with each parent. Based on a hypothetical two-week period, we defined an arrangement as "dual residence" when the child spent 4–10 overnights with the father. "Mother residence" involved 0–3 overnights with the father, and "father residence" 11–14. This measure of the division of time bore a strong relationship to parents' answers when queried directly about where their children resided (that is, with the mother, the father, or each parent part of the time).

When a family had more than one child, different living arrangements for individual children were rare. For all such discrepancies, the raw data were reviewed to determine the reasons for variation and to establish the dominant arrangement, if any. For example, we observed that in some cases, younger children alternated in dual arrangements while an older sibling established residence with just one parent. When some children lived with their mother and others with their father, the residence was labeled "split." When some children's residence was dual and the others sole, the family was labeled "dual residence."

Since interviews were done within the school year, the measure of de facto residence applies to the typical division of time during the school year. Summer variations in this arrangement are not incorporated into the measure.

Because the first interview was conducted near the time the legal divorce began, many families had not yet established firm agreements about residence and visitation. In order to determine the best estimate of the number of overnights that the child spent with each parent, we used a hierarchy of indicators. First, we determined overnights from an established schedule of visitation, if one existed. If there was no established schedule, we asked for the times when the visiting parent most commonly saw the child. If there were no common times, we used a record of the beginning and ending times of each visit in the two weeks preceding the interview. If there was no information about the past two weeks, then we used the respondent's description of where the child lived (with mother most of the time, father most of the time, each parent part of the time, or some other arrangement). This method resulted in a residence measure based on the best source of information in each family; 67 percent of the answers were taken from an established schedule, 12 percent from a common pattern, 21 percent from visitation in the preceding two weeks, and a negligible percentage from the label assigned by the parent.

We found a high degree of consensus between the measures of residence derived from the reports of mothers and those of fathers. In the 14 percent of cases in which there were discrepancies between parents, the difference was usually attributable to a residential change in the period between the two interviews. When discrepancies existed in the code for residence derived from two parents' interviews, we selected the answer of the parent who had the highest quality of data, as determined from the hierarchy described above. If two parents had data of equivalent quality, then we selected the answer of the parent timed most closely to the target date of interview. That is, at Time 1 we selected the parent interviewed first (closest to the petition time), and in subsequent waves we selected the parent interviewed last.

Summary Comment

The nature of the information that we wanted to collect imposed certain constraints on our research methods. For example, our need to identify a cohort of divorcing families led us to a court records sampling frame, which in turn led to geographic restrictions of the sample and posed serious challenges for locating a sizable number of eligible families. In addition, our desire to learn the perspectives of both parents led to a complex data structure in which different families have different data configurations. Measured against conventional standards for household surveys of individuals, the rate of families captured in the sample is only moderately high. Yet the data set offers advantages that cannot be realized in a conventional household survey. Among these are the inclusion of both parents in a substantial portion of our cases, the ability to focus on recent divorces while maintaining a substantial sample size, and the ability to follow a cohort of families over time. Although we recognize that we do face limits in making population estimates from these data, the study has three important strengths: the equivalent timetable of families, the heterogeneity of the sample, and the ability to compare the perspectives of both parents. The substantial number of dual-residence families also permits detailed analysis of this emergent family form.

Nonetheless, it is a fair question to ask whether the findings of this study can be generalized to the full divorcing population. Certainly, the study of two counties in California cannot yield sound estimates of the parameters of the population of divorcing families across the nation. Rather, we see our research as an important milestone in the progression toward nationally representative data. By including a wider range of divorcing families than most studies, this investigation can permit the first glimpse at the simultaneous consideration of such factors as custodial arrangements, age of children, social class, and ethnic background. Rich descriptive material can be brought to bear on the study of divorce-engendered family processes. Our work should also generate useful debate about the feasibility of certain methodological approaches and the suitability of the strategies we have developed to work with the methodological limitations.

Notes

1. Introduction

1. California Civil Code, Section 4600 (A).
2. See, for example, Wallerstein and Kelly (1980); Hetherington, Cox, and Cox (1982).
3. Family historians have claimed that the bonds of kinship have long counted for less in the United States than in Western Europe, and that American and English marriages have been premised on "affective individualism" in which emotional bonds between spouses were important. See Stone (1977) and Shorter (1975).
4. Furstenberg and Cherlin suggest that "attitude change is partly a circular process" (1991, p. 7). "Behavior influences attitudes which in turn influence behavior." We suspect that the law was part of this cycle as well: the increase in divorce rates and the softening of attitudes helped to make possible the no-fault legal reforms, which in turn may have contributed to a further softening of attitudes.
5. For a general discussion of the significance of gender roles on family law development, see Rhode (1989, chap. 7) and Fineman (1991).
6. For a discussion of the widespread adoption of legislation favoring joint custody, see Folberg (1984, 1991); Scott and Derdeyn (1984, p. 456); and Singer and Reynolds (1988, pp. 497–498).
7. "The most persistent change in gender roles," according to economist Victor Fuchs, has been the dramatic increase of women into paid employment (1988, p. 10). He notes that the most dramatic increase has occurred among married women with husbands and children in the home.
8. See Hochschild (1989, pp. 277–282) for a discussion of research on who does child care and housework.
9. For an excellent history of the social and political movement establishing no-fault divorce, see Jacob (1988).
10. Emphasis added.
11. California Statute, 1970, Chapter 1545, Paragraph 3139, § 2.
12. California Statute, 1972, Chapter 1007, Paragraph 1855, § 1.
13. See California Civil Code, Section 4600(b)(1).

14. California Civil Code, Section 4600 (emphasis added).
15. California Civil Code, Section 4600.5(b). Effective January 1, 1989, a new provision states that the existing custody standard "established neither a preference nor a presumption for or against joint legal custody, joint physical custody, or sole custody, but allows the court and the family the widest discretion to choose a parenting plan which is in the best interest of the children." S.B. 2510 (Robbins), enacted by 1988 California Statute 1550, codified in California Civil Code, Section 4600(d). (West Supp. 1992).
16. Physical custody involves responsibility for the child's day-to-day care, and under joint physical custody arrangements each parent is responsible for the child for "significant" although not necessarily equal periods. Under joint legal custody, the parents share "the right and the responsibility to make decisions relating to the health, education, and welfare of a child." California Civil Code, Section 4600.5. The statute makes clear, however, that when parents have joint legal custody, either parent acting alone may exercise legal control unless the order specifies that the consent of both parents is required.
17. California Civil Code, Section 4600.5. Effective January 1, 1989, Civil Code Section 4607(a) was amended to make it plain that the mediator was to use his or her best efforts to bring about a settlement "that is in the best interests of the child or children," and the language was deleted that suggested that the resolution should necessarily ensure contact with both parents.
18. A mediator helps parents clarify and discuss the issues in their conflict in order to reach an agreement. The mediator also serves as a resource, providing information about the various custodial arrangements available to the family. In contrast, evaluators are professionals appointed to determine, using interviews and observation of parent-child interactions, the best possible custody arrangement in order to make a recommendation to the judge. Often mediators and evaluators are part of a separate department attached to the court, such as Family Court Services in San Mateo and Santa Clara counties. It is the county's local option whether one person can be both mediator and evaluator for a family.
19. Even though they are unable to agree before the trial, parents may come to an agreement during the trial as a result of the advice of their lawyers or an informal conference in the judge's chambers in which the judge indicates that he intends to follow the guidelines set forth in the evaluator's report should he have to decide custody.
20. Gender-neutrality has been strongly criticized by some scholars who argue that ignoring gender means ignoring the real disadvantage women face in the labor market, the greater child-rearing burdens generally assumed by mothers, and the fact that their greater experience may make mothers better single parents than fathers: see Rhode (1987, pp. 521–534); Bartlett and Stack (1986, p. 14) ("In making custody decisions and enforcing the rights of fathers, courts have tended to be too easily impressed by the good intentions of fathers and have exaggerated the credit due them for their newfound willingness to assume some active role in parenting.").

Professor Olsen has argued that gender neutrality is a misnomer because any perceived neutrality will be male-biased in a patriarchal society; see Olsen (1984). Finally, several critics contend that the result of gender neutrality is to punish mothers who have not fulfilled traditional feminine roles by refusing to grant them custody; see Neely (1984, pp. 177–183).

21. For example, see Bartlett and Stack (1986) (arguing that gender neutrality has placed women in the position of having to "negotiate away economic for custodial rights"); Mnookin and Kornhauser (1979); and Rhode (1987, p. 531).

22. On the fathers' rights side, some advocates have argued that while many state statutes are gender-neutral in form, since some include a primary caretaker presumption, men are unlikely to be given custody of younger children. They argue that this is unfair because who took care of the children *before* the divorce is not necessarily the best indicator of which parent is better capable of doing so. See Atkinson (1984, pp. 8–13).

23. See Mnookin and Kornhauser (1979, p. 951, note 2). Most claims about the proportion of custody cases that are adjudicated are not based on empirical research. There are few empirical studies. See McIsaac (1983); Weitzman and Dixon (1979); Graham (1985).

24. Both the gender-conscious (tender years doctrine/maternal presumption) *and* the gender-neutral approaches may have potential advantages and disadvantages for men and women. See Roth (1977, p. 423); Sheppard (1982, p. 229); Uviller (1978, p. 107). Indeed, feminist scholars and fathers' rights advocates are divided on this issue precisely because plausible theoretical arguments can be made either way. Empirical evidence would inform this debate, though clearly not resolve it. The conflicting claims involve value judgments that are not subject to falsification by data, and long-run predictions concerning social change.

25. See Levy (1968); Mnookin (1975).

26. See, for example, Scott and Derdeyn (1984).

27. See Hetherington et al. (1982); Santrock, Warshak, and Elliott (1982).

28. See Emery (1988) for a summary.

2. Understanding the Processes of Divorce

1. For similar distinctions see also Bohannan (1979, pp. 29–55).

2. A great deal of research and scholarly debate has surrounded the issue of gender division of labor. In 1981, Gary Becker's *A Treatise on the Family* provided a theoretical rationalization (human capital theory) for the sexual division of labor in families. Barrett (1982) criticizes Becker's explanation of the sexual division of labor: "Although [his] analysis is intuitively appealing in its explanation of past practice, its prediction that the distribution of housework between men and women should be substantially different where women work outside the home relative to when they do not, and where the wife's relative earnings are high versus when they are low is not borne out by the facts. Instead, in the face of a mass exodus of married women into paid employment, there has been relatively little

change in familial economic gender roles." (In fact, Barrett claims that "until we are willing to restructure the household economy as an egalitarian institution, for instance, by mandating equal time spent in child care and other unpaid activities, economic parity for women will never be fully realized.") Becker, in a later piece, responds to some of the criticisms by arguing that the division is more a result of the lower opportunity cost for women of pursuing household work (Becker, 1985).

3. W. J. Goode first pointed out the significant economic impact of divorce in 1956. He challenged others "to recognize the financial difficulties that ensue for both parties to the divorce . . . In most cases they were barely able to get along when the household was intact, and did not accumulate much property. Husband and wife divide the administrative problems of the household, contributing 'unpaid' services toward its continuity. When the divorce occurs, the gap cannot be filled . . . The expenses of each human unit are greater in the separated or divorced family than in the ongoing family, but the income may not increase to meet the greater demands."

4. See also Parke and Sawin (1976).

5. One sees some kinship here with the position advocated by Goldstein, Freud, and Solnit.

6. See Maccoby and Martin (1983) for a review of research on the effects of stress on parent-child interaction.

7. Much of the discussion that follows draws on and extends Mnookin and Kornhauser's 1979 article "Bargaining in the Shadow of the Law: The Case of Divorce."

8. The impact of the law and of legal institutions on divorce bargaining has received further attention since Mnookin and Kornhauser published "Bargaining in the Shadow of the Law: The Case of Divorce" in 1979. See, for example, Mnookin (1984); Griffiths (1985); Melli, Erlanger, and Chambliss (1988); Sarat and Felstiner (1988).

9. Some scholars and judges have suggested a legal framework that would treat divorce with kids and divorce without kids as two completely distinct legal problems. See Glendon (1986).

10. The role of judges is further highlighted by the broad discretion which they have been granted in this field. See Glendon (1986); Mnookin (1975).

11. For a description of the child support guidelines in effect at the time of our study, and the subsequent evolution of California guidelines, see pp. 116, and 352 n. 14.

   Before the 1980s, state court judges characteristically had very broad discretion to establish the amount of child support awards under vague state legislation. As a result of federal legislation enacted in the 1980s, states are now required to establish "guidelines" that operate as rebuttable presumptions in all support proceedings. The Child Support Enforcement Amendments, enacted in 1984, required guidelines as a condition of participating in the Aid to Families with Dependent Children program but did not require states to make the guidelines mandatory. As of October 1,

1989, the Family Support Act of 1988 required states to adopt mandatory guidelines that would operate as rebuttable presumptions in all support proceedings.

Most states now have child support guidelines that establish presumptive support awards based on the combined income of the two parents and their relative shares. While state guidelines vary considerably, as of February 1990, 32 states had some form of an "income shares" model in which the amount of the total support obligation under the guidelines depends upon the combined income of both spouses. This total support obligation, often specified in a table, is allocated between the two parents in proportion to their relative income. The non-custodial parent is then ordered to pay his (or her) share to the custodial parent. Some 15 states have adopted a model in which the child support award depends *only* on the non-custodial parent's income. See Munsterman et al., *A Guide to Child Support Guidelines* (National Center for State Courts, 1990).

Should the fact that the children are spending time in both households affect the level of child support awards established by the guidelines? Should a non-custodial parent get "credit" for his expected expenditures on the child while the child visits? How should joint custody affect the level of support awards? Once again, states vary (see Munsterman et al., 1990, pp. 23–26), although most permit some sort of adjustment when parents share custody. The evolution of the California guidelines since our study was completed suggests the range of possibilities. See note 14, p. 352.

12. The term "preferences" is being used very loosely here. Parenting is an activity requiring considerable self-sacrifice in the interests of children. Traditional exchange-bargaining theory does not easily encompass altruistic behavior, although a number of recent writers have dealt with the issue thoughtfully.

3. Characteristics of the Families Studied

1. See Chapter 2, "Land of Dreams and Disaster: Postindustrial Living in the Silicon Valley," in Judith Stacey's book *Brave New Families* (1990).
2. See the Current Population Survey conducted in March and April, 1986. Earnings and labor force participation refer to the year 1985.
3. See also Jessie Barnard on "his and her marriages" in *The Future of Marriage* (1972).
4. We asked each parent about his/her working hours at Time 1, and also asked whether the hours had changed since the pre-separation period, so that for each respondent we were able to work backward to an estimate of pre-separation working hours. However, we did not ask respondents to give this information about the former spouse, so we do not have "proxy" information about working hours for the non-interviewed spouse in cases where only one parent was interviewed, as we do for income and involvement in child care.

4. Initial Residence and Visitation

1. This proportion closely approximates the cutoff point of at least one-third time with each parent informally used in California to define joint custody. Other researchers (for example, Camera and Resnick, 1988) also use the "at least two-thirds" definition to distinguish sole from dual residence.

5. Child Custody

1. If every father for whom we had no information had desired mother custody, then 59 percent of all fathers would have wanted mother custody.
2. In theory, parental requests could conflict for either of two reasons: (1) the petitioner might have sought more custody for himself or herself than the respondent had requested; or (2) the petitioner might have been seeking *less* custody for himself or herself than the respondent had requested. In practice, nearly all the conflicts involved each parent wanting *more* custody than the other would provide. In fewer than 1 percent of the cases was there a conflict between the petition and the response because one parent was requesting a form of custody that would give the other parent more custody than he or she had requested.
3. The absence of conflicting requests does not necessarily mean, of course, that it was easy for all these parents to agree on the custodial arrangement, or that there was never significant legal conflict. As we show in Chapter 7, intense and bitter bargaining over custody sometimes results in a negotiated resolution before a petition or response is filed.
4. These pilot studies were conducted by Michael Wald and Eleanor Maccoby, with their seminar students. In 1979, 21.2 percent of the final decrees provided for mother physical custody and joint legal custody; 4.4 percent provided for joint physical custody, which necessarily includes joint legal custody.
5. In 1981, 23.9 percent of the final decrees provided for mother physical custody and joint legal custody; 13 percent provided for joint physical and legal custody.
6. Because of the large number of fathers failing to make a specific request, this relationship is significant for mothers only.

6. The Economic Provisions of the Divorce Decree

1. For a description of the evolution of California guidelines and Federal legislation see p. 342 n. 11 and p. 352 n. 14.
2. In almost half the cases in which the father received sole physical custody, the court reserved judgment on child support. By contrast, when the mother received sole physical custody, the child support issue was decided in 92 percent of the cases. In joint custody cases, support was usually decided, but not quite so often as in the mother-custody cases. It appears that the court was reluctant to issue a final order providing that no child support would be paid in cases involving less traditional and possibly less stable custody arrangements.

3. This rate of spousal support is almost five times higher than that found in the rest of the country (see Table 6.3). Nevertheless, it is low compared to the rate of child support.

4. It should be noted that our sample excluded all divorcing couples without a minor child under 16. Some of these, especially those involving marriages of long duration with grown children, may have awarded spousal support.

5. *Current Population Survey,* March/April Batch File: Alimony and Child Support (machine readable data file) conducted by the Bureau of the Census for the Bureau of Labor Statistics. Washington: Bureau of the Census (producer and distributor), 1988.

6. The compliance numbers in our sample are somewhat higher than those calculated for the United States because we average the reports of payments by mothers and fathers, whereas the national sample has only the reports of the mothers. Our numbers reflect the fact that fathers report higher compliance on average than do mothers.

7. Conflict over the Terms of the Divorce Decree

1. Sarat and Felstiner (1986); Sarat and Felstiner (1989) are exceptions in that they focus on the office practice of divorce lawyers.

2. For those families where only one parent was interviewed, that parent's score became the family score. The scores for these families did not differ significantly from the scores for families where both parents were interviewed. In families where both parents were interviewed, the correlations between mother's and father's ratings were as follows: custody, $R = 0.52$; visitation, $R = 0.41$; child support, $R = 0.30$; spousal support, $R = 0.53$; family home, $R = 0.31$.

3. Because parental conflict ratings were only available for families interviewed at Time 3, Figure 7.2 represents the distribution of conflict for 802 families. The number of responses to the family home questions is smaller because families that did not own a home did not respond to this question.

4. We were able to determine the disposition of the family home for 411 of the families that owned homes. The mother kept the home in 37 percent of these cases and the father in 26 percent. In 38 percent of the cases, the home was sold and (usually) the spouses split the proceeds. Needless to say, families that own homes have somewhat different characteristics from families that do not. The former tend to have longer marriages and more children, and both fathers and mothers in these families tend to earn more than their counterparts who are not homeowners. Chapter 6 discusses these relationships in detail.

5. See Hart and Sacks (1978).

6. For comparison with the court record information, we selected the higher of the two custody conflict ratings (custody conflict and visitation conflict).

7. The roman numerals in Table 7.A1 (in Appendix A) indicate the conflict level assigned by our combined measure; the arabic numbers show the number of families in each cell.

8. We may underestimate the amount of legal conflict, since we are dealing only with those families whose decree was final by the end of our study. We have 917 cases for whom we had T-3 interview data, and of this number 799 had final divorces by September 1989 and 118 did not. Their respective means on the questions where they were asked to rate themselves on a 10-point scale with respect to how much difficulty they had had arriving at agreement over custody and visitation are as follows:

	Divorce final ($N = 799$)	Divorce not final ($N = 118$)	
Mean difficulty			
Custody	3.12	4.12	($p = .004$)
Visitation	3.43	4.25	($p = .015$)

9. Appendix A contains Tables 7.A2 to 7.A3, which show the *t*-test results and the significance of the differences between intense-conflict families and other families for various variables.

10. We also explored the relationship between parental attitudes toward the divorce process itself and the degree of legal conflict. Not surprisingly, intense-conflict fathers rated themselves as more determined to get the custody they wanted, more willing to involve the courts, and more willing to take risks than their lower-conflict counterparts. Intense-conflict mothers were also more determined to get the custody they wanted and more willing to involve the courts than lower-conflict mothers.

11. Age of youngest child and length of marriage are substantially correlated, but when both are entered into a regression predicting legal conflict, the age of the youngest child is the only significant predictor.

12. See Ash and Guyer (in press).

13. A multiple regression predicting the amount of legal conflict, using only those families in which both parents had a standard interview, yielded the following standardized beta weights:

Father concerned: child's well-being in mother's household	.22
Father's hostility toward mother, T-1	.17
Mother concerned: child's well-being in father's household	.11
Discrepancy: perceptions of pre-separation involvement	.10
Age of youngest child	−.07
Mother's hostility toward father	.02

14. See, for example, Priest and Klein (1984).

15. Note that in divorce, since neither side is typically a repeat player who has reputational interests, a 50-50 set of outcomes is plausible. Contrast T. Eisenberg's (1990) recent findings from a study of dispositions of federal court cases.

16. We began by asking a straightforward question: Is it the case that when parents fight about one distributional issue, they tend to fight about all issues? Or do different families fight over different issues? To assess the likelihood of trade-offs between custody and money issues, we first consid-

ered whether there is any relationship between conflict over one issue and conflict over another. The correlation between conflict over custody and conflict over visitation was especially large ($R = 0.73$). Conflicts over the various money issues were also reasonably related (child support and spousal support, $R = 0.51$; child support and family home, $R = 0.49$; spousal support and family home, $R = 0.44$). Conflicts over custody or visitation and conflicts over spousal support and disposition of the family home were only slightly related, but the correlations between conflict over custody issues and conflict over child support were reasonably large (custody, $R = 0.44$; visitation, $R = 0.47$). This is in itself equivocal, however, for the amount of child support may necessarily be affected by the custodial outcome. For example, if a father is claiming sole father custody, and the mother is claiming sole mother custody, obviously the amount of child support will be affected by the custody outcome.

17. There are, of course, three different elements to the money issue: child support, spousal support, and community property. In this analysis, we considered only child support and spousal support because we were unable to collect information about each family's existing stock of marital property, or its division. We think it very unlikely that the result would be different if we had been able to take the property elements into account. First, only a small portion of divorcing families do have substantial property assets other than a house and pension rights. Second, California community property rules provide a clear entitlement to half the value of the communal property. Therefore, for most families there is little uncertainty about the respective entitlement of each spouse.

18. If the child spent the same amount of time in each parent's household, the amount of scheduled child support received by the lower-income parent was less than if that parent had full custody. See p. 352 n. 14.

19. Because the children in all these cases resided with the mother, and therefore the number of overnights with the father by definition had to be three or fewer per two-week period, the "number of overnights with father" was not a significant predictor of the level of support. This was as expected since for these cases there was little variation in the number of overnights.

20. The regression in Table 7.7 also suggests the possibility of a joint decree effect because the joint decree variable approaches significance. We are unpersuaded that simply having a joint decree in itself reduces the expected child support award after one corrects for overnights with the father. When we ran a regression using a joint decree variable, the custody conflict variable, and a dummy variable representing the interaction between the two using all cases where the children resided either with the mother or in both households, none of these three variables proved to be significant.

8. Continuity and Change in Children's Residence and Visitation

1. The change in percentage in father residence is of borderline significance: $F = 2.91$, $p \leqslant .06$.

2. We saw earlier in this chapter that some families shifted the children's residence after Time 1; thus, for example, the families with mother residence at Time 2 are not always the same families as those having this residence at Time 1, although most of them did remain in mother residence at all three time periods. The question addressed in Figure 8.4 is the following: at each time period, given that a child is living with the mother (or father), regardless of how long that residence pattern has been maintained, what is the probability that the child will have overnight visits, daytime visits, or no visits with the father during the regular school year? And does this probability change as the time since parental separation lengthens?

3. The time change in visitation was significantly different in direction when visitation with fathers by mother-resident children was compared with visitation with mothers by father-resident children. "No visitation" with fathers increased significantly, while "no visitation" with mothers decreased (F for the interaction of time by sex of resident parent was 7.26, $p \leq .001$), and the interaction for daytime visits was of comparable strength.

4. Higher rates of visitation with non-resident mothers than non-resident fathers have also been reported by other researchers, for example, Furstenberg et al. (1983); Seltzer and Bianchi (1988).

5. The parallel question about father-resident children could also be posed: whether a mother's having joint legal custody makes a difference in visitation with her. However, almost all the father-resident families in our sample had joint legal custody, so comparisons with father legal custody are not possible.

6. The F value for income is 6.62, $p \leq .01$; the F for legal custody is 2.18, n.s.

7. There were only 37 girls (from 31 families) who lived with their fathers at all three time periods of the study, and 61 boys (from 47 families). With such small sample sizes, sex differences among subgroups can only be interpreted tentatively. The differences were not statistically significant (see Table 8.A3 in Appendix A).

8. When only one parent was interviewed, that parent could usually tell us about the current marital status of his/her former spouse. But in some cases (more women than men) our respondent had lost track of the former spouse and could not provide information on remarriage; our N's for the remarriage analysis are therefore somewhat lower than the total N for families at Time 3.

9. For families initially in dual residence, the relationship between mother's T-1 hostility and decrease in time with father was significant: Chi square 10.4, $p \leq .01$. The Chi square for father hostility, for those with initial father residence, was 6.1, $p \leq .05$.

10. It is interesting to ask whether continued contact might affect hostility, rather than the reverse. Perhaps continuing contact by children with a non-resident parent could soften interparental hostility through the necessity of cooperation; or, conversely, hostility could be exacerbated when

parents are forced into continued contact through their co-responsibility for children. We find that neither occurs: when we look at the sample as a whole, changes in interparental hostility are not predicted either by the initial distribution of the children's time between the two households, or by changes in this distribution. As we will see in Chapter 9, there are many parents who manage the exchange of children with minimal contact with each other, thus reducing the opportunities for hostility to be either aroused or moderated by co-parental transactions.

11. Such information should soon be available from a longitudinal project in Arizona, directed by Sanford Braver and associates.

9. Parenting and Co-parenting Apart

1. Some co-parenting data presented in this chapter were published in Maccoby, Depner, and Mnookin, 1990.
2. The F for time is 4.67, $p \leq .05$.
3. We find a significant increase in difficulty in monitoring with children's age.
4. A 3×2 analysis of variance (three coparenting patterns: cooperative, conflicted, and disengaged; and two residential groups: sole versus dual) yields a significant interaction: $F = 3.78$, $p \leq .05$.
5. See Steinman, Zemmelman, and Knoblauch (1985); Ahrons (1981).
6. For the purposes of this analysis, if the parents disagreed, their replies were averaged.
7. For the data supporting this conclusion, see Albiston, Maccoby, and Mnookin (1990).
8. In Chapter 4 we combined the parents who said yes to this question with an additional group who spontaneously mentioned concerns about the other household elsewhere in the interview. We reported there that two-thirds of the mothers and 40 percent of the fathers expressed such concerns. In the following analysis, however, we deal only with the answers to the specific question about what parents found upsetting.
9. On some items the two parents' reports were moderately well correlated (for example, on the frequency of talking about the children, and the frequency of arguments). On other items, the correlations were low though significant (for example, on the severity of logistical problems, and whether rules were coordinated). Principal components analysis done separately for mother and father reports yielded almost identical factors and item weightings for the two parents. Furthermore, after the effect of residential arrangement had been partialled out, the two parent reports had similar means and standard deviations on the items making up the two factors. Therefore we judged it to be legitimate to combine the reports of the two parents to obtain a score representing the co-parenting of a parental couple.
10. Items were recoded so as to have comparable means and standard deviations, and were then factor-analyzed. A principal components analysis (with varimax rotation) was done, first for Time 2 data, then for Time 3.

The same two major factors emerged for the two time periods, with the eight items having nearly identical factor loadings on the two factors at the two times.

11. The two factor scores were not unrelated (Pearson $r = -.39$ at Time 2, $-.46$ at Time 3), but the correlations were low enough to permit the two scales to make independent contributions to the variance of other measures.

12. When percentages are computed on the basis of all the families in the study, including those in which the children did not go back and forth, the figures are as follows: Cooperative: 19 percent at Time 1, 21 percent at Time 2; Conflicted: 25 percent and 19 percent; Disengaged: 20 percent and 28 percent; Mixed: 8 percent and 3 percent; Children not spending time in both households: 26 percent and 30 percent.

13. This relationship was not significant at Time 2, and was significant at the .05 level at Time 3.

14. There were two significant main effects and no interaction.

15. Significant at $p = .05$.

16. A regression based on the 223 families where both mothers and fathers were interviewed at Time 1, where co-parenting measures were available for Time 2 (that is, children were spending time in both households), and where legal conflict measures were available (based on Time 3 and court record data) yielded the following values for variable predicting Time 2 discord:

	Standardized betas	R^2
Mother's hostility, Time 1	.28***	
Father's hostility, Time 1	.30***	.42
Legal conflict	.38***	

Comparable figures for a prediction of Time 3 discord from T-2 hostility of the two parents and legal conflict were as follows ($N = .21$):

	Standardized betas	R^2
Mother's hostility, Time 2	.31***	
Father's hostility, Time 2	.09	.21
Legal conflict	.17**	

17. The Chi square for this analysis is 16.5, $p = .01$.

10. Economic Changes over Time

1. *Current Population Reports:* "Child Support and Alimony : 1985," Series P23, No. 152, U.S. Department of Commerce, Bureau of the Census, 1987, report that approximately 50 percent of non-custodial fathers who are required to pay child support do not pay the full amount, and that 25 percent of these fathers pay nothing at all. Several writers have examined factors related to compliance or noncompliance with support awards (Chambers, 1979; Furstenberg et al., 1983; Weiss and Willis, 1985).

2. In the Time 2 interview, respondents were asked to report the amount of child support paid or received per child. Close examination of the data reveals that some respondents misunderstood the question and reported total amounts for all children. Therefore, in Time 2 the data on child support compliance are reliable only for one-child families. To avoid this problem, the question was reworded in Time 3. However, in comparisons of Time 2 and Time 3 we limit the analysis to the one-child families in both periods.

3. This adjustment is calculated from questions in the Time 3 survey which asked if finances have "worked out differently from the way they are stated in the agreement on file in court." If the answer to that question is yes, then the respondent is asked if either or both parents agreed to the change. If both parents agreed to the change, the family is assigned an informal compliance rate of one (full compliance). The lower bound on the proportion of families with modifications is calculated from the number of families in which both parents (if interviewed) said they agreed to the change; the upper bound is calculated from the number of families in which *either* parent said he or she agreed to the change.

4. Although there was little change in median working hours, mothers' *mean* working hours did increase slightly (by 2 to 3 hours per week) over pre-separation levels, indicating that some women who had been working part time (a relatively small group) had moved into full-time employment.

5. Because many children spent time with both parents, we measured the number of children in each household as the proportion of time the children spent with each parent times the number of children. To adjust for the resulting fractional number of children, we used a linear interpolation of the equivalency scales used by the Bureau of the Census in calculating poverty thresholds (*Current Population Reports:* "Characteristics of the Population below the Poverty Level: 1984," Series P-60, No. 152, U.S. Department of Commerce, Bureau of the Census, June 1986). The mean number of children in our sample families was 1.7, so the pre-separation family size was 3.7. Our calculations yielded post-separation family sizes averaging 2.3 for mothers, 1.4 for fathers.

11. Facing the Dilemmas of Child Custody

1. For additional general information on divorce mediation, see Coogler (1978); Emery, Matthews, and Wyer (1991) (confirming earlier findings that mediation "greatly reduced the need for custody hearings and that agreements were reached more quickly in mediation"); Spencer and Zammitt (1976); Winks (1980–81). For information on California's Mediation Program, see Duryee (1991).

2. For arguments supporting the contention that father-child contact declines over time, refer to Folberg and Graham (1979); Atkin and Rubin (1976, p. 29); Hetherington, Cox, and Cox (1976, p. 421). But for some counter-evidence, see Keshet and Rosenthal (1978), whose study found some increases in contact.

3. Some articles which argue that economic support is more likely to continue

where the father has contact with the child include: Abraham (1989); Cza-panskiy (1989); Ellis (1990, p. 86 n. 69) (discussing the heated debate over the validity of empirical work testing the hypothesis that increasing paternal contact increases the likelihood of compliance with child support orders).

4. The power of law to achieve cooperative co-parenting is severely re-strained by an obvious but often overlooked point: some of these families were unable to cooperate *prior* to divorce. Divorcing couples often do not have a history of positive co-parenting or even positive relations; thus it would seem optimistic to expect the law to create post-divorce relations that were not present pre-divorce. (See Cherlin 1991.)

5. See also the summary of research on divorce mediation in Emery (1988).

6. For sources that outline child custody law developments, refer to Cochran (1985, pp. 6–14) and Freed and Walker (1989).

7. For a discussion of the problems of judicial discretion and vagueness in the best interests standard, see Mnookin (1975); Chambers (1984) (while the best interests standard seems "wonderfully simple, egalitarian, and flexible," Chambers notes that it is too broad, allowing for too much judicial discretion, as well as unclear, not elucidating what should be con-sidered; pp. 478, 481, 487–499); Cochran (1985) (standard is the source of great uncertainty); and Crippen (1990).

8. In fact many observers have concluded that the best interests standard still retains gender bias: see Cochran (1985) and Crippen (1990, p. 462) ("Evaluations of parental roles inevitably introduce distortions based on gender stereotyping. Stereotyping of family relationships commonly favors mothers. In fact, the caretaker preference is often described as a presump-tion for mothers").

9. The wisdom of a presumption in favor of joint custody has been hotly debated by legal scholars. See Folberg and Graham (1979); Schulman and Pitt (1982); Scott and Derdeyn (1984); Singer and Reynolds (1988).

10. See, for example, Cochran (1985, p. 54 n. 255) and Singer and Reynolds (1988, pp. 509–511).

11. For arguments and evidence of such benefits, consult the discussion and cited sources in Roth (1977, pp. 450–451, notes 104–105).

12. California Civil Code, Section 4600.5 (West 1983).

13. In theory at least, joint legal custody can play a significant role by making the non-custodial parent (typically the father) feel more responsible and connected to the child. See Robinson (1982–83, pp. 670–671).

14. Recent changes in California child support schedules have modified the structure of the schedules in effect at the time of our study. Because of these changes, the amounts of child support awarded to custodial mothers should increase.

At the time the families in our study were securing a divorce, child support guidelines represented a complicated amalgam of state law and county practice. The Agnos Child Support Standards Act established cer-tain mandatory statewide support minimums below which courts could not go. These minimums, enacted primarily to protect mothers who might otherwise require AFDC, were based on an income schedule that "topped out'' at low income levels. California Civil Code §§ 4720 et seq. Although California had no statewide child support guidelines above these Agnos Act minimums, state law authorized individual counties to adopt "discretionary guidelines" setting higher support levels. The Superior courts in both San Mateo and Santa Clara counties did adopt such schedules to provide guidelines for child support during the pendency of the divorce proceedings. While not identical, the county guidelines incorporated a formula that made child support dependent on (1) the number of children; (2) the combined income of the two parents; (3) the relative incomes of each parent; and (4) the proportion of time the children spent with each parent. The time share adjustment factor meant that the support that the higher-earning spouse would otherwise be required to pay the lower-earning spouse would be adjusted downward to reflect the percentage of time the high-earning parent had primary responsibility for the children. See Norton (1987).

After our study was completed, the California legislature mandated the Judicial Council to adopt a uniform statewide child support guideline, which among other things reflected the "net disposable income of each parent" and "the percentage of time each parent has primary responsibility for the children." California Civil Code, Section 4720.2 (c). Effective March 1, 1991, the Judicial Council adopted a uniform statewide child support guideline that incorporated a formula similar to that previously underlying the San Mateo and Santa Clara county schedules. The statewide formula included a "timeshare adjustment" factor. See Rules of Court, rule 1274.

In response to advocates' concerns that California support orders were too low, and that the expenses of the custodial parent are not in fact usually reduced by reason of the fact that the child spent more time with the non-custodial parent, later in 1991, the California legislature enacted legislation (SB 101) that would have removed the "timeshare adjustment" factor as of July 1, 1992. See California Family Law Report, Vol. 15, No. 9, September 1991. However, SB 101 was subsequently repealed before it ever went into effect, and instead a new law was enacted (SB 370) incorporating a formula that includes a timeshare adjustment based on the actual "percentage of time" each parent is expected to have "physical custody" of the children. This percentage must be specified in the court record. Because of other changes contained in SB 370, the new formula is expected typically to result in higher amounts of child support than would have been required by Rule 1274 or by the old county guidelines in effect during our study. See California Family Law Report, Vol. 16, No. 6, June 1992.

References

Abraham, K. 1989. The divorce revolution revisited: A counter-revolutionary critique. *Northern Illinois University Law Review* 9:251.

Ahrons, C. R. 1981. The continuing coparental relationship between divorced spouses. *American Journal of Orthopsychiatry* 51:416–428.

Ahrons, C. R., and R. H. Rodgers. 1987. *Divorced families: A multidisciplinary developmental view.* New York: W. W. Norton.

Albiston, C. R., E. E. Maccoby, and R. H. Mnookin. 1990. Does joint legal custody matter? *Stanford Law and Policy Review* 2:167–179.

Ambert, A. 1982. Differences in children's behavior toward custodial mothers and custodial fathers. *Journal of Marriage and the Family* 44:73–86.

Ash, P., and M. Guyer. In press. Biased reporting by parents undergoing child custody evaluations. *Journal of the American Academy of Child and Adolescent Psychiatry.*

Atkin, E., and E. Rubin. 1976. *Part-time father.* New York: Vanguard Press.

Atkinson, M. 1984. Criteria for deciding child custody in the trial and appellate courts. *Family Law Quarterly* 28:8.

Barnard, J. 1972. *The future of marriage.* New York: Bantam.

Barrett, N. S. 1982. Obstacles to economic parity for women. *American Economics Review* 72:160–165.

Bartlett, K. T., and C. B. Stack. 1986. Joint custody, feminism and the dependency dilemma. *Berkeley Women's Law Journal* 2:9–41.

Becker, G. S. 1981. *A treatise on the family.* Cambridge, Mass.: Harvard University Press.

——— 1985. Human capital, effort, and the sexual division of labor. *Journal of Labor Economics* 3:S33–S58.

Bohannan, P. 1979. The six stations of divorce. In *Divorce and after,* ed. P. Bohannan, pp. 29–55. Garden City, N.Y.: Doubleday.

Bowman, M. E., and C. R. Ahrons. 1985. Impact of legal custody status on fathers' parenting postdivorce. *Journal of Marriage and the Family* 47(2):481–488.

Braver, S. L., P. J. Fitzpatrick, and R. C. Bay. 1988. *Non-custodial parent's report of child support payments*. Paper presented at the 96th Annual Meeting of the American Psychological Association, Atlanta.

Broderick, C. B. 1975. Power in the governance of families. In *Power in families,* ed. R. E. Cromwell and D. H. Olson. New York: Sage Publications, Halstead Press Division, John Wiley and Sons.

Buchanan, C. M., E. E. Maccoby, and S. M. Dornbusch. 1991. Caught between parents: Adolescents' experience in divorced homes. *Child Development* 62(5):1008–1029.

Cahn, N. R. 1991. Civil images of battered women: The impact of domestic violence on child custody decisions. *Vanderbilt Law Review* 44(5):1041–1097.

California Family Law Report. 1991. Vol. 15(9), September 1991.

Camera, K., and G. Resnick. 1988. Interparental conflict and cooperation: Factors moderating children's post-divorce adjustment. In *Impact of divorce, single parenting, and stepparenting on children,* chap. 9, pp. 169–196, ed. E. M. Hetherington and J. D. Arasteh. Hillsdale, N.J.: Lawrence Erlbaum Associates.

Cannell, C. F., P. V. Miller, and L. Oksenberg. 1981. Research on interviewing techniques. In *Sociological methodology,* ed. S. Leinhardt. San Francisco: Jossey-Bass.

Chambers, D. L. 1979. *Making fathers pay: The enforcement of child support.* Chicago: The University of Chicago Press.

———— 1984. Rethinking the substantive roles for custody disputes in divorce. *Michigan Law Review* 83:477–569.

Cherlin, A. J., F. F. Furstenberg, Jr., P. L. Chase-Lansdale, K. E. Kiernan, P. K. Robins, D. R. Morrison, and J. O. Teitler. 1991. Longitudinal studies of effects of divorce on children in Great Britain and the United States. *Science* 252:1386–1389.

Clingempeel, W. G., and N. D. Reppucci. 1982. Joint custody after divorce: Major issues and goals for research. *Psychological Bulletin* 91(1):102–127.

Cochran, R. F., Jr. 1985. The search for guidance in determining the best interests of the child at divorce: Reconciling the primary caretaker and joint custody preferences. *University of Richmond Law Review* 20:1–65.

Coogler, O. 1978. *Structured mediation in divorce.* Lexington, Mass.: Lexington Books.

Cowan, G., J. Drinkard, and L. MacGavin. 1984. The effects of target, age and gender on use of power strategies. *Journal of Personality and Social Psychology* 47:1391–1398.

Crippen, G. 1990. Stumbling beyond best interests of the child: Reexamining child custody standard-setting in the wake of Minnesota's four year experiment with the primary caretaker preference. *Minnesota Law Review* 75:427–503.

Czapanskiy, K. 1989. Child support and visitation: Rethinking the connections. *Rutgers Law Journal* 20:619–665.

Depner, C. E., K. V. Cannata, and M. B. Simon. In press. Building a uniform statistical reporting system: A snapshot of California Family Court Service. *Family and Conciliation Court Review*.

Duryee, M. A. 1991a. "Demographic and outcome data of a court mediation program." Unpublished report. San Francisco: Judicial Council of California.

———— 1991b. "A consumer evaluation of a court mediation service and a comparison of mandatory court mediation with private voluntary mediation." Unpublished report. San Francisco: Judicial Council of California.

Eisenberg, T. 1990. Testing the selection effect: A new theoretical framework with empirical tests. *Journal of Legal Studies* 19(2):Part I:337–358.

Ellis, J. W. 1990. Plans, protections, and professional intervention: Innovations in divorce custody reform and the role of legal professionals. *University of Michigan Journal of Law Reform* 24:65–188.

Emery, R. E. 1982. Interparental conflict and the children of discord and divorce. *Psychological Bulletin* 92(2):310–330.

———— 1988. *Marriage, divorce, and children's adjustment.* Newbury Park, Calif.: Sage Publications.

Emery, R. E., S. G. Matthews, and M. M. Wyer. 1991. Child custody mediation and litigation: Further evidence on the differing views of mothers and fathers. *Journal of Consulting and Clinical Psychology* 59(3):001–009.

Feldman, S. S., and T. Gehring. 1988. Changing perceptions of family cohesion and power across adolescence. *Child Development* 59:1034–1045.

Fineman, M. A. 1991. *The illusion of equality: The rhetoric and reality of divorce reform.* Chicago: The University of Chicago Press.

Freedman, D. S., A. Thornton, and D. Camburn. 1980. Maintaining response rates in longitudinal studies. *Sociological Methods and Research* 6:87–98.

Folberg, J. 1984. Joint custody law—the second wave. *Journal of Family Law* 23:1–55.

———— 1991. *Joint custody and shared parenting,* 2nd ed., ed. J. Folberg. New York: The Guilford Press.

Folberg, J., and B. Graham. 1979. Joint custody of children following divorce. *University of California Davis Law Review* 12:523.

Freed, D. J., and T. B. Walker. 1989. Family law in the fifty states: An overview. *Family Law Quarterly* 22:367–528.

Fuchs, V. R. 1988. *Women's quest for economic equality,* chap. 1. Cambridge, Mass.: Harvard University Press.

Funder, K. 1986. Work and the marriage partnership. In *Settling up: Property and income distribution on divorce in Australia,* ed. P. McDonald. Australian Institute of Family Studies. Sydney: Prentice-Hall.

———— 1991. Children's constructions of their post-divorce families: A family sculpture approach. In *Images of Australian families,* ed. K. Funder. Australian Institute of Family Studies. Melbourne: Longman-Cheshire.

Furstenberg, F. F., Jr., and A. J. Cherlin. 1991. *Divided families: What happens to children when parents part,* pp. 41–44. Cambridge, Mass.: Harvard University Press.

Furstenberg, F. F., Jr., C. W. Nord, J. L. Peterson, and N. Zill. 1983. The life course of children of divorce. *American Sociological Review* 48:656–668.

Furstenberg, F. F., Jr., and G. B. Spanier. 1984. *Recycling the family: Remarriage after divorce.* Beverly Hills: Sage Publications.

Gjerde, P. F. 1986. The interpersonal structure of family interaction settings: Parent-adolescent relations in dyads and triads. *Developmental Psychology* 22:297–304.

Gleason, J. B. 1987. Sex differences in parent-child interaction. In *Language, gender and sex in comparative perspective,* ed. S. U. Philips, S. Steele, and C. Tanz. Cambridge: Cambridge University Press.

Glendon, M. A. 1986. Fixed rules and discretion in contemporary family law and succession law. *Tulane Law Review* 60:1165–1197.

Goldberg, W. A. 1990. Marital quality, parental personality, and spousal agreement about perceptions and expectations for children. *Merrill-Palmer Quarterly* 36:531–556.

Goldstein, J., A. Freud, and A. J. Solnit. 1973. *Beyond the best interests of the child.* New York: Free Press.

Goode, W. J. 1986. *Women in divorce.* New York: The Free Press.

Graham, B. 1985. Dispute resolution in dissolution cases: A Marion County profile. *Willamette Law Review* 21:551–568.

Griffiths, J. 1985. What do Dutch lawyers actually do in divorce cases? *Law and Society Review* 20:135.

Grillo, T. 1991. The mediation alternative: Process dangers for women. The *Yale Law Journal* 100:1545–1610.

Groves, R. M., and R. L. Kahn. 1979. *Surveys by telephone: A natural comparison with personal interviews.* New York: Academic Press.

Gusfield, J. R. 1963. *Symbolic crusade: Status politics and the American temperance movement.* Urbana: University of Illinois Press.

Hart, H., and A. Sacks. (tentative ed. 1978). *The legal process: Basic problems in making and application of law.* Cambridge, Mass.

Hetherington, E. M. 1988. Parents, children and siblings six years after divorce. In *The impact of divorce, single parenting, and step-parenting on children,* ed. E. M. Hetherington and J. D. Arasteh. Hillsdale, N.J.: Lawrence Erlbaum Associates.

———— 1989. Coping with family transitions: Winners, losers, and survivors. *Child Development* 60:1–14.

Hetherington, E. M., and W. G. Clingempeel. In press. Coping with marital transitions: A family systems perspective. *Monographs of the Society for Research in Child Development.*

Hetherington, E. M., M. Cox, and R. Cox. 1976. Divorced fathers. *Family Coordinator* 25:477.

———— 1982. Effects of divorce on parents and children. In *Nontraditional families,* ed. M. E. Lamb. Hillsdale, N.J.: Lawrence Erlbaum Associates.

Hiller, D. V., and W. W. Philliber. 1985. Maximizing confidence in married couple samples. *Journal of Marriage and the Family* 47:729–732.

Hochschild, A. 1989. *The second shift,* pp. 277–282. New York: Viking.

Hodgson, J. W., and R. A. Lewis. 1979. Pilgrim's progress III: A trend analysis of family theory and methodology. *Family Process* 18:163–174.

Isaacs, M. B., B. Montalvo, and D. Abelsohn. 1986. *The difficult divorce: Therapy for children and families.* New York: Basic Books.

Jacob, H. 1988. *Silent revolution: The transformation of divorce law in the United States.* Chicago: University of Chicago Press.

Johnston, J. R. In press. *Guidelines for the resolution of disputed custody and visitation for children of domestic violence.* Section 1, final report to Judicial Council of California.

Johnston, J. R., and L. E. G. Campbell. 1988. *Impasses of divorce: The dynamics and resolution of family conflict.* New York: Free Press.

Johnston, J. R., L. E. G. Campbell, and S. Mayes. 1985. Latency children in post-separation and divorce disputes. *Journal of the American Academy of Child Psychiatry* 24:563–574.

Joshi, H. 1984. *Women's participation in paid work: Further analysis of the women and employment survey.* Research paper No. 45, Department of Employment, HMSO, London.

Kay, H. H. 1990. Beyond no-fault: New directions in divorce reform. In *Divorce reform at the crossroads,* ed. S. Sugarman and H. H. Kay. New Haven: Yale University Press.

Kelly, J. B. 1980. Divorce: The adult experience. In *Handbook of developmental psychology,* ed. B. Wolman and G. Stricker. Englewood Cliffs, N.J.: Prentice-Hall.

——— 1990. *Mediated and adversarial divorce resolution processes: An analysis of post-divorce outcomes.* Final report prepared for the Fund for Research in Dispute Resolution, December 1990.

Keshet, H. F., and K. M. Rosenthal. 1978. Fathering after marital separation. *Social Work* 23:11–18.

Kessler, R. C. 1983. Methodological issues in the study of psychological stress. In *Psychological stress: Trends in theory and research,* ed. H. B. Kaplan. New York: Academic Press.

Koch, M. A. P., and C. R. Lowery. 1984. Visitation and the noncustodial father. *Journal of Divorce* 8(2):47–65.

Lamb, M. E., J. H. Pleck, E. L. Chernov, and J. A. Levine. 1987. A biosocial perspective on paternal behavior and involvement. In *Parenting across the lifespan: A biosocial perspective,* ed. J. B. Lancaster, A. Rossi, J. Altman, and L. Sherrod. New York: Aldine de Gruyter.

Laosa, L. N. 1988. Ethnicity and single parenting in the United States. In *The impact of divorce, single parenting and stepparenting on children,* ed. E. M. Hetherington and J. D. Arasteh. Hillsdale, N.J.: Lawrence Erlbaum Associates.

Lax, D. A., and J. K. Sebenius. 1986. *The manager as negotiator,* p. 33. New York: Free Press.

Levy, R. 1969. *Uniform marriage and divorce legislation: A preliminary analysis,* chap. 1. Unpublished manuscript prepared for the Special Committee on Divorce of the National Conference of Commissioners on Uniform State Laws.

Lowery, C. R. 1986. Maternal and joint custody: Differences in the decision process. *Law and Human Behavior* 10:303–315.

Lytton, H. 1979. Disciplinary encounters between young boys and their mothers: Is there a contingency system? *Developmental Psychology* 15:256–268.

Maccoby, E. E., and C. N. Jacklin. 1983. The "person" characteristics of children and the family as environment. In *Human development: An interactional perspective,* ed. D. Magnusson and V. Allen. New York: Academic Press.

Maccoby, E. E., and J. Martin. 1983. Parent-child interaction. In *Charmichael's manual of child psychology,* vol. 4, ed. P. Mussen. New York: Wiley.

Maccoby, E. E., C. E. Depner, and R. H. Mnookin. 1990. Coparenting in the second year after divorce. *Journal of Marriage and the Family* 52: 141–155.

McDonald, P. F. 1986. Property division. In *Settling up: Property and income distribution in divorce in Australia,* ed. P. F. McDonald. Australia and the Australian Institute of Family Studies. Sydney: Prentice-Hall.

McIsaac, H. 1983. Court-connected mediation. *Conciliation Courts Review* 21(2):49–59.

McKinnon, R., and J. S. Wallerstein. 1986. Joint custody and the preschool child. *Behavioral Sciences and the Law* 4:169–183.

Melli, M. S., H. S. Erlanger, and E. Chambliss. 1988. The process of negotiation: An exploratory investigation in the context of no-fault divorce. *Rutgers Law Review* 40:1133–1172.

Minuchin, P. 1985. Families and individual development: Provocations from the field of family therapy. *Child Development* 56:289–302.

Mnookin, R. H. 1975. Child custody adjudication: Judicial functions in the face of indeterminacy. *Law and Contemporary Problems* 39(3):226–293.

——— 1985. Divorce bargaining: The limits of private ordering. *University of Michigan Journal of Law Reform* 18:1015–1037.

Mnookin, R. H., and L. Kornhauser. 1979. Bargaining in the shadow of the law: The case of divorce. *Yale Law Journal* 88:950–997.

Monroe, P. A., J. L. Bokemeier, J. M. Kotchen, and H. McKean. 1985. Spousal response consistency in decision-making research. *Journal of Marriage and the Family* 47:733–738.

Munsterman, X., et al. 1990. *A guide to child support guidelines.* National Center for State Courts.

Neely, R. 1984. The primary caretaker parent rule: Child custody and the dynamics of greed. *Yale Law and Public Policy Review* 3:168–186.

Norton, G. H. 1987a. Support schedules in California: Selected custody and spousal support issues. *California Family Law Monthly* 4:57–74.

Norton, G. H. 1987b. Explaining and comparing the California child and spousal support schedules. *California Family Law Monthly* 4:1–22.

Olsen, F. 1984. The politics of family law. *Law and Inequality* 2:119.

Parke, R. D., and S. O'Leary. 1976. Father-mother-infant interaction in the newborn period: Some findings, some observations and some unresolved issues. In *The developing individual in a changing world,* vol. 2, *Social and environmental issues,* ed. K. A. Riegel and J. Meacham. The Hague: Mouton.

Parke, R. D., and D. B. Sawin. 1976. The father's role in infancy: A re-evaluation. *The Family Coordinator* 25:365–371.

———— 1980. The family in early infancy: Social interactional and attitudinal analysis. In *The father-infant relationship: Observational studies in the family setting,* ed. F. A. Pedersen. New York: Praeger.

Parke, R. D., and B. R. Tinsley. 1981. The father's role in infancy: Determinants of involvement in caregiving and play. In *The role of the father in child development,* ed. M. E. Lamb, 2nd ed. New York: John Wiley and Sons.

Parker, H., and S. Parker. 1986. Father-daughter sexual abuse: An emerging perspective. *American Journal of Orthopsychiatry* 56:531–549.

Peters, H. E., L. M. Argys, E. E. Maccoby, and R. H. Mnookin. Cooperative and non-cooperative contracting at divorce: Evidence from child support compliance and award modifications. Presented at the annual meeting of the Population Association of America, March 1991 (revised February 1992), Washington, D.C.

Pleck, J. 1983. Husbands' paid work and family roles: Current research issues. In *Research in the interweave of social roles,* vol. 3, *Families and jobs,* ed. H. Lopata and J. H. Pleck. Greenwich, Conn.: JAI Press.

Polikoff, N. D. 1982. Why are mothers losing? A brief analysis of criteria used in child custody determinations. *Women's Rights Law Reporter* 7(3): 235–243.

Preston, G., and M. Madison. 1984. Access disputes in the context of the family structure after marital separation. *Australian Journal of Sex, Marriage and Family* 5(1):37–45.

Priest, G. L., and B. Klein. 1984. The selection of disputes for litigation. *Journal of Legal Studies* 13:1.

Ransom, D. C., L. Fisher, S. Phillips, R. F. Kokes, and R. Weiss. In press. The logic of family measurement: An approach to avoiding type III errors in family research. *Family Systems Medicine.*

Rhode, D. L. 1987. Gender and jurisprudence: An agenda for research. *Cincinnati Law Review* 56:521–534.

Robinson, H. L. 1982–83. Joint custody: An idea whose time has come. *Journal of Family Law* 21:641–685.

Roman, M., and W. Haddad. 1978. *The disposable parent: The case for joint custody.* New York: Penguin Books.

Ross, M., and F. Sicoly. 1979. Egocentric biases in availability and attribution. *Journal of Personality and Social Psychology* 37:322–336.

Roth, A. 1977. The tender years presumption in child custody disputes. *Journal of Family Law* 15:423–462.

Rothberg, B. 1983. Joint custody: Parental problems and satisfactions. *Family Process* 22:43.

Russell, G. 1982. Shared-caregiving families: An Australian study. In *Nontra-*

ditional families: Parenting and child development, ed. M. E. Lamb. Hillsdale, N.J.: Lawrence Erlbaum Associates.

Russell, G., and A. Russell. 1987. Mother-child and father-child relationships in middle childhood. *Child Development* 58:1573–1585.

Safilios-Rothschild, C. 1969. Family sociology or wives' family sociology? A cross-cultural examination of decision-making. *Journal of Marriage and the Family* 31:290–301.

Santrock, J. W., R. A. Warshak, and G. L. Elliott. 1982. Social development and parent-child interaction in father custody and step-mother families. In *Nontraditional families,* ed. M. E. Lamb. Hillsdale, N.J.: Lawrence Erlbaum Associates.

Sarat, A., and W. L. F. Felstiner. 1986. Law and strategy in the divorce lawyer's office. *Law and Society Review* 20(1):93–134.

——— 1988. Law and social relations: Vocabularies of motive in lawyer/client interaction. *Law and Society Review* 22:737–769.

——— 1989. Lawyers and legal consciousness: Lawtalk in the divorce lawyer's office. *Yale Law Journal* 98(8):1663–1688.

Scanzoni, J. 1965. A note on the sufficiency of wife responses in family research. *Pacific Sociological Association Review* 8:109–115.

Schulman, J., and V. Pitt. 1982. Second thoughts on joint child custody: Analysis of legislation and its implications for women and children. *Golden Gate University Law Review* 12:538–577.

Scott, E., and A. P. Derdeyn. 1984. Rethinking joint custody. *Ohio State Law Journal* 45:455–498.

Seltzer, J. A., and S. M. Bianchi. 1988. Children's contact with absent parents. *Journal of Marriage and the Family* 50:663–677.

Shaffer, M. 1988. Divorce mediation: A feminist perspective. *University of Toronto Faculty of Law Review* 4:162–200.

Sheppard, A. 1982. Unspoken premises in custody litigation. *Women's Rights Law Reporter* 7:229.

Shorter, E. 1975. *The making of the modern family.* New York: Basic Books.

Singer, J. B., and W. L. Reynolds. 1988. A dissent on joint custody. *Maryland Law Review* 47:497–523.

Spanier, G. B., and L. Thompson. 1984. *Parting: The aftermath of separation and divorce.* Beverly Hills: Sage Publications.

Spencer, J. M., and J. P. Zammit. 1976. Mediation-arbitration: A proposal for private resolution of disputes between divorced or separated parents. *Duke University Law Journal* (December): 911–939.

Stacey, J. 1990. Land of dreams and disaster: Postindustrial living in the Silicon Valley, chap. 2. In *Brave New Families.* New York: Basic Books.

Steinman, S. 1981. The experience of children in a joint custody arrangement: A report of a study. *American Journal of Orthopsychiatry* 51:403–414.

Steinman, S. B., S. E. Zemmelman, and T. M. Knoblauch. 1985. A study of parents who sought joint custody following divorce: Who reaches agreement and sustains joint custody and who returns to court. *Journal of the American Academy of Child Psychiatry* 24:554–562.

Stone, L. 1977. *The family, sex, and marriage in England: 1500–1800*. New York: Harper and Row.

Straus, M. A., R. J. Gelles, and S. K. Steinmetz. 1981. *Behind closed doors: Violence in the American family*. Newbury Park, Calif.: Sage Publications.

Strauss, P., and J. Strauss. 1974. Review of "Beyond the best interests of the child." *Columbia Law Review* 996:1002–1004.

Sudman, S., and G. Kalton. 1986. New developments in the sampling of special populations. *Annual Review of Sociology* 12:401–429.

Sweet, J. A., and L. L. Bumpass. 1987. *American families and households*. New York: Russell Sage Foundation.

Thompson, L., and A. J. Walker. 1989. Gender in families: Women and men in marriage, work and parenthood. *Journal of Marriage and the Family* 51:873–893.

Townsend, A. L., and G. T. Deimling. 1983. *Family problem-solving effectiveness: The complexity of transforming individual data into family measures*. Paper presented for the Preconference Workshop on Theory Construction and Research Methodology, Annual Meeting of the National Council on Family Relations, St. Paul, Minnesota.

U.S. Department of Commerce, Bureau of the Census. June 1986. Characteristics of the population below the poverty level. *Current Population Reports*, Series P-60, No. 152.

——— 1987. Child support and alimony: 1985. *Current Population Reports*, Series P-2, No. 152.

Uviler, R. K. 1978. Fathers' rights and feminism: The maternal presumption revisited. *Harvard Women's Law Journal* 1(1):107–130.

Wallerstein, J. S., and J. B. Kelly. 1980. *Surviving the breakup: How children and parents cope with divorce*. New York: Basic Books.

Watson, M. 1981. Custody alternatives: Defining the best interests of the child. *Family Relations* 30:474.

Weiss, R. 1975. *Marital separation*. New York: Basic Books.

Weiss, Y., and R. J. Willis. 1985. Children as collective goods in divorce settlements. *Journal of Labor Economics* 3(3):268–292.

Weitzman, L. J. 1985. *The divorce revolution: The unexpected social and economic consequences for women and children in America*, p. 243. New York: The Free Press.

Weitzman, L. J., and R. B. Dixon. 1979. Child custody awards: Legal standards and empirical patterns for child custody, support and visitation after divorce. *University of California–Davis, Law Review* 12(2):473–521.

Youniss, J., and J. Smollar. 1985. *Adolescent relations with mothers, fathers and friends*. Chicago: University of Chicago Press.

Zill, N., and J. L. Peterson. 1982. *Trends in the behavior and emotional well-being of U.S. children: Findings from a national survey*. Paper presented at the annual meeting of the American Association for the Advancement of Science, Washington, D.C.

Index

Abelsohn, D., 32

Adolescents. *See* Teenagers

AFDC (Aid to Families with Dependent Children), 342n11, 352n14

Age and gender of children: in sample, 61, 63, 313; as factors in residence and visitation, 77–79, 177–178, 199–200, 201, 269, 303–307, 320; as factors in co-parenting and conflict, 144–145, 206–209, 238–239, 247, 277

Age distribution: sample and U.S. data, 316

Agnos Child Support Standards Act (Calif.; 1984), 352n14

Alimony. *See* Spousal support

Anglo-American divorce law tradition, 5–7

Bargaining: as continuing process, 11, 199, 202, 210–211, 251, 256–257, 264; economic factors in, 48–49, 50–51, 53, 154, 160 (*see also* Money-custody link); risk aversion in, 49–50, 51; and conflict level, 57, 155–159, 271–273; petitions as tool in, 102; and compliance, 251, 264, 278–280

Barrett, N. S., 341n2

Becker, G. S., 341n2

Best interest of child: as legal standard, 9, 44, 49, 273, 282, 340nn15,17; criticisms of, 11–12, 282–283, 340n20, 341n22, 352nn7,8; as parental standard, 102, 195–197, 200–201, 273, 282, 292

Buffering, parental, 31, 38–39, 211, 227–228, 247–248, 295

California statutes, 3, 5; reforms, 9–10, 107–108, 288–289; considerations and goals of, 41–43, 119, 155, 175, 271, 274; criticisms of, 41–45, 153, 271; successes and failures of, 113–114, 271–274, 279–281, 289; processes under, 133; recent changes, 342n16, 352n14

Camera, K., 12

Chambers, D., 283

Cherlin, A. J., 64

Chernov, E. L., 26

Child support: and legal rights, 48, 115, 116, 118–119, 136, 290–291, 342n11, 352n14; factors influencing, 57, 116–123 passim, 130–131, 135–136, 155–159, 250–257, 274, 347nn19,20; gender differences in, 116–119, 130, 132, 270; as related to income, 120–123, 256, 261–262, 265; in U.S. sample, 128–130; as source of legal conflict, 135–136; recommendations on, 290–291

Child Support Enforcement Amendments (U.S.; 1984), 342n11

Children, influencing features of. *See* Age and gender of children; Family size; Teenagers

Children's attitudes, 3, 4, 36, 89–90, 193–195, 200. *See also* Teenagers

Clingempeel, W. G., 65

Communication. *See under* Cooperation

Compliance: factors influencing, 116–123 passim, 131, 156–157, 190–197, 199, 251–257, 263–264, 278, 345n6 (chap. 6); U.S. studies, 129, 350n1; effect of

238. *See also specific types of physical custody by name*
Residential moves. *See* Relocations
Resnick, G., 12
"Reversed" households, 267, 269
Reynolds, W. L., 11
Risk aversion in bargaining, 49–50, 51
Ross, M., 65
Rothberg, B., 76
Rule enforcement, 218, 225–230, 232, 248, 281–282
Russell, A., 29
Russell, G., 29

Safilios-Rothschild, C., 310
Sample: described, 13–15, 58–70, 294, 313–319; subgroups, 15–16, 162–163, 165, 335–336; vs. U.S. sample, 62; exclusions from, 313, 319–322, 345n4; refusal rate, 317; attrition rate, 323–324
Scanzoni, J., 311
Sebenius, J. K., 55
Separation, residential arrangements during: sample and U.S. study, 74; perceptions influencing, 79–97, 145–147
Sicoly, F., 65
Singer, J. B., 11
Solnit, A. J., 3, 285, 286
Spanier, G. B., 316, 317
"Split" residence and custody, 74 (table note), 151, 166, 336; as preference, 99
Spousal support, 7–8, 48, 123–124, 129, 130, 135, 136, 250, 257, 260, 261, 265, 345n3
Stanford Child Custody Study. *See* Follow-up study
Steinman, S., 80
Stepchildren, 79, 94, 185, 187
Strauss, J., 3
Strauss, P., 3

T-1, T-2, T-3, 13–14
Teenagers: in follow-up study, 15, 248, 275, 284, 285, 291; in intact families, 29; and residence decisions, 77–79, 177, 269; and visitation, 193–195, 200, 275

Thompson, L., 316, 317
"Traditional" (intact) families, 267; division of labor in, 22–29 passim, 35, 63–68, 212–214
Trial settlements, incidence of, 149–151
Transportation and logistical issues, 79–80, 96–97, 183–184, 185–187, 200, 214–217, 275, 295

Uncontested cases, custody outcomes in, 103, 137, 300
Undermining. *See* Hostility
"Undifferentiated" households, 267
United States: national studies, 62, 74, 128–130, 197–198, 316–317; child support guidelines, 116, 342n11

Visitation: as policy issue, 3–4, 285–286, 293; and child support, 42, 45–46, 120, 122, 123, 130–131, 155–159 passim, 251, 253–257, 263–264, 276, 347nn19,20; as legal right, 45, 48, 278, 280, 287–288; pending final settlement, 74, 75; as source of conflict, 135, 137, 140–141, 191–193, 280–281, 284–285, 286, 287, 346n8; changes in over time, 171–176 passim, 191–193, 194, 197–200, 274–276; incidence of by type (overnight, daytime, etc.), 172–175; gender differences in, 172–176, 183–187; factors influencing, 177–180, 183–190, 192–201, 276; father-contact index, 181–182; in national study, 197–198; sample's schedule, 304, 305, 307

Wald, M., 344n4
Wallerstein, J. S., 80
Watson, M., 80
Weitzman, L. J., 316, 317
Welfare income, 258, 260
Working mothers. *See* Education and employment; Income

Zill, N., 197, 314